W9-DBJ-416
TALLAHASSEE
COMMUNITY COLLEGE

Celibacy and Religious Traditions

Celibacy and Religious Traditions

EDITED BY CARL OLSON

OXFORD
UNIVERSITY PRESS
2008

OXFORD
UNIVERSITY PRESS

Oxford University Press, Inc., publishes works that further
Oxford University's objective of excellence
in research, scholarship, and education.

Oxford New York
Auckland Cape Town Dar es Salaam Hong Kong Karachi
Kuala Lumpur Madrid Melbourne Mexico City Nairobi
New Delhi Shanghai Taipei Toronto

With offices in
Argentina Austria Brazil Chile Czech Republic France Greece
Guatemala Hungary Italy Japan Poland Portugal Singapore
South Korea Switzerland Thailand Turkey Ukraine Vietnam

Published by Oxford University Press, Inc.
198 Madison Avenue, New York, New York 10016

www.oup.com

Library of Congress Cataloging-in-Publication Data
Celibacy and religious traditions / Carl Olson, editor.
p. cm.
Includes index.
ISBN 978-0-19-530631-6; 978-0-19-530632-3 (pbk.)
1. Sexual abstinence—Religious aspects. 2. Celibacy.
I. Olson, Carl.
BL65.S4C45 2007
204'.47—dc22 2007009931

9 8 7 6 5 4 3 2 1

Printed in the United States of America
on acid-free paper

This book is dedicated to the memory of Louise and Warren Eisenhower for their love, hospitality, and good cheer

Preface

This book is intended for an educated general readership and for use in college courses. It is also intended to be a supplement to other texts in introductory courses in various religious traditions, because the issues raised by its essays play pivotal roles in many cultures. Moreover, the chapters in this book are intended to introduce students to the role of celibacy, or a lack of it, in various religious traditions, and the contributors present the rationale for its observance (or not) within the context of each tradition. Scholars writing about religious traditions that do not advocate celibacy for its followers call attention to exceptions to this general trend and what lessons can be learned from the absence of celibacy from a culture.

This book grew from my own teaching of courses in various religions (such as Hinduism, Buddhism, Islam, and Taoism, as well as Native American Indian and African religions). During the course of my teaching, I was not surprised to discover that students are very interested in topics related to human sexuality. Celibacy provides a way to discuss a topic directly related to human sexuality. It also is a way to learn something valuable about the worldview and value system of particular religious traditions.

Using the expertise of scholars in various religious traditions encompassing East and West, ancient and modern, moribund and living, this collection of essays addresses certain questions such as the following: Why do some members of a religious community decide to maintain a celibate style of religious life? Is celibacy a prerequisite for religious office or status? Are there different contexts within a given religious tradition for the practice of celibacy? Are there gestures or actions that can replace the absence of sexual activity? What is the symbolic significance of celibacy within a particular religious tradition? Besides such questions, these chapters will also address issues about the symbolic significance of celibacy, its function within a religious tradition, its connection to the acquisition of power, and the physical or spiritual benefits of celibacy. In addition to addressing implications for the practice or nonpractice of celibacy within various traditions, this work will enhance our understanding of spirituality, and contribute to our knowledge of asceticism in the East and West.

In a collaborative work of this nature, I need initially to thank the contributors from all over the globe for their hard work, insights, creativity, and willingness to share their knowledge with a wider audience. At Oxford University Press, my gratitude goes to Cynthia Read and others at the press for their faith in and support for this project, such as Meechal Hoffman for her early work on this book and Christine Dahlin for steering it through the production process. This book marks the fifth time that Margaret Case has served as my copyeditor, and I am deeply in her debt. When some contributors were tardy, Peggy helped to keep me sane. I am also thankful to my colleague Glenn Holland for coming through in the clutch, and I am delighted that we could work together on a writing project after being together for so many years at the college on the hill. Finally, I want to extend my thanks to President Richard Cook and Dean Linda DeMerritt of Allegheny College for moving the college forward and allowing me to continue to do what I love. Finally, I want to thank Richard and his wife, Terri, for their many contributions to the college and specifically for his help with my work by offering me a humanities chair. Richard's decision to retire from the college creates a huge gap that we hope will be filled by someone as talented and successful in the near future.

Contents

Contributors

Shahzad Bashir is associate professor of religion studies at Stanford University. He is the author of *Messianic Hopes and Mystical Visions: The Nurbakhshiya between Medieval and Modern Islam* and *Fazlallah Astarabadi and the Hurufis*. He is currently finishing a book entitled *Bodies of God's Friends: Sufism and Society in Medieval Islam* that explores the treatment of the human body in hagiographical narratives produced in Iran and central Asia during the later medieval period (ca. 1300–1600).

Willi Braun is professor of religion in the Department of History and Classics and director of the Interdisciplinary Program of Religious Studies at the University of Alberta, Edmonton. His books include *Feasting and Social Rhetoric in Luke 14*, *Rhetoric and Reality in Early Christianities*, and *Guide to the Study of Religion* (coedited with Russell McCutcheon). He has served many years as editor of *Method & Theory in the Study of Religion* and *Studies in Religion/Sciences Religieuses*. With support of a grant from the Social Sciences and Humanities Research Council of Canada, he is currently preparing a monograph on the social history of Roman-period Christianity.

M. Darrol Bryant is professor of religion and culture at Renison College, University of Waterloo, Ontario. He is the author of more than twenty volumes in the study of religion, including *God, The*

Contemporary Discussion; Jonathan Edwards' Grammar of Time; Self & Society: Muslim-Christian Dialogue; Woven on the Loom of Time: Many Faiths and One Divine Purpose; Religious Conversion; and *Religion in a New Key*. He has been a visiting scholar at Cambridge University, Hamdard University, Mahatma Gandhi University, University of Madras, and Nairobi University. Central to his research and publication is the interfaith encounter and dialogue of religions.

Karen Cheatham is completing her doctoral degree at the Centre for the Study of Religion, University of Toronto. She received her master's degree from the Graduate Theological Union in Berkeley, California. Cheatham's research focus is the religious discourse on male virginity and chastity in eleventh- and twelfth-century Western Europe. Her essay "Rupert of Deutz on Masturbation and Virginity" appears in *Rule Makers and Rule Breakers: 7th Annual St. Michael's College Symposium Papers.*

Eliezer Diamond is the Rabbi Judah A. Nadich Associate Professor of Talmud and Rabbinics at the Jewish Theological Seminary in New York City. He is the author of articles on the rabbinic period in *The Schocken Guide to Jewish Books* and essays in *The Reader's Guide to Judaism*, and he is author of the book *Holy Men and Hunger Artists: Fasting and Asceticism in Rabbinic Culture.*

Paul Dundas is a reader in Sanskrit at Edinburgh University. Besides publishing numerous essays in journals and books, he is the author of *The Jains* (second edition, 2002; Italian translation, 2005) and the forthcoming *History, Scripture and Controversy in a Medieval Jain Sect.* He is widely recognized as an international authority on Jain religion.

Jeanne L. Gillespie serves as associate dean of the College of Arts and Letters and associate professor of Spanish and women's studies at the University of Southern Mississippi. Her book *Saints and Warriors: Tlaxcalan Perspectives on the Conquest of Tenochtitlan* explores the Amerindian responses to the encounter with Europeans in the voices of the Tlaxcalans, who allied themselves with Cortés in the defeat of the Mexica empire. Current research projects include the decimal tradition of the Isleños of south Louisiana, Portuguese and Spanish narratives of Asian exploration, and Nahuatl poetic forms in women's voices.

Glenn Holland is Bishop James Mills Thoburn Professor of Religious Studies at Allegheny College. He is author of *The Tradition That You Received from Us* and *Divine Irony* and is coeditor with John T. Fitzgerald and Dirk Obink of *Philodemus and the New Testament World.*

John Kieschnick teaches at the University of Sterling in the United Kingdom. He previously held the position of associate research fellow at the Institute of History and Philology at Academia Sinica in Taipei. In addition to journal and encyclopedia essays, he is the author of *The Impact of Buddhism on Chinese Material Culture* and *The Eminent Monk: Buddhist Ideals in Medieval Chinese Hagiography.*

Livia Kohn is professor of religion and East Asian studies at Boston University. She is a prolific scholar with such recently published books as *Daoism and Chinese Culture; Daoist Monastic Life;* and *Health and Long Life: The Chinese Way.* She was editor of *Daoist Body Cultivation.*

C. Scott Littleton is professor of anthropology emeritus at Occidental College in Los Angeles. A specialist in Japanese religion and culture, the origin and distribution of the Arthurian and Holy Grail legends, and comparative Indo-European mythology, he is the author of the *New Comparative Mythology: An Anthropological Assessment of the Theories of Georges Dumézil;* (with Linda A. Malcor) *From Sythia to Camelot: A Radical Reassessment of the Legends of King Arthur, the Knights of the Round Table, and the Holy Grail; Shinto: Origins, Rituals, Festivals, Spirits, Sacred Places.* He was editor of *The Sacred East.*

Oyeronke Olajubu is a senior lecturer at the University of Ilorin in Nigeria. She has published essays in European, American, and African journals, and chapters for books on such topics as Yoruba religion, gender, feminism, culture, and other topics. She has also published a book entitled *Women in the Yoruba Religious Sphere.*

Patrick Olivelle is the chair of the Department of Asian Studies at the University of Texas at Austin, where he is also professor of Sanskrit and Indian religions and holder of the Jacob and Frances Sanger Chair in the Humanities. His work has covered the ascetical traditions of India. Among his major publications are *The Āśrama System: History and Hermeneutics of a Religious Institution; Pañcatantra; The Early Upaniṣads: Annotated Text and Translation; Dharmasūtras: The Law Codes of Āpastamba, Gautama, Baudhāyana, and Vasiṣṭha; Manu's Code of Law: A Critical Edition and Translation of the Mānava-Dharmaśāstra*; and *Language, Texts, and Society: Explorations in Ancient Indian Culture and Religion.*

Carl Olson is professor of religious studies at Allegheny College, Meadville, Pennsylvania, where he has held the National Endowment for the Humanities Chair; the Teacher-Scholar Professorship of the Humanities; and a visiting fellowship at Clare Hall, University of Cambridge. He is now a permanent fellow of Clare Hall. He has published many essays for journals, books, and encyclopedias, and he has served as review editor for many years of the *International Journal of Hindu Studies.* He has published a couple of books on method and theory, a couple of books on comparative philosophy, and most recently *The Different Paths of Buddhism: A Narrative-Historical Introduction; Original Buddhist Sources: A Reader*; *The Many Colors of Hinduism: A Thematic-Historical Introduction*; and *Primary Hindu Sources: A Sectarian Reader.*

John Powers is a reader in the Faculty of Asian Studies at Australian National University. He is the author of more than sixty articles and fourteen books, including *History as Propaganda: Tibetan Exiles versus the People's Republic of China.* He specializes in Indian and Tibetan Buddhist history of ideas.

Celibacy and Religious Traditions

I

Celibacy and the Human Body: An Introduction

Carl Olson

It is biologically natural for human beings to engage in sexual relationships for the procreation of the species, impelled by motives of lust, pleasure, enjoyment, comfort, companionship, relaxation, or a combination of these drives and needs. Upon reaching adolescence, it is not unusual to experience sexual urges due to chemical changes within one's body that for some people can be overwhelming and difficult to control. Many societies channel this sexual energy into early marriage, for the welfare of the social fabric. Due to the dangers associated with sexually transmitted diseases, especially the deadly scourge of AIDS, contemporary governments have encouraged programs of sexual abstinence or protected sex as preferable ways to prevent such hazards. Certain religious organizations have advocated lifelong celibacy for spiritual reasons, whereas some religious traditions that oppose the practice in general allow for instances or exceptions to the prevailing ban on celibacy.

Being subject to sexual urges presupposes that one is embodied, and our bodies are necessarily embedded in the world. The embodied nature of our sexual drives is, of course, equally true of celibacy. In fact, a discussion of sexuality and celibacy presupposes a conceptual grasp of the human body as a sensitive substance with the ability to produce both pain and pleasure. In addition to being a sensitive substance, the body projects a visible, tangible image of itself in space and time. The body can also transform itself into a sign that functions in a self-referential way and as a referent for others by means of its ability to acquire meaning. If a symbol can be understood as a particular type of sign, the body can be said to symbolize a bridge that connects nature and culture.[1] As a sign or symbol, the body can be an ambivalent entity from a cross-cultural perspective, even as it possesses the potential to embody and reveal cultural values and attitudes.

During the latter half of the twentieth century there has been an acute philosophical interest in the human body. Maurice Merleau-Ponty, for instance, in his work *Phenomenology of Perception* discusses human bodies as organisms capable of perception. The human body and the perceived world form a single system of intentional relations that form correlations, implying that to experience the body is to perceive the world, and vice versa.[2] Therefore, the body and world form an inseparable, internal relationship. Mary Douglas, an anthropologist, views the body as a metaphor for reality and a symbolic system, whereas Michel Foucault concentrates his focus on the body as a product of a relationship between power and knowledge. George Lakoff and Mark Johnson, who are influenced by Merleau-Ponty and second-generation cognitive science, point to the role that the body plays in conceptualization, which is only possible through the body: "Therefore, every understanding that we can have of the world, ourselves, and others can only be framed in terms of concepts shaped by our bodies."[3] Mark Johnson, on the other hand, argues that the human body is in the mind, in the sense that structures of understanding are essential to meaning and reason. But he also explores how the body is in the mind, or how reason and imagination have a bodily basis. He thinks that our bodily, social, linguistic, and intellectual being are interconnected in complex relationships that constitute our understanding of our world.[4] From another perspective, there is also a sense in which one can speak about the history of the body, most clearly evident in the aging process, which demonstrates that the body experiences changes.

In addition to being a sign, symbol, metaphor, mode of conceptualization, and having a history, the body is also flesh, which can express a lustful nature that manifests as threatening and dangerous unless it is controlled and regulated by social processes. Since the body is associated with uncontrollable and irrational passions, desires, and emotions, celibacy is an excellent example of exerting discipline and control upon the human body: "Disciplining is a technical operation designed to form and to fix aptitudes in a body, thus augmenting the body's powers, increasing its functional efficacy. . . . Disciplining makes bodies docile—adapted to instrumental layouts and productive, and also tractable. It makes bodies function as elements that can be programmed and maneuvered."[5] Sexual urges do not cease until weakened by old age, disease, or afflictions associated with medication for high blood pressure or diabetes, and celibacy is often part of a pattern of actions undertaken to control and discipline the body.

The decision by an embodied person to engage in heterosexual or homosexual activity is not only a personal and mutual action but also a social one. Since sexual relations occur within a social context, the human body may in this sense also be thought of as the result of numerous social and cultural practices, behaviors, and discourses, which operate to construct the body as a social artifact.[6] In summary, although our body is biologically given to us, it is socially constructed.

If the human body and sexuality are inherently social, the same thing can be stated about celibacy, although its observance can differ according to individual volition (for example, whether it is elected or imposed) and temporality (for example, whether it is temporary or permanent). For the aspiring Catholic priest, Hindu ascetic, or Buddhist monk, celibacy appears to be an antisocial choice, but such a momentous and personal decision enables the male or female to enter into a new social order and construct a new identity and status. An understanding of celibacy can thus be a useful way to view the significance of the human body and desire within a social context. This book demonstrates how the practice of celibacy differs cross-culturally and historically within different religious traditions, highlighting exceptions to the general ethos of each tradition.

The Nature of Celibacy

Celibacy is commonly understood as entailing a vow to abstain from all sexual relationships. Such a vow or intention does not necessarily mean perpetual virginity, because a person could have been married or simply have engaged in sexual relations before taking a vow to remain celibate. Celibacy does not require a vow, however, when it is forced on a person because of social or religious circumstances, such as being on a religious quest, participating in a hunting expedition, or observing a religious ritual.

Within the Western context, celibacy originates from the Latin term *caelebs*, which means "alone or single."[7] The implications of being alone are a bit misleading, because choosing to be celibate might make a person a member of a community of other celibates. In Hinduism, celibacy is called *brahmacarya*, which is practiced by an ascetic and by a student (*brahmacārin*), which suggests that for a Hindu celibacy is practically synonymous with being a student. These definitions of celibacy from East and West are indicative of cross-cultural differences; the Indian ascetic can choose to live alone or in a group of other wandering ascetics, and students have often lived in the homes of their teachers.

The chapters within this book demonstrate that the practice of celibacy is a complex religious phenomenon. The control of sexual desire can be used, for instance, to divorce oneself from a basic human biological drive, to extricate oneself from what is perceived as impure, or to distance oneself from the transient world. Within some religious traditions, one can find the practice of temporary celibacy, a commitment to long-term permanent celibacy, or an outright condemnation of it. By maintaining a state of virginity, members of some religious traditions imitate divine models, whereas other traditions do not admit the possibility of emulating such paradigms. Whether or not a religious tradition encourages or discourages it, the practice of celibacy gives us insight into its worldview, social values, gender relations, ethical implications, religious roles or offices, understanding of the physical body, and its practitioner's connection to spiritual and political power. Celibacy can contribute to the creation of a certain status and play a role in the construction of identity, while serving as a source of charisma. It can also represent a negotiation regarding social values and cultural attitudes. In some religious traditions, it is possible to renounce sex and gain sacred status and economic support from society.[8]

The practice of celibacy reflects a certain understanding of a particular culture's conception of the human body. In fact, celibacy marks the human body, an inscription that may be accompanied by special modes of dress to differentiate the celibate from ordinary people. This has important implications for understanding the image of the body within each culture. From one perspective, a person's body is presented to him or her, while its meaning is taught by society (such as parents, relatives, and peers). Likewise, a person's attitude about his or her body arises from society's image of itself. The human body is a natural symbol system, even though the body is never experienced naturally because it is always mediated by society. Moreover, an individual's body is patterned in a way analogous to the pattern of the social body. The ways that we are taught to control our bodies, for instance, reflects a general cultural style.

Celibacy, Danger, and Purity

For many religious traditions, the physical human body is a microcosm of society. Therefore, intense social controls will be experienced as demands for strong bodily controls. A good example of the direct correlation between bodily and social control can be found in the military, where soldiers stand rigidly at attention. Because of this correlation, the human body functions as a symbol of society. In fact, the human body is a model that can stand for any bounded system. With such a system in place, this helps us to grasp bodily refuse (such as sweat, saliva, urine, and feces) as symbols of danger. These kinds of bodily refuse are connected to the margins of the body and are considered polluting. By transgressing the boundary of the body, these forms of refuse trigger a concern for purity in religions traditions. In many religious traditions, therefore, celibacy reflects a concern for maintaining purity.

Purity is connected to holiness, whose root meaning implies being set apart. Because holiness is characterized by completeness, it requires that individuals conform to the class or category to which they belong and that classes or categories of things should not be confused.[9] Moreover, holiness represents order, unity, and perfection with respect to a person. In many religious traditions, celibacy is part of the process of becoming holy, complete, perfect, and clean.

In contrast to holiness and purity, pollution is a form of dirt that offends against order. Standing in opposition to holiness, dirt is unclean and a form of danger.[10] Whether it is committed intentionally or inadvertently, pollution is a danger that tends to strike when form or order is attacked, which can result in disorder, a sign of danger. Furthermore, disorder invokes power because it can spoil pattern or order. If order implies restriction, like the practice of celibacy in some religious traditions, disorder implies a limitless potential for destroying pattern. Thus disorder is dangerous. In some religious traditions, the practice of celibacy is one way in which danger can be controlled.

The person practicing celibacy in some instances becomes an embodiment of power; this is especially evident among Hindu ascetics, Buddhist monks, and Sufi mystics. Possessing within itself a drive, impulse, or tendency, power possesses an impetus to empower, which suggests that power gives itself, increases itself, and enhances itself. Power is, however, ambivalent because it is both creative and destructive. By drawing it into us, we can be either strengthened or weakened by it. Thus to encounter or acquire power demands care if one is not to be overwhelmed or overawed by it. Power possesses the ability to affect things or persons by forcing them to move or behave in a certain manner. This points to the dynamic nature of power and its energetic force. Power also has a compulsive aspect because it can coerce actions and even prohibit actions. By means of its force of compulsion, power coerces that which it encounters, and controls it. Celibacy gives a person power, according to evidence from religious traditions of the East and West. And if one possesses power, this gives one control over oneself, over other entities, and even over the cosmos.

Celibacy, Asceticism, Violence, and Pain

Within a personal and social context of inhabiting a human body and being driven by desire, temptation, and possibly transgression, one may choose to practice celibacy in order to control oneself so as to achieve either a short-term goal or a permanent goal beyond the everyday world. In practicing celibacy, one is denying the body what it naturally strives to exercise in terms of its biological urges, with the result that the body is brought to further attention. Thus the ascetic act of denial as evident in the observance of celibacy is another kind of affirmation, a less carnal and more spiritual one.

By agreeing or choosing to be celibate because, for example, one is entering a religious position, such as the priesthood, that demands celibacy as a prerequisite, a person is making a type of decision that is ascetic. This is true even if he or she is not strictly speaking a full-fledged ascetic, that is, one who strives to harness bodily drives and re-channel them into more spiritual ends by denying fundamental biological drives. As some of the chapters in this book attest, some Eastern paths advocate utilization of natural biological drives to achieve their goals, standing in sharp contrast to more conservative traditions. There is a variety of ways to interpret asceticism within different cultural contexts. It is possible to view asceticism as a structure of compensation in which an ascetic both gives up and receives something.[11] Asceticism represents, moreover, a withdrawal from the habitual way of behaving.[12] In some contexts, asceticism is a means of critiquing the dominant society. Or it can be defined as "performances designed to inaugurate an alternative culture, to enable different social relations, and to create a new identity."[13]

Celibacy is not only associated with an ascetic strain within particular religious traditions but it is also a scripted form of violence. Without claiming that violence is innate to human nature, violence can be defined in the following way: "Violence, in both the widest possible and the most elementary senses of the word, entails any cause, any justified or illegitimate force, that is exerted—physically or otherwise—by one thing (event or instance, group or person, and, perhaps, word and object) on another."[14] Of course, by adopting a celibate lifestyle, one is inflicting the violence on oneself, or in the case of institutional celibacy, the violence is already embodied in the religious institution that demands celibacy as a requirement for membership. By practicing celibacy, a person works against the natural inclinations of the human body and its drives, and he or she thereby perpetuates violence on him or herself. With its inherently ascetic and violent features, celibacy causes emotional, mental, and physical discomfort and pain of an often self-inflicted kind. Pain can be defined as "a sensation that is tangled with mental and even cultural experiences."[15] When the practice of celibacy is personally chosen by an individual it represents a form of self-punishment. Pain is, of course, intimately associated with asceticism. Moreover, it is possible for pain to be transformed into power.[16]

Monotheist Traditions

As a context for the discussion of Western and some monotheistic religious attitudes toward the practice of celibacy, the book begins with the classical world of Greece and Rome. In the worlds of Greece and Rome, citizens were expected to reproduce. Those that chose to remain single were penalized by government legislation. An exception to this general social expectation of reproduction was granted the Vestal Virgins by virtue of their religious office. The position of the Vestal Virgins was significant in the ancient world because it was anomalous, even though many of these women married after their thirty years' term of duty was completed.

The stress on reproduction hid a classical cultural conviction that sexual pleasure was potentially dangerous and antisocial. Sexual pleasure was symbolically connected to heat, and orgasm was seen as akin to minor epilepsy. Moreover, sexual intercourse was associated with the loss of a person's vital spirit. The danger associated with sexual pleasure motivated the Stoics, for instance, to advocate sex for the production of children and not the sake of pleasure alone. The emphasis on reproduction contributed to making celibacy an uncommon practice in the Greco-Roman world.

Willi Braun's chapter reviews Greek myths that provide some examples of celibacy, but he warns us not to interpret myths as representative of social practice or as paradigms of human behavior. Braun also reviews ascetic tendencies among philosophers and their stress on self-control and reason, although such thinking did not include renunciation of sexual relations, which was conceived as a civic duty to produce a new generation, promote moderation, and counteract desire, lust, and effeminate attitudes. Since sexual moderation was the cultural norm and celibacy an aberrant practice, Braun devotes much of his essay to examining the important role of celibacy among the Roman Vestal Virgins and the eunuch-priests of the Cybele cult.

Although there was no ambiguity associated with the Vestal Virgins' vow of celibacy, their roles, status, and privileges did create some ambiguity in the minds of others. Eunuchs, however, who were considered strange figures by ancient writers, attracted only disdain, ridicule, and suspicion. Various thinkers classified eunuchs as a third type of human being, and they were viewed as immoral, weak, and low on the social ladder. Braun also discusses the association of eunuchism with purity, chastity, desexualization, and sterility. Since the eunuch was disdained and ridiculed by others, what fascinates Braun is the rationale for the continuation of the eunuch's place in the Greco-Roman world, which he traces both to gender ideology of the historical period together with achievement of male excellence, and to accepted notions of the science of physiognomy, with its presupposition that external bodily characteristics determine internal character.

Judaism represents a religious tradition that is strongly opposed to celibacy. In ancient Judaism, marriage was regarded as both a normal condition and a divine ordinance. The generally accepted opinion was that world creation entailed an injunction to multiply the species (Gen. 1:26). With the destruction of the Temple and the strengthening of the synagogue, Judaism became a religion of the book and of the sanctified, married household. No single aspect of normal life could be renounced if it represented the will of God. From the perspective of rabbinic Judaism, the unmarried man is not a whole person. In fact, the unmarried man diminishes the likeness of God. Therefore, celibacy was not common and was disapproved by the rabbis on moral and theological grounds, and the rabbis equated celibacy with sinfulness, as Eliezer Diamond's chapter reminds us. For rabbinic Judaism, sexual abstinence was not a virtue because it was in conflict with the purpose of creation. Although the Jewish idea of holiness includes a reference to restraint of sexual relations, this does not include becoming celibate.

The Jewish tradition did allow for exceptions, with a temporary practice of celibacy during a woman's menstrual cycle. There were also examples of prophetic figures that practiced celibacy as a result of their direct contact with God. And an individual called a *nazir* took a temporary vow of celibacy in order to attain a state of holiness. Although celibacy played only a minor role in Jewish history, Diamond's chapter calls attention to some exceptions among marginal sects, such as the Therapeutrides, who wanted to develop discipline and remove social obstacles to the study of divine wisdom; the Essences, who were motivated to reject material and sensual pleasure; and the Qumran community, whose practice of celibacy is open to scholarly debate—but each of these exceptions represents a response to catastrophe of some kind.

Diamond's chapter also calls attention to some exceptions in rabbinic Judaism that were associated with studying the Torah. And Diamond draws a distinction between Palestinian and Babylonian rabbinic attitudes. Thus Diamond finds some evidence of celibacy within Judaism, and he attempts to recover the motivations and circumstances behind the rare cases where it occurs.

The emphasis on the virgin birth of Jesus, the apparent celibacy of Jesus due in part to his itinerant lifestyle, and the apparent sexual abstinence of many of his disciples served as models for Christian practice at a later period. The narrative of the virgin birth suggests a mentality that closely linked virginity to the gift of prophecy. In the case of Jesus, his celibacy was an adjunct of his prophetic calling. Glenn Holland contextualizes his essay within Roman culture, with its notions of self-restraint that were connected to self-mastery and the idea that vital energy would be depleted by means of sexual relations, which could thus prove harmful to a person. Holland connects the Christian motivation for celibacy to both a decision to refrain from marriage and eschatological expectations of the early community. The message of Jesus and response to it demanded that the hearers repent, believe, and focus on matters that were beyond ordinary and family concerns. Holland calls attention to the period after the death of Jesus, when it was possible to find examples of married and unmarried male and female ministers, although the women tended to be unmarried or widowed.

In his first letter to the Corinthians, the apostle Paul affirms that sexual renunciation is not essential to his message, although he does refer to sexual continence as a gift and sexual relations as normal. Holland's chapter reminds us that as the early Christian movement developed, the notion of lifelong celibacy became accepted as a higher path to salvation. In fact, different notions about the nature of a follower of Jesus grew along with rationales for voluntary celibacy.

Holland traces the growing emphasis on celibacy and veneration of the ascetic lifestyle. Before long, lifelong celibacy received a theological foundation with important implications for women. In the second-century Christian churches, sexual abstinence became a distinguishing mark, as it established the authority of prophetic figures and church leaders by making the human body a more appropriate vehicle to receive divine inspiration. For Justin Martyr (ca. 100–ca. 165), continence was associated with fundamental simplicity, whereas Tertullian (ca. 160–ca. 225) grasped celibacy as the most effective technique with which to achieve clarity of the soul. If sexuality was symptomatic of humanity's fall into bondage, the renunciation of sexual relations was linked in the Christian imagination with the reestablishment of a lost human freedom, regaining the spirit of God, and the conquest of death. With the growing negative view of sexuality in the fifth century, the works of Jerome, Augustine, and the rule of Benedict, according to Holland, shaped the Latin comprehension of acceptance of celibacy by the church.

Within the context of medieval Christianity, celibacy was increasingly a prerequisite for religious office or position. Celibacy also set a religious person apart from the rest of society. Karen Cheatham's richly nuanced chapter emphasizes change within medieval Christianity, and it calls attention to writers who discussed three orders of the faithful based on sexual lifestyle, with the highest status reserved for those who refrained from sexual activity. Cheatham makes a distinction between virginity, which was mostly associated with women, and chastity, which represented a choice of lifestyle after sexual activity and did not imply lifelong abstinence. These kinds of choices were associated with sexual purity, preparation for an intimate relationship with God, and imitation of angels, and were connected to superior moral and spiritual conditions.

In addition to discussing the diversity of medieval notions of virginity and the theme of spiritual castration, Cheatham stresses that the concepts of virginity and chastity had wide influence on the shaping of the medieval mind in many ways. An obvious example is clerical celibacy, which is traced to the polluting nature of sexual intercourse and is connected to daily performance of the Eucharist service. In addition to the economic factors involved in clerical marriage, there is also evidence of resistance to celibacy enforced by church authorities. For lay members of the church, there developed so-called chaste marriages for devout couples. Cheatham calls attention to lay sanctity movements, such as the Beguines in the thirteenth century—a group of uncloistered religious women for whom chastity and celibacy were fundamental to their lifestyle. Such examples show that the medieval church and the role of celibacy, within it and outside of it, were complex and never static.

Protestant Christianity exemplifies a different attitude toward the practice of celibacy. M. Darrol Bryant begins his chapter by raising the question of whether or not celibacy is a Protestant issue. After surveying the issue of celibacy in early Christianity, Bryant presents celibacy as a path of obedience and service, although troubling questions about sexuality persisted. Martin Luther, a Catholic priest turned reformer, offered a critique of celibacy after becoming convinced on the basis of his study of the Psalms that God's grace, not our acts, redeems us. In his lectures on Galatians in 1519, Luther denounced priestly celibacy, saying it was not good for all priests. Furthermore, the formal vow of celibacy set clergymen apart from the masses of the people. Being opposed to any coercive authority, Luther argued that monastic vows stand against the Word of God and against Christ because they violate the freedom of the gospel and make religion a matter of rules, statues, orders, and divisions rather than a spontaneous relation to God through Christ. Moreover, it is ridiculous, he said, to assume that virginity is superior to marriage. The belief that the celibate person attains a higher stage of perfection than the average person is abhorrent because it involves a conviction that Christ has not done everything sufficient for our salvation. Thus there is a danger that the vow of celibacy could become a substitute for faith itself. In his work the *Babylonian Captivity*, Luther argued that marriage was a natural state, whereas Satan inspired clerical celibacy.

In addition to Luther, Bryant examines other figures, such as the humanistic scholar Erasmus, the Swiss reformer Ulrich Zwingli, French reformer John Calvin (who pointed to the corruption in the church and lack of scriptural basis for celibacy), and Menno Simons, a Dutch Anabaptist. Bryant points out the Protestant undermining of the distinction between priests and laity that contrasts a celibate priesthood with a married ministry. After reviewing examples of lay spiritual and lay-centered movements among the Puritans, Pietists, and Methodists, as well as John Wesley's call for perfection, which had no connection with celibacy, Bryant discusses the neo-orthodox Protestant thinker and pastor Karl Barth (d. 1968), who strikes a balance between the options to marry or remain single. Bryant views Barth's position as a correction to the Protestant tradition, before he concludes with a look at male-centrist thinking in the twenty-first century.

In contrast to Roman Catholicism, the Eastern Orthodox Church does not insist on celibacy for all clergy. They allow some clergy who are content to remain among the "lower" clergy to marry. This attitude toward celibacy reflects in part the tendency of individual Eastern Orthodox Churches to practice independence from each other by forming bodies that more or less correspond to the national states in which they exist.

In contrast to Christianity and the model of Jesus, the prophet Muhammad was a model for married life, a position shared with Judaism. The Qur'an (57:27) denounces celibacy as a human invention. Hence, ascetic practices tend to be un-Islamic from an orthodox perspective. Although the Shiite Muslims are an exception with respect to mortification of the flesh, there is in Islam generally no injunction to mortify the body, because such practice does not allow a person to perform ritual duties. In his chapter, Shahzad Bashir shows that the Islamic situation is more complex with respect to celibacy.

In contrast to the orthodox tradition, the Sufi movement expresses more negative attitudes toward the body. Sufi religious leaders express a variety of opinions about whether or not a Sufi should lead a celibate life. In addition to contested ascetic practices among Sufis on the basis of Qur'anic injunctions and personal choice, Bashir finds that celibacy functions as a form of social protest by Sufi groups, and that there is a relation between forced celibacy and political power during the medieval period. Bashir points out that most Sufis marry, with the exception of the Bektashi order in Turkey, although antinomian Sufi groups have arisen that were more radical and insistent on celibacy.

Other exceptions to the Islamic tradition included eunuchs, who served in the military and as government officials and had status in the society and real influence on kings. Bashir also balances his chapter by discussing the female Sufi saint Rabi'a and works that discuss advantages of marriage and celibacy to promote religious life.

Eastern Religious Traditions

In his chapter, which focuses on classical Hinduism, Patrick Olivelle draws a distinction between the terms *chaste* and *celibate*; he views the latter category as a social institution within the Hindu context. Knowing the important role played by celibacy in Indian history, Olivelle finds it ironic that there is no specific term for celibacy, although the term *brahmacārya*, which is later adopted by Buddhists, comes to approximate celibacy—it entails an initiation that requires a celibate lifestyle for several years during a young man's life as a student. In comparison to the minor role of celibacy in vedic religion, the embrace of celibacy by members of newer religious groups, such as Buddhists, Jains, and Ājīvikas, influenced the later Brahmanical tradition.

The importance of celibacy in Indian culture was embedded in the stages of life (*āśramas*) of a student, forest dweller, and renouncer, the sole exception being that of the life of a householder. According to Olivelle, the āśrama system was crucial for the development of celibacy in Indian culture, where it evolved from a permanent commitment to temporary stages of life, although the value of celibacy changed when it was domesticated. Olivelle discusses the tension between the values of domestic life and ascetic values. Overall, Olivelle shows how ascetic values were incorporated into the stages of life and also relegated to later in life after a person had been able to meet social obligations. The classical Hindu attitude toward celibacy is captured nicely in the *Āpastamba Dharmasūtra* (2.13.3–6), where it affirms that those practicing celibacy attain immortality and acquire superhuman powers on earth.

Although the cultural attitude toward the value of celibacy continued in later Hinduism, the picture became more complex with the advent of devotional religious movements and Tantra. The various devotional movements have tended to be more life affirming and use sexual imagery in poetry to express the erotic and devotional relationship between a person and his or her deity. Devotional Hinduism also tends to be more sensual, with an emphasis on seeing and touching the deities.

The Tantric movement in its so-called left-handed form embraces sexual relations and other forbidden things as a means to achieve liberation. In

Tantra, the human body is considered a microcosm of the divine pair represented by Śiva and Śakti. By engaging in a ritualistic practice of sexual intercourse, a couple imitates the divine paradigm. This forbidden and illicit form of sexuality increases one's spiritual progress and prefigures the union of the divine masculine and feminine forces within one's body; final liberation is conceived as an androgynous condition and the overcoming of one's fragmented condition. The use of sexual relations to achieve liberation stands in sharp contrast to classical yogic techniques.

Celibacy is integral to the religious way of the Jain ascetic. There is a conviction that celibacy protects the soul from the harm associated with passion connected to sexual activity. The Jains also believe that there is a direct connection between celibacy and nonviolence (*ahiṃsā*). They believe that the act of sexual intercourse destroys numerous single-sense creatures believed to dwell in the generative organs of couples.

Paul Dundas makes creative use of the narrative of the Jain monk Sthūlabhadra to illustrate the struggle against sexual desire and a test of the vow of celibacy. The story suggests a juxtaposition of two opposing conceptual realms: urban sexual relations and renunciation, with the latter being the heroic choice to conquer desire. Dundas places the Jain attitude within its historical context and takes Olivelle's discussion in a previous chapter in another direction by discussing women as sources of temptation and roots of violence, and the monastic guidelines for relating to women. Dundas also connects food with erotic desire because food conditions sexual activity, both promote satisfaction, and both threaten the soul. In addition, Dundas examines the relationship between monks and nuns and the relationship between women and sexual restraint.

Instead of being in sharp contrast to the Jain ascetic, a Jain householder could choose to limit sexual activity to certain times, have a single partner, and curb the sexual drive. These are examples of the strong influence that celibacy has over the Jain religious imagination. Dundas calls attention to the negative view of sexual intercourse that shaped lay attitudes. And he reminds us that attitudes about celibacy are presented from a male perspective.

Similar to ascetic Jainism, a fundamental ethical precept embodied in the message of the Buddha involved the practice of celibacy for those who choose to become monks or nuns. Since ignorant craving was by definition essential to the arising of suffering, it was absolutely necessary for a monk or nun to become detached from sensual pleasure. Moreover, sexual relationships entailed social and family responsibilities and functioned as obstacles to mental concentration. Householders were not expected to share in the latter because they were expected to have sexual relations, although a householder might practice celibacy on special occasions or for a specific purpose for a specific period of time. John Powers uses narratives to illustrate Buddhist attitudes and monastic rules, and he unpacks various rules and regulations in an attempt to comprehend why celibacy is essential for liberation. Powers discusses instructions for overcoming desire that are directed to the brain instead of the sexual organ, because it is the source of desire.

If we compare the formative period of Buddhism with its later development in Tibet, we find a more complex situation, because some schools of Tibetan Buddhism insisted on celibacy while some schools allowed sexual intercourse within a ritualistic context. Some more elite, advanced practitioners under the influence of Tantric thought imitated the Buddha, who is depicted as engaged in sexual relations with consorts. There were also some sects of Tibetan Buddhism that allowed for married clergy, in sharp contrast to the formative tradition. Powers skillfully distinguishes between Vajrayāna sexual techniques and more popular forms in the West.

In addition to India and Tibet, China and Japan hosted further developments within Buddhism. With respect to the practice of celibacy, there was wide diversity within these countries. John Kieschnick demonstrates the many obstacles to celibacy in China, where sexual activity was encouraged by the culture, was considered healthy, and played an important role in the social-lineage ancestor cult. From the Chinese perspective, celibacy was antireligious and antisocial, although a layman might produce a son to protect his lineage and take a vow of celibacy afterward. Kieschnick also calls attention to the sexual misconduct of monks that harmed the image of Buddhism, the work of critical literary figures, and the fabrication for political reasons of stories about wayward monks.

Although the practice of celibacy spread with Buddhism to Japan, with the advent of devotional movements and an emphasis on the role of lay people the Japanese abandoned celibacy for a married clergy. As Kieschnick observes, the practice of allowing a married clergy needs to be comprehended within the context of a belief in the decline of the Buddhist doctrine. The practice of celibacy never completely died out in Japan, however, as evident in the development of Zen Buddhism, and Korean Buddhism represented a counter movement back to celibacy.

Kieschnick's essay on East Asian Buddhism is complemented by Livia Kohn's essay on Daoism. Celibacy is not central to Daoist ethos or to Confucianism. A basic conviction holds that the family represents the basis of Chinese society; this is an attitude that gives paramount importance to the role of filial piety and marriage in ensuring the continuation of the paternal lineage and perpetuation of the ancestral cult. Nonetheless, the harnessing and refining of sexual energy, a basic power of life, is essential to Daoism. Inner alchemy schools stress female superiority in harnessing the primal sexual energy, and influenced the bedchamber arts. The practice of inner alchemy is intended to stimulate sexual energy and to transform it into a spirit that creates an immortal embryo. This type of practice is also associated with longevity techniques and mental concentration. Kohn shows that sexual techniques do not completely eliminate celibacy because they are used as a prelude to enhancing concentration and meditation practices, which are not intended to devalue sexuality but rather to gain inner strength. With the body forming the basis for transformation, sexuality becomes internalized into a refined sexual practice.

Shinto, an indigenous religious tradition of Japan, represents another religious tradition that is opposed to celibacy. C. Scott Littleton indicates that Shinto celebrates life and procreation. Littleton places Shinto into a historical and cultural context by reviewing its mythology, divine beings, belief system, shrines, priesthood, relationship between women and religions, and the cultural institution of the *miko*, who must be virgins in order to assist priests. Littleton also discusses the religion's attitude toward marriage and its relationship to the state, and he makes a brief comparison to Judaism. The Shinto tradition stands in sharp contrast to some forms of the Buddhist tradition that exerted an equally profound influence on Japan.

Non-Asian Indigenous Religious Traditions

Within African indigenous religions, celibacy is not viewed with favor because it upsets the social and religious order and the necessity to propagate the species. In African cultural traditions, celibate individuals are treated with contempt to the extent of being ostracized by their families and society. Likewise, sterile people are also despised, and they are compared to unproductive earth that possesses no value. For example, although in some religious traditions celibacy can symbolize purity, it is the emitting of semen that functions as a form of purification among the Zulu of southern Africa. When a Zulu male fears that he has been treated negatively with secret medicines, he does not sleep with his wife. Rather he goes to another woman and has sexual relations with her. Thereby, he expels his evil into her.[17] Such a scenario gives rise to questions about the connection between celibacy and social habits, and the extent of social control over human bodies by the individual and the collective.

Concentrating her essay on the Yoruba society of Nigeria, Oyeronke Olajubu stresses the importance of procreation to perpetuate family and lineages in order to ensure biological immortality. She examines sexuality as it is connected to the maturation process for males and females, which is also connected to the rhythm of life and ancestors. She also explores the importance of children and the dire consequences of not producing any children. She finds that sex is conceived as a divine gift that must not be abused by the Yoruba.

Contextualizing celibacy among the Yoruba, Olajubu finds it among servant and slave groups within the society, which calls attention to sociopolitical problems related to class, power, and the status of the celibate person as subject to force. Within a religious context, on the other hand, celibacy is not a lifelong commitment; religious functionaries are required to practice it for periods of time when they assume roles as intermediaries between divine beings and worshipers. Some elderly, who dedicate themselves to a deity, also practice celibacy, along with young girls dedicated to goddesses. From the perspective of her sociocultural analysis, Olajubu argues that celibacy is a matter of class and not religion among the Yoruba, and it is connected to the need for loyalty, trust, and protection of royal blood.

As a general statement that invites qualification, Native American Indians do not embrace or stress celibacy because it is not creative, whereas sex is a natural act that is encouraged. Among Native Americans, there is a cultural expectation to gratify one's passions, although there tends to be a double standard for men and women, with the former allowed to be promiscuous while the latter are expected to remain pure, unless women want to compromise their future marital status. Moreover, the dichotomy of body and soul that Native Americans believe in does not contribute to an emphasis on celibacy because sexuality is conceptualized as a creative power.

The cultural encouragement of sexual relations among Native American Indians is sometimes interrupted by short-term celibacy, such as the game played by the Cherokee and by the Eskimo at their Bladder Festival. In another instance, married Cheyenne abstain from sexual relations for long periods of time after the birth of a child and conception of another. Within the context of the Sun Dance ritual, celibacy is imposed by the rigors of the rite and is not specifically required. The Sun Dance also paradoxically embodies numerous sexual aspects that tend to dominate the ascetic aspects of the rite. In general, Native American Indians tend to respect those that choose celibacy, but they do not emulate celibates as a general rule.

Some Native American Indian peoples give overt expression to sexuality in their cultural figures, such as the trickster with his insatiable sexual appetite, which reflects universal human biological urges that need to be addressed before cosmic and social equilibrium can be achieved by members of a society. Trickster narratives are indicative of the ambivalent and dangerous nature of sexuality. It is also important to mention the role of clowns and their often sexually obscene antics.

As we move from North America to Mesoamerica, we encounter peoples who celebrated sexual pleasure, which placed them into opposition with Catholic priests' intent on converting them. Mesoamericans believed that sexual relations between married couples were healthy, harmonious, and positive, whereas sexual transgressions threatened the social fabric. Jeanne Gillespie calls attention in her chapter to the connection between abstinence and purity; uncleanness is caused by excess and imbalance, creating the general rule that sexual moderation is to be preferred. For unclean individuals, sweat baths were used for purification.

Even though sexual relations are tied to pleasure, harmony, and moderation, there were exceptions to the general social pattern among Mesoamericans. Gillespie calls attention to the practice of periodic celibacy by warriors, the finite nature of bodily fluids, and the necessity for abstinence during some festivals. In fact, celibacy was connected to a return to social and cosmic balance.

NOTES

1. T. N. Madan, *Non-renunciation: Themes and Interpretations of Hindu Culture* (Delhi: Oxford University Press, 1987), 95.

2. Maurice Merleau-Ponty, *Phenomenology of Perception*, translated by Colin Smith (London: Routledge and Kegan Paul, 1962), 205.

3. George Lakoff and Mark Johnson, *Philosophy in the Flesh: The Embodied Mind and Its Challenge to Western Thought* (New York: Basic Books, 1999), 555.

4. Mark Johnson, *The Body in the Mind: The Bodily Basis of Meaning, Imagination, and Reason* (Chicago: University of Chicago Press, 1987).

5. Alphonso Lingis, *Foreign Bodies* (New York: Routledge, 1994), 58–59.

6. Bryan S. Turner, "The Body in Western Society: Social Theory and Its Perspectives," in *Religion and the Body*, edited by Sarah Coakley (Cambridge: Cambridge University Press, 1997), 19.

7. Sandra Bell and Elisa J. Sobo, "Celibacy in Cross-Cultural Perspective: An Overview," in *Celibacy, Culture, and Society: The Anthropology of Sexual Abstinence*, edited by Elisa J. Sobo and Sandra Bell (Madison: University of Wisconsin Press, 2001), 11.

8. Ibid., 8.

9. Mary Douglas, *Purity and Danger: An Analysis of Concepts of Pollution and Taboo* (New York: Praeger, 1966), 2.

10. Ibid., 96–97.

11. See Geoffrey Galt Harpham, *The Ascetic Imperative in Culture and Criticism* (Chicago: University of Chicago Press, 1987), and "Asceticism and the Compensation of Art" in *Asceticism*, edited by Vincent L. Wimbush and Richard Valantasis (New York: Oxford University Press, 1995), 357–368.

12. Robert A. F. Thurman, "Tibetan Buddhist Perspectives on Asceticism," in *Asceticism*, edited by Vincent L. Wimbush and Richard Valantasis (New York: Oxford University Press, 1995), 108–118.

13. Richard Valantasis, "A Theory of the Social Function of Asceticism," in *Asceticism*, edited by Vincent L. Wimbush and Richard Valantasis (New York: Oxford University Press, 1995), 548.

14. Hent de Vries, *Religion and Violence: Philosophical Perspectives from Kant to Derrida* (Baltimore: Johns Hopkins University Press, 2002), 1.

15. Ariel Glucklich, *Sacred Pain: Hurting the Body for the Sake of the Soul* (Oxford: Oxford University Press, 2001), 11.

16. Ibid., 81.

17. Axel-Ivar Berglund, *Zulu Thought-Patterns and Symbolism* (Bloomington: Indiana University Press, 1989), 332.

2

Celibacy in the Greco-Roman World

Willi Braun

Using the word "celibacy" to isolate a list of phenomena in ancient Greco-Roman societies depends almost entirely on how we define the term, which in Western usage has been deeply impregnated with the Christian imagination (*imaginaire*). The Greek language speaks of the "unwed" (*agamos*), but it is not an equivalent term. The Latin *caelebs*, etymological ancestor to "celibate," refers to a man unwed, either by preference or by circumstance, which may, but commonly does not, imply abstinence from sexual activity.[1] If we restrict celibacy to mean, say, "deliberate abstinence from sexual activity,"[2] we may be scooping water from the Tiber with a sieve, so to speak, retrieving from the various classes of ancient sources a few isolated solid bits that for that reason cannot lead to generalizations about celibate practices in ancient Mediterranean societies as a whole, perhaps not even at all.[3] In the cultural pools of the ancient Mediterranean, deliberate sexual continence was hardly a commonplace in practice, although it was always a topic of conversation, proscription, and varied worry from ancient periods until well into the period of Christianity, when celibacy became a defining bodily and rhetorical mark on which Christians staked their difference.[4]

The Greek mythic corpus displays some fascination for renunciation of marriage and sex. Among its female deities, Athena (Roman Minerva), known both as Athena Parthenos (Virgin Athena) and Athena Polias (Athena of the City), is born without a mother; she is a lover of man and manliness but renouncer of marriage, yet defender of patrilineality and patriarchy, the touchstones of ancient Greek social structure.[5] Artemis (Roman Diana), as aggressively virginal and unmarried as Athena, is the patron of untamed nature, where she is *primus inter alia* of "the countless anonymous nymphs of forests, rivers, and mountains, who are all pictured as virginal creatures of the wild."[6] Hestia (Roman Vesta), goddess of hearth and home, is sexually inactive, the stable, immovable, female element in patrilocal marriage, in which women were movable goods. Thus she is, paradoxically, the promoter of patrilineal descent and, if Vernant has it right, the divine warrant for the patriarchal fantasial desire for producing offspring and securing patrimony without the help of women.[7]

Outside the club of the Olympian gods, we might note the immensely popular Anatolian Attis myth complex, variedly narrated but widely disseminated in iconography and cults throughout the Greco-Roman regions. Attis, often thought to be the eponymous inspiration for the familiar emasculated eunuch-priests in the Greco-Roman goddess cults (see below), was, as everyone knew, the demigod "whose genitals had been harvested by a potsherd" (Minucius Felix, *Octavius* 24.12), either in a fit of madness or in remorse for a horny lapse in his chaste devotion to Cybele.[8] The Pythia, Apollo's priestess, who occupied the bronze oracular tripod at Delphi, was a complexly ambiguous virgin (Plutarch, *Pythian Dialogues*; Pindar, *Pythian Odes*), closed to male penetration but vaginally open to divine possession and thought to be in a hierogamous relationship with the god.[9] Dire consequences of lost virginity are among the matters for thought also in the tale of the Danaides in the demogonic myth of the Mycenaean city of Argos.[10] Here the fifty daughters of King Danaus of Argos were forced to marry on a single occasion the fifty sons of Aegyptus. Instructed by their father, all but one of them killed their newly wed man on the wedding bed. As a result, the women were condemned to an afterlife of endless and futile chores, carrying water from the Styx in perforated jars or sieves, thus displaying in their fruitless bodies and pointless activity who they really were: no longer virgins, never to be mothers, hence "mythological prototypes" of all unproductive *agamoi*, unweds, and understandably also associated with the uninitiated in the Eleusinian mysteries.[11] In another version of the Danaides' crime, their infernal banishment to eternal unproductive labor is replaced with a restoration of the Danaides to remarriage and motherhood. It is this version, perhaps, that makes it possible for Herodotus (*Histories* 2.171) and others to credit the Danaides with bringing the *Thesmophoria* to Greece, which appeared also in Rome as the festival of the Bona—a festival, honoring Demeter, where participation was limited to married women who prepared themselves for the rituals by temporary sexual abstinence.

These are mere tidbits from the ancient myths, legends, and commentaries on them. They are replete with divine, quasi-divine, and heroic figures that are set apart in terms of their sexual activities or renunciation thereof, their ambiguously gendered bodies and "unnatural" sexual proclivities and preferences. But gods, like heroes and ancestral prototypes, are not necessarily role models or paradigms of human gender identity and behavior; in Greco-Roman societies these mythological figures were normally revered not by emulation but by placation.[12] In resistance to one long scholarly tradition, one ought not hasten to interpret the meaning of myths and mythemes as symbolic images of the society that hosts these myths, much less as a coded charter for human behavior.[13] Certainly celibacy of varying kinds, linked to diverse motives and effects, is a recurring motif in the mythological and ritual repertoire. Although it is possible with a dash of interpretive ingenuity to presume that celibacy in myth and ritual is a means for thought about gender, sex, division of labor, the viability of communal identities, and the ideals of household and civic organization, "good for thought" is not equivalent to "good in practice."

Greco-Roman philosophical discourses too are replete with worries about sex and the renunciation of it. Although the philosophers did not fear sex, they agreed on the deleterious effects of unregulated passions in the pursuit of a rational, temperate, self-controlled moral character. In matters of sex, then, as in other appetites *kata to sôma* (of the body), philosophers from Plato and Aristotle to the Pythagoreans, Stoics, Cynics, and later Platonists, held that an ascetic impulse, a countermanding *enkrateia* (self-mastery), was to be cultivated as the foundation for the virtue of *autarkeia* (self-determination) that marks the man of reason who is fit for intellectual or political callings. With the exception of a few elite "holy men" (such as Apollonius of Tyana), however, *enkrateia* in sexual matters did not entail the renunciation of sex altogether. Legitimate marriage and decent, restrained sexual union was, after all, requisite for reproduction, a civic duty. Sexual intercourse in accordance with "natural love," the human procreative mandate, was entirely compatible with an ascetically cultivated human dignity. Nothing is wrong with sex as such, the philosophers agreed. Rather than harboring qualms about sex itself, the philosophers wanted to regulate it so as to fit it to their imagined, ideal, self-reliant, rational man. The aim was not abstinence from sex, but rather a therapeutic regime aimed at the higher cultural value of robustly masculine character uninfected by corrosive desires and passions, character-consuming appetites, effeminate affectations, and animalistic lust.[14] That is, celibate tendencies in philosophic thought were contemplated, and occasionally practiced, not as a way of avoiding sexual activities but as a way of "making men," which, in late Hellenistic antiquity, was among the most anxiously pursued forms of self-care.[15]

To this philosophical preoccupation with the pursuit of self-mastery (*enkrateia*) and a nothing-in-excess moral sanity (*sophrosyne*), medical-gynecological "science" would add additional impetus with its theories on the relationship between the spilling of seed and the loss of vital spirit—a relationship that entailed moderation in sexual activity, even occasionally and eccentrically counsel to give up sexual intercourse entirely, such as Soranus gives (*Gynecology* 1.7.32). All this, however, does not amount to evidence of celibacy that is more than exceptional in Greco-Roman practice, although one is surely obliged to agree with Peter Brown that these cultural discourses gave sexual continence "a firm foothold in the folk wisdom of the world in which Christian celibacy would soon be preached."[16]

From the general chatter and static on sex and sexual renunciation on the Greco-Roman broadband, I now turn to inspect what appear to be two spectacular displays of celibacy: the Roman Vestal Virgins and the eunuch-priests of Cybele and her various incarnations.

The Case of the Vestal Virgins

The Vestal Virgins have been among the most scrutinized Roman celibates, for reasons that are easily generalized.[17] The virginal priesthood of Vesta Hestia, goddess of the domestic and "public hearth" (Cicero, *de Legibus* 2.20), was closely associated with the mythic origins of the Roman state and its evolution at least from the time of the early Republic to the end of the fourth century CE when it, along with so many other pagan cults, was terminated by the Christian emperor Theodotius I (394 CE). Aetiological and historical source materials have lent themselves to reconstructing a thousand-year evolutionary genealogy of a particular cultus and the history of religion generally, such that the cult of Vesta offered itself as an ideal example for a " 'paleontological' approach to the study of religion."[18] It is an approach, now waning, that is associated with the nineteenth-century interest in the evolutionary tracking of religious phenomena, an interest that conceded expository power, often in terms of authentic meaning, to origins.[19] Too, the modern take on Vestal Virgins has been dyed in the hues of the centuries-old highbrow Western imaginaire of noble Rome and its "spinster dons" or in admiration, surely spun out of the fantasia of Christian mariology, for "the pagan nuns of the Roman forum—Christian holiness and self-denial *avant la letterlettre*."[20] All this complements the sense that there is "something queer" about the Vestal Virgins (*virgo vestalis*) phenomenon, something "most extraordinary" and weird.[21]

This consternation is due to the peculiar features of Vesta's priesthood. The six Vestals constituted the only female priesthood at Rome and, although the internal supervision of the College—which had eighteen members, but only six cult-performing Vestals at any given time—fell to a superior Vestal, the maximum Vestal Virgin (*virgo vestalis maxima*). She and her colleagues carried on their duties under ultimate jurisdiction of the maximum leader (*pontifex maximus*), that is, the emperor himself. Selection for service as a Vestal was done by the emperor by means of a legal kidnapping, by capturing (*capere*) a prepubescent girl between the age of six and ten who had no bodily defects and came from a patrician family, with both parents alive.[22] The *captio* ceremony, with similarities to Roman marriage rituals, released the initiate from the legal entity of the "power of the father" (*patria potestas*) and the authority of her agnatic family generally and transferred her to the power (*potestas*) of the Roman state and to the Roman collectivity as her substitute agnates.[23] The girl was taken to the Vestal house (*atrium Vestae*) adjacent to the Temple of Vesta, itself located near Rome's Forum and the Regia, the emperor's precinct. Here the Vestal was committed to a thirty-year term of service, during which she was subject to an ironclad vow of chastity. As Plutarch summarizes: "It was ordained by the king that the sacred virgins should vow themselves to chastity for thirty years; during the first decade they are to learn their duties, during the second to perform the duties they have learned, and during the third to teach others these duties" (*Life of Numa* 10.1). "Then, the thirty years having passed," Plutarch continues, "any one who wishes is free to marry and adopt a different mode of life, after laying down her sacred office. We are told, however, that few have welcomed the allowance, and that those who did so were not happy, but were a prey to repentance and dejection for the rest of their lives, thereby inspiring the rest with superstitious fears, so that until old age and death they remained steadfast in their virginity" (*Life of Numa* 10.2). Hence, for most Vestals "their association with the cult remained a lifelong commitment" to celibacy and chastity, first by legal imposition, then objectively imposed by long corporeal practice and post-Vestal life-stage circumstances.[24]

Virgin (*Virgo*) is in fact the sine qua non of the Vestal's status, implying perpetual (prepubescent) maidenhood, physical virginity, and chastity. As Ariadne Staples has rightly underscored, "virginity was not merely a necessary attribute of the Vestals, it was reified."[25] Physiologically it was ensured by prepuberty induction into the Vestal. While in office, the Vestals' virginity was guarded by the Roman surveillance apparatus, including escort by a *lictor*, a ceremonial attendant and bodyguard (Plutarch, *Life of Numa* 10.3).[26] Harsh punishment for violation (*crimen incesti*), that is, failure to preserve actual and perceived chastity, was severely punished, most drastically in a ritual execution by being buried alive—a spectacle, Plutarch notes, that is "more appalling and brings more gloom to the city than any other" (*Life of Numa* 10.5). The gloom, though surely commenting on the brutality of the Vestal's execution, is all the weightier because trials and penalization of Vestals occurred during times of political instability, civil unrest, and military defeat; transgression of a Vestal was thus associated with a failure of the state itself, and her punishment "was intended as expiation for the Roman state as a whole."[27] Not least important, lifelong celibacy was assured by the thirty-year hiatus between presexual girlhood and the Vestal's retirement, which about corresponded to the period of a woman's child-bearing capacity. The term of conscription, that is, largely suppressed the possibility of productive sex and the natural physiological and status progression from virgin (*virgo*) to woman (*matrona*).[28]

This virginal status is confounded, however, by the fact that the Vestals' chief symbolic and ritual functions were matronal in nature: they had to perform various duties associated with Vesta's role as guardian of "the hearth of the city," chief among which was tending the sacred fire burning in the Temple of Vesta; they prepared the *mola salsa* (salt cakes) used in the sacrificial rites during the annual Vestalia; they performed the annual ritual cleaning of the temple on the last day of the Vestalia. Tending hearth, preparing food, cleaning—all core household duties of the Roman married woman. Additional ambiguity is imposed by the peculiar privileges of the Vestals. The right to give testimony in court, ability to make their own wills, and exemption from *tutela* bequeathing their property, as crucial examples, usually were granted only to men.

The Vestal thus was an ambiguous figure; she was in a "position of perpetual rite of passage (*rite de passage*)," as Mary Beard has influentially argued. She was suspended between several sexual and gender categories, "perpetually on the brink, perpetually fixed at the moment of transition from one category to another."[29] She belonged to several classes but to none exclusively and unambiguously. She partook symbolically and legally in any and all conventional sex, gender, and status classifications but could not be fully assigned to a single one of them. She was every significant Roman, but not definitively a single type of Roman. In Holt Parker's concise summary: "A Roman woman existed legally only in relation to a man.... The act of freeing a Vestal from any man so that she was free to incarnate all men removed her from all conventional classifications, including the fundamental distinction between the living and the dead.[30] Thus she was unmarried and so not a wife; a virgin and so not a mother; she was outside *patria potestas* and so not a daughter; she underwent no *emancipatio*, no *coemptio* and so not a ward."[31] Hence her representational value was metonymic: the Vestal is Rome (*Romanitas*).[32] She was the totem of Rome, in Durkheim's definition of a thing that represents the social whole including its genealogical foundation, the ancestral spirits of dead Romans.[33]

It should be stressed, however, that virginity is not merely just another aspect of the Vestal's totemic value. She served the ideology of the impenetrability of the Roman state. Her perfection and purity, along with her unclassifiability, made her the perfect sacrificial victim, a scapegoat (*pharmakos*), when Rome found itself in what R. Girard calls a "sacrificial crisis."[34] The representational value of the Vestal, her categorically liminal status, her ritual duties, and the possibility, occasionally the reality, of her victimization by the very state she represented and embodied must be seen as a dense metonymic cluster of idealized Roman nature. The Vestals' virginity was not, after all, "a matter of free choice to them. No heroic freedom of the individual will was made plain" in their celibacy.[35] Rome captured them, set them apart, and inscribed itself ideologically and ritually on the physiological and symbolic body of the female virgins.

The Case of Eunuchs

In 1925, A. D. Nock wrote that since religious castration is Oriental in origin, "eunuchs have no place in purely Greek and Roman cults."[36] Let us allow that he was correct on the question of provenance. Eunuchs were a fixture in the royal establishments of the ancient Near East.[37] The eunuch priests, the Galli, of the Anatolian mother goddess variously called Kybele, Agditis, Rhea, Magna Mater, Cybele, Artemis, and other names over time (but depicted with a consistent iconography) are of neolithic central Anatolian origin. The Sumerian *gala*, castrated priests in the service of the Sumerian goddess Inanna and Akkadian Ishtar, are documented in Mesopotamian temple records of the third millennium, and the analogous eunuchs (*hijra*) associated with the Indian mother goddess Bahuchara Mata may have roots as old as the Anatolian Galli.[38] Be that as it may ("origin" and "purity" are in any case overrated, even overthrown, explanatory concepts in the study of cultural phenomena), the figure of the eunuch was well known from archaic antiquity to late antiquity, from Assyria to Rome and Byzantium, an important figure in the monarchic palaces and bureaucracies, and in the cults of Attis and Cybele, which entered Rome in the late third century BCE.[39] Eunuchs also appear in the cults of the Syrian goddess Ephesian Artemis and other incarnations of the Anatolian Magna Mater, in popular imagination as reflected in its cultural productions, both literary (Lucian of Samosata, Terence, Apuleius) and iconographic.[40] By the first and second centuries CE, the figure of the eunuch—the Gallus of course, but also as a human gender classification problem—was a stock figure in the social and representational landscapes of the Greco-Roman world. They were as Greek and Roman as anything else, even though Romans contemptuously regarded the Cybelian eunuch-priest as an alien Phrygian freak and promptly outlawed castration for Romans.[41]

Lucius Apuleius, the second-century CE author of the romping, risqué novel *Metamorphoses*, draws a picture for us that permits us to appreciate the flaunted presence and cultural perception of the eunuch.

> They [the *chorus cinaedorum*, "band of homosexual prostitutes," 8.26] put on varicolored garments and beautified themselves hideously (*deformiter quisque formati*) by daubing clay pigment on their faces and outlining their eyes with greasepaint. Then they set out, wearing turbans and saffron-colored robes and vestments of linen and silk. Some had white tunics decorated with purple lance-shaped designs flowing in every direction, gathered up into a girdle, and on their feet they wore yellow shoes. They wrapped the [Syrian] goddess in a silken mantle and put her on my [Lucius the ass's] back to carry, while they, with arms bared to the shoulders and brandishing frightful swords and axes, chanted and danced, excited by the frenzied beat of the music. . . . [T]hey came to the country house of a rich landowner. As soon as they reached the entranceway they frantically flung themselves forward, filling the place with the sound of their discordant shrieks. For a long time they dropped their heads and rotated their necks in writhing motions, swinging their hanging locks in a circle. Sometimes they bit their own flesh with their teeth, and finally they all began slashing their arms with the two-edged blades they were carrying. . . . One of them started to rave more wildly than the rest, and producing rapid gasps from deep down in his chest, as though he had been filled with the heavenly inspiration of some deity (*divino spiritu repletus*), he simulated a fit of madness (*vecordiam*). . . . Shouting like a prophet, he began to attack and accuse himself with a fabricated lie about how he had perpetrated some sin against the laws of holy religion (*sanctae religionis*); and he went on to demand just punishment for his guilty deed from his own hands. He snatched up the utensil which is the distinctive attribute of these half-men (*semiviris*), a whip with long tassels made of twisted strips of woolly hide studded with numerous sheep's knuckle-bones, and he scourged himself hard.

> ... You could see the ground growing wet with the filthy, effeminate blood (*sanguinis effeminati*) from all this slashing of swords and lashing of whips.... When they had grown tired, or at least sated with self-laceration, they ceased their butchery and took up a collection [i.e., resumed begging]. (*Metamorphoses* 8.27–29)

Even if we discount the Monty Pythonesque excesses in Apuleius's description of these devotees of the Syrian goddess, the tone of derision and language of scorn—half-men, effeminates, mad, hideous offenders of the laws of proper religion—is drawn from a standard thesaurus of slurs by which to hurl contempt at these figures. In Lucian of Samosata's *The Eunuch*, Lycinus describes the eunuch as "neither man nor woman but something composite, hybrid, and monstrous, alien to human nature." He was regarded as "one whom the male sex has discarded and the female will not adopt" (Claudian, *In Eutropium* 1.468) or, as Augustine would quip, upon emasculation "neither is he changed into a woman nor does he remain a man" (*City of God* 7.24). Indeed, ancient authors had to invent a new category of person for the eunuch; he became a member of the *tertium genus hominum*, "third type of human," or *tertium sexus*, the "third sex" (*Historiae Augusta, Alexander Severus* 23.7; Prudentius, *Peristephanon* 10.1071). "Third" also designates their place in the hierarchy of human species: man on top, then woman, then eunuch, such that the aspersion "weaker than a eunuch" could be used to remark on human strength that registered below low (Dio Chrysostom, *Oration* 3.35). David Hester summarizes the suspicious and contemptuous character profile: "Generally, they were viewed as soft (*mollis, eviratus, malakos*), effeminate (*semivir, semimas, effeminatus, androgynos*), sexually passive (*kinaidos*), unkind, immodest (*impudicitia*), ... weak, impotent, deceitful, cowardly and incapable of virtue. Popular novels depicted them as power-seeking, unscrupulous, greedy, untrustworthy and undependable.... Dream interpretation, popular sayings, fables, even popular superstitions, all viewed the eunuch as an object of scorn, bad luck and deception. The eunuch, by definition, was not (could not be) a morally upright and virtuous figure, but was always suspicious."[42] Of course, Hester assembles a mélange that contributes to the stereotype "eunuch" simply by combining bits and pieces of ancient stereotypes; but the Greco-Roman eunuch was in fact not just a man without testicles or a man unable to procreate; his additional burden was precisely "eunuch-as-stereotype."[43] One looks in vain for approving nods or commentary on the eunuch in ancient sources, even though they had traditionally enjoyed status as functionaries in high places, and continued into late antiquity to be employed as attendants in women's quarters—which earned them their appellation in the first place, for eunuch means "keeper of the bed."[44]

Were eunuchs celibates, both in the sense of refraining from sexual activity and in the (often) associated sense of chastity? A long Christian commentarial tradition on the eunuch saying in the New Testament Gospel of Matthew 19:12 has offered the eunuch as "an emblem of extreme chastity"—with spill-over into scholarship on eunuchism in ancient Greek and Roman cultures.[45] Prominently, A. D. Nock, rightly arguing against a favored de jure explanation of castration as the means of assimilating the priest to the goddess, suggests that the motives for the "self-mutilation" by the priests of Cybele, Dea Syria, and other goddesses was to ensure for themselves ritual purity. This he understood as a "negative chastity," negative because "chastity in cultus was commonly regarded as something negative and as an abstention." Equating castration with sexual disablement, he understood the practice as a way of cutting off the source of "the impurity involved in sexual intercourse" rather than as motivated by "peculiar powers resting in the pure."[46] Purity and chastity are not, however, associated with eunuchism in the ancient sources, nor was it a technique for desexualization that was known or believed to entail loss of sexual desire and therefore abstinence from sexual activity, that is, celibacy, as A. Rousselle has influentially shown on historical evidence and medical science.[47] Although the eunuch's sterility is taken for granted in the ancient sources, his sexual ability was debated (could he maintain an erection and be a penetrator or could he only be penetrated?), but rarely doubted, both for the kind of sex they had and the excess of their lust.[48] If sexual contact was considered a source of pollution that disqualifies the devotee from service to the deity, the eunuch was hardly qualified "to serve through his whole life the object of his devotion."[49] But serve he did.

Rather than offering a motive for ritual castration or ablation, much less a "religious" one, I should ask why the eunuch was universally disdained and ridiculed, but why, nevertheless, he was accorded some esteem.[50] The question then becomes why the figure of the eunuch persisted robustly in the Greco-Roman world in all periods, and even increased in popularity once the native palaces, temples, and city-state bureaucracies that had provided the eunuch with function and status were overridden by the colonization and "globalization" of Greek and Roman imperial formations.[51]

The despicable and dangerous eunuch was culturally sustained by the regnant Greco-Roman gender ideology, which idealized maleness and pathologized femaleness at many levels. Let me briefly outline the theory that modulated itself from archaic and classical patrilineal and patriarchal household and civic structures, and firmly linked gender identity to citizenship and the public (male) pursuit of civic virtues, into a more diffused gender ideology in the Greco-Roman regions under the conditions of imperial and colonial realities.

First, at the level of conceptualizing and remodeling the architecture of the cosmos in the late Hellenistic period, precisely when eunuchs assume an increase in social and literary profile, two interlinked problems emerge.[52] One concerns the perceived emigration of the gods, once resident among humans in earthly temple and sacred place, to the superlunar regions of the cosmic sphere. Not only did this leave humans to fend for themselves in the chancy muck of life under the moon but it also left them vulnerable to the *stoicheia*, demonic powers that patrolled the sublunar regions. The other is the recasting of the older concept of *Agathê Tychê*—a notion that sees Fate at worst as benign and at best as a principle of sympathetic providential care—into *Heimarmenê*, an understanding of Fate as a capricious, oppressive feminine principle that manifested itself especially in the incarcerating malevolence and maliciousness of the sublunar powers that separated earthy humanity from the ethereal gods. It is in this intellectual matrix that we see the emergence of the various theologies of male saviors, theologies which incipiently understand "salvation" in gendered terms: "maleness," physiologically complete and properly functioning man, represents the goal (*telos*) on the path to salvation. "Femaleness" represents the highest abstraction of the tyranny of this-worldly, material human existence. The eunuch does not, and cannot, belong to either category. It is not a huge leap from imagining the perceived cosmic conflict as a gender war to identifying gender ambiguity as part of the parcel of human deficiencies that are beyond the natural, moral, civic pale.

A second theoretical base undergirding Greco-Roman gender ideology was constructed in the laboratories of research and philosophical thought on human physiology.[53] Ancient physiological and medical thought was based on a theory of monosexuality—Laqueur calls it the "one-sex" model—"in which men and women were arrayed according to their degree of metaphysical perfection, their vital heat, along an axis whose telos was male."[54] Physiological dimorphism, that is, was not converted into ontological gender dimorphism, into an anthropology in which man and woman are distinct categories of human being that, conceivably, could be valued as physiologically different but equal on scales of virtue, value, nobility, or just plain humanity. On the contrary, human bodies were understood in terms of a continuum running between poles of masculinity and femininity; each body was thought to contain both male and female aspects and "every human body, male or female, occupies some position on the spectrum male-female."[55] The position of bodies on the physiognomic spectrum corresponds to their embodiments of core Mediterranean values of virtue, honor, and nobility, just as body types correspond to a person's location on the social and political spectrum of power and influence. On this spectrum, a range of "blessings" (education, rationality, virtue) that qualified people to be custodians (saviors) of the family, city, and state (Dio Chryosthom, *Orations* 32.3) were firmly associated with the masculine ideal.[56] In theory, the model of monosexuality allowed for, indeed expected, prized masculine qualities in women and despised female qualities in men; it would seem intended to mold men to achieve greater levels of maleness (Galen, *De spermate* 1). But the theory runs squarely against another dimension of ancient gender ideology: the hierarchy of the male-female continuum and the problem of physiology. Female and effeminate bodies, according to Hippocratic philosophical-medical theories, lacked the needed levels of dryness, heat, activeness, strength, and solidity to achieve a male level of masculinity.[57] Although there was not complete agreement among the ancient physiologists on exactly how to take measure of a person's level of maleness or femaleness by means of temperature, humors, and density of body mass, they were agreed that the material apparatus of the body both presents the gauge and sets the limits.[58] An impaired male body, a eunuchized effeminate body, thus blocked access to full manly excellence.

It is true that this theoretical allowance was in fact contradicted by another theory, namely, the theory of commensurability of physiological body surface and inner quality of character (see Ps.-Aristotle, *Physiognômonika* 805a–808b). It is this theory that is behind the popularity of late-Hellenistic physiognomy, the "science" of deducing character from physiology—the art of determining from physiological shape, gestures, deportment, and so forth, which of the sexes prevailed in any given person. The second-century physiognomist Polemo states the principle succinctly: "You may obtain physiognomic signs of masculinity and femininity from your subject's glance, movement, and voice. Then, taking these signs, compare one with another until you are able to satisfy yourself on which of the two sexes prevails. For in the masculine something feminine will be found, and in the feminine something masculine, but the designation "masculine" or "feminine" should be used in accordance with which of the two (sexes) prevails" (Polemo, *Physiognomics* 2). It is not hard to see that, according to Polemo's logic, persons with "effeminate" body markings, accompanied by other ambiguous gender and sex displays, would be hard-pressed to convince anyone that their true or "prevailing" character was anything other than commensurate with their physiognomic signs. Eunuchs would always signal that they were deficient precisely in those character qualities that would most identify them as quintessential human beings because those character qualities were precisely those which were physiologically represented in complete, male bodies, with properly (that is, reproductively) functioning genitals. Not all men, that is, were males.

This whole theoretical package, entirely committed to *andreia* (masculinity) as the divinely and naturally ordained high nobility of the human being, was forcefully represented and reproduced in a host of everyday practices and conventions—from schooling to public discourse and rhetoric, to philosophy, to all kinds of gender-coded and gender-signifying domestic and public spaces and proprieties. The totality of Greco-Roman culture was univocal: humans with effeminate qualities and affectations, for which the female body and femaleness is lowest limit, represented humans of deficient personhood. It is this whole cultural kit that explains why the eunuch was such an itch for all Greeks and Romans who worried about gender, sex, and how these are related to character and virtue, as well as ethnic, civic, and imperial identity.[59] The eunuch, neither fully male nor entirely female, incapable of (re)productive sex but perceived to be enslaved to sexual desire and unconstrained in indulging this desire—a powerful yet feared interstitial figure—threatened to rupture the hegemony of masculinity (*andreia*), and by his very presence exposed masculinity as an ideology that is contestable.[60]

It perhaps for this reason that the eunuchs were not only detested but also had supporters and clients. Apuleius, for example, remarks that people "vied in offering" copper and silver coins and various alimentary goods (wine, milk, cheese, grains) to the band of mendicant eunuch devotees of the goddess at whom he otherwise sneers (*Metamorphoses* 8.28). In an "important town" one of the "leading men (*vir principalis*) there, who besides a general religious disposition showed a special reverence for the goddess (*eximie deam reverens*)" took in "the goddess with devout hospitality" and provided lodging for the troop of eunuchs (*galli*) "within the walls of his extensive domain (*domus*) while striving to win the goddess's favor with the utmost veneration (*summa veneratione*) and sumptuous sacrifices" (8.30). In another hill town, a farmer, fearing what Apuleius construes as a "false prognostication" (*fictae vaticinationis*) performed by the *galli*, donated "his fattest ram for a sacrifice to satisfy the hungry Syrian goddess" (8.29). Assuming Apuleius's ethnographic reliability, more than simple charity for beggarly priests is at work here.[61] Fear of the goddess and her priests is a motive in placating her, or reverence is demonstrated by votive offerings. Other sources indicate that the emasculated beggar-priests were sought out for their skill in conducting contagious magic to ward off calamity for twelve months (Juvenal, *Satura* 6.511–515); they were known for interpreting omens, both avian (Cicero, *On Divination* 1.41) and astral (Pliny, *Natural History* 2.37). All this is to say that the goddess's priests were feared and revered not because of their purity, and certainly not because of their continence or because they were considered exemplary models of honoring the gods, but because they performed various divinatory and magical rites to achieve quotidian benefits for people who subscribed to their services.[62] Horror and clientele-inspiring awe were the cross-eyed gazes directed at the eunuch.

Concluding Remarks

As unchaste and polluted of body, a metonym for Greco-Roman anxieties about gender, which is itself a trope for working on worries about identity—personal, civic, imperial—the eunuch-priest is both kin and alter ego to the Vestal Virgin. Both are simultaneously symptoms and signs of empire. One of them is a totemic emblem of the fantasy of an inviolable, eternal Rome, and its sacrificial scapegoat that reasserted Rome and Romans (*Romanitas*) by expiating its (temporary) failures. The other is a creaking announcement of empire's more fundamental fissures, an exposure of the hegemony of empire as a contestable ideology of stability that could not hold up against a disquieting sense of its frailty—that it was as frail as its people's gender vesture that Greeks and Romans often lethargically regarded as natural, fixed, and stable.

NOTES

1. The Greek term *agamos* means unwed, which may but need not imply sexual abstinence. For the Latin, see, for example, Ovid, *Metamorphoses*, 10: "Pygmalion saw... women waste their lives in wretched shame, and critical of flaws that nature had so deeply planted in their female hearts, he lived in preference, for many years unmarried (*caelebs*)." Pygmalion did not, however, abstain from sexual activity, illustrating a more general observation that in antiquity renunciation of marriage does not usually entail renunciation of sexual activity. He sculpted an ivory statue of a perfect virgin and took her as an artificial sex object, even impregnating her with an assist from Venus.

2. Daniel Gold, "Celibacy," in *Encyclopedia of Religion*, 2nd edition, edited by Lindsay Jones (Detroit: Macmillan, 2005), 1474–1478.

3. The metaphor of the sieve appears in Valerius Maximus's story of the vestal virgin Tuccia, who, when accused of the crime of unchastity, "boldly and rashly" offered to prove her innocence by carrying water from the Tiber to the temple in a sieve, a dare to which "the Nature of Things gave way" (*Valerius Maximus* 8.1.absol. 5; see A. Richlin, "Carrying Water in a Sieve: Class and the Body in Roman Women's Religion," in *Women and Goddess Traditions in Antiquity and Today*, edited by K. King (Minneapolis: Fortress, 1997).

4. Peter Brown, *The Body and Society: Men, Women, and Sexual Renunciation in Early Christianity* (New York: Columbia University Press, 1988).

5. "No mother gave me birth. I honor the male, in all things but marriage. Yes, with all my heart I am my father's child" (Aeschylus, *Eumenides* 751–753).

6. H. S. Versnel, "The Festival for Bona Dea and the Thesmophoria," *Greece and Rome* 2nd Series 39 (1992): 49.

7. J. P. Vernant, "Hestia—Hermes: The Religious Expression of Space and Movement in Ancient Greece," in *Myth and Thought among the Greeks* (London: Routledge, 1983), 127–175.

8. The Attis/Cybele material has produced immense scholarly labor, classically by J. G. Frazer, *Adonis, Osiris: Studies in the History of Oriental Religion* (London: Macmillan, 1906), but see especially M. J. Vermaseren, *Cybele and Attis: The Myth and the Cult* (London: Thames & Hudson, 1977); L. E. Roller, *In Search of God the Mother: The Cult of Anatolian Cybele* (Berkeley: University of California Press, 1999); and M. G. Lancellotti, *Attis between Myth and History: King, Priest and God* (Leiden: E. J. Brill, 2002).

9. The Pythia's ambiguous virginity converges with real-life prenuptial virginity. As Giulia Sissa has shown in her programmatic study, in Greek cultures virginity and sexual intercourse were not incompatible once one looks beneath the surface of custom, law, and dissimulating rhetoric. Hence nubile virgins were known to have given birth to a bastard (*parthenios*; child of a virgin) without losing their virginal status. "In literature countless children born to 'virgins' bear witness to a conception of virginity that had nothing to do with the body or sex.... The word *bastard* makes it clear that the Greeks did not expect of their illegitimate children (*parthenoi*) the absolute, unwavering chastity that defines virginity in the Christian ethos." G. Sissa, *Greek Virginity*, translated by A. Goldhammer (Cambridge: Harvard University Press, 1990), 78, 83.

10. Exhaustively studied by C. Bonner, "A Study of the Danaid Myth," *Harvard Studies in Classical Philology* 13 (1902): 129–173.

11. Sissa, *Greek Virginity*, 130.

12. Castrated Attis and the *galli*, eunuch priests of the goddess, may be one exception (see further below).

13. Hans H. Penner, "What a Difference Theory Makes," in *Introducing Religion*, edited by Willi Braun and R. T. McCutcheon (London: Equinox, 2007). Cited from typescript.

14. Martha C. Nussbaum, *The Theory of Desire: Theory and Practice in Hellenistic Ethics* (Princeton: Princeton University Press, 1994); H. Moxnes, "Conventional Values in the Hellenistic World: Masculinity," in *Conventional Values of the Hellenistic Greeks*, edited by P. Bilde et al. (Arhus: Aarhus University Press, 1997), 263–284.

15. M. W. Gleason, *Making Men: Sophists and Self-Presentation in Ancient Rome* (Princeton: Princeton University Press, 1995). See also M. W. Gleason, "The Semiotics of Gender: Physiognomy and Self-fashioning in the Second Century CE," in *Before Sexuality: The Construction of Erotic Experience in the Ancient Greek World*, edited by D. M. Halperin, J. J. Winkler, and F. I. Zeitlin (Princeton: Princeton University Press, 1990), 389–415.

16. Brown, *Body and Society*, 19.

17. Among numerous remarks in the ancient sources on the putative origin, history, features, and function of the cult of Vesta, see especially Plutarch, *Life of Numa Pompilius* 9–10; Aulus Gellius, *Attic Nights* 1.12; and Dionysus of Halicarnassus, *Roman Antiquities* 2.66.1. Cf. the late comparison of the Vestals with Christian virgins in Ambrose's letters (*Ep.* 17 and 18) to the Western emperor Valentinian in 384 CE.

18. H. N. Parker, "Why Were the Vestals Virgins? Or the Chastity of Women and the Safety of the Roman State," *American Journal of Philology* 125 (2004): 565.

19. See T. Masuzama, "Origin," in *Guide to the Study of Religion*, edited by W. Braun and R. T. McCutcheon (London: Cassell, 2000), 209–224. In theory we should expect to find, as we do in fact, that ancestral repertoires (myths, rituals, treasured texts) are not stable but subject to various resignifying and reusing strategies under new conditions and circumstances in the Greco-Roman worlds. See E. R. Wolf, *Europe and the People without History* (Berkeley: University of California Press, 1982), 387: "In the rough-and-tumble of social interaction, groups are known to exploit the ambiguity of inherited forms, to impart new evaluations or valences on them, to borrow forms more expressive of their interest, or to create wholly new forms to answer to changed circumstances. . . . A 'culture' is thus better seen as a series of processes that construct, reconstruct, and dismantle cultural materials, in response to identifiable determinants."

20. M. Beard cites Worsfold in "Re-reading (Vestal) Virginity," in *Women in Antiquity: New Assessments*, edited by R. Hawley and B. Levick (London: Routledge, 1995), 171: "In modern days the sisterhoods of the nuns of the Church of Rome, themselves of great antiquity, offer the closest resemblance."

21. Versnel, "Festival for Bona Dea and the Thesmophoria," 36; A. Staples, *From Good Goddess to Vestal Virgin: Sex and Category in Roman Religion* (London: Routledge, 1998), 129; Beard, "Re-reading (Vestal) Virginity," 166.

22. Staples, *From Good Goddess to Vestal Virgin*, 138–139. Rules of eligibility changed over time; from the fourth century BCE, girls of plebeian rank could be chosen; from Augustus and onward daughters of freedmen could be selected (Cassius Dio, *Roman History* 55.22.5–12; Suetonius, *Divus Augustus* 31.3; see J. E. Thompson, "Images of Vesta and the Vestal Virgins in Roman State Religion and Imperial Policy of the First and Second Centuries A.D.," Ph.D. dissertation, Yale University, 2005, 31 n. 32). The "capturing" of the Vestal is described by Aulus Gellius, *Attic Nights* 1.12.13–14. On the significance of the *captio* ceremony, including required language ("thus I take you, loved one") and the young initiate's bridal coiffure, see Thompson, "Images of Vesta and the Vestal Virgins," 32–33, where he reviews and criticizes the view that the ceremony "would suggest that the Vestal entered into a kind of 'marriage' with the [maximum leader] *pontifex maximus*" (33). See also Staples, *From Good Goddess to Vestal Virgin*, 138–143, for a perceptive discussion of the peculiar legal exceptions applied in the Vestals' release from the power of the father (*patria potestas*).

23. Staples, *From Good Goddess to Vestal Virgin*, 144.

24. Thompson, "Images of Vesta and the Vestal Virgins," 31, 28. Let us translate Plutarch's remarks on the retired Vestal's "dejection" and "superstitious fears" into

Bourdieu's evocation of the Greek term *hexis*, a permanent condition, state of being, brought about, incorporated, through practice: "L'hexis corporelle est la mythologie politique réalisée, *incorporée*, devenue disposition permanente, manière durable" (The bodily hexis is the realized political myth, embodied, becoming a permanent disposition, a lasting manner) (P. Bourdieu, *Le sens pratique* [Paris: Minuit, 1980], 117).

25. Staples, *From Good Goddess to Vestal Virgin*, 129, and see also 147.

26. Since *lictores* also accompanied men of imperial rank, some have suggested that assignment of this privilege to a Vestal contributed to the attribution of a male dimension to the symbolics of the Vestal (G. Dumézil, *Archaic Roman Religion*, 2 vols., translated by P. Knapp (Cambridge: Cambridge University Press, 1970), II:587; M. Beard, "The Sexual Status of Vestal Virgins," *Journal of Roman Studies* 70 (1980): 17). Others think the attendant is a visual symbol of the prestige and set-apart ritual status of the Vestal (Staples, *From Good Goddess to Vestal Virgin*, 145).

27. Thompson, "Images of Vesta and the Vestal Virgins," 35.

28. Beard, "Sexual Status," 14 n. 21; Staples, *From Good Goddess to Vestal Virgin*, 147.

29. Beard, "Sexual Status," 21.

30. In a provocative argument, singularly ignored in subsequent scholarship on the Vestals, K. R. Prowse, "The Vestal Circle," *Greece and Rome* 2nd Series 14 (1967): 174–187, argues that the temple of Vesta shares attributes with other "homes" of Rome's ancestors and that, therefore, "the temple of Vesta guarded within its sacred circle the nameless ancestors upon whose power rested the power of Rome itself" (187). The Vestals' duties were in part to look after the needs of the spirits of the dead. Prowse's argument could be extended with the notice that the highly regulated ritual of live burial of a transgressive Vestal in a subterranean tomb outfitted with minimal furniture and a limited food supply (a scene itself analogous to the ancient hearth-centred house and the Temple of Vesta) takes her beyond the living *and* the dead so as both to join and to placate the powerful spirits of the dead.

31. Parker, "Why Were the Vestals Virgins?" 573.

32. Staples, *From Good Goddess to Vestal Virgin*, 143.

33. Émile Durkheim, *The Elementary Forms of the Religious Life*, translated by J. W. Swain (London: Allen and Unwin, 1915), 123; Parker, "Why Were the Vestals Virgins?" 574.

34. R. Girard, *Violence and the Sacred*, translated by P. Gregory (Baltimore: Johns Hopkins University Press, 1977), 39. Girard's theory of sacrifice is productively and correctively applied to the ritual killing of the Vestal, and by extension to the sacrifice of women, by H. Parker, "Why Were the Vestals Virgins?" 575–578.

35. Brown, *Body and Society*, 8.

36. A. D. Nock, "Eunuchs in Ancient Religion," *Archiv für Religionswissenschaft* 23 (1925): 20.

37. M. Riquet, *La castration* (Paris: P. Lethielleux, 1948).

38. W. Roscoe, "Priests of the Goddess: Gender Transgression in Ancient Religion," *History of Religions* 35 (1996): 198, 206, 213.

39. "Nobles in their togas bare their feet before the car at the rites of the Idaean Mother [epithet for Cybele]" (Prudentius, *Peristephanon* 10.154–155; cited by A. Rousselle, *"Porneia": On Desire and the Body in Antiquity*, translated by F. Pheasant [Oxford: Blackwell, 1988], 201).

40. J. L. Lightfoot, "Sacred Eununchism in the Cult of the Strain Goddess," in *Eunuchs in Antiquity and Beyond*, edited by S. Tougher (London: Classical Press of Wales and Duckworth, 2002), 71–86; G. M. Sanders, "Gallos," in *Reallexikon für Antike und Christentum*, edited by T. Klauser et al. (Leipzig: K. W. Hiersemann, 1972), vol. 8, col. 996; see S. Hales, "Looking for Eunuchs: The Galli and Attis in Roman Art," in *Eunuchs in Antiquity and Beyond*, edited by S. Tougher (London: Classical Press of Wales and Duckworth, 2002), 87–102.

41. Eunuchs inhabited various social positions, ranging from the professional administrative assistants in royal and political administrative offices to the roving bands, probably attached to local shrines of Cybele or the Syrian Goddess, who "ventured to prowl the streets and countryside begging for alms and performing spectacular religious rites" (Roscoe, "Priests of the Goddess," 202). I use the term here without respect either to subtypes or to the distinctions based on the how a male became a eunuch. Ancients did distinguish eunuchic types, even in law: "The name eunuch (*spadonum*) is general; it subsumes who are natural eunuchs (*qui natura spadones sunt*), those who were made eunuchs (*item thlibiae thlasiae*), and any other kind of eunuch" (Ulpian, *Digesta* 50.16.128; discussion in G. R. Brower, "Ambivalent Bodies: Making Christian Eunuchs," Ph.D. dissertation, Duke University, 1996, 155 and n. 27).

42. J. D. Hester, "Eunuchs and the Postgender Jesus: Matthew 19 and Transgressive Sexualities," *Journal for the Study of the New Testament* 28 (2005): 21–22. For the fullest survey of the ancient sources, see P. Guyot, *Eunuchen als Sklaven und Freigelassenen in der griechisch-römishen Antike* (Stuttgart: Stuttgarter Beiträge zur Geschichte und Politk 14, Klett-Cotta, 1980), 42–44, 174–176, on which Hester relies. Transliterations in italics are mine.

43. Brower, "Ambivalent Bodies," 151–153. To wit, "eunuchs, neither woman nor man, lustful, envious, ill-bribed, passionate, effeminate, slaves of the belly, mad for gold, ruthless, grumbling about their dinner, inconstant, stingy, greedy, insatiable, savage, jealous. What more need I say? At their very birth they were condemned to the knife. How can their mind be right when their feet are awry? They are chaste because of the knife, and it is no credit to them. They are lecherous to no purpose, of their own natural vileness" (Basil of Ancyra, *Ep.* CXV [To the heretic Simplicia]).

44. Hester, "Eunuchs and the Postgender Jesus," 19 n. 13): "With respect to eunuchs, during the period under question I have found very few examples in which a eunuch was praised." The examples he did find (Ammianus Marcellinus, *Res Gestae* 16.7; Polybius, *History* 22.22.1) cite eunuchs approvingly for outstanding compensating qualities rather than their emasculated state. Cf. the grudging comment by Sextus Empiricus: "The Mother of the Gods also accepts effeminates (*thêlydrias*), and the goddess would not judge so, if by nature unmanliness (*mê andreion*) were a trivial matter" (*Outlines of Pyrrhonism* 3.217; cited by Roscoe, "Priests of the Goddess," 204).

On their place in women's quarters, see E. Lieber, "The Hippocratic 'Airs, Waters, Places' on Cross-dressing Eunuchs: 'Natural' yet also 'Divine,' " in *Sex and Difference in Ancient Greece and Rome*, edited by M. Golden and P. Toohey (Edinburgh: Edinburgh University Press, 2003), 366.

45. D. F. Caner, "The Practice and Prohibition of Self-Castration in Early Christianity," *Vigiliae Christianae* (1997): 399. See also Hester, "Eunuchs and the Postgender Jesus," 13. The early Christian practice of castration, for which there is evidence from mid-second century onward, demonstrates a mixture of approval and censure.

46. Nock, "Eunuchs in Ancient Religion," 28–32, esp. 30.

47. Rousselle, *"Porneia,"* 121–127. See also G. Casadio, "The Failing Male God: Emasculation, Death, and Other Accidents in the Ancient Mediterranean World," *Numen* 50 (2003): 242, on Nock's views as "anachronistic and ethnocentric. (As it seems to me the British scholar was influenced above all by the model of celibacy laid down for Catholic Priests)." On purity issues in Greek religion, see the standard work of R. Parker, *Miasma: Pollution and Purification in Early Greek Religion* (Oxford: Oxford University Press, 1983).

48. A good collection of evidence is in Brower, "Ambivalent Bodies," 174–178. Apollonius of Tyana, himself a famous sex renouncer, instructs his companion Damis, who assumes that castration means inability to have sexual intercourse, by pointing out that eunuchs too "feel desire" and, therefore, that castration is not a physical shortcut to moral sanity (*sôphrosynê*), which is a matter of "not giving in to sexual intercourse when fueled with desire, but in abstinence and appearing superior to this madness" (Philostratus, *Life of Apollonius* 1.33).

49. Nock, "Eunuchs in Ancient Religion," 31.

50. Positing of motives for the eunuch other than avoiding impurity are available. For example, Burkert's "functional" explanation that aims for coherence between the Antis myth and the ritual castration of the priest suggests cogently that "castration puts a man outside archaic society in an absolutely irrevocable way; being neither man nor woman, but 'nothing,' he has no place to go." This displacement, less cogently, gives him (like Attis's complex dependency on the Magna Mater), "no choice but to adhere to his goddess; . . . the mere act [of castration] makes apostasy impossible" W. Burkert, *Structure and History in Greek Mythology and Ritual* (Berkeley: University of California Press, 1979), 105. See Casadio, "Failing Male God," 235–248, for a survey of other explanations of the motives behind castration and devotion to the goddess.

51. L. H. Martin and P. Pachis, eds., *Hellenisation, Empire and Globalisation: Lessons from Antiquity* (Vanias: Thessaloniki, 2004).

52. See Luther H. Martin, *Hellenistic Religions: An Introduction* (New York: Oxford University Press, 1987).

53. See W. Braun for an elaboration of what follows, in "Fugitives from Femininity: Greco-Roman Gender Ideology and the Limits of Early Christian Women's Emancipation," in *Fabrics of Discourse: Essays in Honor of Vernon K. Robins*, edited by D. G. Gowler et al. (Harrisburg, Pa.: Trinity Press International, 2003), 317–332.

54. T. W. Laqueur, *Making Sex: Body and Gender from the Greeks to Freud* (Cambridge: Harvard University Press, 1990), 5–6.

55. D. B. Martin, *The Corinthian Body* (New Haven: Yale University Press, 1995), 33.

56. Moxnes, "Conventional Values in the Hellenistic World: Masculinity," 273.

57. G. E. R. Lloyd, "The Hot and the Cold, the Dry and the Wet in Greek Philosophy," *Journal of Hellenic Studies* 84 (1964): 92–106; A. Carson, "Dirt and Desire: The Phenomenology of Female Pollution in Antiquity," in *Construction of the Classical Body*, edited by J. I. Porter (Ann Arbor: University of Michigan Press, 1999), 77–100.

58. Martin, *Corinthian Body*, 32.

59. Cf. Hester, "Eunuchs and the Postgender Jesus," 20: "eunuchs were the nightmare embodiment of men's worst fears. Eunuchs had lost their masculinity."

60. I use "hegemony" and "ideology" as related but not identical concepts, under the influence of Antonio Gramsci. Hegemony I take to refer to mass consent, as a matter of course, to a specifiable established order of thinking about everything (from anthropology to cosmology and back again) and ordering oneself morally, socially, politically in accordance with that order of thought. Transgression of hegemonic orders, typically in practice rather than by argument, exposes their ideological foundations, thus rendering them debatable, arguable, and contestable. See Braun, "Fugitives from Femininity," 325–326 and n. 32.

61. Brower, "Ambivalent Bodies," 142.

62. Roscoe ("Priests of the Goddess," 202–203) suggests, plausibly, that the eunuchs (*galli*) were analogous to the Corybantes and Curetes, groups of ritual specialists who were considered dubious in terms of their piety but proficient as what we might think of as mental health specialists who were able to induce a temporary healing form of madness (*mania*) as a means of driving out deleterious psychological distresses.

3

"And Jacob Remained Alone": The Jewish Struggle with Celibacy

Eliezer Diamond

To many readers a chapter about celibacy in Judaism might seem as incongruous as a kosher seafood cookbook. To a degree, the popular conception that Jews have always rejected celibacy as an option is correct—but only to a degree. We have documentation for communities of celibate Jews for the late Second Temple period (second century BCE–first century CE); however, this practice was limited to small and marginal sects. From the time of the temple's destruction and onward we have no record of a celibate community of Jews, although we hear occasionally of individual Jews who did practice celibacy. Moreover, rabbinic Judaism, which slowly became the dominant form of Jewish religious expression from 70 CE onward, understood Genesis 1:28, "Be fertile and increase, fill the earth and master it," to be not only a blessing but also a commandment.[1] The sages also interpreted Exodus 21:10 as establishing an obligation for a husband to have conjugal relations with his wife on a regular basis.[2] The rabbis, who were nothing if not punctilious about detail, even defined the frequency required of men in different professions and social classes. To remain celibate, therefore, was viewed as sinful, as if, say some sages, one had spilt blood or diminished the divine image. To be celibate within marriage, even if one had already had progeny, constituted a breach of the marital contract as defined by the rabbis. Nonetheless, we shall see that the option of abstinence had a powerful attraction for the religious elite of the so-called rabbinic period (70–589 CE) and for members of several religious movements that developed subsequently. This inclination toward celibacy expressed itself both in periodic abstinence and ascetic sexual praxis.

What follows is a description of several Jewish sects of the late Second Temple period (second century BCE–first century CE) that did engage in lifelong celibacy and a delineation of the role of periodic abstinence in the Judaism of the so-called rabbinic period. I will also refer to practices that reflect the ambivalence of some sages toward sexuality. Some isolated instances of celibacy in the medieval and early modern periods will also be mentioned.

Rather than simply present the evidence for the practice of celibacy by Jews I will also attempt to identify the variety of motives for these practices. In a recent essay, the anthropologists Elisa Sobo and Sandra Bell pointed out the importance of understanding that celibacy can have many different motivations and functions.[3] In Judaism as in other religions, celibacy is freighted with a range of meanings.

Therapeutae/Therapeutrides

In his work *On the Contemplative Life*, Philo of Alexandria, a first-century Jewish philosopher and biblical exegete, describes a group of men and women who are celibate, austere in their dining habits (no meat, almost no flavorings, one meal a day), and free of all personal possessions; they devote their entire lives to study, prayers, and hymns. He calls them Therapeutae and Therapeutrides, "either because they profess a healing art [*therapeia*] better than that in the cities—for the latter cures bodies alone, but the former also cures souls . . . or because they have been entrusted by nature and by the holy laws to care for [i.e., worship; *therapeuein*] the Real (το όν)."[4] Concerning the women in particular, he states: "[They] have retained their purity not out of necessity, as some of the priestesses among the Greeks do, but rather of their own free will, out of their zealous desire for Wisdom. Having desired to live with her, they have had no regard for the pleasures of the body, having struggled in the birth pangs, not of mortal offspring but of immortal ones, which the soul that loves God is able to bear on her own, when the Father has sown the rays of mind in her, by which she will be able to contemplate the teachings of Wisdom."[5]

From this last passage, as well as from Philo's contrasting descriptions of the banquets of the Therapeutae and those of the Greeks, and his emphasis on the sect's practice of self-restraint or *encrateia*, it would seem, as Gail Paterson Corrington suggests, that Philo intends to cast the Therapeutae in the mold of Stoic philosophers who are, however, superior to the Stoics themselves in their degree of discipline and self-restraint.[6] One motive for their celibacy, then, is to develop discipline over their natural impulses.

Ross Shepard Kraemer has suggested that the goal of the Therapeutae was to divest their souls of their feminine—that is, sensate—characteristics and to become masculine and then finally virgin, or sexless, so that they could unite with the divine. This notion is suggested by the following Philonic description of the Therapeutae: "Because of their desire for the deathless and blessed life, their mortal life is already over."[7] Kraemer consequently proposes that it was the Therapeutrides' rejection all of the physical aspects of their femininity—they were childless, unmarried, and quite possibly postmenopausal—that allowed them entrance into the community of the Therapeutae. It was this rejection, she adds, that allows Philo, whose general view of women is generally quite negative, to speak positively about the Therapeutrides.[8]

A number of other passages speak of the Therapeutae leaving behind family and friends, bequeathing all their possessions to others. There is also a description of the common meals taken by the sect, during which the young men in the community serve their elders "like true-begotten sons, pleasing to their fathers and mothers, regarding those who they serve as common parents, more their own than those of their blood."[9] Taken together, these passages situate the celibacy of the Therapeutae in the context of a broad rejection of the norms of society, replacing the biologically defined family unit and the individual ownership of goods with a community of novices and elders bound to each other through common belief and practice.[10]

Finally, celibacy is important because familial ties and obligations are obstacles to devoting oneself entirely to the study of divine wisdom and the practice of its dictates. Thus Philo says of the Therapeutae: "[They] pass their time outside the city walls by seeking solitude in garden spots or solitary wild places, not because of some crude or artificial misanthropy, but because they know that intercourse with persons who are dissimilar in habit is unprofitable and harmful."[11] Some scholars have questioned the attribution of this work to Philo; in the late nineteenth century, Paul Lucius suggested that the work was written in the third century and that it describes a Christian monastic community of that era.[12] The present scholarly consensus, however, is that *On the Contemplative Life* was composed by Philo. Another question that scholars have raised is whether the group described by Philo in fact existed or was simply a product of his imagination.[13] Most scholars regard *On the Contemplative Life* as a description of an actual community, in part because of the similarity between the Therapeutae on the one hand and the Essenes and the Qumran community on the other. This last point raises the question of the relationship between the

Therapeutae and the Essenes.[14] Because of the similarity of practices, and perhaps even of names, the weight of scholarly opinion is on the side of assuming some sort of connection between these two groups.[15]

Essenes

Three first-century authors—Pliny the Elder,[16] Philo,[17] and Josephus[18]—describe a Jewish sect called the Essenes. Although there are differences among the accounts, they all agree that at least some of the Essenes were celibate. Pliny states that the sect of the Essenes "has no women and has renounced all sexual desire." Philo also describes the Essene community as consisting entirely of men; Josephus, in his description in *Antiquities*, portrays the Essenes as exclusively male. In his account in *War* he adds: "There is yet another order of Essenes, which, while at one with the rest in its mode of life, customs, and regulations, differs from them in its views on marriage. They think that those who decline to marry cut off the chief function of life, the propagation of the race, and, what is more, that were all to adopt the same view, the whole race would very quickly die out."[19] Even these Essenes, however, only marry women who have proven themselves to be fertile (that is, they have had at lest three regular menstrual periods) and they do not have sex with their wives during pregnancy. Sex, then, is permitted only for the purpose of procreation.[20]

It is striking that the accounts by Philo and Josephus paint an extremely negative picture of women. Although, says Josephus, celibate Essenes are not opposed in principle to marriage and procreation, "they wish to protect themselves against women's wantonness, being persuaded that none of the sex keeps her plighted troth to any one man."[21] In *Antiquities* the reason given for the avoidance of marriage is that a wife "opens the way to a source of dissension."[22] And despite his positive portrait of the Therapeutrides, Philo explains the celibacy of the Essenes with a lengthy diatribe against women, characterizing them as selfish, jealous, and manipulative.[23] Of course, such negative depictions of women can be found in the sapiential literature of the Bible, particularly in Ecclesiastes, and in both Greek and Roman literature beginning with Homer.[24]

Taking these accounts together, it would seem that Essene celibacy resulted mainly from a rejection of material and sensual pleasure and a desire to devote oneself to a life of study, prayer, and honest labor undisturbed by the complications of marriage and family life. Josephus also speaks of the Essenes' focus on ritual purity but he does not link that concern explicitly with their sexual abstinence.[25]

Qumran

The question of celibacy at Qumran has long occupied the attention of scholars.[26] The celibacy of the Qumran community was first assumed because it was hypothesized that they were identical with the Essenes. There is no explicit statement in any of the Qumran scrolls indicating that celibacy was the norm for the members of the community. On the contrary, there are several instances in which some versions of the Damascus Document deal with matters pertaining to married life—although the Rule of the Community makes no reference to women and children, other than an enigmatic mention of a blessing of "long life and fruitfulness of seed."[27]

Nonetheless, there is one passage in the Damascus Document, fragments of which were already discovered in the Cairo Geniza by Solomon Schechter and cited by Louis Ginzberg in the early nineteenth century, that apparently alludes to two groups of Qumran covenanters, one celibate and the other married. The passage reads as follows: "For all those who walk according to these matters in holy perfectness, in accordance with all his teachings, God's covenant is a guarantee for them that they shall live a thousand generations. And if they reside in camps in accordance with the rule of the land, and take women and children, they shall walk in accordance with the law and according to the regulation of the teachings, according to the rule of the law, as he said: 'Between a man and his wife, and between a father and his son.' "[28]

The writer is contrasting "those who walk according to these matters in holy perfectness" with those "resid[ing] in the camps." From the fact that the latter marry and have children, it would appear that part of the "perfectness" of the former group is that they are celibate.[29] The reason for the celibate lifestyle of the former group, Ginzberg suggests, is that they occupy "a sanctuary built by the sect in the land of Damascus." Column 12 lines 1–2 of the document states, "No one should sleep with a woman in the city of the temple, defiling the city of the temple with their impurity"; hence the need for celibacy. Ginzberg's assumption that the sect's final place of settlement was Damascus has been subsequently rejected by scholars on the basis of the findings at Qumran, but the evidence he found for the existence of a celibate community at Qumran has been widely accepted.[30]

We have just seen that Ginzberg connected celibacy at Qumran with purity regulations. Other scholars have suggested other rationales for Qumranite celibacy. Elisha Qimron has offered an argument similar to Ginzberg's. As Ginzberg noted, the Damascus Document forbids intercourse within the city of the temple. Some among the Qumranites, argues Qimron, viewing as they did the Temple and Jerusalem as having been defiled by their opponents, offered to serve as "a temporary substitute for Jerusalem and its Temple" by taking upon themselves the holiness of Jerusalem. This included sexual abstinence.[31]

Albert Marx, who identifies the Qumran community with the Essenes, notes that in connection with the eschatological battle of the Sons of Light against the Sons of Darkness, the War Scroll excludes women and young men from the war camps of the covenanters "when they leave Jerusalem to go to war, until they return."[32] The Qumran community, argues Marx, had already "left Jerusalem" and viewed itself as a war camp preparing for the battle at the end of days. Therefore women were perforce excluded from the community.[33]

A third argument is that of Antoine Guillaumont, who also assumes that the Qumranites are Essenes. He suggests that the members of the Qumran community saw themselves as the recipients of ongoing divine revelation and that therefore, like the Israelites at Sinai, they had to separate themselves from all sexual contact with women.[34]

Recently Michael Satlow has argued that none of the literary evidence for celibacy at Qumran is convincing; rather, the most compelling evidence is archaeological.[35] Excavations at Jerusalem and Jericho have shown that at least wealthier Jews of the first centuries BCE and CE preferred to be buried in family tombs, thus emphasizing the importance for them of the family as an organizing principle and a source of identity. At Qumran, however, the vast majority of the (relatively small) number of graves excavated so far are male, and there are no family plots. Satlow takes this as evidence of a Qumranite rejection of the Greco-Roman ideal of the *oikos*. What was important was not the family unit but rather the community, with fictive familial relationships that supplanted biological ones. From Satlow's perspective, then, the celibacy of the Qumran community was as much a rejection of societal norms as it was an expression of personal piety or purity.

Even for those members of the community who were married, sex was permitted only for procreative purposes. One of the Cave IV fragments of the Damascus Document mentions a prohibition against a husband sleeping with his pregnant wife.[36] There were also other restrictions on married sexual behavior, but the nature of these prohibitions is unclear.[37]

It was mentioned previously that a number of scholars who attributed celibate behavior to the Qumranites did so on the basis of identifying them with the Essenes. This identification itself is far from clear. As in the case of the Therapeutae, it seems reasonable to assume that there is some relationship between the Essenes and the Qumran community but that they are not necessarily identical.[38]

Ascetics and Prophets of the Late Second Temple Period (Second Century BCE–First Century CE)

As noted by Richard Horsley and John Hanson, the direct rule of Judea by the Romans beginning in 6 CE began a period of periodic unrest in the Jewish population that ended in the revolt of 66 CE. This unrest was due to, as they put it, the "colonial situation" of Palestinian Jews under Roman rule. Two major irritants for the Judeans were the tax burden and interference, actual or perceived, in the religious life of the community.[39]

One of the manifestations of this unrest was the appearance of a number of prophetic and messianic figures, including Jesus of Nazareth. There is no explicit mention of the practice of celibacy by any of these figures. However, the ascetic behavior attributed to some of them (such as John the Baptist) and their peripatetic lifestyles make it unlikely that they had wives and children; if they did, they probably had abandoned them in order to preach or simply to live as anchorites far from civilized society.[40] Jesus himself seems never to have married; more to the point, he and his followers personified what Gerd Thiessen has labeled *Wanderradikalismus*.[41] This was a way of living that involved turning away from wealth and possessions and forsaking family ties. As in the case of the Essenes and the Qumran community, this meant substituting the community of believers for one's family of origin. Stephen Patterson adumbrates this ideology as follows: "The rigorous follower of Jesus loses his or her family ties, but is integrated into a new kinship group, articulated in ideal terms and offered as a new construction of reality."[42] Paul, as is well known, favored celibacy and was himself celibate; this suggests that the notion of celibacy was not foreign to the circles, Jewish and Gentile, in which he traveled.

Celibacy as a Response to Catastrophe

Some of the works written in the wake of the Temple's destruction in 70 CE articulate the view that in light of this catastrophe there is no point in continuing normal family life. Thus in the Syriac Apocalypse of Baruch we find the following lament:

> And you, bridegrooms do not enter,
> and do not let the brides adorn themselves.
> And you, wives, do not pray to bear children,
> for the barren will rejoice more.

> And those who have no children will be glad,
> and those who have children will be sad.
> For why do they bear in pain only to bury in grief?
> Or why should men have children again?[43]

Although this is clearly the language of poetic hyperbole, it suggests a response to the calamities of the first and second centuries that some Jews adopted, to a greater or lesser degree, for some time to come. Rabbinic literature records a meeting between R. [= Rabbi] Joshua, a Levite who was a member of the temple choir, and a group of *perushim*—literally, "those who have separated themselves"—who had given up eating meat and drinking wine as a response to the temple's destruction. R. Joshua dissuades them from such extreme behavior and recommends instead a much more modest symbolic commemoration of this event: "Rather, this is what the rabbis said: 'A man plasters his house with plaster and leaves a bit [unplastered] to commemorate Jerusalem.'"[44]

It is true, of course, that celibacy is not mentioned as part of the regimen of the *perushim*. That possibility is raised, at least theoretically, by R. Ishmael (first to second century CE): "He used to say: Because they are uprooting the Torah from our midst we should decree that the world be desolate. We should neither marry nor have children nor perform circumcisions until Abraham's seed comes to an end of its own accord. They said to him: Better that the community should sin unintentionally rather than intentionally."[45]

R. Ishmael's claim that "they [the Roman *imperium*] are uprooting the Torah" probably refers to the Hadrianic decree or decrees forbidding circumcision, and possibly other Jewish practices as well, in the third and fourth decades of the second century.[46] Such legislation made it difficult if not impossible for Jews to carry out their religious obligations; circumcision in particular was viewed as being vital to one's entry into God's covenant with Israel.

The response of R. Ishmael's colleagues is striking. They invoke a principle of rabbinic jurisprudence that discourages religious leaders from publicizing a prohibition when it is likely that it will continue to be flouted nonetheless. Thus they agree with R. Ishmael in theory but view it as impossible to impose such a harsh regimen on the people. Here too one senses the presence of hyperbole; after all, none of the rabbis, including R. Ishmael himself, actually rejected marriage and family despite the dire political and religious situation.

There seems to have been a dissenting view among the rabbis. A rabbinic tradition uses Exodus 2:1 as a pretext for claiming that Amram, Moses' father, separated from his wife, Yocheved; this was done in response to the Pharaonic decree that required all newborn male Israelites to be cast into the Nile. His daughter Miriam took him to task, arguing that her father's decree was harsher than Pharaoh's, who had decreed death for males only; Amram's abstinence precluded the possibility of female children as well. Amram relented, and consequently Moses was conceived.[47] The origin and date of this reading is unclear and it is impossible to know what subtext, if any, is encrypted in this exegesis; nonetheless, it is plausible that biblical interpretation is being employed here to argue against the appropriateness of sexual abstinence as a response to persecution.

The third- to early fourth-century Palestinian rabbi R. Abin proscribes sexual relations during a time of famine or catastrophe.[48] A number of late third-century Palestinian rabbis attribute such behavior to Noah during the flood and Joseph during the years of famine in Egypt.[49] It is likely that these traditions were meant to be understood as paradigms that should be imitated. Although this response to calamity is identical with R. Ishmael's reaction, the motivation seems to be different. This prohibition could be understood in part as a practical measure: one ought not to bring more children into the world when there is insufficient food for those already living or when conditions are horrific. More likely, however, celibacy serves here as a means of identifying with communal suffering, or as a penitential act.[50] The former interpretation seems to emerge from the Palestinian (or Yerushalmi) Talmud. There it is stated that one who desires children may engage in intercourse; however, this permission is limited to the night a woman immerses in the *miqveh* or ritual bath to end her status as a menstruant forbidden to her husband. The rabbis believed—correctly—that this was a particularly propitious time for conception. In this way the Yerushalmi is ensuring that sex will take place only for procreative purposes and not for pleasure's sake.

The Rabbis and the Problematization of Sex

The rabbis inherited a biblical tradition in which chastity plays an important role. Leviticus in particular lists a host of sexual restrictions and makes residence in the land of Israel dependent on the fulfillment of these commandments. However, to use Foucault's distinction, these restrictions constitute a code, not a sexual ethic. Certain acts and relations are forbidden; there is no broader discussion of how one should conduct oneself sexually, nor are any modes of self-discipline proposed. The one example of the voluntary ascetic in biblical literature, the Nazi rite, is restricted in the realms of food, drink, and purity but has no special sexual restrictions placed on the individual.

Nonetheless, we must not forget that the Hebrew Bible already requires periodic abstinence within marriage; Leviticus 18:19 and 20:18 forbid intercourse with a *niddah*, or menstruant; from Leviticus 15:24 it appears that this prohibition is in force for seven days beginning with the onset of menstruation. Moreover, as Leviticus 20:26 explains, it is the observance of this restriction as well as others concerning food and sex that constitute Israel's holiness. A further link between holiness and sexual restriction is found in Leviticus 21; women that are permitted to the Israelites are forbidden to the priests because they have been chosen to "be holy to their God."[51]

The rabbis understood these verses as signifying that restrictions on sexual behavior are the cause of holiness as well as its expression. Hence the rabbis interpret the biblical imperative "you shall be holy" (Lev. 19:1) as specifically forbidding sexual immorality.[52] As a logical consequence of this view they seek out ways to limit sexual expression beyond the proscriptions in Leviticus. Some restrictions were encoded as universal obligations. Thus the rabbis created significant stringencies that increased the monthly period of forced abstinence, requiring that seven days pass without any bleeding before a couple resumes conjugal relations. Jewish males and females were forbidden to be alone with each other in a secluded venue. A man was not permitted to listen to a woman singing. Men were warned not to walk behind women.

However, the rabbis also developed a sexual ethos encapsulated in a statement by the fourth-century Babylonian rabbi Rava: "Sanctify yourself within what is permitted to you."[53] This meant that beyond specific prohibitions some rabbis sought to attain greater holiness through the ascetic stylization of their sexual behavior and the monitoring of their thoughts. "Sinful thoughts," says the Talmud, are worse that sin itself."[54] In the sections that follow we will see the specific ways in which this attitude expresses itself in rabbinic thought and legislation.

The Ordinance Attributed to Ezra

The Mishnah (composed ca. 200 CE), one of the foundational documents of the rabbinic movement, prescribes that a *ba'al qeri*—literally, "one who has had an event," a euphemism for one who has engaged in sex or had a nocturnal emission—may not pray or recite the biblical verses known as the Shema until after having immersed himself in a *miqveh*, a ritual bath. A number of contemporaneous sources forbid a *ba'al qeri* to study Torah, although there is significant debate about what genres of Torah he may or may not study.[55] An anonymous tradition in the Babylonian Talmud attributes this ordinance to Ezra, which simply means that the practice is assumed to have been quite old.[56]

Very little is clear about the history, the significance, and the parameters of this ordinance. Presumably it is based on Leviticus 15:16, which requires a man who has emitted semen to immerse himself; he is considered ritually impure until evening. However, the requirement to purify oneself is mentioned in the Hebrew Bible only in connection with the consumption of sanctified food (that is, some of the agricultural apportionments given to the priests and the flesh of sacrificial animals), and entering or serving in the sanctuary or temple. Nowhere does the Torah suggest that purification is required in order to pray and study. The rabbis themselves were well aware of this anomaly; they note that those who are considered impure because of genital flux, menstrual flow, or having had sexual relations with a menstruant may all study Torah but a *ba'al qeri* may not.[57]

Nonetheless, earlier rabbinic sources (in other words those dating from before 200) seem to understand this ordinance as motivated by purity. In discussing who is considered a *ba'al qeri*, the rabbis use the terms *tamei*, ritually pure, and *tahor*, ritually impure.[58] Even the words of a second-century opponent of the ordinance, R. Judah b. Betera—"words of Torah cannot contract impurity"—assume that its proponents are framing it as a purity regulation. Perhaps, as Louis Ginzberg suggests, this was a means of protecting the sanctity of God's name and of the words of Torah.[59] Ironically, Ginzberg notes, this would place this practice in the same orbit as the *tovelei shacharit* or Hemerobaptists, whom the rabbis clearly considered sectarians. The rabbis themselves record a dispute between the *tovelei shacharit* and the Pharisees (with whose position the rabbis identified) in which the Pharisees are accused of pronouncing the divine name without having previously immersed themselves. Some of the rabbis involved in discussing the *ba'al qeri* ordinance adopt the position of the Hemerobaptists explicitly, if not intentionally; they restrict the requirement for immersion to one who wishes to pronounce God's name. If we assume, however, that the ordinance dates from after the destruction of the temple in 70 CE, after which time this sect presumably disappeared, it may be, as Ginzberg theorizes, that the rabbis had no compunctions about adopting a stringency that was previously the hallmark of a group that they considered heterodox.[60]

The Amoraim (the post-Mishnaic rabbis), however, offer other explanations. One view recorded in the Babylonian Talmud is that engaging in sex puts one in a frivolous frame of mind that is incompatible with prayer and study. Immersion is apparently viewed as an aid in making the appropriate psychological and spiritual transition from one activity to the next. Another view recorded there is that the ordinance's intent is to prevent Torah scholars from, as the Talmud puts it, adopting the lusty sexual habits of roosters; that is, it is viewed as a *delirium* that the sexual activity of Torah scholars be held to a minimum. Requiring one to immerse before study—a significant inconvenience at a time when immersion pools were of necessity outdoors and unheated—has the effect of forcing students of Torah to choose between sex and study; the rabbis' confident expectation was that the latter would prevail.

A similar but somewhat different explanation is given in the Yerushalmi. The concern is that one will have sex with his wife while assuring himself that he will study later that evening; in reality this probably will not happen. The added burden of immersion will dissuade the Torah scholar from engaging in sex, and he will go straight to his studies.

Whether or not these later explanations are historically accurate—and they well may not be—they reflect the mindset of rabbis in Palestine and Babylonia in the third and fourth centuries. They view study and sexuality as being inimical to each other, both because the physical and emotional milieu of sex is seen as being incompatible with or potentially detrimental to study (Babylonian Talmud) and because the use of one's allotted time on earth is a zero-sum game. Time and energy devoted to sex are lost to study. One thinks of Woody Allen's postcoital observation in *Annie Hall*: "As Balzac would say, 'There goes another novel.' "

Am I saying that rabbis were celibate as a result of this ordinance? No. The rabbis understood themselves to subject to the obligations of marriage, procreation, and fulfilling their conjugal debt to their wives. However, one might say that Ezra's ordinance, or more accurately the later rabbinic understanding of this proscription, reveals the existence of what I would call a celibate impulse within rabbinic culture. This impulse is almost never followed to its extreme conclusion, but it makes for an ongoing tension between (holy) work and love (or at least sex).[61]

Torah Study versus Marriage and Family

Daniel Boyarin has described Torah as "the other woman."[62] Although a Christian saint can imagine herself as Christ's bride or beloved, a rabbi who envisions himself as being romantically involved with Torah—and Torah is generally given a feminine *persona* by the sages—is creating potential conflict between his celestial beloved and his earthly spouse. The most powerful formulation of this idea appears in a story told about the only explicitly celibate sage in rabbinic literature, Ben Azzai.[63] After one of his colleagues says that one who fails to heed the obligation to reproduce is likened to a murderer, and another that he is regarded as having diminished the divine image, Ben Azzai declares that both are true. At that a colleague, with the incongruity between

Ben Azzai's declaration and his celibacy in mind, turns to Ben Azzai saying, "You preach well but you do not do well." To this Ben Azzai answers, "What shall I do? My soul lusts for Torah. Let the obligation of procreation be fulfilled by others." Ben Azzai describes himself as being too bound up with his celestial love, Torah, to have any time or emotion for a relationship with a woman of flesh and blood.

On the one hand, Ben Azzai is the exception that proves the rule; on the other, the impulse he describes is present in many of his peers. As Boyarin puts it, "The story of Ben-Azzai is an index of how much energy was required to combat the attractiveness of the celibate life."[64] It was expected of most disciples of the rabbis in third-century Palestine that they take upon themselves a significant period of celibacy in order to devote themselves to Torah study. Isaiah Gafni has suggested that this system was a partial adoption of Ben Azzai's philosophy.[65]

This being said, it is important to distinguish between the celibacy of young students of Torah in Late Antique Palestine and that practiced by Christian monastics and the like. For the fourth-century Egyptian hermits and monks, celibacy was part a larger program of *anachoresis* or withdrawal from the world. This included an abandonment of any material goods or somatic concerns that were not necessary for bare survival. In a religious culture in which celibacy was an acceptable, even honorable option, rejecting sexuality was one more way of disentangling oneself from unnecessary physicality and emotion.

On the whole, the rabbis had no interest in celibacy as a spiritual discipline. Rather, their intense commitment to Torah study, on the one hand, and their sexual code, on the other, made it necessary for them to do without sex for long periods of time. The ideals that motivated their behavior were a love of Torah and a commitment to the virtue of chastity and its attendant obligations, not an acceptance, even temporarily, of the discipline of celibacy.[66] Elsewhere I have called this type of abstinence incidental or instrumental asceticism.[67] The ethos of the Palestinian practice is best summed up by a statement attributed to the third-century Palestinian sage R. Yohanan: "Shall one study with a millstone [i.e., family responsibilities] around his neck?!"[68]

Sex as Obligation, Not as Pleasure

Some Palestinian sages conducted themselves sexually in a manner that minimized the pleasurable component of sex, emphasizing that it its permissibility was limited to reproduction and fulfilling one's marital obligation to one's wife. Thus, R. Eliezer's wife attributed the pleasing appearance of her sons to the chaste sexual habits of her husband, which included having intercourse "as though compelled by a demon"—in other words as though it were against his will.[69] In the same Talmudic passage, R. Yohanan b. Dehabai reports a communication he received from the ministering angels that those who engage in unconventional forms of sexual behavior (such as cunnilingus) will have children with birth defects.

This restrictive attitude toward sexual conduct was, however a minority view. R. Yohanan (mentioned above) says that the majority view is that "whatever a man wishes to do with his wife he may do." It is no different, he says, than the consumption of meat; some like it roasted while some like it cooked. The androcentric nature of R. Yohanan's analogy may offend the modern ear; what is important, however, is that he is normalizing sexual appetite by treating it as no different from the gustatory instinct.

Michael Satlow suggests that we understand the attitude of the Palestinian sages as reflecting the Greco-Roman ideal of the *oikos*, the household, which includes the obligation to procreate and thereby perpetuate the family and the *polis*. In this context, the major function of sex is procreation, a notion emphasized by Palestinian sources to the virtual exclusion of any discussion of sexual intimacy or pleasure.[70]

I would add that the Palestinian rabbinic attitude can be further illuminated by Foucault's exegesis of Xenophon's *Oeconomicus*, a prescription for the proper management of one's estate.[71] The arts of ruling that one must develop to be a successful landholder must be applied to marriage and civic life as well. To rule—over one's workers, one's wife or one's fellow citizens—one must first have demonstrated, through the control of one's passions and impulses, the ability to rule oneself. Only one who is not enslaved to his own desires has the ability and the respect necessary to manage domestic and communal affairs. Consequently, the ability to view sex as the fulfillment of a duty rather than as a pleasurable pastime is part of Xenophon's portrait of the ideal manager, and this is so for the Palestinian rabbis as well. One is reminded of the teaching of the second-century Palestinian sage Ben Zoma: "Who is mighty? He who conquers his impulses."[72]

Finally, we should mention Boyarin's citation of a number of Hellenistic Jewish texts that suggest that first-century Palestinian Judaism was "at best, powerfully ambivalent about sexuality."[73] The term often used by the earliest rabbis to refer to sexual desire is, in fact, יצר הרע, or "the evil inclination"; surely this does not bespeak a positive attitude toward sexuality. Boyarin goes on to argue that Paul's negative view of sex was a natural outgrowth of the Palestinian Jewish culture of his time; he sees the more positive attitudes of later rabbis as a reaction to this perspective.

The Babylonian View

The Babylonian practice, beginning in the first half of the third century or perhaps earlier, was for students of Torah to marry and then to spend years in study, often far from home.[74] There were two motivations for this approach. The first was the Babylonian rabbinic view, consistent with the views of the surrounding Zoroastrian culture,[75] that the only possible antidote to sexual temptation was early marriage. The late-third-century Babylonian sage R. Hisda states, "I am better than my fellows because I married at sixteen; had I married at fourteen I would have been able to say to Satan: 'An arrow in your eye!' "[76] The second was the belief that one who had "a loaf in his basket," that is, someone to whom sex was generally available, would be better able to withstand periods of sexual deprivation.[77]

The Babylonians are aware of the toll that such an arrangement can take on the wife. They consider this issue through the medium of stories concerning various rabbis who spent long periods of time away from home. These range from romanticizing the love between R. Aqiba and his wife, Rachel, which transcends a separation of twenty-four years, to an implicit indictment of those who abandon their families.[78] The expectation seems to have been that a good wife would support a husband in his decision to absent himself for the sake of Torah study; that husband, in turn, was expected to be considerate and appreciative of the sacrifices made by his wife. The following story sums up these themes neatly: "R. Hiyya's wife would torment him. [Nonetheless] when he would find something [appropriate for her] he would wrap it in his scarf and bring it to her. Rab said to him, 'But, sir, doesn't she torment you?' He replied, 'It is as much as we deserve that [our wives] raise our children and save us from sin.' "[79]

There is a series of narratives in the Babylonian Talmud that have as their common theme the invincibility of the sexual impulse.[80] We hear of R. Amram the Pious who, entrusted to protect redeemed female captives from molestation, falls victim to his own desires. He stops himself from acting upon them only by confessing his intentions and bringing shame on himself and his colleagues. The great sages R. Aqiba and R. Meir think themselves immune from the blandishments of sex; however, when Satan appears to them in the guise of a beautiful woman they are saved from sin only through God's grace. The rabbi Polemo is shown, in a Rabelaisian tale that ends with him falling into a latrine, that he cannot hope to defeat the evil impulse decisively.

The final story is about R. Hiyya b. Ashi, who despite the fact that he has separated from his wife, asks God daily to be saved from the *yetzer hara*, the evil inclination. The story continues as follows:

> One day his wife heard him. She said, "Given that he has separated himself from me for quite some time, why does he say this?"
>
> One day he was studying in his garden. She adorned herself and passed before him several times.
>
> He said to her, "Who are you?" She said, "I am Harutah who has returned just today." He propositioned her. She said, "Bring me that pomegranate from the top of the tree." He hastened to bring her the fruit.
>
> When he came home, his wife was putting fuel in the oven. He went and sat inside it. She said to him, "What is this?" He said, "Thus and thus occurred." She said to him, "It was I." He paid no attention to her until she produced evidence that this was so. He said to her, "Nonetheless my intention was to sin." This righteous man fasted all his days until he died of that.[81]

It is not clear why R. Hiyya b. Ashi has stopped sleeping with his wife. Rashi (French, eleventh century), one of the premier medieval commentators on the Talmud, suggests that this was a result of incapacity due to old age. The point of the story would then be that if sufficiently inflamed with lust even the old and feeble can, as it were, rise to the occasion. Once again, we are being told that only the dead are free from the tug of sexual desire.

However, I prefer a reading suggested recently by Shlomo Naeh.[82] He assumes that R. Hiyya b. Ashi has intentionally taken celibacy upon himself. The narrative, suggests Naeh, is a polemic against those Babylonian rabbis attracted to the sexual asceticism of the *qadishayya* and *ihidayya*, the celibates of Syriac Christianity. I will not rehearse Naeh's subtle and complex interpretation of the narrative; I wish simply to emphasize that his interpretation turns the story into an argument that any attempt to practice celibacy will actually result in greater sinfulness.

Let us be clear that the Babylonian view that sexual desire cannot be fully contained is not simply a variation on Paul's declaration that although it is better to remain unmarried "it is better to be married than to be burnt up."[83] In general the rabbis celebrate reproduction as a positive good as well as a commandment, and they recognize the crucial role of sexual desire in the building of society: "If it were not for the evil [read: sexual] impulse, a man would not build a house, marry a wife, and have children."[84] Moreover the Babylonian sages, more than their Palestine colleagues, look favorably on sexual pleasure.[85] Rather, even as they understand the benefits and pleasures of sex and sexuality, the Babylonian rabbis are acutely aware of its destructive—often self-destructive—potential. For some this leads to a deep desire to be done with sex, to be liberated from its bonds. The counsel of the Babylonian rabbis is: We understand your yearning; nonetheless, we urge you to accept your sexual urges as a divinely ordained component of human identity that cannot be ignored or denied, only properly channeled.

The Babylonian rabbis express this attitude most vividly by means of a legend. The beginning of the legend deals with a problem that arose for the rabbis because of their belief that the earlier generations of Jews had been more righteous than the later ones. How, then, were they to explain that the Israelites of the First Temple period worshiped idols whereas Jews of the Second Temple era did not? The rabbinic explanation, based on an interpretation of some impenetrable verses in Zechariah, is that the spirit of idolatry was exorcised from the people through the prophet's agency, upon their return from exile in Babylonia. They mean to say that subsequent generations were able to eschew the practice of idolatry not because of their merit or piety but through a divine act of grace. The legend then goes on to report an attempt to subject the spirit of sexual desire to exorcism:

> [The Jews returning from the Babylonian exile in the late sixth century] said, "Because it is a time of favor let us pray [to be released from] the impulse to sin [sexually]. They prayed and the evil impulse was handed over to them. [The prophet Zechariah] said to them, "Be careful, for if you kill it the world will come to an end."
>
> They imprisoned it for three days; they then searched for a newly laid egg throughout the land of Israel and they could find none. They said, "What shall we do? If we kill it the world will be destroyed. If we ask for half [i.e., only to have licit sexual desires]—heaven does not grant by halves."
>
> They put kohl in its eyes [and blinded it]. It helped to the extent that one is no longer sexually aroused by one's close kin.[86]

The rabbis fantasize here about a scenario in which they are given control of their own sexual urges. Yet, they realize, what would they do if they were indeed granted this power? To destroy sexuality is to destroy the world. To expect that one will only experience "good" sexual impulses is unrealistic; desire is an undifferentiated force that does not make distinctions between the permitted and the forbidden. They therefore conclude that we can only be thankful for the few realms in which desire has little power to undo us; and as for the rest, we face the daily task of wrestling with our sexual instincts and doing our best to harness them for our own good and the god of those around us. More than that, says our narrator, we cannot do.

Conclusion

In its general outlines, then, the assumption that celibacy plays a marginal role in Jewish spiritual practice is correct. When one looks more closely, however, one sees that for many Jews, particularly the religious elite, the tension between sex and spirituality never disappears. The mystics of thirteenth-century Spain and sixteenth-century Safed developed a deeply erotic mythology concerning the masculine and feminine aspects of the Godhead, and they viewed their own sexual relations with their wives as performing the holy task of reuniting the Shekhinah, the divine presence, with her male counterpart in the divine constellation. At the same time, this sacralization of sex led these same mystics to forswear sex on any day other than the Sabbath and to avoid deriving pleasure from intercourse.[87] A number of Hasidic masters of the eighteenth and nineteenth centuries contracted celibate marriages with their wives.[88] The Lithuanian *yeshivot* or Talmudic academies of the 1800s had their *perushim* ("abstinent ones") who followed the Babylonian rabbinic practice of spending years at a time away from their wives and families.[89] Even among the eighteenth- and nineteenth-century Maskilim, the "enlightened" Jewish intellectuals who saw themselves as rebels against traditionalism and staunch foes of the Hassidim, there was a widespread sentiment that marriage should be set aside in favor of male fellowship and intellectual pursuits.[90]

A recent development in American Judaism has added a new element to the situation. Much of the conflict between study and family within Judaism is connected to the assumption that only men are obligated to engage in intensive Torah study. That assumption is being challenged today, even—and in some respects especially—within the Orthodox world. (Although only the non-Orthodox movements have been willing to grant ordination to women, most of the intensive Talmud study among women is taking place in Orthodox circles.) Married women are now being supported by their husbands in their efforts to become Talmud scholars and ordained rabbis. This support undoubtedly includes holding the fort at home while one's spouse pursues her studies. Will we see the emergence of female *perushot* who spend long periods away from their families engaged in study? Only time will tell.

Every religious tradition must address the question of sex. Judaism came to value two conflicting sets of obligations—marriage and procreation on the one hand, and study and prayer on the other—with equal fervor and intensity.

Some unresolved queries in the Babylonian Talmud end with the word *teyku*, "let it stand." A fanciful interpretation of this word parses it as an acronym signifying, "[Elijah] the Tishbite [the forerunner of the Messiah] will resolve all difficulties and questions." Until the arrival of Elijah one can expect the question of what constitutes an appropriate balance of family and spiritual endeavor within Jewish practice to remain a *teyku*.

NOTES

1. For an exhaustive discussion of Jewish and Christian exegesis of this verse, see Jeremy Cohen, *"Be Fertile and Increase, Fill the Earth and Master It": The Ancient and Medieval Career of a Biblical Text* (Ithaca: Cornell University Press, 1989). See in particular 158–165, where Cohen considers possible motivations for the rabbinic understanding of Genesis 1:28 as having legal force.

2. Unless otherwise indicated, the terms "sage" and "rabbi" refer to the virtuosi who constituted the rabbinic movement in its first phase, which began with the destruction of the temple in 70 CE (or perhaps somewhat earlier) and ended sometime in the late sixth or early seventh century.

3. Elisa J. Sobo and Sandra Bell, "Celibacy in Cross-Cultural Perspective: An Overview," in Elisa J. Sobo and Sandra Bell, ed., *Celibacy, Culture and Society: The Anthropology of Sexual Abstinence* (Madison: University of Wisconsin Press, 2001), 3–23.

4. *On the Contemplative Life* 2. Translations of *On the Contemplative Life* are from Gail Paterson Corrington, "Philo, On the Contemplative Life: Or, On the Suppliants (The Fourth Book of Virtue)," in Vincent Wimbush, ed., *Ascetic Behavior in Greco-Roman Antiquity: A Sourcebook* (Minneapolis: Fortress, 1990), 134–155. All other translations of Philo's writings are from the Loeb Classical Library edition.

5. *On the Contemplative Life* 68.

6. Paterson Corrington, "Philo, On the Contemplative Life," 135–136. Compare Philo, *The Life of Moses* 2.216: "For what are our places of prayer throughout the cities but schools of prudence and courage and temperance and justice [i.e., the four virtues of the Stoics], etc."

7. *On the Contemplative Life* 13.

8. Ross Shepard Kraemer, *Her Share of the Blessings: Women's Religious among Pagans, Jews, and Christians in the Greco-Roman World* (New York: Oxford University Press, 1992), 114–115. See also her discussion of Mary Douglas's theory concerning the combined role of minimal ascribed status and stratification ("low grid") and strong communal identity ("strong group") in creating an egalitarian environment (14–19, 199–208).

9. *On the Contemplative Life* 72.

10. The Shakers make their case for celibacy along these lines, although they provide other rationales as well; see Peter Collins, "Virgins in the Spirit," in Sobo and Bell, *Celibacy, Culture, and Society*, 104–121.

11. *On the Contemplative Life* 20. Compare Philo's observation concerning the Essenes in *Quod Omnus Probus* 76.

12. Paul Ernst Lucius, *Die Therapeuten und ihre Stellung in der Geschichte der Askese. Eine kritische Untersuchung der Schrift De vita contemplativa* (Strassburg: C. F. Schmidt, 1879). The church historian Eusebius (third–fourth centuries) accepted the attribution of the work to Philo but preserved Philo's description of the Therapeutae in his *Historia Ecclesia* (2.17) because he believed that Philo was actually describing early Christian monastics.

13. This possibility has been raised most recently by T. Engbert-Pedersen, "Philo's *De Vita contemplative* as a Philosopher's Dream," *Journal for the Study of Judaism* 30 (1999): 40–64.

14. The relationship between the Essenes and the Qumran community will be addressed below.

15. It is possible that the appellation *Εσσηνοί* or *Εσσαîοι* is derived from the Aramaic אסיא, "healers." See Geza Vermes, "The Etymology of 'Essenes,' " *Revue de Qumran* 2 (1960): 427–443. On the connection between the groups, see Emil Schürer, *The History of the Jewish People in the Age of Jesus Christ*, revised and edited by Geza Vermes et al. (Edinburgh: T & T Clark, 1973–1987), 593–597; and Lester Grabbe, *Judaism from Cyrus to Hadrian*, vol. 2 *The Roman Period* (Minneapolis: Fortress, 1992), 499. See, however, his cautionary remark in Grabbe, *Judaic Religion in the Second Temple Period* (London: Routledge, 2000), 206.

16. *Natural History* 5.73.

17. *Quod Omnis Probus*, 75–87; *Hypothetica* (cited by Eusebius, *Praeparatio Evangelica* 8).

18. *War* 2.120–161; *Antiquities* 18.18–22.

19. *War* 2.160. This and all subsequent translations of Josephus are from the Loeb Classical Library edition. Note that earlier in his account in *War* (2.120) he tells us that the Essenes "adopt other men's children . . . and regard them as their kin and mold them in accordance with their own principles."

20. *War* 2.161.

21. *War* 2.121.

22. *Antiquities* 18.21.

23. *Hypothetica* 11.14–17.

24. See Eva Cantarella, *Pandora's Daughters*, translated by Maureen B. Fant (Baltimore: Johns Hopkins University Press, 1987).

25. See *War* 2.123, 129, 150 and *Antiquities* 18.19.

26. This section is an expanded version of my discussion of celibacy at Qumran in Eliezer Diamond, *Holy Men and Hunger Artists: Fasting and Asceticism in Rabbinic Culture* (Oxford: Oxford University Press, 2004), 33–34; for a summary of the evidence see Joseph M. Baumgarten, "Celibacy," in Lawrence H. Schiffman and James C. VanderKam, eds., *Encyclopedia of the Dead Sea Scrolls* (Oxford: Oxford University Press, 2000), 1:123–124.

27. 1QRule of the Community, column 4 line 7. However, 1QRule of the Congregation, which contains the rule for "the final days," marriage, and family are mentioned; the minimum age for marriage is set at twenty (column 1 lines 9–10).

28. Cairo Damascus Document MS A, column vii lines 4–9. This and all subsequent translations of the Damascus Document and Qumran texts are from Florentino García Martinez and Eibert J. C. Tigchelaar, eds. and trans., *The Dead Sea Scrolls: Study Edition* (Leiden: E. J. Brill, 1997).

29. See Louis Ginzberg, *An Unknown Jewish Sect*, translated and edited by Ralph Marcus et al. (New York: Jewish Theological Seminary of America, 1976), 32–33. See Eli Ginzberg's foreword, ix–xi, for a history of the genesis of this work.

30. See Eli Ginzberg's foreword, xiii. The precise meaning of "Damascus" in the Qumran documents has been the subject of much debate; see Jerome Murphy-O'Connor, "Damascus," in Schiffman and VanderKam, *Encyclopedia of the Dead Sea Scrolls*, 1:165–166.

31. Elisha Qimron, "Celibacy in the Dead Sea Scrolls and the Two Kinds of Sectarians," in J. T. Barrera and L. V. Montaner, eds., *The Madrid Qumran Congress: Proceedings of the International Congress on the Dead Sea Scrolls, Madrid 18–21 March, 1991* (New York: E. J. Brill and Editorial Complutense, 1992) 1:287–294, esp. 291. See the passage in the Damascus Document cited above, the Temple Scroll, column 45 lines 7–12, and other sources cited by Qimron.

32. War Scroll (1QM), column 7 lines 3–4.

33. Albert Marx, "Les racines du célibat essénien," *Revue de Qumran* 7 (1970): 338–342.

34. Antoine Guillamont, "A propos du celibate des Esséniens," in *Homage á André Dupont-Sommer* (Paris: Adrien Maisonneuve, 1971), 395–404.

35. Michael Satlow, *Jewish Marriage in Antiquity* (Princeton: Princeton University Press, 2001), 21–24.

36. 4Q270 fragment 2 II lines 15–16. As was mentioned previously, Josephus describes the Essenes as abiding by this restriction. One should also note that in the apocryphal work *The History of the Rechabites*, a work of uncertain date that clearly has Christian interpolations but may have a Jewish core, some of the community is designated as celibate while other members marry but have intercourse with their wives only once in order to procreate.

37. 4Q267 fragment 9 vi lines 4–5 (= 4Q270 fragment 7 column I lines 12–13). It has been suggested that the rather opaque statement that "no one should intermingle [יתערב] voluntarily on the Sabbath" (Cairo Damascus Document MS A column XI line 4) is a prohibition of sexual activity on the Shabbat, but this is mere speculation.

38. See Grabbe, *Judaism from Cyrus to Hadrian*, 2:496.

39. Robert A. Horsley with John S. Hanson, *Bandits, Prophets, and Messiahs: Popular Movements at the Time of Jesus* (San Francisco: Harper and Row, 1985), 35.

40. Note, for example, Josephus's description of the ascetic Bannus in *Life* 2: "[He] dwelt in the wilderness, wearing only such things as trees provided, feeding on such things as grew of themselves, and using frequent ablutions of cold water by day and night for purity's sake."

41. Gerd Thiessen, *The Sociology of Palestinian Christianity*, translated by John Bowden (Philadelphia: Fortress, 1978).

42. Stephen J. Patterson, "*Askesis* and the Early Jesus Tradition," in Leif E. Vaage and Vincent L. Wimbush, eds., *Asceticism and the New Testament* (New York: Routledge, 1999), 64.

43. 2 Baruch 10:13–16a. This translation is from James Charlesworth, ed., *The Old Testament Pseudepigrapha* (Garden City, N.Y.: Doubleday, 1983).

44. Tosefta Sotah 15.11–12. The date of the Tosefta's composition has not been determined definitively; I assume that it dates from the mid-third century. This and all subsequent translations of rabbinic texts are my own.

45. Tosefta Sotah 15.10.

46. There is reason to question whether these were actually imperial rescripts or the work of the provincial governor Tinnaeus Rufus; see Y. Geiger, "The Decree against Circumcision and the Bar-Kochva Revolt" (in Hebrew) in A. Oppenheimer, ed., *Mered Bar Kokhva* (Jerusalem: Zalman Shazar Center, 1980), 85–93. In rabbinic literature, the period of the Hadrianic persecutions is known as שעת השמד, "the time of utter destruction." Saul Lieberman points out that this phrase is equivalent to the Latin *extirpatio*, a term used by the Romans to describe the uprooting of a religion. See Saul Lieberman, "The Persecution of the Jewish Faith" (in Hebrew), in *Salo Whittmayer Baron Jubilee Volume on the Occasion of His Eightieth Birthday*, edited by Saul Lieberman, Hebrew Section (Jerusalem: American Academy for Jewish Research, 1974), 228–229. See Lieberman, "Persecution," for a full discussion of this question.

47. BT (Babylonian Talmud; final editing in sixth century [?]) Sotah 12a and parallels. A particularly interesting version of this legend is found in a midrashic collection of uncertain date and provenance, *Pesiqta Rabbati* (Pisqa 43), where it is said that Moses' father Amram, in conjunction with his fellow elders, actually issued a decree forbidding Israelite men to have relations with their wives because of Pharaoh's decree.

48. *Genesis Rabbah* (fifth-century Palestinian midrashic collection) 31:12 and parallels.

49. PT (Palestinian Talmud, edited in final third of fourth century [?]) Ta'anit 1:6 (64d) and parallels.

50. Sexual relations were forbidden by the rabbis during the later and more stringent of the fasts that were instituted in case of drought or famine (Mishnah Ta'anit 1:6). The rabbis also defined the biblical requirement that on Yom Kippur "you shall afflict yourselves" as including a prohibition of sex.

51. Leviticus 21:6.

52. See Diamond, *Holy Men and Hunger Artists*, 78.

53. BT Yebamot 20a.

54. BT Yoma 29a.

55. Tosefta Berakhot 2:12, PT Berakhot 3:4 (6b), BT Berakhot 22a. All subsequent citations of and references to rabbinic discussion of this subject can be found in the PT or the BT at these locations.

56. BT Bava Qamma 82a. The Palestinian Talmud (Shabbat 1.4, 3c) lists this as one of the eighteen ordinances decreed by the disciples of Shammai despite the opposition of the disciples of Hillel in the early first century.

57. Tosefta and parallels.

58. Mishnah Miqva'ot 8:2–4.

59. Louis Ginzberg, *A Commentary on the Palestinian Talmud, Tractate Berakhot* (in Hebrew; New York: Ktav, 1941), 2:234, 269.

60. Ibid., 2:240, 271.

61. See Steven Fraade, "Ascetical Aspects of Ancient Judaism," in Arthur Green, ed., *Jewish Spirituality from the Bible through the Middle Ages* (New York: Crossroad, 1988), 275.

62. Daniel Boyarin, *Carnal Israel: Reading Sex in Talmudic Culture* (Berkeley: University of California Press, 1993), 134.

63. Tosefta Yebamot 8:7. This story has been analyzed numerous times. See Boyarin, *Carnal Israel*, 134–136, and Diamond, *Holy Men and Hunger Artists*, 35–38.

64. Boyarin, *Carnal Israel*, 136.

65. Isaiah Gafni, *The Jews in Babylonia in the Talmudic Era: A Social and Cultural History* (in Hebrew; Jerusalem: Zalman Shazar Center for Jewish History, 1990), 267–268.

66. I am paraphrasing here the distinction made by Paul Southgate in "A Swallow in Winter: A Catholic Priesthood Viewpoint," in Sobo and Bell, *Celibacy, Culture, and Society*, 248.

67. Diamond, *Holy Men and Hunger Artists*, 16.

68. BT Qiddushin 29b.

69. BT Nedarim 20a–b.

70. Satlow, *Jewish Marriage*, 12–21, esp. 19, 280 n. 109; Satlow, *Tasting the Dish: Rabbinic Rhetorics of Sexuality* (Atlanta: Scholars Press, 1995), 290–294.

71. Michel Foucault, *The Use of Pleasure: The History of Sexuality*, volume 2, translated by Robert Hurley (New York: Vintage, 1990), 152–165.

72. Mishnah Abot 4:1.

73. Daniel Boyarin, "Body Politic among the Brides of Christ: Paul and the Origins of Christian Sexual Renunciation, in V. Wimbush and R. Valantasis, eds., *Asceticism* (New York: Oxford University Press, 1995), 460.

74. Boyarin, *Carnal Israel*, 159–165, by comparing the Palestinian and Babylonian versions of the midrash that Moses separated himself from Zippora permanently after the revelation at Sinai, shows that the Palestinian version probably reflects Palestinian disapproval of this Babylonian practice.

75. See the observation of Anne Drafthorn Kilmer, reported in Boyarin, *Carnal Israel*, 140 n. 13, that from a very early date Babylonian culture and religion view sex as a necessity for everyone. See also Diamond, *Holy Men and Hunger Artists*, 131.

76. BT Qiddushin 29b–30a.

77. See BT Ketubot 62a–b and 63a–b.

78. See the series of stories in Bavli Ketubot 62b–63a and the analysis in Boyarin, *Carnal Israel*, 146–158.

79. BT Yebamot 63a–b.

80. BT Qiddushin 81a–b.

81. BT Qiddushin 81b.

82. Shlomo Naeh, "Freedom and Celibacy: A Talmudic Variation on Tales of Temptation and Fall in Genesis and Its Syrian Background," in J. Frishman and L. Van Rompay, eds., *The Book of Genesis in Jewish and Oriental Christian Interpretation* (Louvain: n.p., 1997), 73–89.

83. I Corinthians 7:9.

84. *Genesis Rabbah* 9:7 and parallels.

85. See Boyarin, *Carnal Israel*, 56 and passim; Satlow, *Tasting the Dish*, 315–327 and passim.

86. BT Yoma 69b.

87. See David Biale, *Eros and the Jews: From Biblical Israel to Contemporary America* (New York: Basic Books, 1992), 109–118.

88. Ibid., 137–141.

89. Ibid., 147–148.

90. Ibid., 157–158.

4

Celibacy in the Early Christian Church

Glenn Holland

Celibacy in early Christianity had substantial points of contact with the practice of sexual restraint in the Roman philosophical context as well as in ascetic forms of Judaism. The Roman model was the philosophical notion of self-mastery displayed in self-restraint. In the case of sexual behavior, this restraint was allied with the idea that sexual activity depleted the male body's vital energy (its *pneuma* or "animal spirit") and could prove harmful.[1] The Jewish model was more equivocal. Although apparently there were ascetic groups among the Jews of the first century CE that practiced celibacy, notably the Essenes and the Therapeutae, the primary expectation for sexual behavior among pious Jews was chastity (that is, sexual fidelity) within marriage.[2] The purity laws in Torah associated with sexuality in general appear to assume sexual activity within marriage as the norm, with abstinence at particular times and for particular purposes. Most regulation of a couple's sexual life was concerned with the procreation of legitimate offspring as a means of establishing and enlarging the People of the Covenant, a dominant concern in the patriarchal narratives of the Hebrew Bible, for example. This meant both a rejection of sexual practices not conducive to reproduction (such as intercourse during menstruation or homosexual intercourse) and the practice of both divorce and polygamy if one's wife was unable to conceive.[3]

But despite substantial points of contact with ideas of sexual restraint already current at the turn of the age, the motivation for and practice of sexual restraint and celibacy within the early Christian context appear to have been unique in at least two major respects. On the one hand, the commitment to celibacy is often difficult to distinguish from the decision not to marry and, by doing so, to assume the responsibilities of the household. In such a case, celibacy is less a choice than the necessary consequence of another choice, the choice not to marry. On the other hand, within early Christianity there ultimately develops a widespread and deeply ingrained ideal of lifelong celibacy as the foundation of an ascetic lifestyle that offers a "higher way" toward salvation. What follows is an attempt to place celibacy in its historical and cultural context as a component of Christian faith and practice during the ancient period, from the origins of the Jesus movement to the end of the ancient period around 500 CE.

The Idea of Sexual Restraint in the Jesus Movement

The practice of sexual restraint in the Jesus movement and the early Church has its origins in Jesus' teaching and the practices of his disciples. Jesus not only proclaimed the imminent arrival of the Kingdom and the imposition of God's sovereignty over his creation but also demanded a response from those who heard his proclamation (as in the summary of his message in Mark 1:14–15). The response of repentance and belief led his followers away from preoccupation with everyday responsibilities, including the responsibilities attendant on marriage. All evidence indicates that Jesus himself was unmarried and celibate, a status consistent with the demands of his peripatetic ministry and his role as a prophet dedicated to proclaiming the word of God. Although earlier prophets of Israel and Judah had married and fathered children, and sometimes even made their families a part of their prophetic ministry (see, for example, the "prophetic actions" described in Hosea 1–3 and Isaiah 8, with the symbolic names given to children), the urgent demands of proclaiming the imminent Kingdom seems to have precluded marriage. John the Baptist was another major prophetic figure of Jesus' era who was unmarried and celibate as a result of his commitment to proclaiming God's imminent Kingdom.

But the group of Jesus' disciples, and notably the inner circle of twelve, included married men (cf. Mark 1:29–31, 1 Cor. 9:5). Whether or not the wives of disciples were included among their number (cf. Mark 3:33–35) or among the women who traveled with the disciples and saw to their needs (Luke 8:1–3) is unknown. In Mark 10:28–30, Peter refers to the disciples leaving "all" behind to follow Jesus, and the parallel story in Luke explicitly includes wives (Luke 18:29–30). Presumably the disciples' travels with Jesus imposed at least a temporary celibacy on them, although they were not otherwise ascetic. In fact, Jesus was apparently reviled by some who acted as "a glutton and a drunkard" (Matt. 11:19).[4]

Jesus' teaching also touched explicitly on matters of sexual morality and restraint. His prohibition of divorce in Matthew 19:1–9 (cf. Mark 10:1–12) leads the disciples to declare that it would be better not to marry (Matt. 19:10). Jesus' response refers in part to those "who have made themselves eunuchs for the sake of the kingdom of heaven" (Matt. 19:12c). This is a call to forsake voluntarily what is expected and "natural" in regards to sexuality, specifically within the Jewish context (Matt. 19:4–9), and even to assume an "excluded" status, since Torah excluded eunuchs (or better, the "sexually damaged") from the Temple (Deut. 23:1; cf. Isa. 56:1–8, esp. 3–5).

Jesus calls all those who repent and believe into the "family" of the Jesus congregation, a family whose claims must take priority over those of the natural family (cf. Mark 6:4–6, Matt. 10:37–39, Luke 9:59–62). Jesus even grants the family of his followers priority over his own family (Mark 3:20–21, 31–35). As a result, Jesus stands in contrast to the mainstream Judaism of his time and its emphasis on procreation—and thus family life—as a universal responsibility. Generally Jesus radicalized the call to serve God and to seek his Kingdom above all else, and this of course had direct consequences for what could be considered all "normal" aspects of life, especially marriage, children, household, and the attendant responsibilities. But the radical call to serve God does not necessarily call for the elimination of other priorities; it may instead be understood as a demand for their reorientation toward preparation for and service to the impending Kingdom of God.

Jesus' apocalyptic outlook—his anticipation of the end of the current age and the establishment of God's sovereignty over the earth—provides the context for much of the content and urgency of his moral demands. Those who wished to follow Jesus had to make their moral decisions and act within the "temporary" conditions that would prevail until the impending advent of the Kingdom. After the experience of Jesus' resurrection, his followers apparently understood their moral decisions and action within the context of the "temporary" conditions prevailing between Jesus' resurrection and his imminent return.[5] As a result, Jesus' call to grant priority to the claims of the impending Kingdom over all other considerations—including those of marriage, children and household—retained its commanding urgency.

Apostolic missionaries, who spread the gospel in the decades following Jesus' crucifixion ("apostles" in the broader sense), were the members of the Jesus movement, whose way of life closely approximated that of Jesus' own ministry. Yet we find the missionary apostles, including Peter and others who were married, apparently traveled with their wives and were supported by the congregations they visited (1 Cor. 9:4–7).[6] Their presence indicates that "proclaiming the gospel" did not preclude the responsibilities of marriage, but doubtless the apostolic ministry redefined them to a certain extent. There are also prominent examples of unmarried male missionaries, notably Paul and Barnabas (1 Cor. 7:7, 9:6, 15) and of female missionaries apparently unattached to any man—either unmarried women or widows (cf. Phoebe, Rom. 16:1–2). Similarly, local leadership of congregations was apparently in some cases taken up by single women, again either unmarried or widows (cf. Phoebe, Rom. 16:1–2; Chloe, 1 Cor. 1:11). Their prominence within the early Jesus movement seems to indicate at the very least that both men and women without a marriage partner were held in equal esteem as the married.[7]

The apostle Paul's reflections on sexual restraint should be understood in the context of life in the Jesus congregations, both those Paul himself established and others. The dominant pattern among the Jesus congregations founded by Paul appears to have been a continuation of the patterns of daily life, including the responsibilities of family, work, and society, but with the focus now on the risen Christ and his imminent return (cf. 1 Cor. 7:8–11, 17–24, 29–31). For the most part, Christian ethics appear to have taken much of their substance from prevailing Hellenistic morality, with its emphasis on sexual continence, hard work, and service to others.[8] Distinguishing characteristics included strict chastity within marriage and celibacy for the unmarried, but there appears to have been no emphasis on voluntary chastity beyond that. Paul, true to his Jewish identity, believed that monogamous marriage was the natural state for men and women, and that marriage inevitably involved sexual intercourse as a way of satisfying both partners' natural needs (1 Cor. 7:1–5, 36–38). Paul identified the ability to remain celibate as a "gift" (χάρισμα) from God, one granted to him but not to everyone; still he writes, "I wish that all were as I myself am" (1 Cor. 7:7), specifically because he felt the single life made it easier to serve God wholeheartedly (1 Cor. 7:29–35).

In 1 Corinthians 7, the regulation of sexuality and Paul's preference for the single life are both discussed entirely within the context of marriage. Paul is in fact participating in a long-standing contemporary discussion of the desirability of marriage for those devoted to a particular way of life; most often such discussion focused on the responsibilities of the Stoic philosopher.[9] There appears to be no consideration in Paul's writings of the desirability of celibacy per se, but only the ability to remain unmarried and yet not "burn" (1 Cor. 7:8–9).

The second generation of the Jesus movement (ca. 70 to 100 CE) faced a new situation, one that more closely resembled that of later generations than that of the previous generation. Once the natural leaders of the Jesus movement—his original followers—had died, there was no single model for deriving and exercising authority among the Jesus congregations. On the one hand, there was an emphasis on continuity with the apostolic witness that was generally taken as the authentic, authoritative interpretation of Jesus' life and ministry, but on the other there was also an emphasis on the moral standing of those who would assume leadership, most notably in regard to marital status (cf. 1 Tim. 3:2, 12). The expectation that a male leader be "the husband of one wife" implies a model of marital fidelity parallel to one's exclusive covenantal fidelity to the Lord, exalting the relationship of a husband and even an infertile wife over the desire for procreation. This may represent a new attitude toward the bond of affection between a husband and wife, but more likely reflects the decreased interest in procreation among members of a group looking for an early end to the current age, a group whose growth was sustained by converts as well as by the birth of children to faithful couples.

External forces also shaped the development of the Jesus movement. The Jewish War (66–70 CE) ended in Rome's victory over the Jews and the destruction of the Jerusalem Temple. The catastrophe effectively left the Pharisees alone of all of the major factions of first-century Judaism to determine its future.[10] They appear often to have done so in conscious contrast to the development of the Jesus movement.[11] Persecution of Jesus' followers, now known as "Christians," sporadic for years under Jewish and Roman authorities, became an imperial matter for the first time with the persecution in the city of Rome under Nero in 64 CE.[12] Finally, the delay of Jesus' second coming (the *parousia*) forced Christian leaders to reevaluate the situation of the Church as a continuing institution in the world, while still awaiting Jesus' eventual return. The delay of the *parousia* meant the Church depended on the establishment of Christian families living in households in the everyday world. But the delay also fed apocalyptic expectations among some Christians who undertook ascetic practices, including celibacy, in specific anticipation of the *parousia*. For the most part, however, Christian leaders at the end of the first century encouraged Christians to follow the Lord's will in the context of families living in well-ordered households.[13]

At the same time, the experience of official Roman persecution gave an urgent cast to an ethic of self-denial; the behavior of persecuted Christians was expected to be exemplary in all respects. The martyr's rejection of worldly pleasure, family, liberty, and ultimately life itself for the sake of Christian confession would set an example of renunciation for all believers. But in fact there were Christians who recanted under persecution, leading to debates over whether those who later wished to repent and return to the Church community could do so. Ultimately a policy of leniency prevailed over the demands of the "rigorists," marking a clear distinction between those who felt the believer's life inevitably followed a pattern of sin, repentance, and rededication, and those who demanded consistent adherence to a higher standard of morality as proof that one's faith and confession were genuine.

So there arose different ideas of what it meant to be a faithful follower of Jesus. A constant factor, however, was a distinctive sexual morality, with an emphasis on chastity within marriage, in contrast to the prevailing standards of Roman society, and rejection of divorce and remarriage, in contrast to Roman and Jewish practice. A corollary of this standard was celibacy until marriage and often also after the death of a spouse, creating perforce a major subclass of celibate men and women among the members of the Church.

Celibacy in Christian Communities during the Second Century

By the end of the first century, there were several reasons a Christian might decide to practice voluntary celibacy as a form of self-denial. First was a heightened expectation of the impending end of the age, the reason Paul had given when urging others not to marry. Second was the dualistic point of view that set "this world" and its demands in contrast to the demands of "the Kingdom" and the world to come. Most often this dualism set "the things of the spirit" in opposition to "the things of the flesh" conceived of specifically as the demands of the body, most notably in terms of its (sexual) desires that could theoretically be partially or entirely suppressed. A final motivation for voluntary celibacy was self-definition, both of the Christian movement in contrast to the other religious and philosophical movements of the time, and of individual Christians as those particularly devoted to the Lord.

Already during the early second century, there were those in the Christian community who attempted to set themselves apart through special ascetic practices. Some possessed special spiritual gifts (*charismata*), such as prophecy, that were considered especially beneficial for the community. Christians set apart by their possession of such spiritual gifts lived in such a way as to elevate and refine their receptivity to the Spirit, most often by ascetic practices. Celibacy was a common ascetic discipline; it eliminated the distracting demands not only of the household, as Paul had argued, but also those of the flesh, allowing the mind and soul to attend to the promptings of the Spirit with singleness of heart. Tertullian (ca. 160–c. 230) argued that celibacy and the exercise of spiritual gifts went hand in hand, since, in the words of Peter Brown, "it was directly through the body and its sensations that the soul was tuned to the high pitch required for it to vibrate to the Spirit of God."[14] Tertullian attributed the widely spread gift of prophecy among the followers of the heterodox teacher Montanus to their celibacy, itself a result in turn of their openness to the Holy Spirit.[15]

Voluntary forms of ascetic renunciation appear to have increased even as the threat of persecution decreased. Ascetics were venerated because they gave up the normal pleasures of life, just as the martyrs gave up life itself under persecution. During the second century, ascetics most often remained as members of local congregations and served as reminders to their fellow Christians of the "higher calling" to renounce worldly pleasures in service to Christ. Individual ascetics often served as spiritual counselors to married members of the congregation.

The growing emphasis on celibacy as an expression of religious devotion among Christians was consistent with the new wave of sexual restraint that arose in the Roman Empire during the second century CE. The new attitude is evident not only in the works of philosophers in the first two centuries of the Common Era but also in those of physicians; both groups were concerned with personal conduct as means of subduing the body to the control of the inner self.[16] Michel Foucault attributes this general trend as part of "an intensification of the relation to oneself by which one constituted oneself as the subject of one's acts," that is, by the greater emphasis on the individual as a moral agent.[17] It is not difficult to see why this was so. Sexual desire is the only "natural" appetite that can be entirely suppressed (in contrast with hunger and thirst), and so sexual restraint became the sine qua non of self-containment. Moreover, sexual desire cannot be satisfied by limited indulgence short of the act of completion; in fact, limited sexual activity (comparable to "nibbling" as a way of curbing appetite) enhances sexual desire rather than kills it. This fact makes sexual desire a paradigm for the general temptation to sin, since once initiated, sexual desire finds its satisfaction only in the act of completion. Further, sexual desire has no natural point of surfeit, as hunger and thirst do, since one can easily sense with those desires when one is "full." On the other hand, one can be rendered physically incapable of sex, but not (normally) of eating or drinking, and still be otherwise in good health. Moreover, the fact that personal control over one's sexuality is necessary for the larger social good (unlike control over one's consumption of food and drink, strictly a personal good) makes sexual restraint socially useful and so also morally good.

But this is not all. A person's decision to remain celibate appears also to have been a conscious appropriation of spiritual power, not only of the power necessary to remain celibate but also of the power that arises from celibacy as a manifestation both of social independence and of religious purity. Social independence meant, especially for women, that they were not identified in terms of their association with a male but rather valued for their independent decision to maintain their virginity intact, that is, against the wishes of males. Stories of Christian women who refused to marry or, if forced to marry, refused to have sexual intercourse with their husbands, are stories of female independence and self-assertion, even if understood within the context of submission to (a male) God.[18] Virginity is one way a woman might "become male" in the sense that she could act as an independent authority and source of power (a possibility open only to men in imperial society) within the Christian community.[19] Jo Ann McNamara argues that virginity was a basis of equality between men and women. When the Fathers refer to women who "play the man," they are attempting, in the terms of their language and presuppositions, to offer essentially nongendered praise, since both men and women were expected to "play the man" against the Devil and the temptations of this world. The goal virginal women sought to achieve was not the "male mind" but the "celestial mind," the mind that acts in agreement with and in adoration of God.[20]

Both mainstream and heterodox groups during the second century adopted as one of their defining attributes a commitment to celibacy among their members, most often as part of a rigorist interpretation of Christian ethics. Among such groups, celibacy represented a rejection of commitment to life in this world and the entangling presence of sin inevitably tied up with sexuality. The essence of human nature was invariably explained by reference to the story of Adam and Eve, and humanity's fall in Eden was already identified by some with sexuality; to reject sexuality was to reject Adam's claims on the renewed believer.[21] Christian ascetics identified by their contemporaries as Encratites (from *enkrateia*, continence) associated sexuality with other aspects of humanity's "animal" nature they blamed for the Fall.[22] They were not only celibate but also practiced dietary restrictions, including those they believed would help to suppress sexual desires.[23] The Marcionites and other nonconforming groups included celibacy as a necessary requirement for membership. The idea of lifelong celibacy began its long ascendancy, expressed primarily in terms of female virginity. This ideal was promulgated by literary works such as the mid-second century *Acts of Paul and Thecla*, with its adamantly virginal heroine who rejected marriage in favor of a chaste infatuation with the Apostle Paul that led her to survive several attempts to make her a bride or a martyr before she ultimately assumed the life of a solitary ascetic.

Toward the end of the second century, the great increase in the membership of the Church led to widespread acceptance of two distinct standards of Christian ethics, each based on a distinctive way of life. One was the way of life of the common Christian living in the world, and the other was the ascetic way of life adopted by the spiritual adept, including notably and inevitably the commitment to sexual abstinence. The basis of the different ethical standards was a widely accepted distinction between those Christians who did what was required and those who wished to do more. The common Christian was obliged to do all that Christ commanded, but could do so as a spouse and householder with children and slaves. But it was also possible to do more than Christ commanded in the way of self-denial and devotion to God, and in that way to attain "perfection."

To some extent this double standard represented a protest against the accommodation of the Christian movement to the prevailing culture of the Roman Empire, at a time when "common" Christians had become harder to distinguish from other Roman citizens. But the double standard also had its practical side: those who distinguished themselves from other Christians through acts of renunciation also depended on those "ordinary" Christians to maintain the larger Church by providing monetary support and the children who would become its new members. The double standard provoked a continuing debate. Some believed the life of the common Christian and that of the ascetic represented two stages in the believer's progression toward salvation, while others believed there were essentially two sorts of Christian: common Christians and ascetics, those "perfected" Christians called to a higher level of obedience. This division, some argued, would continue even in Heaven as an eternal distinction among believers.

It was an increasingly common expectation during the later second century that members of the clergy would be celibate. Clergy were often drawn from the ranks of Christian widowers. Widows likewise continued to serve as patronesses of congregations, and in so doing exercised some degree of authority and influence, at least in the congregations under their patronage. Here again, celibacy was deeply intertwined with related issues of marriage, the more so since sexual restraint in marriage was the expectation among both Christian and pagan Roman couples. After producing several offspring, couples were expected to give up sexual activity, incidentally also preparing themselves for a celibate life after the death of a spouse. Although celibacy was associated with spiritual purity and moral restraint, it appears to have remained for many Christians primarily the consequence of a decision not to (re)marry.

The Ideal of Christian Celibacy in the Third Century

During the third century, again partly because of the growing numbers of those joining the Church, ascetics began to separate themselves in large numbers from congregations of "common" Christians and live apart. Ascetics would still devote themselves to works of charity among members of local congregations, but increasingly they withdrew from the daily life of those congregations, and in fact set themselves in contrast to the life of common Christians. Although ascetic withdrawal meant the loss of the leadership example provided by the spiritually mature ascetic, common Christians continued to regard such people with deep respect, and believed their words possessed particular wisdom and power.

The ideal of lifelong celibacy began to acquire a theological underpinning and justification. Origen of Alexandria (ca. 185–ca. 254) had an elaborate theory of the soul, its fall and redemption, which presented bodily existence as only a brief episode in the soul's long progress toward eventual restoration to its prelapsarian purity. Lifelong celibacy suppressed the claims of the body and so enabled the speedier progress of the soul toward its ultimate, posthumous reconciliation with God. Moreover, celibacy broke down the barriers that separated men and women by subjugating the functions of sexuality to the higher calling of the soul, granting the celibate the freedom from the body for which the soul yearned. Methodius of Olympus (d. ca. 311) wrote *Symposium, or Banquet of the Ten Virgins*, a dialogue based on Plato's *Symposium*, itself a reconsideration of the true nature of *eros* that transcended the merely sexual. In Methodius's *Symposium*, each of ten virgins, including the legendary Thecla, offers a discourse in praise of virginity, combining allegorical interpretations of Scripture with attacks against false teachers (including Origen) and exhortations to the moral effort to live a life of perfect celibacy, the life most pleasing to God.

As the *Symposium* demonstrates, by the mid-third century, virginity for both men and women had emerged as the ideal for those who aspired to wholehearted devotion to God, and celibacy was considered a primary virtue among those who sought to renew their lives and purify themselves of sin through renunciation. Cyprian, bishop of Carthage from 248 to 258, saw the body as the battleground in the struggle between the soul and the world, with sexuality one of the many temptations the world might bring to bear to overcome the good intentions of the soul. He gave careful instructions for the dress and behavior of virgins, intended to help them avoid "deadly snares and death-bringing pleasures."[24] The Jewish-Christian heterodox teacher Mani (216/17–276) developed the strict theological dualism of Manichaeism. Mani understood the cosmos and the material world as the site of an eternal struggle between the equal but opposed forces of Light and Darkness. The Manichean Elect played their part for Light in this struggle by keeping themselves pure through fasting and celibacy. Other members of the group, the *auditors*, were generally married, but would also fast and would refrain from sexual activity for set periods of time, in the hope of some day being joined to the Elect.[25] Mani's primary influence on later orthodox theories of sexuality was through the erstwhile Manichean Augustine of Hippo, who even after his conversion to a Neoplatonic understanding of Christianity retained a Manichean antipathy for those aspects of creation he felt were estranged from the light of the true God.

The groups both within and outside mainstream Christianity that emphasized the opposition between flesh and spirit, between the claims of this world and those of the world to come, most often—although not unanimously—focused on sexuality as the primary example of the inner conflict Christians had to face and overcome. As a result, by the end of the third century, both models of the Christian life—the common Christian and the perfected Christian—were dominated by a notion of sexual restraint, either inside or outside of marriage, as the clearest evidence of pious self-command.

Celibacy and Asceticism in the Fourth Century

Celibacy was a necessary concomitant of the abandonment of worldly wealth and status embraced by those ascetics who retreated into the desert toward the end of the third century and the beginning of the fourth century. The most notable of these, Antony (251?–356), was born to wealth but gave away his possessions and retired to the edges of the Egyptian desert to live as a hermit. The desert or wilderness had associations with spiritual struggle and enlightenment that stretched back to the history of Israel's wanderings, and had been sanctified by Jesus' temptation by the devil in the desert (Matt. 4:1–11). Antony, like the Cynic philosophers before him, sought to reduce the physical demands of life to a bare minimum, but did so in a solitary existence in a harsh environment that forced him back entirely on his own physical and spiritual resources. The ultimate goal of the desert ascetic was to allow the body to find its "natural" level of need, need that would be met by the simplest of food and drink, in stark contrast to the sensual eating and drinking of the civilized world the hermit had left behind. Antony believed his sparse diet aided in suppressing sexual urges, a suppression further assisted by his removal from society and the presence of women. The fourth-century desert ascetics of Syria were regarded as "angels" by the lay people whom they counseled and supported through their intercessions with God, in that they had surpassed the bonds of human existence by celibacy, fasting, and diligent prayer.

About 320, Pachomius (ca. 290–346) founded a monastery at Tabennisi in the Thebaid near the Nile in Egypt, where strenuous manual labor and strict discipline provided the basis for what was basically an ascetic community of hermits (*coenobium*). The ascetic community shared the ideals and the intentions of the solitary hermit, but with the additional obligations imposed by membership in a community: obedience, fellowship, humility, forbearance, interdependence, stability. Although a hermit was free to engage in spiritual warfare for the betterment of his soul, a monk was part of a social network of mutual obligation, a man who surrendered the austere privacy of his inmost self to the community and to God. Celibacy was an integral part of the discipline of the monastery, but so also was the humble surrender of the self where sexual desire originates. But the monastery also provided a refuge from society for those wishing to escape the censure of Roman society. Even at its best, the monastery was always composed both of those led to the ascetic life primarily by spiritual considerations and those drawn to it by more purely personal motives.

The rigorous demands of the celibate life and the inevitable temptations to be overcome by the spiritually strong were perennial topics in the literature that exhorted the faithful to follow the ascetic path. Women were most often portrayed in this body of literature as a source of sexual temptation for men, a means by which even the most faithful man might easily fall. Women were not the only or the worst danger for the ascetic man, but they were often employed in the literature as the embodiment of all that would distract the ascetic from his avowed desire to live exclusively in devotion to his Lord. Yet this symbolic use of women was not necessarily intended to condemn women as a sex, but rather to warn men that separation from women, and indeed separation from all earthly affections, was the clearest and safest path to staunch celibacy and so also to spiritual purity.[26]

The situation of young Christian women in the fourth century was still closely tied to the consequences of the family's choice to give them in marriage or not. The two acceptable roles for Christian women were the chaste wife and mother and the dedicated virgin, both examples of sexual continence. But this status was subject to change: young women of marriageable age might be given to the service of the Church if marriage did not seem a suitable choice to their families, and perhaps later reclaimed if the family found a suitable match. This may explain why Fathers such as Gregory of Nyssa and Ambrose are careful not to disparage matrimony even as they praise virginity.[27] So even as late as the fourth century, the primary sexual virtue for a Christian woman was chastity, either exclusive fidelity to her husband or maintenance of her virginity intact, rather than virginity per se, as highly praised as that was.[28]

When young aristocratic women sought out ascetic vocations, they did so in social contexts different from those of their male counterparts; they either remained within the paternal household or established an association with a congregation. Within the paternal household, a dedicated virgin was a living expression of her family's piety as well as her own. Such women often lived as recluses within their own homes, secluded from the outside world except for participation in worship services in church. Another possibility was to form larger or smaller associations with other celibate women. Virginity was the primary trait of the women in such communities, because it was also the basis of the women's social independence. Removal from the paternal household presented an opportunity for celibate women to free themselves from the supervision and authority of men and so become autonomous individuals. As such, celibate women were free also to become associates of men likewise dedicated to the Church, and to enter the literate world of intellectual engagement. In the Latin West, aristocratic virgins became influential as patrons of the Church in the fourth century, forming a financial and intellectual alliance with male clergy and monks.[29] Their virginity was an essential part of their identity and independence, and part and parcel of their spiritual authority as examples and as counselors.

These aristocratic women were comparable to the dedicated widows of earlier centuries, but because of their uncompromised virginal state, were perceived as symbols of pious constancy and lifelong dedication to God's will. It was in this context that the perpetual virginity of Mary also became particularly important, as an example of both the chaste mother and the dedicated virgin. The Holy Mother offered an example of the virgin "bride" whose unsullied fidelity was dedicated exclusively to God.

Lifelong celibacy in the context of a life dedicated to God's service was supported by theological justifications based on one of two models of idealized human existence: either the prelapsarian state of Adam in Eden or the reiteration of that state in the sinless person of Jesus. Gregory of Nyssa (ca. 330–ca. 395), for example, himself a married man, attributed the division of the sexes, and so also human sexuality, to the fallen state of humanity. Sexuality was intended for procreation, and procreation itself was a drive arising from Adam's loss of his original state and fall into sin and death.[30] To suppress the procreative urge, according to Gregory, was to trust in the future provided by God for a redeemed humanity, rather than to participate in the futile human attempt to overcome mortality by producing offspring.[31]

In the West, Ambrose of Milan (ca. 339–397) saw the incarnate Christ as the model for redeemed humanity, a model toward which the believer advanced from the moment of his or her baptism. The primary distinction between the body of the believer and the body of Christ, according to Ambrose, was the believer's entrapment in sexuality, the primary instance of the unfortunate effects of the Fall.[32] Moreover, involvement with sexuality represented for Ambrose a compromise with the world, an action belonging more properly to nonbelievers than to Christians, and therefore not worthy of Christians.[33]

Ambrose saw virginity as the purest expression of *integritas*, the wholehearted devotion of body and mind to a single master, without concession to the powers that dominate the current age.[34]

Development of a theological foundation for lifelong celibacy was a necessary prologue to the debate over celibacy among the clergy that simmered in the church for many years before breaking out in earnest in the late fourth century. On the one hand, celibacy had emerged as the deepest expression of commitment to the Lord, symbolic of the renunciation of normal life in "the world," and a means of recapturing the prelapsarian state of bodily integrity. On the other, lay people who themselves lived "in the world" felt that celibacy was typical of ascetics who, they believed, had little understanding of, or sympathy with, the problems of most common Christians. Married clergy, on the other hand, knew the situation of the common Christian much better. Underlying the debate over clerical celibacy was the conviction among many that one's progress in the Christian life could be measured by one's withdrawal from sexual activity, either as a virgin from birth or as a celibate partner within a marriage after producing children. But the married state remained a constant incitement to sin because of mutual sexual attraction between husband and wife, an attraction that remained even if the couple's wish was to remain celibate. The safest choice therefore for a mature life of virtue untainted by sexual desire or activity was lifelong virginity. Clerical celibacy won increasing favor in the West, even as married lower clergy remained the rule in the East.

The Rejection of Sexuality in Fifth-Century Christianity

At the beginning of the fifth century, the Western church adopted an increasingly negative view of sexuality as the primary example of how "the flesh" worked against the devout intentions of the mind and spirit. Jerome (ca. 342–420), a contemporary and friend of Augustine of Hippo, offered a severe attitude toward sexuality not untypical of the West in his time. Jerome had been born into a wealthy family and was well educated before devoting himself to the ascetic life in the wilderness of Palestine. Jerome was ordained a priest in Antioch but from 382 served as secretary to Pope Damasus in Rome. Despite his impressive knowledge of Latin literature, Jerome absolutely denied there was any value in secular Roman culture. He also rejected marriage of the sort the average married Roman Christian enjoyed as no more than a capitulation to the desires of the flesh. He supported lifelong celibacy for priests and other clergy, regarding celibacy as a necessary foundation for a holy life. Although Jerome had female friends who were his intellectual companions, he also feared the sexual temptation that the presence of even the holiest of women presented to the male believer.[35] Contrary to many theologians in the East, Jerome postulated that sexual differences between men and women were eternal, a distinction between them that would remain even in Heaven.[36]

Augustine of Hippo (354–430) formulated the theory of human sexuality that was to have definitive influence on the religious consciousness of the West. Augustine's ideas were shaped both by his time as a Manichaean and by his early struggles with sexual temptation, a temptation to which he often yielded. Augustine had a long and apparently monogamous relationship with a mistress who was also the mother of his son, but although he accepted the son he found himself unable either to marry or to reject his mistress. When he was first converted to Christianity, Augustine broke off the relationship with his mistress to immerse himself in an ascetic community similar to a Neoplatonic philosophical community. Later, after what he regarded as a second conversion experience, Augustine moved into the all-male world of the Christian clergy, where celibacy was reinforced by separation from the company of women.

Unlike Gregory of Nyssa and Ambrose, Augustine believed sexuality and marriage had been a part of the created order from the beginning. But he also believed sexuality, like every other aspect of the created order, had suffered corruption as a result of humanity's fall. Although originally the human body, its senses, and its desires had been under the control of Adam and Eve's rational will, after the fall the human will became corrupt, and the harmony of body and soul had been disrupted, leaving the soul prey to bodily desire.

In the Neoplatonic view Augustine adopted, all good came from God and reflected God, who was thus himself the source of all good. God created the world good, but meant the good things in the world to point human beings toward God as the origin of the good within them and as the sum of all good. When human beings sought out and enjoyed an earthly good—the pleasure of sexual intercourse, for example—for its own sake rather than as a way to glorify God, this was concupiscence, the essential nature of sin. Sexuality became for Augustine the primary example of concupiscence, the desire for some good other than God for its own sake. Proof of the corruption of sexual desire in human beings was the way the body failed to respond to the promptings of the will to engage in sexual intercourse (as in the case of male impotence) or, by contrast, the way the body manifested sexual excitement against the desire of the will (for example, by a man's spontaneous erection). So every male experienced in his own body the clear evidence that the body's desires were not subject to the promptings of the will.[37]

Augustine's view of human sexuality provoked a dispute with the Pelagian teacher Julian of Eclanum over whether human sexuality was inherently disordered and sinful after the Fall, or unaffected and morally neutral. Julian maintained that sexuality was just another realm of human choice, and had not been essentially altered by the Fall. It could be a cause of sin, but it could also be domesticated in chaste Christian marriage. Its moral standing was a matter of human choice. Augustine in contrast believed sexuality was invariably tainted by lust as a result of the Fall, but that marriage provided the one correct use of the desire engendered by lust: "A man turns to use the evil of concupiscence, and is not overcome by it, when he bridles and restrains its rage . . . and never relaxes his hold upon it except when intent on offspring, and then controls and applies it to the carnal generation of children to be spiritually regenerated, not to the subjection of the spirit to the flesh in a sordid servitude."[38] But corruption was the condition of all desires of the body. Before the Fall the human body had been in harmony with the human will and under its control. But now, after the Fall, the human body was a deceiver, a mocker of the will that could no longer control it because of its own corrupt nature; the harmony was broken. Mistrust of the human body led to a mistrust and suspicion of all bodily pleasures, most notably those associated with sexuality.[39] Bodily pleasures were a danger to a man's social position, his domestic happiness, and the eternal fate of his soul. With the eclipse of Palagianism in the West, Augustine's position on human sexuality became dominant. With Augustine's theological foundation, the ascetic suspicion of pleasure typical of the medieval era was fully in place in the Latin West, and formed a counterpoint to the theological glorification of the virginal life for both women and men that was a foundation for monasticism.

Although a number of prominent theologians had written their own monastic rules, including Basil of Caesarea and Augustine himself, it was Benedict of Nursia (ca. 480–ca. 550) whose experience as leader of a group of hermits led him to create "a simple rule for beginners," including "nothing harsh, nothing burdensome," that became the model for medieval monasticism.[40] Benedict's rule provided both a justification and a model for a community of ascetics. Celibacy was so fundamental to the monastic life that Benedict does not mention it explicitly, but subsumes it, along with poverty, under obedience, specifically obedience to the abbot.[42] Celibacy is part of the monk's humility, his self-surrender, his renunciation of the world and its ways. Even here, then, at the end of the ancient period, celibacy is once again an expression of a commitment to a church family rather than to a natural family and a household. The monk rejects a life as head of his own household by swearing obedience to the abbot, by embracing poverty, and by forswearing the desire to produce heirs. It was in the context of the monastery and the convent that celibacy found its most natural home and highest expression in the Middle Ages, bequeathing to the new era the most enduring institutional expression of late antique Christian piety.

NOTES

1. Aline Rousselle, *"Porneia": On Desire and the Body in Antiquity*, translated by Felicia Pheasant (New York: Barnes & Noble, 1996), 5–23.

2. For the Essenes, see Josephus, *Jewish Antiquities* 18.18–22, and *Jewish War* 2.119–161; Philo of Alexandria, quoted in Eusebius, *Preparation for the Gospel* 8.6–7; Pliny the Elder, *Natural History* 5.17. The Essenes are often identified with the members of the Qumran community that produced the Dead Sea Scrolls, cf. Geza Vermes, *The Dead Sea Scrolls in English*, 4th ed. (New York: Penguin, 1995), 20–22. The Theraputae are the sole subject of Philo's *The Contemplative Life*.

3. Elaine Pagels, *Adam, Eve, and the Serpent* (New York: Random House, 1988), 11.

4. References to Jesus' ministry and teaching are here presented as they appear in the gospels and other New Testament literature, without consideration of how accurately the traditions of the Jesus movement reflect the attitudes and teachings of Jesus himself. The subsequent development of attitudes about sexual behavior in the Jesus movement and early Christianity were based on the received traditions about Jesus without consideration of how his historical person may have differed from the Jesus of the traditions.

5. This idea of an "age of the church" separate from the period of Jesus' ministry but preliminary to his return is apparent in both Matthew's and Luke's presentation of salvation history; see Werner Georg Kümmel, *Introduction to the New Testament*, revised edition, translated by Howard Clark Kee (Nashville: Abingdon: 1975), 118–119, 144–147.

6. The literal equivalent to the Greek phrase in 1 Corinthians 9:5 is "a sister wife"; Paul's genuine letters are our best source for the conditions prevailing during the first generation of the Jesus movement.

7. Elizabeth Schüssler Fiorenza, *In Memory of Her: A Feminist Theological Reconstruction of Christian Origins*, 10th anniversary edition (New York: Crossroad, 1994), 160–204.

8. Abraham Malherbe, *Paul and the Thessalonians: The Philosophic Tradition of Pastoral Care* (Philadelphia: Fortress, 1987), esp. 95–107; Wayne Meeks, *The Origins of Christian Morality: The First Two Centuries* (New Haven: Yale University Press, 1993), 37–51.

9. Will Deming, *Paul on Marriage and Celibacy: The Hellenistic Background of 1 Corinthians 7*, 2nd ed. (Grand Rapids, Mich.: William B. Eerdmans, 2004), 47–104.

10. For the factions in first-century Judaism, see Josephus, *Jewish Antiquities* 18.1.2–6 (11–25); D. S. Russell, *The Jews from Alexander to Herod* (Oxford: Oxford University Press, 1967), 155–174. Of these, the Essenes and Zealots were apparently wiped out as a result of the Roman victory, while the Sadducees, identified with the

high priestly families, lost their base of power with the destruction of the Temple and the suspension of its sacrificial rituals.

11. This was, of course, characteristic of both religious movements, as they defined themselves away from each other in terms of a recasting and refocusing of the traditions of early first-century Judaism they had both inherited; cf. Jesus' sustained attack on the "hypocrisy" of the scribes (i.e., experts in Torah) and Pharisees in Matthew 23.

12. Tacitus, *Annals* 15.44.2–8; Suetonius, *Life of Nero* 16.2.

13. We can see this tendency at work in the so-called household code found in the pseudo-Pauline letters, Ephesians 5:21–6:9, Colossians 3:18–4:1.

14. Peter Brown, *The Body and Society: Men, Women and Sexual Renunciation in Early Christianity* (New York: Columbia University Press, 1988), 77.

15. Ibid., 76. Montanus began his prophetic ministry in Phrygia (central and northwestern Asia Minor) in the last third of the second century. Tertullian ultimately left the Christian church to became a Montanist.

16. For more on this shift in attitude, see Michel Foucault, *The Care of the Self*, vol. 3 of *The History of Sexuality*, translated by Robert Hurley (New York: Pantheon, 1986), 39–68; Rouselle, *"Porneia,"* 5–23.

17. Foucault, *Care of the Self*, 41.

18. Gail Patterson Corrington, "The 'Divine Woman'? Propaganda and the Power of Celibacy in the New Testament Apocrypha: A Reconstruction," in *Women in Early Christianity*, edited by David M. Scholer (New York: Garland, 1993), 174–176 and the chart on 181–182.

19. Corrington, "'Divine Woman'?" 179–180.

20. Jo Ann McNamara, "Sexual Equality and the Cult of Virginity in Early Christian Thought," in *Women in Early Christianity*, edited by David M. Scholer (New York: Garland, 1993), 226–229.

21. Pagels, *Adam, Eve, and the Serpent*, xxv–xxvi.

22. Brown, *Body and Society*, 92; cf. Irenaeus, *Against Heresies* 1.26.1, cited in Eusebius, *History of the Church* 4.29.1–2.

23. For a detailed investigation of the ancient connection between fasting and celibacy, see Teresa M. Shaw, *The Burden of the Flesh: Fasting and Sexuality in Early Christianity* (Minneapolis: Fortress, 1998). There she notes: "ancient insights concerning the control of desires that lead to pleasure (and pain) and concerning the careful management and training of the body with the soul, as well as ancient anthropological and physiological models, give much of the shape and contours to early Christian understandings of the body, creation, and indeed, salvation" (7).

24. Cyprian, *On the Dress of Virgins* 21.

25. Brown, *Body and Society*, 200–201.

26. This point is well illustrated by an anecdote about Abbot Sisois, a fourth-century monk: "Abraham, the disciple of Abbot Sisois, said to him: Father, you are an old man. Let's go back to the world. Abbot Sisois replied: Very well, we'll go where there are no women. His disciple said: What is the place in which there are no women, except the desert alone? The elder replied to him: Therefore take me into the

desert." *The Wisdom of the Desert: Sayings from the Desert Fathers of the Fourth Century*, translated by Thomas Merton (Norfolk, Conn.: New Directions, 1960), lxx, 49.

27. Cf. Gregory of Nyssa, *On Virginity* 7; Ambrose of Milan, *Concerning Virgins* 1.24–31.

28. Gregory of Nyssa, himself a married man, offers an interesting point of view in the encomium *On Virginity*, written before 371. Gregory compares the blessedness of the celibate life to the inevitable difficulties attendant upon marriage (a topic also taken up by Ambrose in *Concerning Virgins* 6.24–29), and laments that he and other like him "are only spectators of the beauty belonging to others and witnesses of the blessedness of others" because "we are kept as if by an abyss from the boast of virginity to which one cannot return once he has set his foot upon the path of the worldly life." *On Virginity* 3, translated by Virginia Woods Callahan, *Saint Gregory of Nyssa: Ascetical Works* (Washington, D.C.: Catholic University of America Press, 1967), 12.

29. Brown, *Body and Society*, 266.

30. Gregory of Nyssa, *On the Making of Man* 16.4–17.5; Brown, *Body and Society*, 293–294.

31. Gregory of Nyssa, *On Virginity* 3 (Callahan, *Saint Gregory of Nyssa*, 15–16).

32. Ambrose of Milan, *Concerning Virgins* 1.21; see Brown, *Body and Society*, 351.

33. Ambrose of Milan, *Concerning Virgins* 1.62–66; Brown, *Body and Society*, 348.

34. Ambrose of Milan, *Concerning Virgins* 1.10–13; Brown, *Body and Society*, 354.

35. For Jerome's intellectual circle, see Elizabeth A. Clark, *The Origenist Controversy: The Cultural Construction of an Early Christian Debate* (Princeton: Princeton University Press, 1992), 25–35.

36. Brown, *Body and Society*, 382–383.

37. Augustine, *On Marriage and Concupiscence* 1.6.

38. Ibid. 1.8.

39. Ibid. 1.23.

40. *The Rule of St. Benedict* 73.8, Prologue 46.

41. Ibid. 5.1–13.

5

"Let Anyone Accept This Who Can": Medieval Christian Virginity, Chastity, and Celibacy in the Latin West

Karen Cheatham

"The entire company of the catholic church are either virgins or continent or married. Whoever is outside these three orders, therefore, is not numbered among the sons of the church or within the limits of the Christian religion."[1] This excerpt from a letter written by Pope Gregory VII in 1075 demonstrates the importance given by the medieval Church to categorizations based on sexual status—a pattern that dates back to the early Church Fathers. Nearly a century earlier, in a work written for the kings Hugh Capet and Robert the Pious, Abbo of Fleury (d. 1004) illustrated the same tripartite division—virgins, continent, or married—with greater elaboration: "We know that there are from either sex, three orders of the faithful, and if three orders, three grades in the holy and universal church; although none of them is without sin, nevertheless, the first is good, the second better, the third best. And, indeed, the first [order] in either sex is of the married, the second of the continent or widowed, the third of virgins or nuns."[2]

Here Abbo categorizes and ranks Christians of both sexes. In his schema, the order of virgins, composed of virginal monks and nuns, is the most revered; the order of the continent and widowed, which includes clerics and widowed women, is good but inferior to the first; and that of married men and women, who are understood to be sexually active, garners the least respect; that is, the more removed a person is from the sexual economy the more esteemed he or she is.[3] Another traditional tripartite representation united virgins and the continent as one order of contemplative religious, and designated rectors (prelates, preachers, and so on) and married people as the second and third orders, respectively.[4] This was the idea Elizabeth of Schönau (d. 1164), a Benedictine nun and renowned visionary, enlisted when she described her vision of three paths representing the nature of the orders of the Church. She saw the married, whose path was surrounded with thorns; the continent, whose route was free from brambles and bedecked with flowers; and rectors, who forged a middle way between the others.[5] Clearly, sexual status was an integral component of Christian society during the Middle Ages. Indeed, as we will see in the following pages, such was the value attributed to sexual abstinence that chastity was taken up by all manner of Christians from monks, nuns, recluses, and hermits to priests and other secular clergymen, to the nobility, royalty, and everyday laypeople.

Virginity and Chastity—Withdrawal from the World

Sexual renunciation became a Christian ideal during the religion's earliest days, and it continued to flourish and change over the course of the Middle Ages.[6] Virginity, lifelong sexual abstinence for religious reasons, was the most revered form of renunciation, but chastity, a permanent state of continence after an earlier period of sexual activity, carried a similar significance. Both forms of sexual renunciation were meaningful because they entailed a permanent state of sexual purity.[7] Perpetual sexual renunciation was an ideal for religious men as well as women, but men usually opted for continence, whereas virginity was chiefly associated with women. Indeed, virginity came to be treated as the essence of a woman's spirituality, whereas for men, it was certainly a virtue to be cultivated but rarely the focal point of their religious endeavor.[8]

Virginity and chastity were important because they brought human beings closer to God. According to Christian belief, Adam and Eve's fall corrupted the human race, causing alienation from God. The goal for Christians was to recover through God's grace that lost pure state and reestablish union with God, as far as humanly possible. Grace was understood as a free and unmerited gift from God that required no individual action; however, human beings could make themselves worthy of grace through intense renunciation and mortification. The more a person disassociated him- or herself from worldly desires, the more he or she prepared the body and soul for an intimate connection with

God.[9] For the religious, renunciation encompassed every facet of life—in addition to sexual renunciation, they restricted their diet; wore coarse, simple clothing; avoided daily comforts; and limited social relationships—but sexual renunciation was the most significant symbol of the ascetic's spiritual endeavor.

When ascetics practiced chastity and virginity, they believed they were imitating the lives of angels. "For the life you profess is very high," wrote William of Saint-Thierry (d. 1148) to his Carthusian brethren at Mont Dieu, "it surpasses the heavens, it is on par with the angels, it is similar in its angelic purity."[10] Angels, ascetics maintained, are unencumbered by carnal passions; furthermore, they are distinguished by their uninterrupted contemplation of God. The monastic life of sexual renunciation and continual prayer, then, was modeled on angelic existence.[11] Describing the effect of chastity as he understood it, the Cistercian abbot Bernard of Clairvaux (d. 1153) enthused: "And why should you not be, even today, what all the elect will be some day after the resurrection, like to the angels of heaven, since like them you are unmarried? . . . Embrace that holiness of life which makes you similar to the blessed and which puts you in God's house, according to the words of the Scripture: 'Purity brings man close to God.'"[12]

The Christian conception of virginity relates to the body and its sexual innocence, but it goes far beyond the merely physical.[13] Virginity also has a spiritual component, which takes into account an individual's moral or spiritual state. Christian thinkers have always understood that virginity entailed both physical and spiritual qualities, but in their writings some emphasized one and some the other. Medieval writers who placed primary emphasis on physical virginity looked first to the body for evidence of a person's virginal status. For example, in his treatise *De laesione virginitatis*, Rupert of Deutz (d. 1129) argues explicitly against those who elevate spiritual virginity, claiming that a narrative in Deuteronomy (22:13–29) establishes that the physical component is what matters. As the story goes, a newly married man sought to annul his marriage on grounds that his bride had not been a virgin on their wedding night. When the case was brought before the town elders, they judged that the young woman had indeed been a virgin, and they based their decision on the evidence of the couple's bloodied bed sheets. The elders never inquired about her spiritual state, Rupert rebukes; they only looked for physical evidence.[14]

On the other hand, medieval authors who underscored virginity's spiritual nature chiefly took into account the individual's virtue and probity. For example, Anselm of Canterbury (d. 1093) assured the lapsed nun Gunhilda that physical integrity was not God's principal concern. He wrote: "For we know of many holy women who, having lost their virginity, were more pleasing to God and were closer to him through penitence in their chastity than many others, even though holy in their virginity."[15] Also, the English Abbot Aldhelm (d. 709) averred: "Therefore carnal integrity is in no way approved of, unless spiritual purity is associated with it as a companion."[16] The diversity of this discourse is intriguing and can serve as a valuable tool for studying the past. In fact, many modern scholars who examine the subject have concluded that the representation of virginity as physical predominated in texts until the twelfth or thirteenth century, when the spiritual component became paramount, and they associate the change with contemporary cultural developments.[17] Although the trend observed by these scholars is generally acknowledged, the argument can be overstrained. During the twelfth and thirteenth centuries, many writers did indeed stress spiritual virginity; nonetheless, others emphasized physical virginity and sometimes both characterizations coexisted in one text. Additionally, the representation of virginity as spiritual is not exclusive to the later Middle Ages—it appears in works as early as the fifth century. Because of these qualifications, it is critical to be mindful of the diversity of medieval conceptions of virginity and study each case on its own merits.[18]

Few challenges threatened the ascetic's spiritual endeavor more than the libido. For it was not enough for religious men and women to eschew sexual activity; they also had to extirpate all improper thoughts and behavior. Even sexual dreams and nocturnal emissions could arouse anxiety. Could a person celebrate or receive the Eucharist after experiencing a nocturnal emission? Was such an occurrence sinful? A letter to Augustine of Canterbury from Pope Gregory the Great (d. 604) set the tone for most medieval discussions of the matter. According to Gregory, nocturnal emissions were polluting if the person in question had experienced lustful feelings or indulged in too much food or drink while awake (overindulgence was thought to fuel a person's sexual drive). Still, the dreamer was sinless as long as he or she did not invite the evil thought that caused the orgasm. On the other hand, a nocturnal emission was sinful if the individual consented to it.[19] Gregory's assessment was remarkably evenhanded: though monks who experienced involuntary seminal emissions could be accused, perhaps unjustly, of moral transgressions, Gregory acknowledged that these nocturnal events were natural physiological processes, not always subject to a person's will.

With freedom from sexual desire as a goal, spiritual castration emerged as a theme in religious literature. Christ had proclaimed: "For there are eunuchs who have been so from birth, and there are eunuchs who have been made eunuchs by others, and there are eunuchs who have made themselves eunuchs for the sake of the kingdom of heaven. Let anyone accept this who can" (Matt.

19:12). Taking Jesus' statement literally, Origen of Alexandria (d. 254) had himself castrated so he could provide religious direction to women without provoking scandal.[20] To be sure, the Church did not look upon self-inflicted castration as an honorable palliative for sexual desire. In fact, in 325, the Council of Nicaea pronounced that intentional castration was grounds for dismissal from the clergy and an impediment to clerical promotion.[21] Nonetheless, ascetics emulated (rather than imitated) Origen as an exemplar of spiritual virtuosity.[22] Furthermore, interpreting Jesus' statement about eunuchs as a call for sexual abstinence, Christians admired *spiritual* castration as an ideal state free of sexual desire. As such, stories of spiritual castration made their way into medieval religious texts. The monk Caesarius of Heisterbach (d. 1240) included numerous stories of this mystical remedy for desire in his thirteenth-century works. In his *Dialogue on Miracles*, Caesarius tells of a monk named Bernard who was so beleaguered by sexual yearning that he was prepared to return to the secular world and take a wife. Persuaded by the monastery's prior to delay his departure, the monk retired to his bedchamber and experienced a beneficent dream. In the dream, he was being chased by a fearsome, knife-wielding man and a black dog. Eventually, the man caught up with the monk, castrated him, and fed his testicles to the dog. Upon waking, Bernard discovered to his delight and relief that he was physically unharmed but permanently liberated from the ache of desire that had been plaguing him.[23]

Though religious men and women aimed to eradicate improper desire, desire was a passion not entirely without use to the individual soul. The challenge it posed was crucial for the individual's spiritual development. In one of Caesarius of Heisterbach's tales, for example, a monk opines that a virgin would choose to endure the trials of lust rather than being delivered from them because, "temptation is the guardian of humility and the means of practicing virtue."[24] Some writers even compared their own status with that of the angels, declaring that their own chastity deserved more reverence than an angel's chastity since angels were naturally continent and did not have to battle earthly passion. Bernard of Clairvaux echoed this sentiment when he reflected: "a person living in the way I have described [with chastity and love] has greater merit than an angel who does so because for a human being this is a matter of virtue, while for an angel it is a matter of office."[25] Similarly, the author of the thirteenth-century Middle English treatise *Holy Maidenhood* (or *Hali Meidhad*) assured his virginal audience that "angel and maiden are equal by virtue of the power of maidenhood . . . and though their [the angels'] maidenhood is more blessed now, yours is kept with greater effort, and more reward shall be given you."[26]

So significant was the ideal of virginity in Christian thought that by the fifth century it had developed into a genre of discourse that persisted into the medieval period and flourished during the later Middle Ages. Monks and religious leaders addressed countless letters, treatises, guidebooks, and rules about virginity to nuns, recluses, and less often monks, who frequently requested spiritual guidance. Those who penned these works praised virginity extravagantly and expected the preservation of virginity to be at the very core of women's religious lives. "Let the virgin always consider that all her members are consecrated to God, incorporated in Christ, dedicated to the Holy Spirit," wrote Aelred of Rievaulx (d. 1167), "let the whole object then of her striving and of her thoughts be the preservation of her virginity."[27] Commonly, those who wrote virginity texts warned their audiences of the dire consequences connected with a loss of virginal perfection: lost virginity and the special status it conferred could never be recovered.[28] They also cautioned their virginal addressees that pride would destroy virginity just as surely as any lubricious encounter. "Truly a humble and penitent widow is more pleasing to God than an insolent and proud virgin," instructs the *Speculum virginum*, a twelfth-century guide for religious women.[29] Frequently, they enticed their readers to choose virginity or chastity by portraying marriage in the worst possible light, a rhetorical device that was well developed by the late antique period.[30] Religious writers addressed this sort of discourse, known as the *molestiae nuptiarum* or the woes of marriage, to both men and women, but when men were the audience marriage was discouraged not for the sake of preserving virginity but because bachelorhood was a way of life suited for the man of philosophy.[31] Tracts written to women warned against oppressive husbands and cautioned that even good husbands could die leaving wives to raise families on their own. They also lectured wives about the discomforts of pregnancy, the perils of childbirth, the aggravation of children, and the burdens of running a household. Alan of Lille (d. 1202) employed this motif in his preaching manual, the *Ars praedicandi*. In it, he persuades virgins to preserve virginity by contrasting carnal marriage with a spiritual marriage to Christ. (A common medieval metaphor for the spiritual relationship between Christ and a religious was that of the ascetic as a bride of Christ.) "Oh virgin," Alan implored, "if you wish to marry an earthly husband because he is in the flower of youth, consider how death will pluck away that flower, or else it will wither in any case in the winter of old age. Marry, then, that Husband who alone has immortality." The passage continues in this vein, touching on the ephemeral nature of wealth, a husband's good looks, noble ancestry, and worldly honor.[32] These authors were playing, of course, on women's very real concerns: in the Middle Ages, in the highest echelons of society, women were often not able to select their own marriage partners, and childbirth was responsible for countless deaths.

Works about virginity were predominantly male-authored, but some women joined the discussion as well. In the late tenth century, the German canoness Hrotswitha of Gandersheim wrote a number of plays that stressed the significance of female virginity and made many of the same points expressed by her male counterparts. In her works, Hrotswitha depicted strong, independent women who heroically defend their virginity against lust and seduction. Despite her positive portrayal of women, Hrotswitha was nevertheless influenced by the values and traditions of her era; thus her depictions also incorporate aspects of the traditional misogynistic tradition.[33] Though perhaps paradoxical for us, her tales would have been empowering for nuns and probably laywomen too.

Despite the obvious preoccupation with female virginity in medieval discourse, evidence shows that men were prepared to learn from tracts originally written for women and that virginity was relevant for their religious pursuit as well. For example, the *Speculum virginum* has been found in the medieval libraries of numerous male religious houses.[34] Furthermore, works such as the treatise on virginity by Guibert of Nogent (d. 1124), written for a male audience at the request of a fellow monk, and the missive dealing with the impact of masturbation on both male and female virginity by Rupert of Deutz (d. ca. 1129) attest that virginity and chastity were meaningful ideals for cloistered men and not just women.[35]

Virginity and chastity were concepts invested with profound meaning for medieval Christians. They were weighty symbols of a paradigmatic relationship between human beings and God. But they were also much more. Their impact reverberated far beyond the realm of spirituality and theology, creating ripples that affected the social outlook and mental attitude of the Christian community, shaping perceptions about sexuality, gender roles and expectations, assessments of natural human physiology, and ultimately influencing what was perceived as valuable in Christian society.

Clerical Celibacy

One of the most well-known elements of the Roman Catholic Church is a celibate priesthood. The origins of this practice are rooted in the early fourth century, when the sexual behavior of the clergy became a concern for Christian leaders.[36] A key reason for their consternation was sexual intercourse: they believed it was a pollutant and thus incompatible with the duties of the clerical office. According to the Old Testament, certain categories of objects and activities were unclean.[37] Among the things it deemed unclean were discharge from sexual organs, menstruation, childbirth, and sexual intercourse. After an unclean activity, a person was polluted for the rest of day and was required to bathe; priests could not serve at the altar until they were purified.[38] From the Christian perspective, this meant that clergymen needed to maintain a constant state of purity, through chastity. Both Pope Siricius (d. 398) and Pope Innocent I (d. 417) explained the Christian reasoning in influential letters to fellow Christians. Comparing Christian ministers with Jewish priests from the Old Testament, they argued that the latter were banned from having sexual relations with their wives before performing religious services; therefore, perpetual chastity was obligatory for Christian ministers because they celebrated the Eucharist daily.[39] The concern of these popes and other like-minded men was not celibacy (abstinence from marriage) but chastity (abstinence from sexual activity). They accepted that Church ministers would have wives but expected them to abstain permanently from sexual intercourse.

Over the course of the medieval centuries, the behavior identified by the early Church leaders as proper for the clergy endured. Reform-minded men continued to pass legislation against clerical fornication, and at times they organized programs of reform. The Carolingian era was one such period of vigorous reform activity.[40] Still, overall efforts to eradicate clerical incontinence were inconsistent and ineffective. In fact, evidence suggests that from the seventh to the eleventh century a majority of clergymen (especially those in rural areas) were married and enjoyed an active sexual relationship with their wives.[41] This general state of affairs is attested by Rather of Verona's late tenth-century carp that if he deposed all priests who lived with women or who married after ordination, no one but young boys would be left to serve the Church.[42]

The Church in the East also labored to reach a definitive position about clerical chastity during the early centuries of the Middle Ages, but unlike the Roman Church, it was able to settle the matter swiftly and decisively. Decisions made at the Council of Trullo in 692 determined the final word on the subject. According to Trullo's decrees, priests, deacons, and subdeacons could marry before but not after ordination. Clergymen were allowed (expected even) to cohabitate with their wives, and sexual activity was licit except on days when religious services were being performed. Celibacy was compulsory for bishops, and if married when elected they were obliged to separate from their wives.[43] Trullo's decrees endured in the East throughout the Middle Ages and into the modern era with little change.

Around the middle of the eleventh century in the West, the ineffectual enforcement of celibacy that characterized earlier medieval centuries became a thing of the past as popes and Christian leaders galvanized around a call for reform. As we have seen, throughout the late antique and early medieval centuries, clerical chastity was promoted because of anxiety about the polluting effects of coitus. However, during the eleventh-century reform there were added concerns. Purity remained an issue, but it was invested with even more meaning. Typically, purity laws had to do with a priest's suitability to celebrate mass—he needed to be ritually clean to handle the sacred objects and speak the holy words. During the eleventh century, purity also became important for priests as a moral virtue. Like monks and nuns, clerics were now expected to be pure in order to have a proper relationship with God.[44] In addition to the matter of ritual pollution, apprehensions about the loss of Church property and income came into play. Over the centuries, ecclesiastical property and offices had increasingly become hereditary, passing from priests to their children, thus dissipating the power and unity of the Church. As well, married clerics supported their families with Church resources, and Christian leaders dreaded the effect this might have on the Church's prosperity.[45] Both concerns, economic and ritual, were reactions to the fact that Church officials and institutions had become inextricably involved in the affairs of the secular world, and both motivated men to seek reform in the middle of the eleventh century.

The task undertaken by these men was not easy. Spanning the decades between 1049 and 1139, it took the efforts of several popes and countless reform-minded Christians to achieve a positive outcome. In addition to the new motivations just discussed, what distinguishes this era from earlier reform efforts is a marked shift in focus. Whereas earlier legislation primarily targeted the sex life of the clergy, seeking to enforce chastity, eleventh-century lawmakers endeavored to eliminate clerical marriage.[46] Furthermore, these reformers initiated fresh strategies for executing their edicts. Building on legislation promulgated by Leo IX (1049–1054) and Stephen IX (1057–1058), the 1059 Lateran council under Pope Nicholas II (1059–1061) disallowed marriage for members of the higher clergy (bishops, priests, deacons, and subdeacons), banned unchaste clerics from serving at the altar, and incited parishioners to boycott masses celebrated by married priests.[47] It was not long before some members of the laity began to sympathize with the reformers' cause and responded to their call for a boycott. In one case, during the mid-1050s, a group in Milan known as the Patarenes banned together against clerics and their families and sought to implement clerical chastity by force. Believing that sacraments performed by unchaste clerics were inefficacious, they boycotted the churches of those who were unchaste, constrained clergymen to sign an oath of chastity, and kept those who refused to comply from approaching the altar.[48]

The role of Pope Gregory VII (1073–1085) in the clerical reform was also critical. Indeed, before he took the lead in the reform as pope, he lent a hand to Leo IX's reforming enterprise. Little about Gregory's legislation was novel, but his method of enforcement was. Determined that his celibacy laws not be ignored, Gregory circulated his decrees to the bishops of Western Europe with instructions to publicize and enforce them. He also appointed permanent legates in various regions to see to it that canons were obeyed.[49] Furthermore, he instructed the laity to refuse the ministrations of unchaste clergymen and bade them air their grievances in public assemblies and courtrooms.[50] Gregory has regularly been credited as the key force behind the drive for clerical celibacy (hence its common moniker, the Gregorian Reform). In fact, his effort was part of a much larger movement that did not originate with him, and his reign did not see clerical celibacy eradicated. Nonetheless, Gregory's tenacity and rigorous enforcement strategies helped him succeed where others had failed and paved the way for the successes of the subsequent century.[51]

Under the auspices of Innocent II, the First and Second Lateran Councils (1123 and 1139, respectively) promulgated decisive legislation that effectively and finally eradicated clerical marriage in the Christian West. The relevant canon of Lateran I states: "We absolutely forbid priests, deacons, subdeacons and monks to have concubines or to contract marriages. We adjudge . . . that marriage contracts between such persons should be made void and the persons ought to undergo penance."[52] The seventh canon of the Second Lateran Council took the earlier council's pronouncements a step further. After declaring that all married members of the higher clergy should be separated from their wives, it proclaims: "For a union of this kind which has been contracted in violation of the ecclesiastical law, we do not regard as matrimony."[53] Until this time, clerical marriages were illegal but sacramentally valid. In other words, canon law prohibited clerics from marrying (it was illegal), but if a clergyman married in spite of the ban the union was acknowledged as true and binding (it was valid). However, these two councils ended the concessionary atmosphere of earlier years and made clerical celibacy an absolute requirement for membership in the clergy. The pronouncements have remained the official position of the Catholic Church in the West to the present day.

Clerics were not the only people affected by this campaign against clerical marriage; so too were their wives and children. Over the centuries, as the drive for clerical continence escalated, reformers attacked clerics' families with increasingly truculent language. A cleric's spouse was no longer a wife (*uxor*); instead, she was a concubine (*concubina*), harlot (*meretrix*), prostitute (*scortum*), or mistress (*pellex*)—all words suggestive of a nonmarital and immoral relationship based essentially on carnality.[54] An excerpt from a vitriolic attack on clerical wives by Peter Damian (d. 1071) is illustrative of the rhetoric of the age: "So come and listen to me, you strumpets, prostitutes waiting to be kissed, you wallow for fat pigs, den of unclean spirits, nymphs, sirens, witches, forest goddesses of the night, and if there are yet other monstrous titles of ill-omen that one can find, they should well be ascribed to you.... You furious vipers, by the ardor of your impatient lust you dismember your lovers by cutting them off from Christ who is the head of the clergy."[55]

Not only were clerical wives demeaned by Christian moralists but they also suffered at the hands of lawmakers. For instance, Leo IX is said to have ordered women who lived with priests to be made servants (*ancillae*) of the Church.[56] Urban II made Leo's order official at a synod in 1089.[57] Because of reformers' efforts, many respectable women were cast out of their homes, separated from their families, and denied their social status. The children of these ostracized couples were targeted as well: they were deemed illegitimate, denied inheritance rights, and could not be ordained.

In spite of the official attack on clerics' concubines (clerics could not marry, thus their female partners were considered concubines), there is evidence that some of these women may have been less stigmatized than the Church would have liked. From the late twelfth to the mid-fourteenth century in France, writers produced vernacular narratives known as fabliaux, which tell ribald stories of cuckolded husbands, insatiable wives, simple-minded peasants, and greedy, lascivious priests. Stories about the clergy describe lustful priests on the hunt for sexual adventures with their female parishioners. If these portrayals sprang even partially from priests' actual behavior, one cannot help wondering if the laity would not have preferred a priest with a steady partner to a priest lurking among the wives of the community.[58] Additionally, in her study of clerics' female companions from the early-fourteenth-century diocese of Barcelona, M. A. Kelleher has determined that even though concubines had no official status in their communities, their illicit unions did not necessarily draw reproach from fellow townspeople. In fact, evidence shows that some communities offered assistance to concubines and their children when their clerical partners abandoned them.[59] Therefore, despite their marginal status and the Church's strong position against them, some clerics' concubines may still have been able to garner respect from fellow Christians as quasi wives.

The reformers were the victors in the conflict over clerical celibacy and chastity, but their success was not without obstacle. In France, Germany, England, and elsewhere the clergy reacted to the decisive reform legislation with violence as well as simple resistance.[60] For example, the English Church did not issue decrees against clerical marriage until 1076, and even then, the legislation fell short of Gregory's lofty expectations. According to a decree promulgated by Lanfranc, the archbishop of Canterbury, married priests in England could keep their wives as long as future priests remained unmarried.[61] At the council of Paris in 1074, Abbot Walter of Saint-Martin of Pontoise took up Gregory's position against the majority of churchmen, who believed the pope's demands were unreasonable. When he urged those present to obey Gregory's rulings, they "seized him, dragged him around, struck him, boxed him about the ears, spat at him, and lead him weakened with many insults to the king's palace."[62] Dissenters also circulated pamphlets opposing the reform. The first promarriage tract, composed around 1060 by Ulric of Imola, argued that neither scripture nor tradition demanded continence, and that though the pope could counsel chastity, he could not demand it. His critique was influential enough that it provoked condemnation from a Roman synod in 1079.[63] These overt challenges to the rigorous enforcement of clerical celibacy died out fairly quickly, but resistance of a more subtle nature persisted to the end of the Middle Ages (and in into the modern age).

Although reformers had successfully changed the behavior of clergymen, compelling them to comply with the Church's celibacy laws, they had less success changing their convictions. Clergymen who believed they should be allowed to marry were not immoral or dissolute: they were simply men who thought that clerical marriage was a valid and honorable institution. Reformers saw the matter differently. They deemed celibacy imperative for the proper execution of the clerical office and right ordering of the Church. The gulf dividing the two positions was expansive and complicated and, in spite of a favorable conclusion for reformers, continues to challenge the Roman Catholic Church to this day.

Chaste Marriage

The medieval Church considered marriage a sacred institution and sexual intercourse a fundamental component of married life. Nonetheless, the bias in favor of celibacy and chastity that pervaded Christian thought was manifest in much of the Church's discourse about marriage and must have affected the laity's perceptions of marriage and marital relations. In his first letter to the Corinthians, the Apostle Paul expressed his apprehensions about the married state: unmarried men and women could give their full attention to pleasing God, whereas married people were concerned about the affairs of the world and satisfying their spouse—their interests were divided (7:32–34). In the same letter, Paul allowed that marriage was expedient for those unable to exercise self-control and avoid fornication, but he did not attach any inherent value to it

(7:9). The judgments of St. Augustine (d. 430), a relatively optimistic voice on marriage, would also have reminded laypeople that the Church looked askance at matrimony and sexual activity. In the fifth century, Augustine wrote two treatises on marriage that shaped Christian thought throughout the Middle Ages. In them, he named three positive ends of marriage: procreation, fidelity between spouses, and the bond of love. These three goods, as he called them, could be achieved despite—not because of—the sexual component of the married state. Furthermore, the goods of marriage made the institution laudable because it turned the iniquity of sex into something of value. Even within marriage, however, sex was only moral if couples observed certain guidelines. Sex for reasons of procreation was sinless, sex for pleasure was sinful but only a minor peccadillo, but any sex that involved the attempt to avoid procreation was a mortal sin.[64]

The Church also imparted its misgivings about sexual activity to the lay community with the very rules that governed licit sexual practice, as evidenced by the penitentials. Penitentials were practical handbooks, produced from the late sixth to the early eleventh centuries, that provided confessors with lists of sins and their accompanying penances. Among the myriad subjects covered by the penitentials was the issue of sexual abstinence in marriage. Marital sex was permitted, but penitentials severely restricted the lawful times for sexual activity: Lent and other significant points in the religious year, feast days, Sundays, and several days prior to communion were all occasions that demanded sexual abstinence.[65] With respect to the penitentials' perspective on married sex, James Brundage has noted: "[According to the authors,] even in marriage sex is always pleasurable, always impure, and always sinful. Marital sex was a concession, they believed: God allowed married persons to have sex only for procreation, never for pleasure."[66]

Inculcated with a belief that sexual activity was polluting and an impediment to spiritual growth, some laypeople resolved to observe permanent sexual abstinence within marriage, a practice known as chaste marriage.[67] Although originally proposed by Eusebius of Caesarea in the fourth century as an option for married clergymen (rather than commanding married priests to separate from their wives, he suggested that they refrain permanently from marital relations), chaste marriage resonated with some devout laypeople.[68] It may have been particularly attractive to women. For one, the practice enabled women who were not able to enter a convent and who could not independently pursue a religious calling, to live pious lives while married. Furthermore, by abstaining from sex, women could avoid childbirth and the very real hazards that accompanied it. Finally, chastity within marriage may have made for a more equitable relationship between husband and wife; some who wrote about chaste marriage likened the relationship to one of siblings and maintained that, in this sisterly role, the chaste wife was no longer subordinate to her husband.[69]

Even though for a time Christian leaders had advocated chaste marriage for members of the clergy, it was not a practice they promoted for the laity. In part, they feared that ordinary Christians would succumb to carnal desire and break their vows of chastity. This was cause for alarm because in the medieval world vows were solemn and irrevocable. Although some could be commuted for other forms of penance—for instance, in certain cases fasting could substitute for pilgrimage—an oath of chastity was not negotiable because no other practice surpassed it.[70] The penalty for breaking a vow of chastity varied from authority to authority, but according to the Dominican friar John of Freiburg (d. 1314), even a promise of chastity made privately between a couple was binding before God and violating it constituted a mortal sin.[71] Churchmen may also have feared that the laity's renunciation of sexual activity might blur the distinction between the clergy and the laity and undermine the clergy's exalted status. Furthermore, because of the relationship's brother/sister quality, they may have worried that it could weaken male authority within marriage.[72]

Scholars who have studied accounts of chaste marriage in hagiographical sources (saints' Lives) have determined that two diverse characterizations of it appear in the texts, and that one type was predominant during the early Middle Ages and another during the later medieval period.[73] In the first type, chaste marriage is depicted as an unconsummated virginal union: the spouse with a religious calling, usually the woman, is typically forced to marry by her parents, and on her wedding night she persuades her husband to take a vow of chastity. Often these virgins die triumphantly and heroically as Christian martyrs. The legend of Saint Cecilia—an early text that remained a "bestseller" throughout the Middle Ages—is an ideal example of this first type.[74] In spite of her wish to remain a virgin and dedicate her life to God, Cecilia's parents betrothed her to a young pagan youth named Valerian. After the wedding, however, when they retired to the bridal chamber, she told him of an angel that watched over her and cautioned that the angel would slay him if he touched her sexually. So warned, Valerian submitted to his wife's wishes, quickly converting to Christianity and swearing an oath of chastity. Eventually, both Valerian and Cecilia met with martyrs' deaths.

On occasion, men were also depicted as the instigators of virginal chaste marriages. Yet, more commonly, when the male saint had a religious calling he either abandoned his wife immediately after the wedding or fled from his fiancée before the nuptials to retire as a hermit or monk.[75] The paradigm for this model of behavior was St. Alexis. According to his legend, Alexis submitted to his parents' wishes and married the girl they chose for him, despite his religious calling. Nevertheless, as soon as they were wed, he gave his new bride his ring and the tie from his waist and fled to the desert to serve God as a hermit and later a beggar in his parent's home.[76] Alexis's legend was exceedingly influential, especially during the eleventh century.[77] Indeed, according to one of his medieval biographers, upon hearing Alexis's legend sung by a minstrel, Waldo (the founder of one of the most important heretical groups of the Middle Ages, the Waldensians) was inspired to abandon his wife and his wealth to become a wandering preacher and ascetic.[78]

The second type of chaste marriage predominates in saints' Lives from the thirteenth century and beyond.[79] In this case, couples make a vow of abstinence following an initial period of sexual activity, often after having children. Here, marriage is no longer portrayed as an impediment to holiness. Although hagiographers continued to produce accounts that extolled virginal marriages, that type was eclipsed by this latter characterization. The life of Bridget of Sweden (d. 1373) typifies this new model. Bridget, whose saintliness was augured even before her birth, vowed to preserve her virginity when she was still young; however, disregarding her oath, her parents compelled her to marry a virginal knight named Ulf. For two years, they lived together chastely, but eventually, after first praying to God that they might engage in coitus without sin, they consummated their marriage and produced eight children. After bearing her last child, Bridget persuaded her spouse to join her in a vow of chastity, a state they maintained until Ulf's death.[80]

The appearance of this new portrait of chaste marriage coincides with a lay-religious movement that swept across Christian society during the thirteenth century. Influenced by the ethos of the mendicant orders, the new lay sanctity was characterized by a drive to imitate Christ both in his sufferings and in his activity and behavior in life. Seized by this new fervor, devout Christians rushed to enter religious orders in unparalleled numbers, and new mendicant orders such as the Franciscans and Dominicans grew to accommodate the demand. Both groups developed a second order for cloistered women and a third order for pious lay men and women, who lived religious lives while remaining in their homes. Among those who became tertiaries were single women and men who had made the decision never to marry. While some women joined religious third orders, others opted for the anchoritic life: with the approval of their local religious authority, these women confined themselves in cells, usually flanking the town chapel, to live chaste and penitential lives.[81] Some embraced a life of married chastity.

An especially noteworthy example of those who led devout and chaste married lives are a group of religious women known as the Beguines, who emerged at the beginning of the thirteenth century in Liège and the southern Low Countries.[82] Beguines were a quasi-religious group of loosely connected uncloistered women, not bound by a Rule or permanent vows. They expressed their religiosity diversely: some worked in hospitals and cared for lepers, some pursued penitential lives in the world, and some became anchoresses and nuns after a period of religious engagement with the world. Whatever way they chose to live, chastity and celibacy were fundamental to them. For instance, Mary of Oignies (d. 1213), one of the Beguines' most charismatic figures, was married at the age of fourteen but quickly convinced her husband to join her in a life of poverty and chastity. The couple eventually separated so Mary could live out the last part her life as an anchoress. Other Beguines, including Juetta of Huy and Odilia of Liège, were also married women who took vows of chastity and lived holy and penitential lives.

Drawing prudently on evidence gleaned from saints' Lives, scholars have been able to make some astute determinations about the ideals of sanctity and the evolution of those beliefs during the medieval period.[83] They think that the second model of chaste marriage exemplified by Bridget of Sweden and the Beguines illustrates that a new criterion for sanctity had developed in the thirteenth century. In this new model, holiness was linked with an imitation of the poor and humble Christ and was available to anyone, including married people—virgins and chaste alike.[84] These scholars' conclusions are born out by Jacques de Vitry's passionate depiction of the Beguines: "You also saw holy women (and you rejoiced), serving the Lord devoutly in matrimony, raising their children in fear of God, guarding an honest marriage and an immaculate marriage bed. . . . [F]or many, abstaining from licit embraces with the consent of their husbands, and leading a celibate and truly Angelic life were so much the more worthy of the greater crown, the more they were placed in the fire that did not burn."[85] These women may not have been virgins, but they were venerated as saintly and no less praiseworthy than any of their virginal counterparts. Indeed, their marriages augmented their sanctity because, for them, temptation was a daily trial.

Laypeople were expected to marry, but at the same time Christian moralists saw marriage as the least worthy form of Christian life. Ordinary Christians wanted to participate in the religious life but most could not abandon the responsibilities of the secular world to dedicate their lives to Christ. Chaste marriage offered a solution to the predicament, and as the medieval centuries progressed, those who had embraced this form of life found themselves part of a growing number and variety of devout Christians who were honored and admired for their extraordinary piety.

From its earliest days, the Catholic Church linked sexual renunciation with holiness and upheld virginity, chastity, and celibacy as ideals to emulate and admire. Still, over the centuries, while always remaining fundamental to medieval Christian life and thought, these ideals were reconsidered, reimagined, and transformed. For instance, as we have seen, in the last centuries of the Middle Ages virginity, although still considered a woman's prized possession, had lost its luster as the sine qua non of holiness and, conversely, the clergy's physical chastity had become more meaningful. However, as the sun set on the medieval period and the early modern era dawned, these deep-seated ideals about sexual renunciation were shaken to the core by Protestant reformers whose criticism of the medieval Church's principal traditions and beliefs opened a new discourse about the value and place of virginity, chastity, and celibacy in the Christian world.

NOTES

1. *Epistolae Vagantes of Pope Gregory VII*, edited by H. E. J. Cowdrey, Oxford Medieval Texts 20 (Oxford: Oxford University Press, 1972), 9; translated by Giles Constable, "The Orders of Society," in *Three Studies in Medieval Religious and Social Thought* (Cambridge: Cambridge University Press, 1995), 305.

2. *Liber Apologeticus* in *Patrologia Latina* (hereafter *PL*), edited by J. P. Migne, 1st ed. (ca. 1849–1855), 139: 463A–B. Translated by Elizabeth Dachowski, "*Tertius est optimus*: Marriage, Continence and Virginity in the Politics of Late Tenth- and Early Eleventh-Century Francia," in *Medieval Purity and Piety: Essays on Medieval Clerical Celibacy and Religious Reform*, edited by Michael Frassetto (New York: Garland, 1998), 119.

3. See Constable, "Orders of Society," 283.

4. Ibid., 306.

5. Ekbert of Schönau, *Sanctae Elizabeth vita* 6.90 in *PL*: 166C–167A/*Elisabeth of Schönau: The Complete Works*, translated by Anne L. Clark (New York: Paulist Press, 2000), 164.

6. For more on sexual renunciation during the early Christian centuries, see chapter 4 in this volume. Also, Peter Brown, *The Body and Society: Men, Women, and Sexual Renunciation in Early Christianity* (New York: Columbia University Press, 1988).

7. Peter Brown, "The Notion of Virginity in the Early Church," in *Christian Spirituality: Origins to the Twelfth Century*, edited by Bernard McGinn et al. (New York: Crossroad, 1985), 427–428.

8. Barbara Newman, *From Virile Woman to WomanChrist: Studies in Medieval Religion and Literature* (Philadelphia: University of Pennsylvania Press, 1995), 28–34.

9. Jean Leclercq, *The Life of Perfection: Points of View on the Essence of the Religious State*, translated by Leonard J. Doyle (Collegeville, Minn.: Liturgical Press, 1961), 17–19. The exemplars for this type of ascetic striving were the desert Fathers and

Mothers of late antiquity. For more on the desert ascetics, see David Brakke, *Demons and the Making of the Monk: Spiritual Combat in Early Christianity* (Cambridge: Harvard University Press, 2006); Brown, *Body and Society*, 213–240; David G. R. Keller, *Oasis of Wisdom: The Worlds of the Desert Fathers and Mothers* (Collegeville, Minn.: Liturgical Press, 2005).

10. *Un traité de la vie solitaire*, edited by M.-M Davy (Paris: Librairie Philosophique J. Vrin, 1940), 1: 73.

11. Brown, "Notion of Virginity"; Leclercq, *Life of Perfection*, 26–33.

12. 3–*In Lab* 7 in *Sancti Bernardi Opera Omnia* (hereafter *SBO*), edited by Jean Leclercq et al. (Rome: Editiones Cistercienses, 1957–1980), 5: 225; translated by Leclercq, *Life of Perfection*, 30.

13. Caroline Walker Bynum writes about the medieval body as a contested site in *Holy Feast and Holy Fast: The Religious Significance of Food to Medieval Women* (Berkeley: University of California Press, 1987).

14. *De laesione* in *PL* 170: 549B–C. See also *Hali meidhad*, edited by Bella Millett (New York: Oxford University Press for the Early English Text Society, 1982), 6; and "Holy Maidenhood," in *Anchoritic Spirituality: Ancrene Wisse and Associated Works*, translated by Anne Savage and Nicholas Watson (New York: Paulist Press, 1991), 229.

15. *Ltr* 168 in *S. Anselmi Cantuariensis archiepiscopi opera omnia*, edited by Franciscus Salesius Schmitt (Stuttgart-Bad Cannstatt: F. Frommann Verlag, 1984), 4: 45; and *The Letters of Saint Anselm of Canterbury*, translated by Walter Fröhlich (Kalamazoo, Mich.: Cistercian, 1990), 2: 66–67.

16. *De laude virginitate* 16 in *Aldhelm, The Prose Works*, translated by Michael Lapidge and Michael Herren (Totowa, N.J.: Rowman & Littlefield, 1979), 72; and *Aldhelmi Opera*, edited by Rudolfus Ehwald, *Monumenta Germaniae Historica* (hereafter *MGH*) *Auctorum Antiquissimorum* 15 (Berlin: Weidmannsche Verlagsbuchhandlung, 1919), 245.

17. See Clarissa Atkinson, "Precious Balsam in a Fragile Glass: The Ideology of Virginity in the Later Middle Ages," *Journal of Family History* 8 (1983): 131–143; John M. Bugge, *Virginitas: An Essay in the History of a Medieval Ideal* (The Hague: Martinus Nijhoff, 1975); Dyan Elliott, *Spiritual Marriage: Sexual Abstinence in Medieval Wedlock* (Princeton: Princeton University Press, 1993), 266–274; Newman, *From Virile Woman to WomanChrist*, 30–31.

18. For scholars who stress this perspective, see *Medieval Virginities*, edited by Anke Bernau, Ruth Evans, and Sarah Salih (Toronto: University of Toronto Press, 2003); Kathleen Coyne Kelly, *Performing Virginity and Testing Chastity in the Middle Ages* (London: Routledge, 2000); Sarah Salih, *Versions of Virginity in Late Medieval England* (Cambridge: D. S. Brewer, 2001).

19. Bede, *Ecclesiastical History of the English People*, edited by Bertram Colgrave et al. (Oxford: Clarendon Press, 1969), 1.27, 99–103 (English and Latin). Medieval writers recognized that both women and men could experience involuntary orgasms, but their discussions usually focused on men; Dyan Elliott, *Fallen Bodies: Pollution, Sexuality, and Demonology in the Middle Ages* (Philadelphia: University of Pennsylvania Press, 1999), 15. On nocturnal emissions, see Elliott, *Fallen Bodies*, 14–34; Jacqueline

Murray, "Men's Bodies, Men's Minds: Seminal Emissions and Sexual Anxiety in the Middle Ages," *Annual Review of Sex Research Mount Vernon* 8 (1997), 1–26.

20. Eusebius, *Hist Eccl* 6.8 in *The History of the Church from Christ to Constantine*, translated by G. A. Williamson (Minneapolis: Augsburg, 1975), 247–248. For more on Origen, see Brown, *Body and Society*, 160–177. On castration, see Mathew Kuefler, "Castration and Eunichism in the Middle Ages," in *Handbook of Medieval Sexuality*, edited by Vern L. Bullough and James A. Brundage (New York: Garland, 1996); Jacqueline Murray, "Mystical Castration: Some Reflections on Peter Abelard, Hugh of Lincoln and Sexual Control," in *Conflicted Identities and Multiple Masculinities: Men in the Medieval West*, edited by Jacqueline Murray (New York: Garland, 1999).

21. Nicaea, 325, c. 1 in Norman P. Tanner, ed., *Decrees of the Ecumenical Councils* (Washington, D.C.: Georgetown University Press, 1990), 1: 6.

22. Jacqueline Murray argues that after being castrated, Abelard looked to Origen as a model: "Mystical Castration," 75–80. See also Eusebius, *Hist Eccl* 6.8 in Williamson, tr., *History of the Church*, 247–248.

23. 4/97 in *Dialogus miraculorum*, edited by Joseph Strange (Cologne: J. M. Heberle, 1851), 1: 265–266/*The Dialogue on Miracles*, translated by Henry von Essen Scott and C. C. Swinton Bland (London: G. Routledge, 1929), 1: 302–303.

24. 8/42 in Strange, *Dialogus miraculorum*, 2: 114/*Dialogue on Miracles*, 2: 41–42.

25. *Sent.* I.38 in *SBO*, 6–2: 20; and ""The Sentences," in *Bernard of Clairvaux: The Parables & the Sentences*, edited by Maureen M. O'Brien, translated by Francis R. Swietek (Kalamazoo, Mich.: Cistercian Publications, 2000), 134.

26. *Hali meidhad*, 6; and Savage, tr., "Holy Maidenhood," 229.

27. *Inst* 15 in *Aelredi Rievallensis Opera Omnia: Opera Ascetica*, edited by Anselm Hoste et al., *Corpus Christianorum. Continuatio Mediaevalis I* (hereafter *CCCM1*) (Turnholt: Brepols, 1971), 651; and "Rule of Life for a Recluse," in *Aelred of Rievaulx: Treatises & Pastoral Prayer*, translated by Mary Paul Macpherson (Spencer, Mass.: Cistercian Publications, 1995), 64.

28. See *Inst* 14 in *CCCM1*, 650; and MacPherson, tr., "Rule of Life for a Recluse," 62–63. Also see *Hali meidhad*, 5–6; and Savage, tr., "Holy Maidenhood," 228–229.

29. *Speculum virginum*, edited by Jutta Seyfarth, *Corpus Christianorum. Continuatio Mediaevalis* 5 (Turnholt: Brepols, 1990), 66. For more on the *Speculum virginum*, see C. J. Mews, ed., *Listen Daughter: The "Speculum Virginum" and the Formation of Religious Women in the Middle Ages* (Houndmills: Palgrave, 2001).

30. On this topos, see Katharina M. Wilson and Elizabeth M. Makowski, *Wykked Wyves and the Woes of Marriage: Misogamous Literature from Juvenal to Chaucer* (Albany: State University of New York Press, 1990), 44–60; Bella Millett, "The Theological Background," introduction to *Hali meidhad*, xxx–xxxviii; Newman, *From Virile Woman to WomanChrist*, 32–34.

31. Wilson and Makowski, *Wykked Wyves*, 61–108.

32. *Ars Praedicandi* 47 in *PL* 210: 194; and *The Art of Preaching*, translated by G. R. Evans (Kalamazoo, Mich.: Cistercian Publications, 1981), 168. See also *Hali meidhad*, 12–20; and Savage, tr., "Holy Maidenhood," 234–240; *Ltr* 40 in *The Letters of*

Osbert of Clare, Prior of Westminster, edited by Edward William Williamson et al. (Oxford: Oxford University Press, 1998), 136.

33. Jane Tibbetts Schulenburg, *Forgetful of Their Sex: Female Sanctity and Society, ca. 500–1100* (Chicago: University of Chicago Press, 1998), 136–138. See *Hrotsvit Opera Omnia* (Munich: Saur, 2001), 132–267; *The Dramas of Hrotsvit*, translated by Katharina M. Wilson (Saskatoon: Peregrina, 1985).

34. Newman, *From Virile Woman to WomanChrist*, 21–22.

35. Guibert, *Opusculum de virginitate* in *PL* 156: 579–608; Rupert, *De laesione*, in *PL* 170: 545–560.

36. For a discussion of clerical chastity during the early Christian period, see chapter 4 in this volume.

37. Although Christians considered themselves exempt from Jewish prescriptions and proscriptions, they nonetheless turned often to the Old Testament for guidance.

38. Charles A. Frazee, "The Origins of Clerical Celibacy in the Western Church," *Church History* 57 (1988): 112–113. For the Old Testament purity laws, see Lev. 7:19–20, 15, 22:3–8; Ex. 19:15; 1 Sam. 21:4.

39. Siricius, *Epist et dec* 1.7.8–11 in *PL* 13: 1138B–1141A. Innocentius, *Epist et dec* 2.9.12 in *PL* 20: 476A–B.

40. For more about the Carolingian reform efforts, see John E. Lynch, "Marriage and Celibacy of the Clergy the Discipline of the Western Church: An Historico-Canonical Synopsis," *The Jurist* 32 (1972): 34–38; M. A. Claussen, *The Reform of the Frankish Church: Chrodegang of Metz and the Regula canonicorum in the Eighth Century* (Cambridge: Cambridge University Press, 2004).

41. Jo Ann McNamara, "Chaste Marriage and Clerical Celibacy," in *Sexual Practices & the Medieval Church*, edited by Vern L. Bullough and James Brundage (Buffalo, NY: Prometheus Books, 1982), 26; Frazee, "Origins of Clerical Celibacy," 118.

42. *Ratherii Romam Euntis Itinerarium* in *PL* 136: 585–586.

43. Trullo, 692, c. 6, 12, 48 in G. D. Mansi, *Sacrorum conciliorum . . . collectio* (Florence, 1759), 11: 944–948, 965.

44. H. E. J. Cowdrey, "Pope Gregory VII and the Chastity of the Clergy," in Frassetto, *Medieval Purity and Piety*, 282–292; Uta-Renate Blumenthal, "Pope Gregory VII and the Prohibition of Nicolaitism," in Frassetto, *Medieval Purity and Piety*, 38.

45. James A. Brundage, *Law, Sex, and Christian Society in Medieval Europe* (Chicago: University of Chicago Press, 1987), 179–187.

46. Brundage, *Law, Sex, and Christian Society*, 214–115; Frazee, "Origins of Clerical Celibacy," 125.

47. Lat. II, 1059, c. 3 in Rudolf Schieffer, *Die Entstehung des Päpstlichen Investiturverbots für den Deutschen König, MGH Schriften* 28 (Stuttgart: Hiersemann, 1981), 218–222. Records of Leo's and Stephen's councils are not extant, but we know of their decrees by way of contemporary sources. Translation and discussion in Blumenthal, "Pope Gregory VII and the Prohibition of Nicolaitism," 243–244.

48. Cowdrey, "Pope Gregory and the Chastity of the Clergy," 271.

49. Anne Llewellyn Barstow, *Married Priests and the Reforming Papacy: The Eleventh-Century Debates* (Toronto: E. Mellen, 1982), 67–74; Henry Charles Lea, *History of Sacerdotal Celibacy in the Christian Church* (London: Williams and Norgate, 1907), 1: 269–271.

50. Cowdrey, "Pope Gregory and the Chastity of the Clergy," 277–278.

51. See Blumenthal, "Pope Gregory VII and the Prohibition of Nicolaitism"; Cowdrey, "Pope Gregory and the Chastity of the Clergy," esp. 290–291.

52. Lat. I, 1123, c. 21 (c. 3 in some manuscripts) in Tanner, *Decrees of the Ecumenical Councils* 1: 194.

53. Lat. II, 1139, c. 7 in Tanner, *Decrees of the Ecumenical Councils* 1: 198. Translated by Paul Beaudette, "'In the world but not of it': Clerical Celibacy as a Symbol of the Medieval Church," in Frassetto, *Medieval Purity and Piety*, 24.

54. Barstow, *Married Priests*, 43.

55. *Ltr* 112 in *Die Briefe Des Petrus Damiani*, edited by Kurt Reindel, *Die Briefe der deutschen Kaiserzeit* (Munich, *Monumenta Germaniae Historica*, 1989), 3: 278; *The Letters of Peter Damian*, translated by Owen J. Blum (Washington, D.C.: Catholic University of America Press, 1989), 5: 276–277.

56. Bernold of St. Blasien, *Chronicon* a. 1049, edited by G. H. Pertz, *MGH SS* (Hannover: Impensis Bibliopolii avlici Hahniani, 1844), 5: 426.

57. Melfi, 1089, c. 12 in Mansi, *Sacrorum conciliorum . . . collectio*, 20: 724.

58. On the depiction of the clergy in the fabliaux, see Daron Lee Burrows, *The Stereotype of the Priest in the Old French Fabliaux: Anticlerical Satire and Lay Identity* (Oxford: P. Lang, 2005).

59. M. A. Kelleher, "'Like man and wife': Clerics' Concubines in the Diocese of Barcelona," *Journal of Medieval History* 28 (2002): 355, 349–60.

60. For more on this topic, see Lynch, "Marriage and Celibacy," 194–197, 199–207; William E. Phipps, *Clerical Celibacy: The Heritage* (New York: Continuum, 2004), 134–136.

61. *Concilia Magnae Britanniae*, edited by D. Wilkins (London, 1737), 1: 367; Barstow, *Married Priests*, 87.

62. Synod of Paris, 1074, in Mansi, *Sacrorum conciliorum . . . collectio*, 20: 437–438.

63. *De continentia clericorum*, edited by Lothar von Heinemann, *MGH Libelli de lite* 1 (Hannover: Impensis Bibliopolii Hahniani, 1891), 254–260. On Ulric's defense, see Barstow, *Married Priests*, 107–140; "Pope Gregory and the Chastity of the Clergy," 288–289. For evidence of the treatise's condemnation, see Bernold, *Chronicon* a. 1079 in *MGH SS* 5: 436.

64. *De bono coniugali* 3.3, 6.6 in *Augustine: De bono coniugali, De sancta virginitate*, edited and translated by P. G. Walsh (Oxford: Clarendon Press, 2001), 6–9, 13–15; *De nupt et concup* 1.7.8, 17.19 in *Corpus scriptorum ecclesiasticorum Latinorum* (Vienna, 1867–), 42: 219–220, 231; and "Marriage and Desire," in *Answer to the Pelagians, II*, translated by Roland J. Teske, *The Works of St Augustine* (New York: New City Press, 1998), 24–1: 33, 40–41; Brundage, *Law, Sex, and Christian Society*, 89–90.

65. See Brundage, *Law, Sex, and Christian Society*, 153–165; Pierre J. Payer, "Early Medieval Regulations Concerning Marital Sexual Relations," *Journal of Medieval History* 6 (1980), 353–376; Payer, *Sex and the Penitentials: The Development of a Sexual Code, 550–1150* (Toronto: University of Toronto Press, 1984).

66. Brundage, *Law, Sex, and Christian Society*, 154–155.

67. Some scholars call this practice spiritual marriage instead of chaste marriage. However, during the Middle Ages, in addition to connoting the sexual abstinence of married couples, spiritual marriage frequently described the allegorical union between Christ and the soul, Christ and the Church, and the bishop and the Church. Because of this, I have chosen to use the term *chaste marriage*. It should be noted, though, that the term *chaste marriage* is not itself without ambiguity. Medieval writers used it when speaking of married couples who abstain from sex, but they also employed it when referring to sexual fidelity within marriage; that is, to couples who only engage in procreative sexual relations with each other.

68. *Demonstratio evangelica* 1.9 in *The Proof of the Gospel being the Demonstratio Evangelica of Eusebius of Caesarea*, translated by W. J. Ferrar (London: Society for the Promotion of Christian Knowledge, 1920), 1: 53–54; McNamara, "Chaste Marriage and Clerical Celibacy," 24.

69. Elliott, *Spiritual Marriage*, 53, 55–58, 246; McNamara, "Chaste Marriage and Clerical Celibacy," 29–30.

70. Elliott, *Spiritual Marriage*, 158–164.

71. *Summa confessorum* 1.8.46 (Rome, 1518), f. 22, p. 43.

72. Elliott, *Spiritual Marriage*, 141; Margaret McGlynn and Richard J. Moll, "Chaste Marriage in the Middle Ages: 'It were to hire a greet merite,'" in Bullough and Brundage, eds., *Handbook of Medieval Sexuality*, 105, 107.

73. See Elliott, *Spiritual Marriage*, 63–73; Marc Glasser, "Marriage in Medieval Hagiography," *Studies in Medieval and Renaissance History* n.s. 4 (1978): 11–19.

74. For one of the most widely read versions of her life, see Jacobus de Voragine, *Legenda aurea*, edited by Giovanni Paolo Maggioni (Firenze: SISMEL, Edizioni del Galluzzo, 1998), 2: 1180–1187; and *The Golden Legend: Readings on the Saints*, translated by. William Granger Ryan (Princeton: Princeton University Press, 1993), 2: 318–322.

75. Glasser, "Marriage in Medieval Hagiography," 18, 9–19. On remaining in the marriage as predominantly woman's behavior, see Elliott, *Spiritual Marriage*, 65.

76. For one of the most widely read versions of his life, see *Legenda aurea*, 1: 621–626; Ryan, tr., *Golden Legend*, 1: 371–374.

77. Elliott, *Spiritual Marriage*, 105–106.

78. He experienced his conversion in 1173. *Chronicon universale anonymi Laudunensis*, edited by Georg Waitz, *MGH SS* 26 (Hannover: Impensis Bibliopolii Hahniani, 1882), 447–448; and R. I. Moore, *The Birth of Popular Heresy* (London: Edward Arnold, 1975), 111–113.

79. Glasser, "Marriage in Medieval Hagiography," 19–32; Elliott, *Spiritual Marriage*, 204, 195–265, 295.

80. *The Life of Saint Birgitta*, edited by Birger Gregersson et al., translated by Julia Bolton Holloway (Toronto: Peregrina, 1991), 13–16, 20–21.

81. On the growth of anchoritism during the twelfth century, see Anneke B. Mulder-Bakker, *Lives of the Anchoresses: The Rise of the Urban Recluse in Medieval Europe*, translated by Myra Heerspink Scholz (Philadelphia: University of Pennsylvania Press, 2005).

82. For more on the Beguines, see Brenda Bolton, "Mulieres Sanctae," in *Women in Medieval Society*, edited by Susan Mosher Stuard (Philadelphia: University of Pennsylvania Press, 1976), 141–157; Walter Simons, *Cities of Ladies: Beguine Communities in the Medieval Low Countries, 1200–1565* (Philadelphia: University of Pennsylvania Press, 2001).

83. Hagiographical sources provide valuable evidence about the Middle Ages, but they must be used cautiously. On this topic, see Schulenburg, *Forgetful of Their Sex*, 17–57.

84. Elliott, *Spiritual Marriage*, 203–205; Glasser, "Marriage in Medieval Hagiography," 22–31; André Vauchez, "Between Virginity and Spiritual Espousals: Models of Feminine Sainthood in the Christian West in the Middle Ages," *Medieval History Journal* 2.2 (1999): 352.

85. Jacques de Vitry, *Vita Mariae Oigniacensis*, edited by D. Papebroeck, *Acta sanctorum bollandiana* June 23 (1867) 5: 547–548. Translated in Elliott, *Spiritual Marriage*, 200.

6

Celibacy and the Protestant Traditions: From Celibacy to the Freedom of the Christian

M. Darrol Bryant

On the question of celibacy, I have no instructions from the Lord.
—I Cor. 7:25a

Is celibacy an issue in the Protestant traditions? In the longer history of the Christian traditions, the issue of celibacy is centered in the celibacy of clergy and those following the monastic traditions. The biblical traditions are silent on the question of the celibacy of priests and monastics, since neither priests nor monks and nuns in the Christian sense are known to the biblical traditions. But at the Council of Nicea (325), shortly after Constantine had fatefully elevated Christianity from an outlawed religion to the religion of the empire, there was a proposal to "compel all clergy to give up cohabitation with their wives"; this proposal was rejected.[1] There were, obviously, married clergy at that time. The position of the Eastern or Orthodox churches came to be that priests and deacons could marry before ordination but not after. And bishops were to be celibate. This has continued to be the tradition among the Eastern or Orthodox churches. In Western or Catholic churches, the issue of celibacy of the clergy has had a long and controversial history. Pope Siricius in 386 ordered celibacy for "priests and levites," and this decree was repeated by Innocent I (402–417).[2] Yet Leo the Great (440–461) forbade the higher clergy to put away their wives on ordination; they were to go on living with them as "brother and sister." The Western church then refused to ordain married men before mutual vows of continence had been exchanged between them, and wives then tended to enter a religious institution. Later in the Lateran Councils, the notion of celibacy for all the clergy was strengthened, and made the rule in the Western church.[3] This, according to the *Oxford Dictionary of the Christian Churches*, was the practice of the Catholic tradition down to 1917, when Canon 132 forbade "altogether the ordination of a married man."[4] Earlier, the Protestant reformers of the sixteenth century had rejected the notion of clerical and monastic celibacy. Behind this history of celibacy in the Christian era lies a complex history of developments, controversies, and conflicts that go to the very beginnings of the Christian traditions.

Celibacy in the Biblical Traditions and Early Christianity

When researching this chapter, I was surprised to discover that the term *celibacy* is not even found in Young's *Analytical Concordance of the Bible*, long a standard concordance. Further conversations with Jewish colleagues assured me that the word does not appear in the Hebrew Bible, and that celibacy as "an unmarried state" played no role in Jewish traditions.[5] The reason, I was told, was simple: it violates the divine command "to be fruitful and multiply" (Gen. 1:28). Further investigation led me to see that in the Jewish traditions, this injunction was understood to make marriage and procreation a fundamental feature of Jewish life and practice. Daniel Gold says simply, "Although traditional Judaism proscribes sexual relations outside marriage, all Jews are expected to marry and engage regularly in conjugal relations."[6] Chapter 15 of Leviticus speaks of the sexual impurities of men and women, and chapter 21, on the "holiness of the priesthood" says that a priest should "not marry a prostitute" but nowhere enjoins "celibacy" as a desired or permanent state for the Jewish priest. And there is also the belief that men involved in a war should remain continent for the duration of the conflict. The situation within the first-century Jewish world, a world of conflicting Jewish groups such as the Pharisees, the Sadducees, the Zealots, and others—the world in which Jesus lived—is, however, somewhat more complicated. There are those who argue that the Qumran community—those of the Dead Sea Scrolls—may have practiced a limited celibacy as "warriors of Israel" during these troubled times, and others have pointed to the practice of celibacy among the Essenes, but these are disputed points and certainly not characteristic of the longer Jewish tradition. If it is not a practice found in Jewish traditions, where does it come from?

Peter Brown in his masterful study *The Body and Society: Men, Women, and Sexual Renunciation in Early Christianity* observes that by the end of the first century, Judaism and the leadership of the Christian churches

> had begun to diverge precisely on the issue of marriage and continence. With the destruction of the Temple and the strengthening of the synagogue and the house of study, Judaism was fast on its way to becoming a religion of the book and of the sanctified married household.... In Judaism, the Law rested equally on every aspect of the human person. It required reverent attention to those things which all human beings were held to share—food, time, and marriage. These kept God's world in being.... They had no intention of bringing the end of the world into the present by breaking with marriage.... They firmly maintained that the life of the married householder, the father of children, was the only life appropriate to a spiritual guide in Israel.... [T]he rabbis of Palestine came to wield influence in Judaism largely because they stood for a world that had no intention of vanishing.[7]

Why did the early Christians diverge? And why over the question of marriage and celibacy? Does the value of celibacy emerge in the early Christian movement as it begins to encounter the Greek and Roman worlds? Again, the historical record is not clear. Although some argue that there are few, if any Roman traditions—for some the exception is the tradition of the Vestal Virgins—that raise celibacy as an ideal or preferred condition for human being, there are others that contend that there were groups in the first century that "advocated celibacy and abstinence from sexual activity for their members."[8] If, as Brown observes, "the pagans of the first century A.D. had not been greatly disturbed by the presence of an animal nature in the act of love," it would seem that many Christians, for diverse reasons, were.[9] Was there something in sexuality that was the source of this unease? Why—and for whom—was marriage an issue?

Some contemporary writers on celibacy within the Catholic traditions will write of early Christianity in ways that suggest that it is simply obvious that celibacy is the ideal taught by Jesus and practiced by the Apostles.[10] But again Jesus, aside from a highly peculiar statement that we find in the Gospel of Matthew (19:12) about being "eunuchs for the Kingdom of Heaven," has no teaching about celibacy, nor do we find this theme prominent in the early Christian writings from the time of Jesus' death until the end of the first century. It is in the second century that this emphasis on celibacy begins to emerge. We see it looming larger in Tertullian and Origen at the end of the second and beginning of the third centuries. This once led James E. Dittes to observe concerning the tradition of priestly celibacy that "in the face of the uncertain warrants in theology, Scripture and early history, the durability [and origin, we might add] of the tradition becomes something of a puzzle and invites explanation on other grounds."[11]

Although the emergence in early Christianity of the idea of celibacy, especially priestly celibacy, remains puzzling, we might begin to unravel some of this puzzle by looking at the thesis found in Peter Brown's study *The Body and Society*. Early Christians, Brown argues, saw in Christ's death and resurrection the end of an age and the dawning of something new. Brown unfolds a long and complex argument about the implications of this end of the age, too long to reproduce here. But a few comments will perhaps suggest something of the ground out of which the notions of celibacy, continence, and virginity emerge. It is to be found, Brown argues, within early Christianity itself. Here we will focus on one moment in Brown's reconstruction of the ministry of Paul, the apostle to the gentiles. Paul had established churches in some of the leading cities of the Roman empire, places such as Ephesus and Corinth. And "in the communities that Paul had founded"—communities outside the orbit of Palestine—"the body . . . was to enjoy none of the carefree moments of indeterminacy allowed it by pagans. The body was not a neutral thing, placed between nature and the city. Paul set it firmly in place as a 'temple of the Holy Spirit.' . . . It belonged to the Lord. It was, indeed, . . . a physical object as totally infused by his spirit as the limb of a body: 'Do you not know that your bodies are members of Christ?' "[12]

For Paul, the human person lived in the tension of "a life lived *in the flesh*" yet "a life of glorious freedom lived in Christ *in the spirit*: "The Spirit of Him who raised Jesus from the dead dwells in you, he will . . . give life to your mortal bodies also." In the fifties Paul wrote a series of letters to his supporters in Corinth. In it, says Brown, "we can glimpse a church where issues of sexual control and renunciation condensed anxieties about the entire structure of the communities that Paul had wished to found." In one sense, the Corinthians were seeking a distinctive mark of this new life *in the spirit*, and some had come up with a "trenchant solution: . . . they would undo the elementary building blocks of conventional society." They would renounce marriage and await the coming of Jesus "holy in body and spirit." This radical option would truly bring an "end to the world," the world that unfolds from generation to generation through procreation. Is this the "new creation" that Paul envisaged? Brown says bluntly that "Paul wanted no part in such a hope." But he had to tread carefully with his Corinthian followers. Part of his response was the seventh chapter in Paul's first letter to the Corinthians, probably "the most important in the entire Bible for the question of marriage and related subjects." Brown observes that "in his other letters, sexual renunciation played no part in Paul's letters," yet here, when challenged by the Corinthians, Paul agreed that "it is good for a man not to touch a woman." But Paul's primary concern was "to deter his correspondents from so radical a remedy for their ills." Although Paul did not set out to praise marriage, he does "point out that marriage was safer than unconsidered celibacy... [and] much of the letter consisted of blocking moves."[13] Here are some of Paul's words:

> Now concerning the matters about which you wrote. It is well for a man not to touch a woman. But because of the temptation to immorality, each man should have his own wife and each woman her own husband. The husband should give to his wife her conjugal rights and likewise the wife to her husband.... Do not refuse one another except for a season that you may devote yourselves to prayer, but then come together again, lest Satan tempt you through lack of control.... I wish that all were as I myself am. But each has his own special gift from God, one of one kind and one of another.... Only, let every one lead the life which the Lord has assigned to him, and in which God has called him. This is my rule in all the churches.... I think that in view of the impending distress it is well for a person to remain as he is. Are you bound to a wife? Do not seek to be free. Are you free from a wife? Do not seek marriage. But if you marry, you do not sin and if a girl marries she does not sin. (I Cor. 7:1–7, 17, 26–28)

His words couched in restraint, Paul says that "married couples should not renounce intercourse," that it is best to "lead the life... assigned," and later that it is "no sin" for the young to marry. But Paul left "a fatal legacy to future ages," even if unintended, when in defending marriage he "slid imperceptibly into an attitude that viewed marriage itself as no more than a defense against desire." "At the time," Brown continues, "fornication and its avoidance did not occupy Paul greatly. He was concerned to emphasize, rather, the continuing validity of all social bonds."[14] Moreover, "Paul was... determined that his own state of celibacy should not be adopted by the church of Corinth... [for] to have done so would have swept away the structures of pious households," and that was not his intention.

This was not the "new creation in Christ" that Paul had proclaimed. But this moment is, I think, illustrative of the diverse ways in which some in the newly forming Christian communities were hearing what Paul proclaimed. Moreover, as these early Christian writings became standardized, circulated, and known in the emerging Christian world at the end of the first century and into the second century, the diverse ways in which this proclamation would be heard would grow. How did the Gentile, not steeped in the Jewish traditions, hear Paul's teaching? How would those influenced by gnostic ideas hear Paul's contrast of "in the flesh" and "in the spirit?" How would those struggling to define leadership in this movement hear Paul's comment about his own celibacy? Here may lie part of the answer to the puzzle of the emergence of the teachings about sexual issues including celibacy and virginity that were to become increasingly prominent throughout the second century of the Christian era.

There are, of course, many more factors, as Brown's study reveals, that lead to the emergence of celibacy and virginity as ideals for the clergy. But there is no question that by the fourth to fifth centuries, the idea of virginity and celibacy were firmly established as ideals for Christians, and for much of the Church, this meant that priests and those in religious orders were to refrain from marriage. Moreover, they were to exhibit in their bodily life something of the world beyond. This view was most commonly argued on the basis of the view that by remaining unmarried—and thus free from the entanglements of family life—the celibate priest would be able to devote himself fully to the work of the church. And within the newly flourishing religious institutions inaugurated by Benedict of Nursia, celibacy was seen as part of the way of obedience, of focusing one's life wholly on loving service to God through the Opus Dei—the eight periods of communal prayer beginning at 2:00 A.M.—that would structure the life of men and women in this "school of God's service."[15] Underlying these more sociological arguments lay the deeper issues of the sexes and sexuality in early Christianity. What was the nature of the human person? Didn't Genesis say that human beings were created in "the image of God . . . male and female he created them" (Gen. 1:27)? And didn't Paul say that we are "God's temple and that God's Spirit dwells" in us? (1 Cor. 3:16). Why should some renounce sexual relations with the opposite sex? Was sex wrong? Evil? Polluting? How does the body, especially its sexual dynamic, compromise the priestly role? Is it not possible to love God and to love a woman or a man at the same time? These were the troubling questions that second- and third-century Christians faced and from which emerged the views that undergirded the practice of celibacy.[16]

Luther and the Protestant Critique of Clerical and Monastic Celibacy

The Protestant rejection of the practice of monastic and clerical celibacy emerges in the reform movement initiated by the Augustinian monk Martin

Luther (1483–1546) in the early 1500s. Although Luther was an outwardly successful member of his Augustinian religious order—he was teaching in the new university at Wittenburg by 1508 and he had been sent by his order to Rome in 1510—he was inwardly troubled. He felt himself to be under the judgment of God, and his efforts to find a resolution to his inward unease and religious anxiety in the sacrament of penance were not successful. His studies of scripture, however, especially the Psalms and then Paul's Letter to the Romans, proved to be existentially transforming for Luther. He was struck in his studies of the Psalms that the Psalmist often found himself abandoned by God—something that Luther felt acutely. But it was Paul's teaching on "justification by faith alone" that unlocked the inner demons that had tormented Luther. Luther suddenly felt freed: it was God's gracious act in Jesus Christ that redeemed us—and not our acts, no matter how noble. God's love for humanity is the gift of God that we must accept in gladness and faith. However, the opening shot of the reform movement Luther unwittingly began was not Luther's insight into the graciousness of God but his opposition to the practice of selling indulgences. This practice within the Catholic tradition was seen as a way to free departed souls from purgatory. It led Luther, then a university professor, to the posting of the Ninety-five Theses—a series of propositions that called into question the very notion of indulgences—on the Wittenberg church door in 1517. Implied in some of the theses was Luther's view that the Christian faith was a deep and inward trusting in the promises of God, an acknowledgment of God's gracious act toward humanity in Jesus Christ, and not any human work or act. This call for scholarly debate quickly became a public controversy—but celibacy, clerical or monastic, was not an issue on the agenda. Indeed, the Reformation came as much a surprise to Luther as to anyone else. As Luther wrote to his monastic spiritual advisor, Spalatin, who had earlier been concerned by Luther's troubled conscience and his inordinate time spent in confession, "Good Heavens! Spalatin, how excited you are! More than I or anyone else. I wrote you before not to assume that this affair was begun or is carried on by your judgment or mine or that of any man. If it is of God, it will be completed contrary to, outside of, above, and below, either your or my understanding.... Let God see to it."[17]

It was some years later, after Luther had been excommunicated and it was clear to all that there would be no resolution of the conflict with Catholic practice and doctrine, that Luther addressed the issue of celibacy. By the early 1520s, Luther, protected by Frederick the Wise and other German princes against the forces of empire and church, found himself struggling to give some leadership to the movement he had unleashed. Not only had priests begun to abandon their vows but many monks and nuns had also begun to leave their religious institutions. Karlstadt, one of Luther's followers, had rejected celibacy for priests and religious, and now monks and nuns were beginning to come to Luther seeking his advice about what they should do and whether marriage was permitted. Already in 1519, Luther had published "A Sermon on the Estate of Marriage" in which he wrote, following his quoting of Genesis 2:18–24, which concludes "the two shall be one flesh," as follows:

> All of this is from God's word. These words teach us where man and woman come from, how they were given to one another, for what purpose a wife was created, and what kind of love there should be in the estate of marriage.... God makes distinctions between the different kinds of love, and shows that the love of a man and woman is (or should be) the greatest and purest of all loves.... [T]here are three kinds of love: false love, natural love, and married love. False love is that which seeks its own, as a man loves money.... Natural love is that between a father and son, brother and sister, friend and relative.... But over and above all these is married love.... All other kinds of love seek something other than the loved one, this kind wants only to have the beloved's own self completely.[18]

But, as Luther points out, we know marriage after the Fall: "If Adam had not fallen, the love of bride and groom would have been the loveliest thing." Note that Luther here ascribes the Fall to Adam and no mention is made of Eve. He then continues, "Now this love is not pure either.... Therefore, the married state is now no longer pure and free from sin. The temptation of the flesh has become so strong... that marriage may be likened to a hospital for incurables."[19] However, marriage is the "estate" or calling that is given by God for humans, but sinful and fallen humans. Moreover, Luther acknowledges that marriage that is for "companionship and children" is also a "sacrament."[20] "It is an outward and spiritual sign of the greatest, holiest, worthiest and noblest thing that has existed or ever will exist: the union of the divine and human natures in Christ," and a married man should "honor it as sacred."[21] And it is a "covenant of fidelity," meaning that "the whole basis and essence of marriage is that each gives himself or herself to the other, and they promise to remain faithful to each other."[22] Although Luther does not address the issue of clerical celibacy here, he does contend that "Before Adam fell it was a simple matter to remain virgin and chaste, but now it is hardly possible, and without special grace from God, quite impossible. For this very reason neither Christ nor the apostles sought to make chastity a matter of obligation. It is true that Christ counseled chastity, and he left it up to each one to test himself, so that if he could not be continent he was free to marry, but if by the grace of God he could be continent, then chastity is better."[23] Later, Luther would alter his position on this issue. But here Luther indirectly criticizes the notion of "obligatory or required celibacy," while he allows that "chastity is better." Finally, Luther nearly concludes his sermon as follows:

> This at least all married people should know. They can do no better work and do nothing more valuable either for God, for Christendom, for all the world, for themselves, and for their children than to bring up their children well. In comparison with this one work... there is nothing at all in pilgrimages to Rome, Jerusalem or Compostella, nothing at all in building churches, endowing masses or whatever good works could be named. For bringing up their children properly is their shortest road to heaven.[24]

In the context of the sixteenth-century Christian world, Luther's sermon is remarkable for the way it rehabilitates marriage, an institution long relegated to a second-place status within Christendom. Moreover, it is moving toward the notion of vocation or *beruf* as central to the Christian life and the context for loving God and the neighbor. And while not fully addressing the issue of celibacy, it places it in a new context: the context of marriage itself. For being chaste or celibate is a virtue to be pursued prior to entering into the state of holy matrimony.

It was not until 1522 that we see the publication of "The Judgment of Martin Luther on Monastic Vows." By this time, monks and nuns were leaving their religious institutions in great numbers in Germany and increasingly turning to Luther for advice. Over the coming years, Luther would often serve as a matchmaker and he would himself marry one of the nuns he could not otherwise place, Katherina von Bora. In his work on monastic vows, Luther says that "there is no doubt that the monastic vow is in itself a most dangerous thing because it is without the authority and example of Scripture. Neither the early church nor the New Testament knows anything at all of the taking of this kind of vow, much less do they approve of a lifelong vow of very rare and remarkable chastity. It is purely a most pernicious invention of men."[25]

Absent here is Luther's earlier acknowledgment that "Christ counseled chastity," for the vow of celibacy is here regarded as a "pernicious" human invention. As Luther remarks, "St Anthony... knew absolutely nothing about monastic vows and ceremonial... but willingly chose to live as a hermit and of his own will chose to live unmarried, after the pattern of the gospel. Pursuing human wishes, his successors made this way of life into a vow, a matter of obligation and compulsion."[26] Here Luther argues his case on different grounds—again not directly against celibacy but rather against vows, and especially the vow of celibacy. Monastic vows, in becoming "a matter of obligation and compulsion," are a kind of "works righteousness," an attempt at righteousness before God on the basis of one's work. Luther had come to see the heart of the Christian Way as faith in the redeeming work of Christ: "it is the gospel that possesses grace. As John says...'Grace and truth came through Jesus Christ.'"[27] And later Luther writes,

> Faith brings Christ to us, makes us one flesh with him, bone of his bones. Faith causes us to have all things in common with him so that our conscience glories in him and on account of him. We live as justified men solely because of his blood and merits, and we shall live redeemed in eternity, without any works of our own or the works of others. Faith in Christ cannot tolerate grace and justification coming from our own works of the works of others, for faith knows and confesses continually that grace and justification come from Christ alone.... This is the definition of being a Christian: simply believing you are justified by the works of Christ alone without any works of our own, believing you have been freed from you sins and saved.[28]

This is the heart of Luther's understanding of the Christian faith, but it is easily misunderstood. Luther's point is not to reject good works as an essential expression of faith—as he makes clear in his 1520 *Treatise on Good Works*—but to deny that our works are what makes us righteous or justified in the eyes of God.[29] For Luther, we are justified and make right with God solely on the basis of God's gracious work in Jesus Christ. Good works then flow from our trust in the promises of God, the gospel, and are for the sake of our neighbors. Our works do not alter our status vis-à-vis God as graciously redeemed and forgiven in and through Jesus Christ, but they do affect our relations with our neighbors and are part of Christian love in the context of our vocations and callings.

Celibacy, for Luther, falls under the category of "works" that presume to make us right with God and is, for this reason, rejected. In his "judgment on Monastic Vows," Luther says "all stations are so oriented that they serve others," and he further makes the bold assertion that there is no difference "in content" between the monk's religious life and the ordinary Christian, worldly life. Some hold, says Luther, "that their own monastic institution is greater ...and that the simple Christian life is the lesser."[30] However, Luther contends it is "obedience to parents and service to neighbor [that] is real and true worship of God" and that the false vows of the monastery have turned it into a "mockery of worship."[31] Vows, by being made external and eternal, have become, according to Luther, the problem. They puff up people and they mislead people into believing that it is the vow that saves them rather than remembering that "it is in Christ alone that all men live, in him all take their vows, in him they all believe and glory and think nothing of their own works." He continues, "Let him be anathema who teaches anything else but that justification and salvation are in faith alone."[32]

By 1630, in Luther's "Exhortation to all Clergy Assembled at Augsburg 1530," any hesitancy about the issue of celibacy—for example, Luther's acknowledgment of the good of chastity that he saw in St. Anthony and St. Benedict, or his earlier view that it was a high calling—has disappeared. Here Luther writes, "Celibacy, that is, the unmarried state or prohibited marriage, as you know, is also one of your papal innovations contrary to God's eternal Word and contrary to the ancient blessed custom of Christendom, contrary to all living creatures and the creation of God himself."[33] There is little wiggle room for the institution of celibacy. In the same exhortation, Luther, who had now been married for five years, sees it important to rehabilitate the status of women. He says that "God has created women to be held in honor and as helpers for man."[34] They are not to be treated as "harlots," since "God wills that they be valued and esteemed as women and that this be done gladly and with love. . . . [O]ne should take them in marriage and remain with them in conjugal love. That pleases God, but it requires skill and grace."[35] Luther would himself remain with Katharina "in conjugal love," together with their children until his death in 1546.

Other Voices from a Time of Reform and Reformation

The sixteenth century was a period of reform across the Western Christian world—and the voices of reform were many and different. They included figures within the Catholic tradition, such as Erasmus. Among those who came to be known as Protestants, I have given pride of place to Luther. But other reform figures—usually the Reformation is said to range across those who became Lutherans, Calvinist or Reformed, Anglican, and Anabaptist—either spoke in their own distinctive ways about reform and the issue of clerical celibacy or were strangely silent.

Even before Luther, Erasmus (1466–1536), the leading light of the new humanistic scholarship, had argued that "the Scriptures alone contained what was necessary to salvation" and had heaped biting satire on the follies and failings of monks, priests, cardinals, and even popes.[36] He was initially supportive of Luther but finally broke with him when he saw that Luther's initiatives were leading to a fracturing of the Church, for Erasmus sought the Church's reform, not its fracture. Ulrich Zwingli, a monk in Zurich and a leading Swiss reformer, along with ten others, had petitioned the bishop of Constance in 1522 requesting permission to marry. They cited Scripture in support of their petition, but in their petition to the Government of the Swiss Confederacy they asked for protection should they decide to marry, and they acknowledged their inability to maintain celibacy. In 1523, Zwingli's foremost disciple married, and in 1524 Zwingli himself took a wife, a widow he had lived with for two years. By the time Jean Calvin, the French reformer then in Geneva, first published his *Institutes of the Christian Religion* in the mid 1530s, the matter of celibacy seems to have become one of the hated practices of the Roman Church that needed not be theoretically addressed but only practically ridiculed. Calvin too had grown up closely connected to the Church and cloister in Noyon in France but now, in the context of discussing the "discipline of the clergy and its degeneration," he wrote of the Catholic traditions that

> in one thing they are extremely rigid and inexorable—in not permitting marriage to priests. But it is needless to speak of the extent to which fornication prevails among them unpunished; and how, relying upon their foul celibacy, they have become callous of all crime. Yet this prohibition clearly shows what a plague all their traditions are.... Surely the forbidding of marriage to priests came about by an impious tyranny not only against God's Word but also against all equity.[37]

According to Calvin, celibacy has no basis in Scripture. Indeed, the crown of his argument are the words of 1 Timothy 4:1ff.: "in later time some will depart from the faith by giving heed to deceitful spirits and doctrines of demons... liars ... who forbid marriage and enjoin abstinence from foods which God created to be received with thanksgiving."[38] This for Calvin was sufficient comment on the practice of clerical celibacy. However, he does acknowledge that the issue was raised at Nicea. As he says, "There are always superstitious little fellows who dream up something new to win admiration for themselves." While the idea of clerical celibacy was rejected at Nicea, Calvin admits that in later years "the too superstitious admiration of celibacy became prevalent" which had a negative impact on the "dignity" and "holiness" of marriage. And even where this "superstition" prevailed, the reality was "abuse."[39] Thus Calvin too affirms the dignity and holiness of marriage. Calvin argues that "man has been created... that... [he] may enjoy a helper joined to himself."[40] And, while Calvin denies that marriage is a sacrament, it is a "good and holy ordinance of God."[41]

Calvin was himself to marry in 1539. And the discipline imposed on the pastoral household, initially in Geneva, and then where Calvinism spread, was very severe. "Any lapse from virtue on the part of a minister was visited with peremptory deposition," observes Henry Charles Lea in his *History of Sacerdotal Celibacy in the Christian Church.*[42] Calvin had come to regard one's station or estate or vocation as fundamental to the Christian life and the means by which God was restoring his fallen creation to Himself. But Calvin emphasized the moral requirements of all God-instituted vocations and insisted that they be lived with discipline, as can be seen in his Geneva.

Menno Simons (ca. 1496–1561) was a Catholic priest in Holland in the 1520s when he was initially shaken by doubts about "transubstantiation" and turned to the study of Scripture. He could not find this doctrine there. Then in 1531, he was further disturbed by reports of those who had been put to death because of their practice of "a second baptism" or adult baptism, and this again had led him to Scripture. Finally in 1536 he left the Catholic Church and joined the Anabaptists. He was then to emerge as one of the leading members of this sect.[43] In his *Complete Writings*, there is no entry for "celibacy," and when he discusses "The Calling of Ministers" he says that they are those who are "ruling their own house well, having a virtuous wife, having the gift of purity, and obedient children. Yes, in all things they are chaste, sober, unblamable, having the Spirit, fear and love of God."[44] And of marriage he says, "We acknowledge, teach, and assent to no other marriage than that which Christ and His apostles publicly and plainly taught in the New Testament, namely, of one man and one woman."[45] A year after leaving the Catholic church and being called to be a minister in the small Anabaptist community, which was much criticized and attacked by both Catholic and Reformed groups, he was married to "a certain Gertrude" who preceded him in death. His was not a very settled marriage, as he was continually on the move on behalf of his community, much persecuted by both Catholics and Protestants. His ministry was concentrated on trying to build up and sustain the Anabaptists.

Henry Charles Lea writes that "the abrogation of celibacy in England was a process of far more perplexity and intricacy than in any other country which adopted the Reformation."[46] In the early 1530s, Henry VIII had come into conflict with the Catholic Church over the issue of yet another annulment. Failing to persuade the Catholic officials on this matter, Henry pushed through Parliament in 1534 the Act of Supremacy, which made the sovereign the head of the Church in England. Though he made some nods to the Continental reformers, Henry was little interested in the doctrinal reforms of Luther or the baptismal reforms of the Anabaptists. And curiously enough, Henry rejected the idea of clerical marriage, even though he had already in the 1520s began to confiscate some church institutions and lands and close some monasteries. The English reforms were more centered in ecclesiology and the reform of the liturgy. It was not until 1549 that an act passed that allowed clergy—and those formerly in orders—to marry.

Reforming the Reformers: Protestant Movements in a Householder Religion

Beyond the period of the major Protestant reformers, the issue of celibacy virtually disappears and seldom emerges in the writings of those who were to reform the reformers in the centuries that followed. One of the central teachings of the European Protestants was the notion of the priesthood of all believers, a conviction that undermined the long-held distinction of the priest and the laity. Theoretically, there was no difference in kind between priest and lay as the leadership in the churches shifted from the celibate priesthood to the married minister. But in social role there was. Luther had argued that the minister was to lead for the sake of "good order" in the church, not because of any difference in nature. Armed with its view of *Sola Scriptura* as the final authority in the life of the Christian, the way was opened to continuing reformation and fragmentation of the Protestant world. These new movements that reformed the reformers all sought to revitalize and extend patterns of lay-oriented spirituality. To borrow a phrase from the Indian religious traditions, the Protestant traditions had become "householder religions." They simply assumed that Christians married and that celibacy, understood as chaste sexual behavior, was a feature of one's premarital life. The very idea of a celibate life that renounced sexuality and was dedicated to God was not even considered. Here we will only briefly comment on these patterns of lay spirituality that emerged in three of many movements within the Protestant world: Puritans, Pietists, and Methodists.

The Puritan movement was initiated in England but had its greatest success in the New World. Initially, the Puritans sought to extend reform beyond the liturgical and ecclesiastical realms characteristic of the Anglican reform to reforms in the world, and thus they have been called "worldly reformers." When some of these English Puritans made their way to the Massachusetts Bay Colony in 1630, John Winthrop, aboard the Arbella, spoke of their purposes as "establishing a City Set upon a Hill," a due form of civil and ecclesiastical government that could undergird this errand into the wilderness. Here the focus of the Christian life was shifted to the transformation of the sociopolitical landscape in the hands of newly born saints.

After a century in the New World, there was a sense that the glorious days might lie in the past. It was then that something quite unexpected happened:

the Connecticut River Valley Awakening of 1734–1735. Out on the frontier, far from Boston, there was a remarkable outpouring of religious enthusiasm that spread up and down the valley. At the center of these events was Jonathan Edwards, a bookish Puritan minister who had succeeded his grandfather, Soloman Stoddard, in the church in Northampton. In a series of sermons on "justification by Faith Alone," the central reformation theme, Edwards found himself confronted with a congregation in turmoil, and people felt themselves affected in unaccustomed ways. No one was more surprised than the scholarly Edwards. Later he would write *A Faithful Narrative of the Surprising Work of God in Northampton* about these times in which there was, Edwards wrote, "a great and earnest concern about the great things of religion and the eternal world." Edwards saw these events as evidence of God's work of awakening and bringing many to a more affecting and vital faith. He reports on a conversation he had with a young woman greatly touched by these events, and it leads Edwards to say "what she gave account of was a glorious work of God's infinite power and sovereign grace.... God had given her *a new heart, truly broken and sanctified*."[47] The events of the Connecticut River Valley were a foreshadowing of the Great Awakening, the period of revival of the 1740s that swept across the American colonies. Edwards was more peripheral to these events, but he wrote an important critical account in his work on the *Religious Affections*. Here he offered an analysis of "true religion" that focused on "the nature and signs of the gracious operations of God's Spirit, by which they are to be distinguished from all things whatsoever that the minds of men are the subjects of, which are not of a saving nature."[48] Here, as young and old were undergoing an experience of "new Birth," the new revival saints were set to continue to construct a new society that would anticipate the Kingdom to come. It was now the inwardly transformed "saint"—lay and minister, married, young, old, male and female—that would extend the Kingdom in the world.

In the lands of Luther there emerged a movement in the seventeenth century that centered around Philipp Jakob Spener (1635–1703), a Lutheran pastor in Frankfurt. It was there that he began to develop a form of congregational and lay life known as the "collegia pietatis." These groups met weekly around the "living Scripture" for prayer and mutual support, thus seeking to deepen and revitalize, Spener hoped, congregational life within the Lutheran world. This innovative movement came at the end of the Thirty Years war that had finally been settled in 1648 at the Peace of Westphalia, where the principle was affirmed that "the religion of the ruler would be the religion of a given territory." But Spener was focused on the revival of a tradition that had become, in his view, overly centred in right belief and doctrine at the expense of the inner life of faith and devotion. Had not Luther taught that faith was an "inward trusting in the promises of God" more than an outward profession of beliefs, Spener wondered? Spener sought a pattern of lay spirituality that could revive his tradition. Spener's views came to be written in a volume called *Pia Desideria* (Pious Desires). In a sermon Spener once said, "how much good it would do if good friends would come together on a Sunday and instead of getting out glasses, cards, or dice would take up a book and read . . . for the edification of all . . . if they would speak together about the divine mysteries, and the one who received most from God would try to instruct the weaker brethren . . . by virtue of their universal Christian priesthood . . . to work with and under us to correct and reform as much in their neighbor as they are able."[49]

In his *Pia Desideria,* this would result in six proposals, including "a more extensive use of the Word of God amongst us," "diligent exercise of the spiritual priesthood," and the reform of preaching so it aims at edification, since "our whole Christian religion consists of the inner man or the new man, whose soul is faith and whose expressions are the fruits of life." A "more extensive use of the Word of God" meant, for Spener, that at home and in meetings members would "take up the Holy Scriptures, read aloud from them, and fraternally discuss each verse in order to discover its simple meaning and whatever may be useful for the edification of all." Here the Bible was really put in the hands of the laity—the printing press now made scripture something you could hold in your hands—to be studied not as an ancient document but as a "Living Word" that could change and deepen one's life.[50] And it was the laity that would discern its meaning and edify one another. Again, this was not a religion of the priestly perfect and the unwashed laity but a "universal priesthood" of lay and married, men and women coming together around the Living Word to build one another up in the faith. Utterly absent are issues of celibacy, it is assumed that we are married people engaged in many different social callings.

Finally, across the channel, John Wesley (1703–1791), an Anglican cleric, would seek to reform his tradition through his Methodist movement. This movement became especially important in the American colonies and in the new republic following the War of Independence in 1774. It too was a lay-centred movement that had what Wesley called "Christian perfection" very close to its heart. Christian perfection, Wesley wrote, was another name for "holiness." And unlike Luther, who argued that the Christian remained *simul iustus et peccator*—at the same time righteous and sinful, saint and sinner—Wesley believed that we could grow in holiness and perfection. Wesley knew that this was a scary topic, since "there is scarce any expression in holy writ, which has given more offence than this. The word *perfect* is what many cannot bear." Moreover, it was a term often used in early Christianity in relation to issues of celibacy and virginity. Nevertheless, Wesley persists since it is a

Biblical phrase, "Be ye perfect, as your heavenly Father is perfect" (Matt. 5:48). But it is not, he points out, "an exemption either from ignorance, or mistakes, or infirmities, or temptations . . . it is only another term for holiness." It is, that is, a perfection of the heart, of the inner man, of the wellsprings of motivation. It is an inward work of Christ and the Spirit since, Wesley explains, "everyone that hath Christ in him, the hope of glory, 'purifieth himself, even as He is pure.'" What does this mean? For Wesley, it means that the Christian can be "purified from pride . . . from self-will, and . . . from anger." Wesley explains that the Christian is one who is "purified from pride, for Christ was lowly of heart. He is pure from self-will . . . for Christ desired only to do the will of His Father. . . . And he is pure from anger . . . for Christ was meek and gentle, patient and long-suffering."[51] These bold claims moved considerably beyond the teachings of the sixteenth-century reformers. And one might expect in this context that Wesley would address issues of celibacy and chastity, but they do not come into the grammar of the working of the Spirit that he outlines in his many sermons and writings.[52] Out of this would grow the Holiness movement in nineteenth-century American Protestantism, as well as the Holiness movement in the United Kingdom. It is the sanctified life in the world of men and women, mostly married, that are moving toward "Christian perfection" that is central for Wesley. That Christians were married, not celibate, had become so much assumed that it never even had to be addressed.

The Return of Celibacy to the Protestant Traditions

Early in the twentieth century there emerged the Swiss Protestant thinker Karl Barth (1886–1968), perhaps the most influential Protestant Christian thinker of the century. Barth had been trained in the liberal tradition of the nineteenth century. He tells us that he suddenly found himself in a quandary on a Sunday morning: he didn't have anything to say to his congregation in the face of the terrible events that were unfolding in the course of the First World War. Like the good Protestant he was, he turned to the study of Scripture, but kept a newspaper in the other hand. The result was a bombshell; it was called the *Epistle to the Romans*. Here, Barth reasserted the "infinite qualitative difference" between God and humanity, something the optimistic theological voices of the nineteenth century had failed to grasp. Paul's Epistle to the Romans had rightly seen that the relationship between God and humanity was a movement from God's side toward humanity in the person of Jesus Christ, redeeming and reconciling humanity with God. This was the "strange and wonderful world of the Bible" that Barth discovered. And over the remainder of his life, volume after volume poured forth, unpacking the wonder of God's gracious action toward humanity in Jesus Christ. In his monumental *Church Dogmatics,* Barth turned to "man and woman" in discussing the doctrine of creation. Here Barth unfolds his account of "man and woman," arguing that "marriage is without doubt the *telos,* goal and centre of the relationship. We may provisionally define it as the form of the encounter of male and female in which the free, mutual, harmonious choice of love on the part of a particular man and woman leads to a responsibly undertaken life-union which is lasting, complete and exclusive."[53]

But then a few sentences later he says, "But it certainly does not belong to every man to enter into the married state and live in it. The decision to do so is not open to each individual and there are reasons why it is open to man not to do so."[54] In Barth's terms, the choice to remain single or unmarried was legitimate. Thus, not all is well, Barth says, with Protestant teaching which often assumes marriage is the only option for man and woman. He explains that the position of the Reformers "arises from the justifiable conflict [they] had to wage against the Roman doctrine of the superior excellence of celibacy and therefore for the equal status of marriage.... This conflict unfortunately led to the inversion which would have it that marriage... is the better state... alone pleasing to God."[55] But this would be to "elevate a human tradition... above Holy Scripture." Rather, Barth argues, the New Testament witness alters the situation: "marriage is no longer an absolute but a relative necessity."[56] We find ourselves, after the life, death, and resurrection of Christ, in an in-between time when both marrying and not marrying are open to us. Barth goes on to offer his interpretation of Jesus' teachings in the following terms: "he expressed himself very definitely about... the sanctity of marriage" and "he did not command anyone to abstain from it," but "he has given reasons which might persuade any one to abstain for marriage."[57] This is not a matter of "prohibitions... but marriage is obviously relativised." Paul's teaching in 1 Corinthians 7 is, Barth argues, a further elaboration on the freedom of a Christian:

> The Christian enters into marriage, not on the basis of a natural necessity, but on that of a special spiritual gift and vocation within his life history and the history of salvation.... He does so in the freedom of the Spirit.... [This same freedom] is recalled by the opposing freedom of the same Spirit... that of not marrying.... There is a genuine Christian obedience which does not lead a man into marriage but past it.... Paul's teaching [in 1 Cor. 7] is the Magna Carta of all who are unmarried, to which we would only add the warning that

they should understand and exercise their voluntary or involuntary celibacy as a matter of Christian obedience as Paul did.[58]

Barth's views are an important corrective in the history of the issue of marriage/celibacy in the Protestant traditions. They move beyond the adversarial spirit that too much characterized the sixteenth-century debates. But this is a theoretical corrective. It does not rehabilitate the practice of monasticism in the Protestant world, nor does it open the issue of clerical celibacy. The return to "religious communities" in the Protestant world had already began in nineteenth-century England as some Anglican woman came together in their service to the poor. In these communities there were vows to a life of simplicity, chastity, and obedience. And in the twentieth century, there are Benedictine monasteries with Anglican and Lutheran monks.

Celibacy Revisited: Sexuality in the Twenty-First Century

Where have we come? What does one say about these Protestant views of celibacy—and marriage—in the light of a more ecumenical age? When we review the origins of the teachings of the sixteenth-century Protestant thinkers in relation to the issue of celibacy, it is clear that their views were forged in the fire of conflict and intra-Christian polemic. Karl Barth already noted this in his *Church Dogmatics*. Although there are enduring insights that emerge, such a context inevitably results in overstatement and a kind of either/or thinking. Thus the conflict became celibacy versus marriage, Scripture versus tradition, our right vision of the Christian faith versus their wrong view of that shared faith. And the victim in such a conflictual situation is the balanced view we might have hoped for, since there are significant issues of gender and sexuality that could have been addressed but do not emerge. For example, we are aware in a way that none of the Reformers could be that there was a strong male centrism pervading their thinking. Only in the nineteenth century in American Protestantism did this male-centrism begin to be challenged. Elizabeth Cady Stanton and other Protestant women produced the Woman's Bible at the end of the century (1898), and we are still dealing with male-centrist issues. Similarly, there is no mention of why women could not be priests and ministers; it was simply assumed that clergy would be men. In 1843, the Congregational Church of Mount Vernon, Ohio, ordained a woman. But it was only in the twentieth century that we began to have the ordination of women in many other Protestant traditions: Anglican in the 1940s in Hong Kong, Lutheran in Canada in the early 1970s, Episcopal in the United States in the 1970s, Presbyterian in

Canada in the 1970s, Anglican in the United Kingdom in 1972. These are developments that were not envisaged in the sixteenth century and that even today remain controversial within the denominations where women serve as priests, ministers, and even bishops.

In these more recent developments, we see how Protestant reflections on celibacy tended to focus more on the *Oxford English Dictionary* definition of celibacy as "remaining in an unmarried state" than it did on celibacy as "a way of living chaste unto God." There are reasons for exploiting this ambiguity in the notion of celibacy: it kept the issues of gender and sexuality in the background. But it is this issue that keeps reemerging even in Protestant traditions that have for centuries now adhered to their rejection of clerical and monastic celibacy and affirmed, in Luther's phrase, the freedom of the Christian. Protestant churches have been challenged to rethink and revise the very notions of sexuality that underlay their earlier teachings about celibacy. If, as Barth insists and earlier Protestant thinkers assumed, we are born male or female—does that mean we are all heterosexual in our sexual orientation? And if some of us are gay or lesbian, what does this mean for our Christian vocations? Or for ministerial offices within the Protestant world? One Protestant denomination in Canada, the United Church of Canada, has argued for the inclusion of gay sexual orientations in our understanding of sexual life and allows the ordination of gay persons. Other denominations are conflicted—as we saw in the uproar over the election of a gay bishop in the Episcopal Church in the United States. Some other denominations refuse to address these issues, insisting that a homosexual orientation is sinful and against the Bible. These are the issues that are confronting and conflicting the Protestant world at the beginning of the third millennium of the Christian era.

NOTES

1. See the entry on the "Celibacy of the Clergy" in the *Oxford Dictionary of the Christian Church* (hereafter *ODCC*), edited by F. L. Cross (London: Oxford University Press, 1958), 255. For a very careful and conservative review of early councils and canons on this issue, see Roman Cholij, *Clerical Celibacy in East and West* (Leominster, Herefordshire: Gracewing, Fowler Wright Books, 1989).

2. See *ODCC*, 255, and the entry on "Siricius," 1261.

3. See Anne L. Barstow, *Married Priests and the Reforming Papacy: The Eleventh-Century Debates* (Lewiston, N.Y.: Edwin Mellen Press, 1982). Barstow observes that "until the twelfth century many of the secular clergy were married," ix. She then notes that it was only with the Second Lateran Council in 1139 that "married clerics" were "prohibited from serving the altar," 1.

4. See *ODCC*, "Celibacy of the Clergy," 255.

5. During warfare, however, it was customary for combatants to refrain from sexual relations during their period of military service; see 2 Samuel 11.

6. Daniel Gold, "Celibacy," in *The Encyclopedia of Religion*, edited by Mircea Eliade (New York: Macmillan, 1987), 3: 146. Gabriel Abdelsayed, writing on "Chastity" in the same volume, writes that the notion of chastity understood as "the adoption of ethical and moral norms in order to achieve a higher and purer life" has been "a dominant theological theme in Judaism" (227–228).

7. Peter Brown, *The Body and Society: Men, Women, and Sexual Renunciation in Early Christianity* (New York: Columbia University Press, 1988), 61–63.

8. While Peter Brown follows the first option, Merry Wiesner-Hanks in "Celibacy and Virginity," in the *Oxford Encyclopedia of the Reformation*, edited by Hans Hillerbrand (Oxford: Oxford University Press, 1996), 1: 296, takes the latter.

9. Brown, *Body and Society*, 432.

10. See the articles in *Priestly Celibacy: Its Scriptural, Historical, Spiritual, and Psychological Roots*, edited by Peter Stravinskas (Pocono, Pa.: Newman House, 2001).

11. James Dittes, "The Symbolic Value of Celibacy for the Catholic Faith," in *Celibacy in the Church*, edited by W. Bassett and P. Huizing (New York: Herder & Herder, 1972), 84.

12. Brown, *Body and Society*, 51.

13. Ibid.; these citations come from pages 49, 52, 53.

14. Ibid., 55.

15. "Prologue," *The Rule of St. Benedict*, translated by A. Meisel and M. del Mastro (Garden City, N.Y.: Image Books), 45. In this edition the term "celibacy" does not appear, though number 63 in the instruments of good works (page 54) says "to love chastity."

16. Some centuries before the emergence of Christian traditions, there were those in the Hindu world who had embraced the practice of *brahmacharya* as an ascetic practice conducive to the spiritual journey. One of India's foremost ashrams, the Divine Life Society in Rishikesh, says that "*brahmacharya* is purity in thought word and deed. In a special sense it is celibacy or control of the sex desire in thought, word and deed. . . . Brahmacharya is absolutely necessary for the attainment of peace and God-vision." Similarly, the Buddhist *Sangha* (monastic community) had enjoined celibacy on those *bikkhus* and *bikkshunis* who would follow the Buddhist Way. As Bhikkhu Bodhi remarks, "the central place of celibacy in the Buddhist spiritual path can be seen in the fact that in Pali both are designed by the same word brahmacariya, meaning *holy conduct*." After his enlightenment, the Awakened One "made celibacy an essential plank of the monastic vocation. . . . [He] knit it into the fabric of monastic life through the disciplinary code of the Vinaya." In these traditions, celibacy is part of the teaching and discipline for those who have chosen the ascetic way of the *sannyasin* or the monastic ways of the *Sangha*. See Swami Shivananda, the *Divine Light Society* at www.hinduism.co.za/celibacy.htm; and Bhikkhu Bodhi, "Celibacy: Buddhist" in *Encyclopedia of Monasticism*, edited by William Johnston (Chicago: Fitzroy & Dearborn, 2000), 263.

17. "Introduction to the Christian in Society," in *Luther's Works*, edited by J. Atkinson, vol. 44 (Philadelphia: Fortress, 1966), xi.

18. Martin Luther, "A Sermon on the Estate of Marriage," in Atkinson, *Luther's Works*, 44: 8–9.

19. Ibid., 9.

20. Ibid., 8.

21. Ibid., 10.

22. Ibid., 10–11.

23. Ibid., 10.

24. Ibid., 12.

25. Martin Luther, "Judgment... on Monastic Vows," in Atkinson, *Luther's Works*, 44: 252.

26. Ibid., 253.

27. Ibid., 257.

28. Ibid., 286–287.

29. Martin Luther, "Treatise on Good Works," in Atkinson, *Luther's Works*, 44: 15–121.

30. Luther, "Judgment... on Monastic Vows," 322–323.

31. Ibid., 331.

32. Ibid., 292.

33. Martin Luther, "Exhortation to All Clergy Assembled at Augsburg 1530," in *Selected Writings of Martin Luther*, edited by T. Tappert (Philadelphia: Fortress, 1967), 92.

34. Ibid., 93.

35. Ibid., 93–94.

36. See Henry Charles Lea, *The History of Sacerdotal Celibacy in the Christian Church* (New York: Russell & Russell, 1957), 351, and Erasmus, *Handbook of the Militant Christian* (Notre Dame, Ind.: Fides, 1962).

37. Jean Calvin, *Institutes of the Christian Religion*, 2 volumes, edited by J. McNeill, translated by F. L. Battles (Philadelphia: Westminster, 1960), 1249–1250.

38. Ibid., 1250.

39. Ibid., 1252, 1253.

40. Ibid., 453.

41. Ibid., 1481.

42. Lea, *History of Sacredotal Celibacy*, 428.

43. See Harold Bender, "A Brief Biography of Menno Simons," in *The Complete Writings of Menno Simons* (Scottdale, Pa.: Herald Press, 1956), 3ff.

44. Menno Simons, "The Calling of the Minister," in *The Complete Writings of Menno Simons*, 441.

45. Simons, *Complete Writings*, 200.

46. Lea, *History of Sacredotal Celibacy*, 378.

47. Jonathan Edwards, *A Faithful Narrative of the Surprising Work of God in The Great Awakening*, edited by C. C. Goen (New Haven: Yale University Press, 1972), 149, emphasis added.

48. Jonathan Edwards, *Religious Affections* (New Haven: Yale University Press, 1959), 89.

49. Philipp Jakob Spener, *Pia Desideria,* translated by T. Tappert (Philadelphia: Fortress, 1967), 13.

50. Ibid., 87, 92, 116ff.

51. John Wesley, "Christian Perfection," in *Readings in Christian Thought,* edited by Hugh Kerr (Nashville: Abingdon, 1990), 195–196.

52. See *The Works of John Wesley,* edited by Albert C. Outler (Nashville: Abingdon, 1967).

53. Karl Barth, *Church Dogmatics,* vol. 3, part 4 (Edinburgh: T. & T. Clark, 1961), 141.

54. Ibid., 144.

55. Ibid., 141.

56. Ibid., 141, 143.

57. Ibid., 144.

58. Ibid., 148.

7

Islamic Tradition and Celibacy

Shahzad Bashir

It may seem, on first consideration, that there is not much to be said about celibacy in the Islamic tradition. Qur'anic verses as well as Muhammad's sayings—including the famous "There is no monasticism in Islam"—express disapproval of restricting sexual activity permanently for religious ends and, on occasion, even enjoin sexual relations between men and women in legitimate relationships as a religious obligation.[1] These canonical statements find frequent mention in the work of medieval and modern Muslim authors, who sometimes present the rejection of celibacy as Islam's distinguishing feature in comparison with competing religions such as Christianity and Buddhism. Muslims have also never developed widespread socioreligious institutions featuring celibacy, and choosing a life of permanent continence has not been, by itself, an established path toward prestige and power in any majority Muslim society.

These facts about the general Islamic orientation toward celibacy are significant, but to leave the matter here would amount to espousing oversimplified views of Islamic thought and the vastly diverse historical realities that have characterized the lives of Muslims over time.[2] Islam emerged from a religious milieu with a long-standing tradition of religious celibacy, and Muslims have continued to engage with the idea in multiple forms over the course of more than fourteen centuries. The place of celibacy in Islamic thought and practice is thus necessarily quite complex. To provide a concrete sense of this, I will treat here three different contexts in which the practice has held a significant place in Muslim understandings. My aim is not to list the numerous cases of famous Muslim men and women who can be shown to have led celibate lives. Instead, I am interested in structural issues surrounding celibacy that can be understood by paying attention to discussions in religious texts as well as by reflecting on historically documented practices in different Muslim societies. I should emphasize that I do not believe that there is a single Islamic position on celibacy or, indeed, any other complex human phenomenon. Rather, the question of celibacy allows us a window into the complicated ways in which Islamic thought and practice have evolved over time.

The three contexts I will treat are the following: celibacy as a component of ascetic practice among Sufis as discussed in classical Sufi sources; celibacy as a form of religious and social protest as adopted by antinomian Sufi groups in the later medieval period; and the relationship between forced celibacy and political power in medieval Islamic societies.[3] I begin with Sufism, a movement with a significant ascetic component that began in Islam's early centuries. Famous Sufi men and women from the past or the present who have chosen celibacy have done so most often to emphasize their ability to live out the imperative to reject the material world advocated in Sufi thought. Many classical Sufi authors concern themselves explicitly with celibacy, but evince a conflicted perspective: on one hand, they must heed the Qur'an and, more significantly, Muhammad's words and practices that reject celibacy; but on the other hand, renouncing material concerns seems to call automatically for celibacy because of its concomitants, the curbing of sexual desire and avoiding the burdens of having a family. In the end, most Sufis who discuss celibacy give their personal opinion on the issue but also emphasize that it is a personal choice faced by every aspiring ascetic. This advice regarding celibacy has worked well over time. Although temporary celibacy has more or less been the norm in the lives of Sufis, only a relatively small number have shunned marriage completely. As a matter of institutionalization, only one branch of the Bektashi Sufi order, influential in Turkey and Eastern Europe from the fifteenth century onward, has required its highest adepts to take a vow of permanent celibacy.

The second context I discuss below takes us to Sufis of a hue different from that of the disciplined ascetics and mystics who produced the immense corpus of literature associated with elite Sufism. Beginning in approximately the twelfth century CE, central Islamic lands from North Africa to India witnessed the rise of antinomian Sufi groups whose proponents adopted unconventional lifestyles as a form of radical critique of other Muslims. They felt that other

Sufis in particular had forsaken their religious obligation to shun the material world and had become devoted to materialistic pursuits. Such groups considered celibacy a mandatory condition for all members, and one among them, called the Haydaris, went as far as to mutilate their sexual organs to ensure it. For such groups, celibacy and other socially opprobrious behavior such as nakedness, shaving off all body hair, begging, and homelessness were ways to reject the claims of society on their minds and bodies.

As discussed in the third section below, celibacy of a different kind from that of the Sufis played a significant role in the functioning of Islamic political arrangements during the medieval period. The foremost case of such politically expedient celibacy was the use of eunuchs as highly placed military commanders and imperial officials in most dynastic empires that flourished in central Islamic lands from the eighth century to the coming of modernity. Eunuchs were male slaves of African or Slavic background who were castrated before being acquired by free Muslim elites and then educated and trained to act as the most trusted administrators of a dynasty or a family. The elites' trust in eunuchs derived fundamentally from the latter's forced celibacy: because they were deemed incapable of acquiring social connections that come with legitimate sexual relations and having children, they could be presumed to remain loyal to their elite patrons. In the religious sphere, the most important group of eunuchs were those entrusted with the guardianship of Islam's holy sanctuaries in Mecca and Medina for more than eight centuries (ca. 1100–1900). In a more limited female counterpart to the eunuchs, women associated with some Islamic ruling houses acquired special political functions through celibacy. Among the Iranian Safavids (1501–1722) and the Indian Mughals (1526–1857), some royal princesses who remained unmarried became royal consorts or the most trusted advisors to kings, who were their close male relatives.

The question of celibacy in Islamic practices relates to sexual desire as well as reproduction, both of which are considered normal aspects of human activity during particular stages of the life cycle. The case studies discussed below suggest that the practice of temporary or permanent celibacy in Islamic contexts is tied heavily to the personal status of the individuals who either choose to or are forced to be celibate. Consequently, whenever celibacy comes into play, we must attend not only to an abstainer's personal religious motivations but also to social factors such as gender, age, slave or free status, and so on, to understand its significance. The focus on celibacy thus provides a view into the larger dynamic between the world of ideas on the one hand and sociohistorical realities on the other.

Celibacy and Asceticism

In general, temporary and permanent celibacy hold quite different places in the Islamic context. Temporary celibacy is mandatory in a number of religious obligations, including in two of the so-called five pillars that form Islam's ritual base. During the month of Ramadan, Muslims are required to abstain from sexual relations during the strict daily fast that extends from daybreak to sundown. Similarly, those who travel to Mecca for the annual Hajj pilgrimage or the lesser pilgrimage called *'umra* are required to abstain from sexual relations while they are in the state of ritual consecration known as *ihram* for a number of days. Pilgrims must enter this state prior to crossing the threshold into the sacred region, and they leave it after fulfilling the necessary ritual requirements.[4] The obligation of celibacy during these rituals has often been extended to other rituals, such as Sufi forty-day retreats, and occasional vows of temporary celibacy have been a normal part of Islamic practice throughout history.[5]

In comparison with this, permanent celibacy has had a more complicated fate. There is no direct criticism against it in the Qur'an, although the text does exhort believers to get married and arrange matches for their dependents, including male and female slaves. Marriage is presumed to entail expense, and those believers who are unable to bear the cost are advised to be abstinent only "until God enriches them of his bounty" (24:33). The only encouragement toward celibacy thus stems from practical considerations rather than from a problem with the exercise of sexuality. Within marriage, if a man takes a vow of celibacy, the Qur'an states that this must not last more than four months. After this period, the woman can be granted a divorce if the man persists (2:226). Marriage and sexual intercourse thus appear as rights belonging to both men and women, something that is reinforced by the example of Muhammad, who married eleven women during his life. As can be seen in the many reports that show the Prophet advocating marriage, celibacy was not a value among the majority in Muhammad's own milieu or among Muslims of the first Islamic century who collected his traditions to use as models for their own lives.[6]

Although celibacy itself lacked significance in Muhammad's times, a few among his companions practiced a stringently ascetic lifestyle, and their example led to the development of a whole movement toward asceticism soon after the Prophet's death. This ascetic tendency eventually evolved into the full-blown mystical movement known as Sufism.[7] Among early Sufis, the person most readily identifiable as an advocate of permanent celibacy is Rabi'a al-'Adawiyya (d. 801), the prototype of female sainthood for later centuries. Most of our information for Rabi'a comes from fragments of her life preserved in works by authors who lived long after her death.[8] As best as we can tell, she was born in a very poor family in Basra, Iraq, and sold into slavery as a child after the death of her parents. She showed a remarkable aptitude toward asceticism from an early age, which compelled her owner to manumit her, so that she lived most of her adult life as a free person devoted to religious pursuits.

Rabi'a's most direct rejection of marriage occurs in her legendary dialogue with Hasan al-Basri (d. 728), an early Muslim intellectual and pious figure whom Sufis regard as an exemplar because of his world-denying attitude. A meeting between Rabi'a and Hasan is impossible on chronological grounds, but the way the encounter is described is instructive for understanding celibacy, particularly with respect to issues involving gender. Farid al-Din 'Attar (d. 1221) writes in his Persian work *Memorial of Saints* (*Tazkirat al-awliya'*): "It is related that Hasan said to Rabi'a, 'Are you inclined that we get married and tie the knot?' She said, 'The marriage knot can only tie one who exists. Here existence has left. I have passed from my own being and exist only through him [i.e., God]. I am completely from him and under his command. Therefore, the permission must be sought from him [and not me].' "[9] On the surface here, Rabi'a says that she cannot marry because she no longer exists as a normal person who is able to exercise her power over her own person. But the more significant message underlying her statement is that marriage would compromise her devotion to God by requiring her to expend time and effort in caring for a husband and possibly a family. It would be difficult to undervalue the significance of this issue for a woman living in a patriarchal setting. Like Rabi'a, many early Sufi women who led ascetic lives seem to have been of slave origin. Freed female slaves had more leeway to choose a celibate, and hence independent, life; first, the process of enslavement cut them off permanently from their natal families, and second, after manumission they were free of the obligation of upholding a family's honor. For a former slave woman who desired freedom of action, for purposes of religion or anything else, marriage would have been an inexpedient choice, since this would have bound her to obedience to a husband, familial duties, and the obligation to uphold the honor of her husband's family.[10]

Rabi'a is a major Sufi figure but exceptional because of her gender. Most early Sufi literature takes men as its standard and represents the male viewpoint exclusively when it comes to discussing sexuality or the responsibilities that become incumbent through marriage. Some handbooks of Sufi thought written in the period 950–1200 CE whose aim was to systemize Sufi ideas contain chapters on marriage and celibacy that claim to set forth the advantages and disadvantages of each practice. Basing themselves on traditions as well as appeals to rationality, these treatments of the question typically portray male sexual lust, inherent in the male psyche, as a problem. Their overall effort is to figure out how to limit the negative effects of sexual desire, particularly its ability to lead away from a singular concentration on God. This can be done through both celibacy and marriage, as argued in the following passage from the highly influential Arabic work *The Sustenance of the Hearts* (*Qut al-qulub*) by Abu Talib al-Makki (d. 996):

> God, may he be praised, has decreed neither marriage nor celibacy, just as he has not made it a duty that every man marry four women. But he has decreed integrity of heart, preservation of faith, a soul at peace, and the execution of commands needed for these. If one's rectitude resides in marriage then that is better for him. If one's uprightness and peacefulness of soul exist with four women, then it is allowable for him to seek his peace and a healthy disposition as long as he fulfills the obligatory conditions. If one is content with one woman then that one is better and more preferred for him since she is more appropriate for his well-being. And if one's healthful condition, integrity of heart, and peace of soul reside in celibacy then that is better for him, since these are the things that are desired of marriage. If one can reach these without marriage then celibacy causes no harm.[11]

Makki is particularly attentive to the weight of tradition, and this statement is preceded by a long discussion listing the various occasions on which Muhammad is supposed to have recommended marriage. He provides some evidence for celibacy as well, but overall he takes marriage to be the standard and allows celibacy only as long as it can be shown to do "no harm."

In comparison with Makki, the slightly later 'Ali b. Usman Hujwiri (d. ca. 1072) states in his Persian work *The Revelation of Mystery* (*Kashf al-mahjub*) that celibacy is the better of the two choices and that original Sufis were all celibate. He considers the appeal to Muhammad's traditions for preferring marriage nothing but a convenience adopted by those who cannot escape their lust, claiming that the Prophet also commanded Muslims toward poverty and spiritual combat, which are more consistent with celibacy. Hujwiri's critique of marriage involves a severe view of women as a class, blaming them for most dissension in the world and for causing men like himself to become ensnared by lust instead of following their higher calling.[12] This misogynistic streak is the norm in almost all works in the genre, where putting up with the wily charms and fractious and deceiving ways of women is presented as one of the trials of men's lives. Even when condoning marriage, Hujwiri's ideal is for both parties to remain celibate, as evident in his story of an earlier Sufi who visited a man and a woman living side by side but without any evidence of a traditional marital relationship. As he was about to leave he asked the old man:

> "What relation is this chaste woman to you?" He answered, "From one side my uncle's daughter from another my wife." I said, "During these three days your interactions with one another have been very like that of strangers." "Yes," said he, "it has been so for sixty-five years." I asked him the cause of this. He replied: "When we were young we fell in love, but her father would not give her to me, for he discovered our fondness for each other. I bore this sorrow for a long while, but on her father's death, my father, who was her uncle, gave me her hand. On the wedding night she said to me: 'You know what happiness God has bestowed upon us in bringing us together and taking all fear away from our hearts. Let us therefore tonight refrain from sensual passion and trample on our desires and worship God in thanksgiving for this happiness.' I said, 'Yes.' Next night she bade me to do the same. On the third night I said, 'Now we have given thanks for two nights for your sake; tonight let us worship God for my sake.' Sixty-five years have passed since then, and we have never touched one another, but spend all our lives in giving thanks for our happiness."[13]

This author thus places celibacy at the very center of Sufi practice. For him conquering sexual lust and the desire for the power that comes with children are necessary preconditions for becoming a true exemplar of the religious path.

One of the most systematic medieval treatments of marriage and celibacy is found in the work of the great scholar and Sufi Muhammad al-Ghazzali (d. 1111), who cites heavily from previous authors such as Makki but brings in other considerations. He assigns five advantages to marriage for men: procreation, warding off excess sexual desire through regulated intercourse in marriage, the comfort and strength that comes from close companionship with another human being, the provision of a wife who takes care of the household, and the opportunity to develop one's reserves of patience and teaching ability through bearing the personalities of women and trying to reform their habits. In comparison, there are three dangers that come with marriage: the necessity of providing for one's dependants can lead one to benefit from unlawful gains; failing to uphold the rights of wives can cause a sense of personal failure; and demands of family life can distract one from God.[14]

For Ghazzali, the best path is to get married and maximize its advantages and minimize the disadvantages. His view is thus substantially different from that of Hujwiri, or even Makki, since he does not endorse celibacy as a viable meritorious path. This is in part because of his understanding of human nature and the construction of the human body. He argues that God was perfectly capable of creating the human species without sexual desire and the need for the use of human sexual organs in order to reproduce. Since he chose not to do so, and, instead, made sexual attraction an inescapable feature of human minds and bodies, there can be nothing wrong with the exercise of sexual capacity. Thus, a person who "marries is seeking to complete what God has desired, and the one who abstains, wastes away what God detests to have wasted."[15] The same theme is echoed by the famous Sufi poet Jalal al-Din Rumi (d. 1274) in his *Masnavi*, where he makes coupling a necessary principle of all existence:

> If there is no friendship between walls
> How can houses and lofty buildings come together?
> If each wall stands apart
> How can the roof remain suspended in the air?
> Without aid from ink and pen
> How can writing appear on the paper's surface?
> This mat that someone spreads in front of us
> Wind would rush away without the intertwining of its warp and woof
> Since for every genus God has created two spouses,
> All results come about by means of unions.[16]

Celibacy then appears as an unnatural choice that goes against both tradition and common logic. Most Sufi practitioners since the time of Ghazzali and Rumi have taken this view on the question of celibacy. They have accepted marriage as a desirable necessity, echoing the words of the early master Junayd (d. 909–910) who reportedly said, "I need sexual intercourse like I need sustenance."[17] There have, nevertheless, been others who have chosen to be celibate, although usually without requiring this of their followers or giving the choice a special value.[18]

A survey of the lives of Sufis who have chosen celibacy over the majority practice indicates that there is a significant structural difference between its implications for men and for women. Among males, vows of celibacy are usually part of the effort to curb sexual desire and include extraordinary efforts to avoid meeting or seeing women.[19] Such mental repression can cause anguish, but in the social sphere, celibacy only occasions the loss of power that may come from not establishing marital connections and having children. The choice to be celibate does not necessarily lead to a loss or gain in men's power over their own persons, an issue that plays out quite differently for women. In patrilineal and patriarchal settings, women move between families headed by men and have much less control over their persons than do men. When available, the choice to remain unmarried can increase a woman's power over her self, making her equal in status to a man. This issue in part explains the celibacy of women such as Rabi'a and others, who are shown interacting as equals with men in early Sufi narratives. A case for this comes also from the story of a Sufi woman named Lalla Zainab (1850–1904), who presided over an affluent Sufi community in Algeria between 1897 and 1904. A significant part of her ability to counter the claims of male relatives derived from the fact that her father regarded her as his successor, and she never married or came under the authority of a male protector in any other way.[20] Women's celibacy is indexed also to the preservation of virginity as a marker of purity, which does not have a similarly valorized male equivalent. This is strikingly evident in the fact that Muhammad's daughter Fatima (d. 632–633) is popularly known among Muslims as the virgin (*batul*) despite the fact that she was married to Muhammad's cousin 'Ali (d. 661) and bore children who founded the only surviving genealogical lines descending from the Prophet. In this context, it seems that a powerful woman has to be regarded as a celibate virgin despite all historical and logical evidence to the contrary.[21]

Celibacy as Social Critique

Starting in the twelfth century CE, a wide swath of Islamic societies from Egypt to India saw the deployment of celibacy as a part of an overall Sufi program substantially different from the kinds of perspectives I have discussed so far. This occurred in the context of the rise of antinomian Sufi groups whose members took it upon themselves to live out the Sufi ideal of poverty and withdrawal from the material world to an extent not evident in prior epochs. Whereas earlier Sufis had practiced asceticism at varying levels, these new Sufis sought to abandon all normative social behavior and, more significantly, flaunt this abandonment in public through practices deemed reprehensible by a majority of the population. Members of these groups went out of their way to wear their religious perspectives on their bodies: they wore no clothing (or an absolute minimum), made a public show of not observing Islamic rituals and dietary strictures, and sometimes used intoxicants openly, to the shock of onlookers. Besides making a mockery of mainstream life, these groups wished to renounce participation in any form of reproduction of society, which included a total commitment to celibacy.

The antinomian movement took its start from the example of radical ascetics who separated themselves from society and attempted to live out, as literally as possible, Muhammad's supposed instruction to his followers to "die before you die." Under mainstream Sufi conditions, this saying implied that Sufis should die to the concerns of the material world through reigning in their concupiscent desires. What was sought, therefore, was a metaphorical death to the material world before physical death. The ascetic virtuosi whose example germinated the antinomian movement took the command more literally, attempting to mortify not just the desires of their minds but also as many aspects of their bodies as could be managed without causing physical death itself. This led to severe fasting and living in graveyards; giving up all clothing even in extreme weather and, at best, wearing animal skins or shirts made of goat hair; absolute refusal to seek any gainful employment; complete severing of ties with family; and denying all desire for sex and children. Over the course of time (and despite the obvious intentions of the virtuosi themselves), these masters began to see developing around themselves communities of followers who attempted to replicate this mode of religious expression. In the approximate period 1200–1500, the social expansion of such groups resulted in the growth of itinerant as well as settled bands of antinomian Sufis who regenerated themselves not through normal human reproduction but by attracting members from all levels of society with kindred views. Some of these groups underwent further institutionalization in later centuries, although that also led to some degree of accommodation to the strictures of normative society.[22]

Antinomian Sufis' religious views precluded writing expositions of their ideology, and our understanding of them derives largely from sources external to the traditions themselves. A rare internal source that describes the life of Jamal al-Din Savi (d. ca. 1232), the inspiration for a group known as the Qalandars, states that he first trained as a mainstream Sufi and a scholar before being attracted to the antinomian path during an encounter with an ascetic in a graveyard in Damascus. All his body hair fell out by divine intervention at the moment of his conversion, and from this point onward he cultivated a bodily aspect that mimicked the condition of a corpse. The author of a verse hagiography in Persian devoted to him purports the master to have proclaimed:

> Die to yourself so that you are set free
> Since no acquaintance ever comes around when one is dead
> Ever since we have died to the world and ourselves
> We have given up the world to those who desire it
> Anyone who wishes to see our trace
> Must leave his world to come to that of the dead
> Ever since this face of ours has become the picture of death
> There is no one left who would have the power of death over us.[23]

Celibacy fits well with this self-portrait, since a dead body has neither sexual desire nor the possibility of procreating through intercourse.

Another antinomian group, founded on the inspiration of Qutb al-Din Haydar (d. ca. 1200) of Zava, Iran, took the matter of celibacy one step further through specific bodily practices directed at sexual functions. Haydar is said to have lived all his mature life in the wilderness, removed from all social interaction, and using only leaves to cover his body. He also made a habit of immersing himself in ice water in winter and walking into fires in summer in order to control his bodily desires. He and his followers are associated particularly with the use of iron, and he is supposed to have had the power to mold the metal with his hands as if it were wax. The Haydaris, his followers, made a point of wearing iron collars, bracelets, and bells to mark this association. Some Haydaris pierced their genitalia with iron rings to preclude any possibility of sexual intercourse.[24]

The antinomian style of Sufism saw its heyday during the period 1200–1500. This correlates with the fact that Sufism underwent extensive institutionalization in these centuries, when famous Sufi masters became major power brokers in the religious, political, and economic life of Muslim societies throughout central Islamic lands.[25] The antinomians are best understood as a reaction against this institutionalization, which they saw as a cooptation of Sufism by worldly people. Although diminished in numbers and social significance, antinomian Sufis have continued to be present in Muslim societies down to the present. Extensive information survives about a Syrian dervish named Abu Bakr b. Abi al-Wafa' (1503–1583), who made his abode in a cemetery outside the city of Aleppo and presided over a community of celibate Sufis.[26] All information about such groups in the premodern period mentions only male actors, but an anthropologist working in the Pakistani city of Lahore in the 1970s reports meeting women antinomian Sufis as well, indicating that they may have been incorporated in such groups at least occasionally.[27]

The only Islamic group to have instituted celibacy as a condition for holding the highest status is one branch of the Bektashi Sufi order that has its roots in the antinomian piety of the later medieval period.[28] The Bektashis trace their origins to Hajji Bektash Vali (d. ca. 1271), an Iranian Sufi with ecstatic tendencies who settled and died in central Anatolia in present-day Turkey. The Bektashis known from Ottoman lands in the fifteenth century exhibited the socially deviant posture characteristic of other antinomian groups. However, they began to institutionalize and became mainstream under the leadership of a master named Balım Sultan (d. ca. 1519) who is buried near the grave of Hajji Bektash himself in the village of Hacıbektaş in central Anatolia.[29] Balım Sultan is claimed to have instituted the initiation rites of a suborder of celibate masters and, since his time, Bektashis have had both celibate and noncelibate leaders. The celibate branch has held particular prestige in Albania, a former Ottoman province where the Bektashi order began to take root among the Muslim population beginning in the sixteenth century.[30] A celibate Baba or master in the Bektashi milieu is identifiable because of a special earring that used to be inserted in a ceremony of investiture at the threshold of Balım Sultan's tomb until the early twentieth century. The rite has since been transferred to other major Bektashi lodges in Albania and elsewhere. Celibate Bektashi Babas continue to be prominent in the religious and political life of modern Albania. One among them, named Baba Rexheb, was transplanted into the migrant Albanian community in Taylor, Michigan. He took the vow of celibacy at the age of twenty-one in 1922 in Albania, and presided over the American hospice between 1954 and 1995. Another celibate initiate named Baba Flamur Shkalla currently leads the community. When criticized for being celibate, and hence childless, he once responded with the retort "Do you think all children are the children of the flesh?"[31] A celibate Bektashi master's position in the community is thus like that of a spiritual father whose very celibacy marks his commitment to the whole community rather than a personal family. Interestingly, this marks an inversion of the meaning of celibacy among the medieval antinomian groups from which the Bektashi order is derived. The radical Sufis became celibate to mark their disassociation from the reproduction of society, while the Bektashi Babas mediate all aspects of society as leaders of noncelibate communal groups.

Celibacy and the Political Sphere

The most radical form of celibacy encountered in the setting of premodern Islamic societies is the widespread use of castrated slaves as trusted servants by ruling houses and the elites from the eighth century until the modern period. Muslim rulers inherited this institution from Near Eastern imperial cultures in place before the rise of Islam. Islamic law prohibits forcible castration, which meant that boys and young men of African and Slavic origins were made eunuchs before entering Islamic domains and, for the same legal reason, Christian doctors usually performed the operation. After being bought, the slaves were vetted for innate aptitudes and then given extensive education and training to become the most trusted protectors and administrators of elite families. In time, the trust invested them meant that they enjoyed many material privileges in the empire and led a life of comfort. However, this came at a severe price: unlike others in society, they had no past in the form of a natal family because of enslavement, and they had no biological future because they could not have children. They were, thus, individuals suspended in time, whose social existence was limited to the years of their own lives.[32]

The value as well as the sacrifice of being a eunuch in the medieval Islamic world can be illustrated by the dramatic case of the Hungarian Gazenfer Agha and his brother Jafer, who were Christian renegades who converted to Islam and were assimilated into the ranks of the ruling class of the Ottoman dynasty. They became confidants to the Prince Selim, who invited them to become members of his household when he ascended the throne as sultan in 1566. As unrelated males, they could do so only by becoming eunuchs, since otherwise their greater loyalty would be presumed to lie with their own households rather than with the dynasty. They thus voluntarily agreed to be castrated, though Jafer died from the operation. Gazenfer, however, "went on to hold two most important offices of the inner service: chief white eunuch and head of the privy chamber. He was one of the most influential persons in government for a period of more than thirty years spanning the reigns of Selim, his son, and his grandson, a tenure longer than that of any grand vezir [prime minister]."[33]

Ruling houses usually employed eunuchs for the preservation of their personal power, but beginning in the twelfth century, the Mamluk rulers of Egypt in particular started appointing eunuchs as guardians of tombs and shrines. Begun at the tomb of the Prophet in Medina, this custom eventually spread to the graves of other religious dignitaries and kings, as well as to the Ka'ba in Mecca, the cubelike shrine that is arguably the symbolic center for the Islamic world. As discussed by Shaun Marmon, the appointment of the eunuchs to religious sanctuaries shows the intersection of a number of factors. To begin with, eunuchs were closely associated with royal power, so that instituting them as guardians of shrines was seen as a way to highlight the importance of the places in question. They were also well suited to the job of maintaining order in the sanctuaries because it was unproblematic for them to cross the boundary between the worlds of men and women. Both in Mecca and Medina, men and women perform rituals together without a strict demarcation of male as against female space. And eunuchs also invoked the world of the dead because of their lack of genealogical connections. In a social context intensely concerned with ancestry and children, individuals deprived of such connections appeared to be virtually dead when seen from the viewpoint of social existence. This quality was seen to be reflected in their physical appearance caused by the lack of male hormones: they usually had no facial hair and, in old age, they suffered from excessively wrinkled skin and bodily deformities caused by osteoporosis.[34]

Evidence from medieval sources indicates that, for eunuchs, being sent to the service of the shrines could be regarded as a special religious boon.

Although this meant being removed from the circles of power surrounding the royal household in the capital or governors' households in provincial centers, the appointment meant acquiring a special proximity to God and the Prophet. From the middle of twelfth century, the tomb of the Prophet in particular was guarded by a society of some forty eunuchs installed in their positions in perpetuity. Members of the society held a particular aura of religious authority since they controlled access to the power (*baraka*) of the sacred shrine. This society enacted ceremonials at the shrine in addition to protecting it, and it also acted as a corporate entity with vested interests, mimicking the functions of a normal family. Through membership in the society, eunuchs who were ordinarily deprived of family connections acquired long-term stakes in the protection and perpetuation of a venerable institution. By becoming attached to Muhammad's shrine eunuchs became, in a way, members of the Prophet's family, acquiring a special religious position that contrasted with their status as individuals who were otherwise deemed deficient in their capacity as fully functional human beings because of the mutilation inflicted on their bodies early in life.

Eunuchs' situation in medieval Islamic political systems was tied fundamentally to their gender. They were expected to perform functions expected of men, but they lacked the liabilities that, in the eyes of the political elites, came with employing free and sexually and reproductively capable men. There is thus no equivalent to eunuchs in the female sphere except for the very limited practice reported from some Islamic dynasties whereby highly educated princesses remained unmarried throughout their lives and, because of this, held positions of power within dynastic and governmental affairs. There are two well-known cases of this in the Iranian Safavid dynasty: the princess Mahin Banu (d. 1561–1562), sister of the king Tahmasp (d. 1576), was betrothed to the mythical figure of the Twelfth Imam as a way to ensure that she would not acquire a real husband. Later, Tahmasp's unmarried daughter Zaynab Begum (d. 1642) had considerable influence in the court of her nephew Shah 'Abbas (d. 1629). A similar pattern can be seen among the Indian Mughals, contemporaries of the Safavids, where the princesses Gulbadan Begum (d. 1603), daughter of the emperor Humayun (d. 1556), and Jahanara Begum (d. 1681), daughter of Shahjahan (d. 1658) and sister to Aurangzeb (d. 1707), never married and exercised considerable political influence.[35] A similar practice is reported also among feudal Sayyid families in Sind province in southern Pakistan, where daughters can be "married to the Qur'an" in order to prevent them making a match that would lead to adulteration of genealogy and the division of property.[36]

Conclusion

The examples I have discussed here strikingly reveal the close connection between celibacy and death in Islamic contexts. Sufi ascetics who began to discuss celibacy as a religious option in the early Islamic centuries were concerned with a proper balance between dying to material concerns and continuing physiological existence. Antinomian Sufis took this issue to its logical conclusion by taking on the characteristics associated with dead bodies. Eunuchs occupied a position simultaneously special and pathetic because of their perceived lack of a past or a future, and they became heavily associated with the graves of those who held religious or political power in the past. These correlations reinforce the socially contextual nature of all sexual activity and its restriction. Whether by choice or by force, restraining sexual desire and procreation is a major defining factor in a human being's profile as a social actor.

These cases reflect also on the malleability of celibacy's meaning for human individual as well as collective life. Depending on social factors, such as gender, or particular sociohistorical situations, celibacy and its association with death can be both empowering and disempowering in terms of personal or social goals. There can thus be no single valorization of celibacy in Islamic contexts. To understand its deployment in any given context, we must pay attention to many different factors, ranging between religious ideology, social institutions and situations, and specific historical circumstances.

NOTES

1. For discussions of the origins and history of the "no monasticism" report, see Louis Massignon, *Essay on the Origins of the Technical Language of Islamic Mysticism*, translated by Benjamin Clark (South Bend: University of Notre Dame Press, 1997), 98–104; and Jane Dammen McAuliffe, *Qur'anic Christians: An Analysis of Classical and Modern Exegesis* (Cambridge: Cambridge University Press, 1991), 263–284.

2. Unfortunately, such oversimplification is a persistent feature of existing discussions of celibacy in Islamic contexts. See, for example, Elizabeth Abbott, *A History of Celibacy* (New York: Da Capo, 2001), 194–195.

3. My comments here are limited to celibacy in the context of heterosexual relationships. The available space does not allow me to enter into a discussion of the complex place of homoeroticism, and allowances and restrictions regarding homosexuality, in Islamic contexts. For a recent overview of issues relevant to this topic, see Khaled el-Rouayheb, *Before Homosexuality in the Arab-Islamic World, 1500–1800* (Chicago: University of Chicago Press, 2005). I am also concerned only with celibacy as

the restriction of sexual acts and desires by individuals for whom sex, and its possible result in the form of children, represents an allowable possibility by the social milieu in which they live. That is, I do not treat the taboo on premarital heterosexual sex as an instance of celibacy. This is not to overlook the fact that such sexual activity can (and does) occur in Muslim societies. However, there is little that can be said about such celibacy beside the fact that it is taken to be the norm in most Muslims societies.

4. For the details of these rituals, see David Waines, *An Introduction to Islam* (Cambridge: Cambridge University Press, 1995), 89–93.

5. For a slightly outdated but still useful discussion of such practices, see Louis Massignon, "Mystique et continence en Islam," *Etudes Carmélitaines* 1 (1952): 93–100.

6. These traditions are collected together in the chapters on marriage (*nikah*) in canonical Sunni collections of hadith such as Bukhari (book 62) and Muslim (book 8). Such traditions were used extensively in later Muslim discussions of the advantages and disadvantages of marriage. See, for example, Muhammad al-Ghazzali, *Marriage and Sexuality in Islam: A Translation of al-Ghazali's Book on the Etiquette of Marriage from the Ihya'* (Salt Lake City: University of Utah Press, 1984).

7. For the general background to the development of Sufism, see Alexander Knysh, *Islamic Mysticism: A Short History* (Leiden: E. J. Brill, 2000); and, for the question of the relationship between asceticism and mysticism, Christopher Melchert, "The Transition from Asceticism to Mysticism at the Middle of the Ninth Century CE," *Studia Islamica* 83 (1996): 51–70.

8. For a survey of Rabi'a's image, see Barbara Lois Helm, "Rabi'ah as Mystic, Muslim, and Woman," *Annual Review of Women in World Religions*, 3 (1994): 1–87.

9. Farid al-Din 'Attar, *Tazkirat al-awliya'*, edited by R. A. Nicholson (Tehran: Intisharat-i Safi 'Ali Shah, 2003), 71. This work exists in multiple versions with significant differences. For an alternative version, which nevertheless has a similar rejection of marriage, see the text translated by Paul Losensky in Michael Sells, *Early Islamic Mysticism* (New York: Paulist Press, 1996), 161–162.

10. For more examples of such women in the early Islamic period, see Jamal Elias, "The Female and the Feminine in Islamic Mysticism," *Muslim World* 78.3–4 (1988): 209–224; and Abu 'Abd ar-Rahman as-Sulami, *Early Sufi Women: Dhikr an-niswa al-muta'abbidat as-suffiyat*, translated by Rkia Cornell (Louisville: Fons Vitae, 1999).

11. Abu Talib al-Makki, *Qut al-qulub*, 2 vols. (Cairo: Mustafa al-Babi al-Halabi, 1961), 2: 528. For a German translation of this text along with explanatory notes, see Richard Gramlich, *Die Nahrung der Herzen*, 4 vols. (Stuttgart: Franz Steiner Verlag, 1992–1995), 3: 601–602.

12. 'Ali b. 'Usman Hujwiri, *Revelation of the Mystery*, translated by R. A. Nicholson (New York: Pir Press, 1999), 364. For a more extensive discussion of misogyny in medieval Arabic literature (including a celibate and male-only utopia), see Fedwa Malti-Douglas, *Woman's Body, Woman's Word: Gender and Discourse in Arabo-Islamic Writing* (Princeton: Princeton University Press, 1991).

13. 'Ali b. 'Usman Hujwiri, *Kashf al-mahjub*, edited by Muhammad Husayn Tasbihi (Lahore: Saman Publications, 1995), 524–525. The cited text is a slightly modified version of the translation given in *Revelation of the Mystery*, 362–363.

14. Ghazzali, *Marriage and Sexuality in Islam*, 53–77.

15. Ibid., 54–55.

16. Jalal al-Din Rumi, *Masnavi-yi ma'navi*, edited by R. A. Nicholson (Tehran: Nashr-i Muhammad, 1995), 920 (verses 519–523). For a complete (but archaic) translation of this passage and the story within which it occurs, see R. A. Nicholson, *The Mathnawi of Jalalu'ddin Rumi*, 6 vols. (London: Gibb Memorial Trust, 1982), 6: 286.

17. Makki, *Qut al-qulub*, 2: 495, and repeated in many later sources.

18. A particularly noteworthy case is Khwaja Nizam al-Din Awliya' (d. 1325), the great master belonging to the Chishti order buried near Delhi, India, who remained celibate throughout his long life on the basis of a command from his master received when he was very young; Carl Ernst and Bruce Lawrence, *Sufi Martyrs of Love: The Chishti Order in South Asia and Beyond* (New York: Palgrave, 2002), 75. Celibacy could sometimes also be a personal choice for a scholar without any religious reasoning, as in the case of the famous jurist and anti-Sufi polemicist Ibn Taymiyya (d. 1328), who apparently never married because it would have taken time away from the pursuit of intellectual causes; David Little, "Did Ibn Taymiyya Have a Screw Loose?" *Studia Islamica* 41 (1975): 105.

19. See, for example, Christopher Taylor, *In the Vicinity of the Righteous: Ziyara and the Veneration of Muslim Saints in Late Medieval Egypt* (Leiden: E. J. Brill, 1999), 93–95, and articles by Jürgen Wasim Frembgen and Katherine Ewing in Pnina Werbner and Helene Basu, eds., *Embodying Charisma: Modernity, Locality and the Performance of Emotion in Sufi Cults* (London: Routledge, 1998).

20. Julia Clancy-Smith, "The House of Zainab: Female Authority and Saintly Succession in Colonial Algeria," in *Women in Middle Eastern History: Shifting Boundaries in Sex and Gender*, edited by Nikki Keddie and Beth Baron (New Haven: Yale University Press, 1991), 254–274.

21. For a summary of the history of Fatima's image, see Laura Veccia Vaglieri, "Fatimah," *Encyclopedia of Islam*, 2nd edition, s.v. For the obvious comparison to be made between Fatima and Mary on this score, see Jane Smith and Yvonne Haddad, "The Virgin Mary in Islamic Tradition and Commentary," *Muslim World* 79.3–4 (1989): 161–187.

22. The most sophisticated treatment of this phenomenon, to which I owe much of my presentation, is Ahmet Karamustafa, *God's Unruly Friends: Dervish Groups in the Islamic Later Middle Period, 1200–1500* (Salt Lake City: University of Utah Press, 1994).

23. Khatib-i Farsi, *Manakib-i Camal al-Din-i Savi*, edited by Tahsin Yazıcı (Ankara: Türk Tarih Kurumu Basımevi, 1972), 45.

24. Karamustafa, *God's Unruly Friends*, 44–46, 67–70. For the internal antinomian justifications for the use of iron and practices relating to the body, see also Persian texts from the Safavid period edited in Sayyid Abu Talib Mir-'Abidini and

Mihran Afshari, eds., *Ayin-i qalandari* (Tehran: Intisharat-i Fararavan, 1996). I am grateful to Farooq Hamid for alerting me to this publication.

25. For a detailed analysis of Sufi intellectual and social life during this period in the Persianate sphere, see my forthcoming work *Bodies of God's Friends: Corporeality and Sainthood in Sufi Islam.*

26. Heghnar Watenpaugh, "Deviant Dervishes: Space, Gender and the Construction of Antinomian Piety in Ottoman Aleppo," *International Journal of Middle East Studies* 37.4 (November 2005): 535–565.

27. Katherine Ewing, *Arguing Sainthood: Modernity, Psychoanalysis, and Islam* (Durham, N.C.: Duke University Press, 1997), 209–217.

28. Ahmet Karamustafa, "*Kalenders, Abdals, Hayderis*: The Formation of the Bektaşiye in the Sixteenth Century," in *Süleyman the Second and His Time,* edited by Halil İnalcık and Cemal Kafadar (Istanbul: Isis Press, 1993), 121–129.

29. John Kingsley Birge, *The Bektashi Order of Dervishes* (London: Luzac, 1937), 56–58.

30. Robert Elsie, *A Dictionary of Albanian Religion, Mythology, and Folk Culture* (New York: New York University Press, 2001), 25–34.

31. Frances Trix, *Spiritual Discourse: Learning with an Islamic Master* (Philadelphia: University of Pennsylvania Press, 1993), 160 n. 4. For Baba Rexheb's interactions with other Muslim groups, see Frances Trix, "Bektashi Tekke and the Sunni Mosque of Albanian Muslims in America," in *Muslim Communities in North America,* edited by Yvonne Yazbeck Haddad and Jane Idleman Smith (Albany: State University of New York Press, 1994), 359–380.

32. For the general background to the use of eunuchs in Islamic political culture, see Jane Hathaway, *Beshir Agha: Chief Eunuch of the Ottoman Imperial Harem* (Oxford: OneWorld, 2005), 7–27.

33. Leslie Peirce, *The Imperial Harem: Women and Sovereignty in the Ottoman Empire* (New York: Oxford University Press, 1993), 12.

34. These and other themes are discussed in various places in Shaun Marmon, *Eunuchs and Sacred Boundaries in Islamic Society* (New York: Oxford University Press, 1995).

35. Kishwar Rizvi, "Gendered Patronage: Women and Benevolence during the Early Safavid Empire," in *Women, Patronage, and Self-Representation in Islamic Societies,* edited by D. Fairchild Ruggles (Albany: State University of New York Press, 2000), 128, 148 n. 28. The author incorrectly identifies Jahanara as the daughter of Akbar rather than of Shahjahan.

36. Such marriages are a subject of critique by human rights activists in Pakistan (www.islamawareness.net/Marriage/Qur'an/married.html, viewed August 10, 2006). The question of division of property is particularly significant since, according to Islamic law, daughters have inalienable shares in parents' property.

8

Celibacy in Classical Hinduism

Patrick Olivelle

A cross-cultural study of a religious institution, such as the one embarked upon in this volume with respect to celibacy, runs the risk of comparing incomparables or of speaking about disparate phenomena. Indeed, until the twentieth century the term "celibate" simply referred to an unmarried person, and "celibacy" to the state of a bachelor. Even the new *Oxford English Dictionary* (1989) defines celibacy as "the state of living unmarried" and celibate as "unmarried, single, bound not to marry." It is only in this last phrase that one detects a shift in meaning from fact to obligation. *The American Heritage Dictionary* (2000) on the other hand, sees "abstaining from sexual intercourse" as the primary meaning of celibate in contemporary usage; 68 percent of its panel of experts rejected the older meaning of bachelor or unmarried. Clearly, the religious use of the term has penetrated the common usage; a celibate is not simply an unmarried person but one who has resolved not to get married, especially for religious reasons. A further problem emerges in differentiating celibacy from its companion term "chastity." The new *OED* defines "chaste" as "pure from unlawful sexual intercourse; continent, virtuous." Yet dictionaries give further meanings of "chaste" to include "celibate," "virginal," and "abstaining from all sexual intercourse," bringing its meaning close to that of celibate. Clearly, we have two terms with a considerable semantic overlap, yet having their own distinctive meanings as well. We can, for example, speak of a chaste wife; it would cause consternation to hear someone speak about a celibate wife.

As a broad distinction, I see celibacy as a social institution; social expectations are created when a person is in a celibate institution or state of life. These expectations are often codified in rules, sometimes with judicial sanction. Thus, for example, in classical India a celibate ascetic in India who gets married (that is, becomes a noncelibate) faces the judicial sanction of becoming the king's slave.[1] A Buddhist monk engaging in sexual intercourse faces the communal sanction of either public penance or expulsion from the community. Chastity, on the other hand, I see as primarily an inner quality; the dictionary definition of "virtuous" points to this characteristic. Clearly, religious institutions dedicated to a celibate mode of life would expect their members to cultivate the inner virtue of chastity, of which the external life of celibacy is a manifestation and affirmation. Chastity, on the other hand, may be practiced without belonging to a celibate institution, as in the case of young persons avoiding premarital sex. Chastity may not always imply complete abstinence from sex, as in the case of the "chaste wife." As a social institution, moreover, celibacy can have social and ideological dimensions different from simple chastity, such as negating the religious value of the institution of marriage and of procreating children.

The confusion between social institution and inner virtue is found also in the ancient Indian discourses on the topic of sexual abstinence. In fact, there is no Sanskrit word for celibacy that would distinguish it from chastity. Monier-Williams, in his dictionary of English and Sanskrit, under "celibacy/celibate" gives seven Sanskrit terms.[2] These are probably terms coined by him; they are never encountered in any Sanskrit discourse on celibacy. The only Sanskrit terms that approximate celibacy/celibate and chastity/chaste is *brahmacarya* and *brahmacārin*. This is true of both the Brahmanical and the Buddhist vocabularies. Etymologically these terms have nothing to do with sexuality; originally they referred to the period following Vedic initiation when the newly initiated adolescent spent several years as a student memorizing the Veda. Such an initiated student was expected to live a strictly chaste/celibate life, and this is the probable reason why the term *brahmacarya* came to refer principally to the student's vow of chastity/celibacy and, by extension, to the celibate lives of Indian ascetics in general. It appears, nevertheless, that this term refers more specifically to the virtue of chastity, although the unmarried and celibate status of the persons in these institutions is clearly part of its semantic range.[3] This is also true of its use in the context of temporary vows that individuals may take as part of their religious regimen. The semantic restriction of *brahmacarya* to celibacy/chastity is indicated in its use in the central vow of Buddhist monks consisting of the ten precepts, where a monk takes the vow to refrain from *abrahmacarya,* that is, offense against chastity.

Thus, there is no term in Sanskrit that directly and exclusively refers to the celibate, that is, the unmarried status of individuals in a variety of religious institutions. Both because of the way our sources deal with the issue, therefore, and because of the large semantic overlap between celibacy and chastity even in contemporary usage, scholarly as well as general, I will address these two areas simultaneously.

Celibate Ideologies and Institutions

The very term *brahmacarya* used in widely different celibate traditions points to the paradigmatic nature of Vedic studentship as the model of celibate living. Yet the period of studentship was generally temporary and, indeed, preparatory to getting married and raising a family as a householder.[4] This institution of celibacy was not ideologically opposed to either the institution or the value system of marriage, sexual engagement, and procreation, but preparatory to it.

Around the middle of the first millennium BCE in the fertile plains watered by the two large rivers of north-central India, the Gaṅgā and the Yamunā, new ideologies and institutions arose that challenged the centrality of the married household life and the significance of children within a religious ideology or system of values. The religious history of India prior to this watershed period is known to us primarily through the literary documents known collectively as the Veda, the Hindu equivalent of revealed scripture. These were produced by a relatively small group of male priests (Brahmins) and largely reflect their priorities, interests, and concerns. Given the prominent, and even hegemonic, role Brahmins have played in the intellectual, cultural, political, and religious history of India, however, the religious ideology presented in the Veda becomes significant for the development of celibate institutions and ideologies.

The ideal and typical religious life within Vedic theology is that of a married householder.[5] The normative character of that life is related to two theologically central religious activities: offering sacrifices and procreating children. Only a married householder, according to that theology, was entitled and qualified to perform either of them. The sacrifice came to be viewed as the source of creative power and the font of immortality for gods and humans. Children, especially sons, were also viewed as ensuring the immortality of the father. Already in the most ancient text of Brahmanism, the *Ṛgveda* (5.4.10) we find the prayer: "Through offspring, O Fire, may we attain immortality."

The completion of a man requires a wife: "A full half of one's self is one's wife. As long as one does not obtain a wife, therefore, for so long one is not reborn and remains incomplete. As soon as he obtains a wife, however, he is reborn and becomes complete" (*Śatapatha Brāhmaṇa* 5.2.1.10). The married householder as the exemplar of the perfect religious life, so central to the Vedic religion, came to be challenged by the emerging ascetic movements around the middle of the second millennium BCE. Such a challenge was probably the background for the defensive tone in a song found in the *Aitareya Brāhmaṇa* (7.13):

Now, since they desire a son,
Both those who are intelligent and those who aren't;
What does one gain by a son?
Tell me that, O Nārada.

A debt he pays in him,
And immortality he gains,
The father who sees the face
Of his son born and alive.

Greater than the delights
That earth, fire, and water
Bring to living beings,
Is a father's delight in his son.

By means of sons have fathers ever
Crossed over the mighty darkness;
For one is born from oneself,
A ferry laden with food.

What is the use of dirt and deer skin?
What profit in beard and austerity?
Seek a son, O Brahmin,
He is the world free of blame.

We see in the last stanza references to dirt, deer skin, beard, and austerity, in all likelihood the hallmarks of the ascetic way that devalues marriage and children.

We can detect a subtext in the late Vedic documents, and they can be interpreted most adequately when viewed within the context of an ongoing debate with those promoting ascetic and celibate ideologies. One significant doctrinal innovation that emerges in the late Vedic period is the theology of debts. It posits that men are born with either three or four debts, according to different formulations.[6] Two of these debts involve offering sacrifices and procreating sons, precisely the obligations that are central to the Vedic ideal of religious living, embodied in the married householder and antithetical to ascetic and celibate modes of life.

When the ascetic ideologies and institutions arose, and within what kinds of social, ethnic, or religious groups, have been matters of controversy. Even though one comes across ascetic or shamanistic figures in the extant Vedic literature, and some practices of sexual abstinence may have been present, it is clear that asceticism and celibacy did not play a significant role in the Vedic religion. Some have seen the new celibate ideologies and institutions as integral developments of the older ritual religion of the Vedas; others have seen them as the assertion of non-Vedic and non-Aryan religious values.[7] I think it is fruitless to speculate on the origins of these new religious movements. The historical reality behind them is a bewildering variety of practices, goals, and ideologies, all of which continued to change over time. Diverse factors surely influenced the history of ascetic institutions, ideologies, and practices, including the interaction among the ethnically diverse populations of India and the new social, political, and economic realities, such as urbanization, expansion of commercial and economic activities, and political consolidations around the middle of the first millennium BCE. The most we can hope to do as historians, modest though it may be, is to unravel and isolate, here and there, some of these possible roots and causes.

The early religious ideology with celibacy as a central value was institutionalized in a variety of new religious groups, including those that came to be labeled as Buddhist, Jain, and Ājīvika, groups that may be called "new religions." Although probably not institutionalized in the same manner, the celibate ideology also influenced the mainstream Brahmanical/Hindu tradition. In the new religions, however, the celibate ascetic stands at the very heart as the embodiment of the new religious ideal and value system. These world-renouncing ascetics, at least ideally, were expected to cut themselves off from all social bonds.[8] They withdrew physically from their homes and villages, gave up all rights to property, led an itinerant life without fixed abodes, begged for their food and necessities, and most significantly were celibate and unmarried (leaving their wives, if they were already married).[9]

The prominence of the celibate ascetic within the new religious ideologies, however, has to be seen within the context of broader developments in the religious cosmology and soteriology of the time. Vedic theology viewed the cosmos as created by some sort of a creator god or through ritual activity (*karma*). The working of the cosmos was also controlled by ritual activity, which also contains the energy that gives immortality to gods and humans. After death, moreover, humans go to the world of the fathers, where they are dependent on the ritual offerings of their sons for their continued felicity. The individual was tied by social and ritual bonds to his or her family and relatives as much after death as while he was alive.

The emerging ideology also viewed the universe as an automatic machine controlled by the energy provided by human activities (*karma*). However, involvement in this cosmic process is viewed negatively; the cosmos and human participation in it are defined now with the new term *saṃsāra,* literally "rolling around." Cosmic and human time is cyclical; both the cosmos and the human individual die and are born again. The rebirth ideology at the heart of the *saṃsāra* conception of the universe viewed human life within *saṃsāra* in essentially negative terms as suffering and bondage. Actions (*karma*), both ritual and moral, that were viewed as assuring immortality in the Vedic ideology are now seen as the basic impediment to human liberation (*mokṣa* or *nirvāna*) from *saṃsāra*. The new ethics is based not on action (ritual, moral, social, economic, or sexual) but on withdrawal from action. As the present state of individuals is determined by their past actions, so also is their future; others, including sons, cannot help or hinder it. It is this autochtonous theory of salvation that made sons and marriage insignificant from a soteriological point of view.

In the early ascetic rhetoric, within both the new religions and in sections of the Brahmanical tradition, the celibate ideal is closely tied to the rejection of ritual activities, which are seen as not only fruitless but also as harmful to spiritual progress. The *Muṇḍaka Upaniṣad* (1.2.6–10) presents a mocking appraisal of the ritual religions:

"Come! Come!" say the oblations shining bright,
as they carry their offerer on the sun's rays of light,
they praise him, telling him flattering things:
    "This is yours, this *brahman's* world,
    built by good deeds and rites well done."

The author retorts:

Surely, they are floating unanchored,
    these eighteen forms of the sacrifice,
    the rites within which are called inferior.
The fools who hail that as the best,
    return once more to old age and death.

Wallowing in ignorance, but calling themselves wise,
thinking they are learned, the fools go around,
hurting themselves badly, like a group of blind men,
  led by a man who is himself blind.
Wallowing in ignorance time and again,
the fools imagine, "We have reached our aim!"
because of their passion, they do not understand,
  these people who are given to rites.
Therefore, they fall, wretched and forlorn,
  when their heavenly stay comes to a close.
Deeming sacrifices and gifts as the best,
the imbeciles know nothing better;
when they have enjoyed their good work,
  atop the firmament,
they return again to this abject world.

The author of the *Muṇḍaka* (1.2.11) presents the new ideal of the world renouncer living in the wilderness:

But those in the wilderness, calm and wise,
  who live a life of penance and faith,
  as they beg their food;
Through the sun's door they go, spotless,
  to where that immortal Person is,
  that immutable self.

The "village," the locus of the married householder and the geographic definition of the ritual ideology, is often contrasted to "wilderness," the locus of the celibate ascetic and of the new religious ideology.[10] Giving an early and rather physical view of the rebirth process after death, an old passage found both in the *Chāndogya* (5.10.1–2) and *Bṛhadāraṇyaka* (6.2.15–16) *Upaniṣads* draws a sharp contrast between the two geographies:

> Now, the people who know this, and the people here in the wilderness who venerate thus: "Austerity is faith"—they pass into the flame, from the flame into the day, from the day into the fortnight of the waxing moon, from the fortnight of the waxing moon into the six months when the sun moves north, from these months into the year, from the year into the sun, from the sun into the moon, and from the moon into lightning. Then a person who is not human—he leads them to *brahman*. This is the path leading to the gods.

> The people here in villages, on the other hand, who venerate thus: "Gift-giving is offerings to gods and to priests"—they pass into the smoke, from the smoke into the night, from the night into the fortnight of the waning moon, and from the fortnight of the waning moon into the six months when the sun moves south. These do not reach the year but from these months pass into the world of the fathers, and from the world of the fathers into space, and from space into the moon. This is King Soma, the food of the gods, and the gods eat it. They remain there as long as there is a residue, and then they return by the same path they went.

The centrality of celibacy within the emergent ascetic ideologies in the middle of the first millennium BCE is highlighted by the Buddhist adaptation of the term *brahmacarya* to refer to the life of a Buddhist monk. Clearly within this context *brahmacarya* is used as a metonym, a single but central aspect of a monk's life expressing the totality of that life.

Structures for Inclusion

Whereas in the institutionalized forms of the new religions, such as Buddhism and Jainism, there was a clear distinction between the fully committed religious aspirant, namely, the celibate monk or nun, and the lay men and women, whose ethic permitted marriage and sexual engagement, within the Brahmanical tradition the institutional structures were vague and there was an ongoing debate about the competing values of celibacy and procreation.

The major structure for inclusion of celibate asceticism into the framework of Brahmanical Hinduism was the system of the *āśramas*. The term *āśrama* within this system has the meaning of a religiously sanctioned mode of life.[11] The system was created as a theological innovation probably around the fourth century BCE. Its inventors and supporters were probably Brahmin scholars partial to the celibate and ascetic lifestyles who wanted to find a place for them within the institutional and theological structures of Brahmanism. In the Vedic religion, as we saw, the only acceptable form of life for an adult male was to be married and to raise a family. The *āśrama* system envisaged four parallel and equally legitimate modes of life for an adult male. The system presupposed that a boy would undergo Vedic initiation and spend some years as a student in his teacher's house. After graduating from school, the young adult took a ritual bath and was known by the name *snātaka* (literally, "bathed person"). In the old system, the parents of such a bath-graduate would find a bride for him, and he would get married. The *āśrama* system, on the other hand, looked at the graduation as the time when the young adult would choose a vocation of life, that is, one of the four *āśramas*. Within this system, then, the initiatory period of studentship was viewed as a time of preparation for choosing one of these adult modes of life.

The four *āśramas* are student, householder, forest hermit, and world renouncer. The first *āśrama,* that of a student, is somewhat confusing, because the period after initiation also was spent by the young man as a student. But as an *āśrama,* studentship was both an adult and a permanent vocation. The young adult then would decide to spend the remainder of his life at his teacher's house dedicated to study and learning. The *āśrama* of a student is the first celibate mode of life in this system.

The sexual life of a forest hermit is somewhat confusing. Some sources permit him to have a wife and family, and the epic depictions of forest hermits indicate that they lived in family groups. But the celibate ideal appears to have influenced at least some sources that recommend a life of celibacy for a forest hermit.

The *āśrama* where celibacy is the hallmark is the world renouncer. The rules for a Brahmanical renouncer are broadly similar to those existing within Buddhism and Jainism for their monks. Not having a family, not being married, and not engaging in sexual activities are fundamental aspects of this form of asceticism.

Sometime toward the beginning of the common era, the *āśrama* system underwent a transformation. The *āśramas* within the reformed system were no longer viewed as adult and permanent vocations but as temporary stages of life. The first *āśrama* is equated to the temporary period of studentship following Vedic initiation. After the completion of this studentship, the young adult gets married and raises a family. When his family obligations are completed, he retires to the forest either with his wife or alone. During the last period of his life, he becomes a world renouncer. In this scheme, celibate modes of life are placed at the very beginning and at the very end of a man's life, leaving the middle and productive years to sexual and economic activities. This is the *āśrama* system that is common in later Hinduism.

Chastity as a Religious Ideal and Virtue

Even though sexual abstinence and rejection of marriage by ascetic communities have to be seen against the background of the Brahmanical emphasis on ritual, marriage, procreation, and family, yet there are other dimensions to ascetic celibacy closely associated with the ascetic techniques for achieving liberation.

The primary condition for renouncing the world is the complete severing of all attachments, especially to sensual objects. That detachment or aversion to the world (*vairāgya*) is the essential prerequisite for renunciation is emphasized in all ascetical treatises. The sexual impulse was viewed as the greatest source of attachment and the greatest impediment to progress on the spiritual path. The body itself is viewed as an impure and dangerous place from which the ascetic should seek to flee as from a burning house.[12] "Lord, this body is produced just by sexual intercourse and is devoid of consciousness; it is a veritable hell. Born through the urinary canal, it is built with bones, plastered with flesh, and covered with skin. It is filled with feces, urine, wind, bile, phlegm, marrow, fat, serum, and many other kinds of filth. In such a body do I live" (*Maitrī Upaniṣad* 108).

The *Mahāsatipaṭṭhāna Sutta* of the Pāli canon, the basic text on which the Theravāda meditative practice is based, echoes the Brahmanical texts in explaining the reality of the human body. "And again, monks, a monk reflects upon this very body, from the soles of his feet up and from the crown of his head down, enclosed by the skin and full of impurities, thinking thus: 'There are in this body: hair of the head, hair of the body, nails, teeth, skin, flesh, sinews, bones, marrow, kidneys, heart, liver, pleura, spleen, lungs, intestines, mesentery, gorge, faeces, bile, phlegm, pus, blood, sweat, solid fat, liquid fat, saliva, mucus, synovic fluid, urine.' "[13] Only one kind of attitude and feeling is appropriate with regard to such a thing: a feeling of disgust accompanied by a desire to be rid of it.

The sexual nature of the body and the natural attraction toward the opposite sex are the greatest obstacles to ascetic detachment. Given that most of the extant ascetic literature was produced by men, there is a marked gynephobic attitude in them. Women are viewed as temptresses waiting to catch the unsuspecting male.

> With stylish hair and painted eyes, hard to touch but pleasing to the eye, women are like the flame of sin and burn a man like straw.
>
> Burning from afar, sweet yet bitter, women indeed are the fuel of hellfire, both lovely and cruel. Foolish women are the nets spread out by the fowler called Kāma,[14] binding the limbs of men as if they were birds.

> A woman is the bait on the fishhook tied to the line of evil tendencies for men who are like fish in the pond of birth, wading in the mud of the mind. (*Yogavāsiṣṭha* 1.21.11, 12, 18, 20)

Meditation on the impure nature of a woman's body beneath the alluring exterior is recommended in many ascetic texts.

> What, pray, is the beauty of a woman, who is a puppet of flesh furnished with tendons, bones, and joints, within a cage of limbs moved by a machine?
>
> Examine her eyes after separating the skin, the flesh, the blood, the tears, and the fluid, and see if there is any charm. Why are you bewitched in vain?
>
> The same breast of a girl, on which we see the brilliant splendor of a pearl necklace comparable to the swift waters of the Gaṅgā rippling down the slopes of mount Meru, is in time eaten with relish by dogs in remote cemeteries as if it were a little morsel of food. (*Yogavāsiṣṭha* 1.21.1–2, 5–6)
>
> Even though a woman's private parts are not different from a deep and festering ulcer, men generally deceive themselves by imagining them to be different.
>
> I salute those who take delight in a piece of skin split in two scented by the breaking of the wind! What could be more rash? (*Nāradaparivrājaka Upaniṣad* 160)

Sexual abstinence, then, was viewed by most Indian religious traditions as a necessary condition for the pursuit of liberation. It was especially necessary for advancement in mental training, which was the central element of the techniques of liberation. In the classical system of Yoga, for example, one of the five preliminary restraints (*yama*) to be cultivated by the mediator is *brahmacarya* or chastity. Without crushing the attraction to sexual and sensual things, especially to women, it is not possible to take even the first steps toward mental discipline.

Within this context it is not surprising that many Indian religious traditions, including the Buddhist and the Jain, denied the possibility of a person reaching liberation while still remaining a householder and engaging in sexual activity, although in the Brahmanical tradition we see a continuing debate on this point. Yet the religious value of celibacy became so ingrained within even the Brahmanical tradition that other religious and moral acts came to be evaluated with the currency of celibacy.

The value placed on celibacy within the broad spectrum of Indian religions resulted in Brahmanical adaptations and reinterpretations of celibate and renunciatory values. These adaptations had the added benefit of making household life "just as good" as that of the celibate ascetic. This is the process that I have elsewhere called the domestication of asceticism, the bringing back of some forms of asceticism from the forest and the wilderness into the home.[15] The interpretive strategy consists in defining elements of domestic life as equal to or even surpassing in excellence parallel elements of asceticism. In the area of sexual control, for example, faithfulness to one's wife and engaging in sexual intercourse only to produce children are presented as domestic equivalents of ascetic celibacy. One Upaniṣad (*Praśna Upaniṣad* 1.13) goes so far as to claim that engaging in sex only at night is the same as celibacy (*brahmacarya*). And Manu (3.50) says that when a householder has sex with his wife only during the permitted nights, he is celibate.

Conclusions

Celibacy as a central virtue in religion arose along with the renunciatory movements in northern India around the middle of the first millennium BCE. Not marrying, not engaging in sexual activity leading to procreation, not engaging in family life were presented within an ideology that deliberately opposed the Vedic theology of the paradigmatic religious life. It is no longer the married householder engaging in procreative and ritual activities who is the epitome of religious living, but the celibate ascetic who has left home, family, and society and lives a solitary, itinerant, and mendicant life. The success of the new religious movements based on these values made celibacy itself a central virtue within the broad spectrum of Indian religions, even that of the Brahmanical tradition that accepted the Vedas as the prime authority in religious matters.

Celibacy, however, also played a positive role within the religious practice of people seeking ways to liberate themselves from the current cycle of transmigratory existence. Most of these technologies of liberation incorporated some form of mental control and training; detachment from sensual things, especially the abstinence from sexual activities and the suppression of sexual impulses, was a basic prerequisite of mental training. Yet the primacy of celibacy as a religious virtue remained in a creative tension with the other and older value placed on getting married and having children, especially sons. Many systems and institutions that sought to bridge this divide were invented over time, the most significant one within the Brahmanical tradition being the system of the *āśramas,* which pushed the ascetic and celibate life to old age when a person would have completed his ritual and procreative obligations. Other traditions saw the rebirth process itself as a way to bridge the divide; if one is unable to undertake the celibate life of a monk in this life, perhaps with adequate accumulation of good *karma* one can hope to be in a situation to do so in the next life. Sexual engagement and celibacy, nevertheless, existed in India—as it did in other religious traditions and in other parts of the world—in a creative tension that was never fully resolved, and is perhaps unresolvable.

NOTES

1. See Patrick Olivelle, "Renouncer and Renunciation in the Dharmaśāstra," in *Studies in Dharmaśāstra,* edited by Richard Lariviere (Calcutta: Firma KLM, 1984), 149.

2. *avivāhaḥ, anudvāhaḥ, apariṇayanam, apāṇigrahaṇam, avivāhāvasthā, akṛtavivāhatvam.* With the privative particle "a" at the beginning, these terms simply state that someone is unmarried. Surprisingly, only two of these, *apariṇayanam* and *apāṇigrahaṇam,* are recorded in Monier-Williams's own Sanskrit dictionary; Monier Monier-Williams, *A Sanskrit-English Dictionary* (Oxford: Clarendon Press, 1899). However, they are absent in the more authoritative dictionary of Böhtlingk and Roth (1855–1875) on which Monier-Williams depended considerably, indicating the artificial nature of these coined terms.

3. Thus, for example, we have penances prescribed for violating *brahmacarya* by Vedic students, violations that include masturbation. Clearly, this has to do with chastity rather than celibacy per se.

4. Permanent studentship was probably an extraordinary institution that was incorporated into the system of the four *āśramas* or vocations of life; see Patrick Olivelle, *The Āśrama System: History and Hermeneutics of a Religious Institution* (New York: Oxford University Press, 1993).

5. Ibid., 35–55.

6. The *Taittirīya Saṃhitā* (6.3.10.5) gives three debts, which becomes the standard in later tradition: "A Brahmin, at his very birth, is born with a triple debt—of studentship to the seers, of sacrifice to the gods, of offspring to the fathers. He is, indeed, free from debt, who has a son, is a sacrificer, and who has lived as a student." *Śatapatha Brāhmaṇa* (1.7.2.1–6) presents the same three debts, with the addition of hospitality to human beings.

7. J. C. Heesterman, "Brahmin, Ritual and Renouncer," *Wiener Zeitschrift fur die Kunde Studasiens* 8 (1964): 1–31; J. Bronkhorst, *The Two Sources of Indian Asceticism* (Bern: Peter Lang, 1993).

8. I say "ideally," because the reality on the ground was clearly more complex. With the rise of organized monastic living, especially in Buddhism, wealth accumulated in monasteries. As Gregory Schopen, *Bones, Stones, and Buddhist Monks: Collected Papers on the Archaeology, Epigraphy, and Texts of Monastic Buddhism in India* (Honolulu: University of Hawai'i Press, 1997) and *Buddhist Monks and Business Matters: Still More Papers on Monastic Buddhism in India* (Honolulu: University of Hawai'i Press, 2004) has shown, many monks did control vast amounts of wealth and gave rich donations.

9. If they were already married, they were expected to leave their wife and family. The most prominent case of such abandonment is by Siddhārtha, the future Buddha. Hindu law also dissolves a marriage ipso facto when the husband becomes an ascetic (Olivelle, "Renouncer and Renunciation," 140–142).

10. Patrick Olivelle, "Village vs. Wilderness: Ascetic Ideals and the Hindu World," in *Monasticism in the Christian and Hindu Traditions: A Comparative Study*, edited by Austin B. Creel and Vasudha Narayanan (Lewiston, N.Y.: Edwin Mellen Press, 1990).

11. Originally the term may have referred primarily to a place where such religious practices were carried out; hence the later meaning of *āśrama* as hermitage. See Olivelle, *Āśrama System*, 8–24.

12. For the conception of the body as a house, see Steven Collins, *Selfless Persons: Imagery and Thought in Theravāda Buddhism* (Cambridge: Cambridge University Press, 1982), 165–176; Patrick Olivelle, "Deconstruction of the Body in Indian Asceticism," in *Asceticism*, edited by Vincent L. Wimbush and Richard Valantasis (New York: Oxford University Press, 1995), 188–210.

13. Translated by Nyanaponika Thera, *The Heart of Buddhist Meditation: A Handbook of Mental Training Based on the Buddha's Way of Mindfulness* ([1962] London: Rider, 1969), 119.

14. The term means both lust and the god of love.

15. Patrick Olivelle, *Rules and Regulations of Brahmanical Asceticism: Critical Edition and Translation of Yādava Prakāśa's Yatidharmasamuccaya* (Albany: State University of New York Press, 1995), 12–26; and Olivelle, "The Ascetic and the Domestic in Brahmanical Religiosity," in *Asceticism and Its Critics: Historical Accounts and Comparative Perspectives*, edited by Oliver Freiberger (New York: Oxford University Press, 2006).

9

Hindu Devotionalism, Tantra, and Celibacy

Carl Olson

The previous chapter, on celibacy in Indian culture by Patrick Olivelle, traces its development in classical Indian religion. Olivelle refers to the domestication of celibacy in Indian culture, and explains how the *āśrama* system incorporates ascetic values, such as celibacy, although it places it as a pursuit proper in the later life of an individual. In addition, the *brahmacarya* ideal embodies the virtue of chastity and the practice of celibacy.

In the classical Hindu tradition, not only was celibacy a prerequisite for attaining liberation but it was also a necessary practice for the attainment of certain mental and physical powers, such as the ability to read other minds, see into the future, acquire prodigious physical strength, or learn to fly. These powers were directly connected to the retention of semen. In other words, sexual relations contributed to a loss of spiritual power, and moreover it can result tragically in premature death or physical or mental impotence. As the Indologist Jan Gonda makes clear, sexuality is a complex notion in Indian culture. Gonda points to the ancient and widespread belief that sexual intercourse is polluting, exposes a person to dangerous powers, and is associated with the loss of vital power and energy—dangers connected to procreative power. He says that "the conviction that any contact with the holy or divine requires purity and the complete concentration of energy, the belief that the holiness of rites and spiritual life is incompatible with sexual power have all over the world led to various forms of ritual chastity and celibacy."[1]

Nonetheless, in the Hindu devotional and tantric traditions celibacy plays a relatively minor role, except for certain strains of asceticism within these traditions. Although classical attitudes about celibacy continue to be embraced by those experiencing initiation, by others during the final years of life, and by holy persons who adopt an ascetic lifestyle, sexuality and the erotic are widely stressed and function to liberate individuals within Hindu devotionalism and Tantra.

Within the context of Vaiṣṇavism, Viṣṇu is depicted with one or more consorts, such as Śrī Lakṣmī or Bhū, who function as paradigms for marital bliss. A similar role is played by the hero Rāma and his wife, Sītā. But the most erotic expression of divine love is provided by the relationship between Krishna and the *gopīs* (young cowherd maidens). Krishna plays pranks on the *gopīs* by suddenly disappearing from their sight and sending them into agonizing searches for him, or while they bathe in a river he steals their clothing, and forces them to retrieve it while he sits waiting in a tree, observing their nakedness.

Within the context of the Śaiva devotional tradition, Śiva plays the contradictory roles of both ascetic deity and married householder. Śiva is sometimes depicted as a prone and inert body who is invigorated by a goddess standing on his chest and having her energy flow into him, which brings him to life, as evident in his open eye and rising phallus. The feminine energy also plays a crucial role in tantric practice. This chapter proposes to survey celibacy in devotional Vaiṣṇavism and Śaivism before considering the tantric movement.

If Hindu ascetic movements emphasize controlling one's senses, devotional movements accentuate the sensual and the importance of the emotion of love.[2] Seeing a divine image, performing a *pūjā* (act of service for a deity), and waving a camphor flame before a divine image appeal to the senses of sight and smell, whereas eating leftovers (*prasāda*) after a *pūjā* ceremony enhances one's sense of taste. People are refreshed and renewed by participating in festivals with their excesses of eating, drinking, dancing, and singing. In contrast to festivals, pilgrimage is frequently an arduous journey to a sacred site that is both a sensual experience and also embodies ascetic features because of the difficulties encountered during the trip.

The classical Hindu tradition recognizes a distinction between the sensual and nonsensual ways of life by generally equating the householder way of life with the senses and the path of the world renouncer with control of the senses, even if it is also possible to find some authorities advocating sensual moderation and even control for householders. The *Laws of Manu* distinguishes, for instance, between the active (*pravṛtti*) and inactive (*nirvṛtti*) ways, respectively, of the householder and renouncer. These represent two different modes of acting, visions of salvation, and general attitudes toward life. While the renouncer is inactive socially, politically, and economically, the householder participates in at least two of these areas of culture by necessity. The renouncer is a noneconomic entity; he does not work and does not place any value on work because it implies the realm of rebirth and additional suffering, and can never become an end in itself. If the focus of the renouncer is beyond this world, associated as it is with suffering, the householder is grounded in the world and family life, which invites a different type of religiosity that is orientated within the world, a realm of god's playground.

The fundamental dichotomy between renouncer and the householder is evident in the practice of celibacy by the former as against the active sexual life of the laity. The sexual restraint of the renouncer not only differentiates him from the householder; celibacy also creates an internal and unnatural heat (*tapas*) that eventually leads to the acquisition of powers. The typical household couple generates a different type of heat associated with their erotic adventures, which is more natural than the heat created by the renouncer. The possibility of a lack of control and excessive indulgence in sexual relations possesses the potential to drain the strength of the householder, whereas the renouncer gains power by restraining himself. This is often symbolically expressed as a difference between the heating of the renouncer and the cooling of the householder. Moreover, the renouncer's celibacy is a danger to the social fabric because it is injurious to the salvific feature of marriage by destroying the social lineage and severing the connection to a person's ancestors.[3] This tension between the renouncer and householder is a theme that runs throughout the history of Indian culture. It is possible to find such a tension within devotional Hinduism, whereas the more radical left-handed type of tantric movement attempts to combine the spirits of the renouncer and the householder by using mundane means and prohibited substances and practices of the orthodox tradition to achieve its salvific goal.

The practice of celibacy does not disappear with the advent of Hindu devotional movements, but its importance is not stressed. It is possible to find some devotional saints adopting celibacy during some period of their lives. Among Śaiva ascetics, there is an emphasis on celibacy in partial imitation of the ascetic deity, although Śaiva householders can also imitate the divine married couple depicted by the tradition. Within the Śaiva tradition, both celibacy and sexual relations are present as valuable and viable lifestyle choices. Left-handed Tantra stresses the necessity of sexual relations as a method of speeding up the process of gaining liberation, although this is a highly refined, complex, and secret practice theoretically reserved for more spiritual advanced practitioners.

Vaiṣṇava Devotional Movements

The *Bhagavad Gītā*, a fundamental Vaiṣṇava text, contains a couple of references to celibacy (8.11; 17.14). In the eighth chapter of the text, there is a reference to *brahmacarya*, or the life of chastity, referring to the period of studentship, and a second reference that suggests becoming chaste. Embodied within the notion of chastity is often the practice of celibacy, which is common during the period of studentship, and is an important virtue. The practice of celibacy and the virtue of chastity are intertwined, if we accept these two references as common.

Significant Vaiṣṇava thinkers composed commentaries on the *Bhagavad Gītā*. Rāmānuja (1050–1137) systematized the work of Yāmuna into a system called qualified nondualism characterized by Brahman, or ultimate reality, as having qualifying characteristics; he responds to these passages in his commentary on the epic text. From his theological position that conceived of God as qualified by the self (*ātman*) and world, Rāmānuja comments that the worship of God includes subduing one's passions and following a vow of chastity.[4] Rāmānuja comments on the second passage (17.14) within the context of discussing the *tapas* (heat of ascetic practice) of the tongue, mind, and body. The bodily *tapas* involves worship of divine beings, gurus, sages, and Brahmins, as well as purification by washing in holy pilgrimage sites, sincerity of bodily actions, nonviolence, and chastity.[5] Rāmānuja's comments can refer to either the practice of celibacy or the virtue of chastity. Nonetheless, Rāmānuja's comments do not shed new light on the importance of celibacy within Vaiṣṇava devotionalism. But such remarks must be placed within the context of his thought that stresses the meditating role of the divine consort (that is, Śrī Lakṣmī) with Viṣṇu and his inclusion of Sanskritic Vedānta philosophy with the Tamil poems of the Āḻvārs.

Mādhva (ca. 1238–1317), whose philosophical theology is called unqualified dualism (*dvaita*) because God, self, and world are seen as different from one another and the latter two are dependent on God, stresses the necessity for God's grace for salvation. Mādhva interprets the term *brahmacarya* as associated with closing the gates of the senses, retraining the mind with a mantra (repeated sacred formula), and fixing one's breath in the mind. Overall, he interprets *brahmacarya* as sending the mind to God.[6] In the second passage from the *Bhagavad Gītā* (17.14) under consideration, Mādhva lists celibacy among virtues and practices, along with purity, uprightness, and homelessness.

Within the cultural context of Hindu devotional religion, celibacy plays a role in the vows (*vratas*) taken by women for virtually any purpose. By directing her vow to a deity, a woman expects the deity to respond with, for instance, protection for her husband's health and long life. By making a vow, a woman exercises personal autonomy and some measure of control over her life. It is not uncommon for a woman to make a vow that includes both fasting and refraining from sexual relations with her husband. This practice thus gives a woman some control over her body. Since vows are often performed for the benefit of male family members, men do not protest the short-term celibacy of their wives.[7] Intertwined with female domestic life and expressions of religious devotion, vows are *dharmic* (righteous) actions conducive to the welfare of the individual, family, and wider society with both mundane and spiritual benefits. Vows are a female domestic kind of *tapas* (heat, asceticism) that confers a transformational power traced to the purifying and perfecting of a woman.

Krishna Devotionalism

The erotic element is no stranger to Krishna devotionalism, which is grounded in the god's playful dalliances with the *gopīs* (cowherding girls) and especially with a favorite *gopī* who is usually identified with Rādhā. Krishna devotionalism moves creatively within a triangle whose three points are playful relationships, separation, and union. The unitive aspect is dramatically expressed symbolically and artistically by the circle dance (*rāsa līlā*), which depicts Krishna situated between each of the gopīs in a circle, in the center of which he also dances.

The predominance of the erotic in Krishna devotionalism is clearly evident in the *Gītāgovinda*, composed by the poet Jayadeva in 1170. This paradigm of erotic devotional poetry depicts the obsession of Rādhā and Krishna with each other. Jayadeva stresses the intense, passionate, sometimes violent, and erotic relationship between the two figures, with Rādhā's jeweled anklets making an erotic sound as the couple reaches a climax of passion. The poet refers to the eight types of sexual intercourse and the eight mysterious kinds of kisses, without detailed descriptions of the different types, and leaves it to the reader's imagination to supply the specific details. Teeth, nail, handmarks, and perspiration are left on the bodies of the divine lovers as proof of their sexual ordeal, which occurs in an ideal realm of joy and bliss. There is no place for the practice of celibacy within this realm of delight. With the emphasis on the power of eroticism within Krishna devotionalism, there is not much focus on celibacy or its practice, even among holy persons of Krishna devotion.

The Bengali saint Caitanya (ca. 1485–1533) was married twice during his life, his first wife having died young. His hagiographical literature states, however, that after 1508, after a trip to Gayā and his encounter with an ascetic, he began to experience ecstatic trance states and divine madness, which suggests that he had no sexual relations with his wife. Caitanya was more absorbed in the love of Krishna than with any mundane love.

Caitanya's life of devotion inspired a religious tradition known as Gauḍīya Vaiṣṇavism, whose underpinnings are the massive theological works of the six Gosvāmins, composed in Sanskrit. If we take the *Bhaktirasāmṛtasindhu* of Rūpa Gosvāmin as a representative work, we find a focus on the practice of devotion, such as surrendering to the feet of the guru, living in sacred places, being generous, wearing sectarian marks on one's body, dancing before God, worshiping, visiting and circumambulating temples, singing praises of God, silent chanting, praying, and serving God in various ways. Rūpa is also concerned about the different kinds of love and emotions. The practice of celibacy does not play a major role on the path of devotion; that is, it does not help a devotee achieve his or her goal, which is the deep love (*rāgānuga*) of God. On the contrary, in following one's emotions, this type of devotion arises spontaneously, and enables devotees a chance to perform parts in the divine play (*līlā*).

As the Caitanya movement evolved, it developed into the Sahajiyā cult, with its emphasis on what is natural, such as human senses and their nonsuppression. The cult stresses the importance of human desire and the necessity of transforming it into pure love (*prema*) by adjusting its motive (devotion) and object (God). The cult accepts Krishna and Rādhā as the divine macrocosmic unity that forms the model for human unity, which is defined by the belief that all males and females are microcosmic, physical manifestations of the divine pair.

A concern for sensual experience is also discovered among the Bāuls of the Bengali region, along with an emphasis on the present moment and living in the world. The Bāuls (literally madmen) are an antinomian and ecstatic group of poet-singers from various socioeconomic backgrounds, who include Hindu and Muslim figures. Within the context of Bāul life, there is no sharp distinction between householder and renouncer, and there is a practice of taking renunciation and initiation together with a partner instead of individually. From the male renouncer's perspective, the partner is a female who serves as his primary guru (teacher), and she is considered his superior.[8] The renouncer's life is not idealized, however. In fact, the flaws of the renouncer lifestyle are openly acknowledged.

In addition to being itinerant composers and singers of devotional works, the Bāuls engage in an esoteric practice called the "four moons *sādhanā*" (practice). The different-colored moons are symbolically associated with bodily secretions, such as excrement, urine, blood, and semen, which are conceived as poisons needed to destroy other poisons within the world and the individual. The practice includes illicit heterosexual relations, oral sex, and consumption of bodily waste products in order for an aspirant to symbolically pierce the four moons and become a *siddha* (perfected or realized one). The esoteric practice involves reversing the downward flow of bodily substances that cause decay and death. By reversing the flow of vital substances, a person gains wholeness (in the case of the male) through the ingestion of menstrual blood and recycling of vital elements. During sexual intercourse, the male partner practices seminal retention, although total seminal retention is not always advocated.[9] Whatever the case, there is no place for the practice of celibacy in such a religious scenario.

Śaiva Devotionalism

In comparison to the Vaiṣṇava tradition, celibacy plays a more prominent role in the Śaiva religious tradition; the deity is both ascetic and householder, and he has inspired ascetic movements, such as the Pāśupatas, Lakulīśas, Kālāmukhas, Kāpālikas, and Nātha-Yogins. Not all of these groups practiced celibacy, however, and celibacy had different meanings, depending on the ascetic's focus.

Worshiping and imitating Śiva as the Lord of Beasts, for instance, the Pāśupatas bathed three times daily in ashes as a form of purification, and at a more advanced stage of spiritual practice acted mad in order to incur the censure of others and thus rid themselves of negative karma. Concurrent with this type of lifestyle was the practice of celibacy, as evident by comments of Kauṇḍinya, a commentator of the *Pāśupata Sūtras.*[10] These types of ascetic practice were part of a regimen of purification, preparation for the acquisition of good karma, and development of a superhuman body that would eventually equate the ascetic with Śiva.[11]

When the founder of the Lakulīśas, a subsect of the Pāśupatas, was depicted possessing two arms, standing naked, carrying a short club, and with an erect penis, this image emphasized the observance of celibacy in a strange way. The erect penis of the founder—Lakulīśa—symbolized priapism and chastity; it had no connection to sexual arousal. Since it was believed that the founder represented an embodiment of Śiva after the deity entered a dead body left at a cremation ground and enlivened the corpse, the erect penis signifies that it was alive, although the body was paradoxically dead. Like the ascetic deity, the erect penis of the iconographical depictions of the founder was indicative of the withholding of semen and its storage within the body. Semen was retained within the body because this practice was associated with the heat generated by *tapas* (ascetic discipline) and thus the acquisition of power.

The Kālāmukhas and the Kāpālikas were additional Śaiva ascetic movements. Members of the former were identified by a black streak on their foreheads; the latter were famous for carrying a human skull with them, from which they ate their meals—a practice modeled on the decapitation of the god Brahmā by Śiva with his thumbnail. Because Śiva was thus guilty of Brahminicide, the ascetic deity atoned for his transgression by wandering homeless, begging for alms, and carrying the divine skull. In addition to carrying a skull and bathing in ashes, the Kāpālikas carried a trident, used wine in their worship, and practiced extreme forms of self-mutilation for sacrificial purposes. Although any literature of these ascetic groups is lost, it is possible to find temple inscriptions and critical references to these ascetics made by opponents. With respect to the central topic of this book, there are inscriptions advising celibacy for Kālāmukha ascetics who decided to live in a monastery.[12] The Kāpālikas also observed celibacy because they also sought magical powers, and they conceived of final liberation as a heavenly bliss defined as perpetual sexual bliss.[13]

When we turn to the great Śaiva poets whose compositions are still sung in temples today, we find that celibacy tends to be neglected and relegated to minor importance. The Nāyaṉār poet-saints traveled throughout southern India singing the praises of their deity and uniting the various locations into a sacred geography.[14] In addition to singing about the ascetic aspects of the deity, these poet-saints referred to God as father and mother, sang of the madness of their love for him and of surrendering to him, and described the unitive experience as a conjugal love relationship. From the seventh to the ninth centuries, Śaiva poets such as Cuntarar imagined himself as a woman in love with her husband, Appar imagined himself as a bridge, and Campantar depicted himself as a lovesick woman. Arguably the greatest Śaiva poet, Māṇikkavācakar composed poems, such as the revered *Tiruvāśagam*, depicting the soul as male and God as its ladylove. It was held to be possible for the soul to attain an androgynous condition analogous to that of Śiva.

Setting aside Śaiva movements that have been heavily influenced by Tantra, such as so-called Kashmir Śaivism, the Vīraśaiva (literally, heroic Śaiva) sect combines the household tradition with that of the wandering ascetic. Vīraśaivas stress the active participation of all members, who wear an *iṣṭaliṅga*, a personal sign of Śiva given to a devotee by his or her teacher at an initiation ceremony; this is considered a dynamic symbol of the deity in contrast to the inert, static, divine image in a temple. This emphasis on dynamic movement is applied to the wandering ascetic, who is free from worldly attachments, impurities, and limiting adjuncts, among which lust is considered an enemy along with others. All impurities place limits on the power of the soul and keep it in a state of bondage, which is overcome by following a well-defined path of devotion that includes ascetic elements. What is unique about the path is the emphasis that it is not necessary to renounce the world to gain liberation, because it is possible to attain liberation while continuing to work within the world, making work a religious calling. As its thought and practices make clear, the Vīraśaiva movement is an attempt to synthesize the ascetic with the household lifestyle and to overcome their dichotomy and tension as embodied by their paradoxical deity.

Tantric Movements

Its name related to a Sanskrit root that means stretching, weaving, and saving, Tantra underwent a long historical evolution to become a distinct religious tradition that deals with the expansion of knowledge. Tantra reached its most creative period during the eighth to fourteenth centuries, developing within clans that originated in ascetic groups who worshiped the terrible form of Śiva-Bhairava along with his consort. Around the ninth century, an unknown reformer stressed the erotic elements of the *yoginī* (feminine spirits) cults associated with the movement, and he created a new clan organizational system that incorporated other clans that developed, focusing on certain goddesses. From the clan tradition, there evolved four transmissions identified with four geographical directions, Śiva, and variously identified consorts. From the eastern transmission, the Trika branch of Kashmir Śaivism developed, which culminated in the work of the great philosopher Abhinavagupta. As it developed from the teachings of inspired yogis and particular texts, Tantra became sectarian and influenced the evolution of Vaiṣṇavism and Śaktism (devotion to the mother goddess).

Secrecy, esoteric teachings, polysemic terminology, a form of yoga called *kuṇḍalinī*, extensive use of *mantras* (repetitive sacred utterances), *maṇḍalas* (sacred diagrams), *mudras* (symbolic hand gestures that could be channeled toward spiritual liberation or mundane goals, such as knowledge of the future, healing, and means of manipulating life)—all are dominant features of Tantra. The left-handed (inauspicious) type of Tantra is radical and excessive when compared to orthodox practice, because it advocates the use of forbidden and impure substances and practices called the five Ms: wine (*madya*), meat (*mamsa*), fish (*matsya*), parched grain (*mudrā*)—which is probably an intoxicant—and sex (*maithuna*), which all violate religious and social norms. The forbidden nature of the five Ms hides their energy, which the tantric practitioner attempts to utilize to his advantage. With respect to sexual transgression, the tantric embraces desire and eroticism and uses them to achieve liberation. Rather than practicing celibacy, the tantric harnesses basic human impulses and instincts and uses them for a higher purpose. With Tantra's macro-microcosmic symbolism forming the background, when tantric aspirants engage in sexual relations they are imitating the divine—Śiva and Śakti—copulating couple, and they are accessing the feminine energy that pervades the entire universe.

In his classic work *Tantrāloka*, Abhinavagupta contrasts the *brahmacāryin* (the initiate leading a life of celibacy and chastity) with an animal confined by bonds, such as an ox, which he defines as a person who either does not use the three Ms (meat, wine, and sexual intercourse) or refuses the three Ms during ritual, even though such a person uses them outside of a ritual context.[15] Abhinavagupta thus redefines the *brahmacāryin* as someone who partakes of the three Ms and not as someone who practices celibacy.

Tantric practice is based on a notion of the complex subtle body, which is located within the gross external body that is perceptible to everyone. Without going into great depth, the subtle body consists of numerous channels of breath forming an intricate network, which makes it possible to circulate the breath within the subtle body. This interior body also consists of seven centers (*cakras*, literally wheels) located along the spinal column. At the base of the spinal column is located the *kuṇḍalinī* in the form of a snake, representing symbolically the goddess, her energy (*śakti*), and chaos (an unlimited source of creativity). The goddess is described as sleeping and blocking the door of the central column with her mouth. In this inert condition, the goddess symbolically represents poison, but when she is awakened she is compared to nectar rising through the channels of the human body. Because the inert condition of the goddess means that nothing is happening to bring release from the suffering of human existence, the tanric yogin needs to stimulate her arousal and get her to rise up the central channel toward the top of the head, which is considered the abode of Śiva and site of blissful union. When the *kuṇḍalinī* unites with the male principle at the top of the human head, this represents the symbolic union of Śiva and Śakti, and the aspirant's realization of his or her androgynous nature, which was previously only latent. The feminine principle is stimulated by a process of meditation, breath control, and breath circulation throughout the various channels in the subtle body. Tantric texts teach a so-called left-handed method, which utilizes the five Ms, in order to speed the process and the ascent of the *kuṇḍalinī*.

Of the five Ms, the practice most pertinent for the topic of this chapter is sexual congress, which is an intentional rejection of celibacy in order to increase an aspirant's progress on the path to liberation. Needless to say, illicit sexual relations, even those performed within a structured ritual context, are scandalous to ordinary people and an intentional violation of traditional social norms. How, then, can tantric practitioners justify illicit sexual relations? From the tantric perspective, everything in the universe is pervaded by Śiva and Śakti, a unity and androgynous energy that transforms everything and all actions into something sacred and whole. Those subject to the bond of ignorance cannot see wholeness because their knowledge has not been expanded by the tantric experience.

Tantric Sexual Practice

Before an aspirant can commence tantric practice, it is absolutely necessary to secure a teacher (*guru*) and be initiated. Next the aspirant is transformed into a deity by means of meditation, reciting of *mantras* (sacred formulas), mentally placing the letters of the name of the deity on each limb of the body (*nyāsa*), hand gestures, and purification of gross bodily elements. Finally, an internal sacrifice enables one to have a direct experience of the deity within oneself. An external aspect of the rite involves a sacred diagram (*maṇḍala*) and the visualization of the deity on the diagram before it is enlivened by one's breath.

Besides the male, the female partner needs to be purified because she is the source of the sacrificial fire that is equated with her vulva, whereas an unpurified woman must be avoided because her condition would render her body fluid useless.[16] By providing her sexual fluid, the female (*śakti*) partner helps to bring the male to a higher consciousness. This makes her both the cause and the caused of the male's enlightenment because her partner's experience also affects her. This scenario makes the female partner superior to the male guru.

When these propaedeutic steps are concluded, the aspirant is prepared for sexual congress and the overt rejection of celibacy so important to many strands of Indian asceticism. It needs to be stressed that heterosexual relations are performed within a highly ritualized context, devoid of raw lust, and enacted with detachment. The sexual rite can be performed by a couple either secretly or in a collective manner that is called "worship in a circle" (*cakra-pūjā*). The collective version of the rite involves couples sitting in a circle and performing the rite.

Some tantric texts specify that the female partner be a woman from a lower caste because such a choice is a radical violation of social norms about contact between castes, whereas some authorities affirm that a female from any caste is qualified. Oftentimes, tantric authors insist that appearance is unimportant, although the excellent quality of the woman's mind is essential.

After a proper partner is found, the couple begins by engaging in mutual worship, which is often called *yonipūjā* (worship of the female sexual organ, or *yoni*). The female sexual organ is equated with the ancient Vedic sacrificial altar on which a male makes an offering of his semen. According to some authorities, worship of the female sexual organ involves the consumption of female bodily fluid by the male practitioner.[17] For a person outside of the tantric clan, such a practice would be disgusting and vile. From the tantric perspective, this type of negative reaction represents a distortion of their practice and manifests the critic's ignorance and lack of understanding. If the female is transformed into a goddess by tantric ritual, her bodily fluids and waste products are products that have been transformed from carnal dirt to divine nectar. Moreover, the female sexual organ is symbolically connected to the third eye located on the forehead of Śiva, which is directly connected with the sixth center of the human body, where the deity enjoys sexual union with his consort.[18] Besides the female organ's association with the third eye of the deity and the sixth center of the human body, it is also considered to be very dangerous, as well as a location for blissful experience.[19] In order to avoid any misimpression, sexual congress cannot be perform with the purpose of sensual pleasure. Even though celibacy is rejected by left-handed tantrics, the normal ascetic practice of self-control is maintained within a context that makes restraint very difficult and an immense challenge. From one perspective, tantric authors teach that illicit sexual relations embrace desire and transform it for the purpose of an aspirant's salvation, whereas desire normally keeps one in a state of bondage.

According to the *Yonitantra* text, night is the best choice for the timing of the rite because of its secret nature, dangers associated with darkness in the popular imagination, and its connection with ghosts and demons that dominate this period of time. Placing the female in the center of a sacred diagram and giving her a narcotic, the male places his female partner on his left thigh (an inauspicious part of the body) and worships her unshaven sexual organ, which recalls an association to the sacred *kuśa* grass of ancient Vedic ritual. After anointing the female organ with sandal paste, which transforms it into a beautiful flower, the male shares wine with his partner, paints a sacred sign on her forehead with vermilion, places his hands on her breasts and recites a seed *mantra* many times, kisses her, and fondles her breasts. In turn, the female aspirant anoints the male's sexual organ with sandal paste and saffron (*kumkum*). While reciting a sacred *mantra*, the male simultaneously inserts his organ into the female for the purpose of producing female fluid, which is also called clan fluid. A drop of this nectar represents the being, energy, pure consciousness of the divine, and a union of pale white semen with red menstrual blood, which represents the union of opposites. Sexual congress is also indicative of the arousal of desire in order to use divine desire to transcend mundane desire.

Abhinavagupta identifies three moments of sexual intercourse: (1) contact of sexual organs; (2) emission of the moon (male) and sun (female) fluids; (3) uniting of sexual fluids.[20] What happens when sexual intercourse results in procreation? Abhinavagupta allows for this possibility in the *Tantrāloka*.[21] From his perspective, the important thing is that the sexual act must be performed without the intent of achieving pleasure, whereas procreation is an accidental possibility from the process. If pleasure is the intention of the practitioners, the ritual fails to enhance consciousness because sexual fluids are not properly stimulated and thus useless, which therefore requires purification of the participants.

The exchange of bodily fluids can occur through sexual intercourse or drinking of fluids. According to the Kaula sect, it is possible for a male to use a method called urethral suction that functions like a vacuum cleaner by drawing the discharged female fluid up the penis and into the males' body, where it is then circulated. It is obvious that this procedure benefits the male and not the female. In fact, the male partner uses the female as a means to the goal of liberation. Some tantric authorities caution that it is best to practice sexual congress with an inexperienced female. Otherwise, she could reap the spiritual benefits instead of the male partner.

The Strange Case of Rāmakrishna

According to a movement that he helped to inspire, the Bengali saint Rāmakrishna (1836–1886) was a follower and advocate of the nondualism of the Advaita Vedānta school of thought. There is evidence that Rāmakrishna studied with a philosopher of this school, but he also worshiped the goddess Kālī, and he served as a priest in her temple in Dakshineswar, a town north of the city of Calcutta. Thus an argument could be made that he represents a devotee of the goddess and practiced a devotional type of Hinduism through his life.[22] Rāmakrishna's eclectic religious nature is also evident in his devotion to the Hindu god Rāma, as well as to Krishna, a vision of Jesus, and another vision of Muhammad. In addition to these forms of devotion, he studied the tantric path with a female teacher in 1861. When his tantric instructor attempted to initiate him into its sexual practice he vigorously resisted because he apparently possessed an inherent fear of contact with women and an acute fear of sex. When he touched a woman he experienced a burning or painful bodily sensation. According to tradition, he thus remained celibate throughout his life.

After his strange behavior manifested itself, others became concerned for his mental stability and attempted to assist him. A superior tried to cure him of his mental stress by sending two prostitutes to visit him, but he ran out of his room to embrace the feet of the statue of the goddess in the temple. His mother also became concerned about his odd behavior, and she arranged a marriage in 1859 with a five-year-old girl, Sarada Devi, who did not join him until she was thirteen years of age. The marriage was, however, allegedly never consummated, even though they often sleep in the same bed. If Rāmakrishna was a failed tantric practitioner because he could not complete the higher and secret sexual congress, it is possible to attribute his failure to his own conflicted sexual identity.[23] In place of engaging in heterosexual relationships, Rāmakrishna was more comfortable in ecstatic trances, having visions, and worshiping the goddess. Thus Rāmakrishna's celibacy is attributable to his personal mental quarks, and he represents an exception to the normal, left-handed tantric practice.

Conclusion

Celibacy continues to be present in Indian religious culture, but it has ceased to be a dominant force in devotional forms of Hinduism, with some exceptions in Śaivism and among some devotional saints.

Devotional forms of Hinduism have not placed great significance on celibacy because the many manifestations of devotion, generally speaking, represent a world-affirming religiosity that embraces the erotic, especially with respect to devotion to Krishna. For some Hindus, asceticism and the practice of celibacy continue to be a religious lifestyle. Thus among Hindus a world-affirming emphasis coexists with the world-negating tendency of the world renouncer. Although there are exceptions among some devotional saints who dedicated themselves to their deity, celibacy is not a viable option for practitioners of devotionalism, with its emphasis on family and communal worship. The Śaiva ascetics are an exception among devotional Hindus, with their adoption of celibacy and other distinctive practices. At the same time, most Śaivas follow the paradigm of their deity as a married householder. Thus, in devotional Hinduism, celibacy continues to be a feasible life option for some followers, although married life is the choice for the vast majority of devotees.

Tantric practice and ideas have exerted a pervasive influence on Hindu devotionalism and other aspects of Indian culture. The left-handed, or more radical, form of Tantra embraces erotic desire to transform it from an element of bondage to an element of liberation. With the guru (teacher) functioning as an embodiment of Śiva and the male and female adepts transformed into Śiva-Śakti by means of ritual, the couple engage in illicit sexual relations with the purpose of untying binding knots, getting their energy and breath to circulate, awakening the *kuṇḍalinī*, eventually uniting their male and female principles in a blissful union, and realizing their androgynous natures. Although desire is a form of bondage for many segments of Hinduism, tantrics use it and transform it into a means of liberation. For the path of radical Tantra, the practice of celibacy is a dead end, and it represents a continuation of bondage.

If we grasp Tantra within the context of its macrocosmic (Śiva-Śakti) and microcosmic (male-female) worldview and its attempt to unite these principles, the radical practice of ingesting impure substances and engaging in illicit sexual relations can be grasped as an exercise in hastening progress toward one's goal instead of the pursuit of hedonistic ends in themselves. This secret path is very dangerous, and the threat of a person becoming mad instead of liberated is an ever-present possibility.

In sum, the radical nature of the tantric path suggests that celibacy blocks the flow of creative liberating energy, whereas sexual intercourse within a ritualistic context unlocks internal energy with the human body and sets one free.

NOTES

1. Jan Gonda, *Change and Continuity in Indian Religion* (The Hague: Mouton, 1965), 293.

2. See chapter 6 of my book, *The Many Colors of Hinduism: An Introduction* (New Brunswick: Rutgers University Press, 2007).

3. William P. Harman, *The Sacred Marriage of a Hindu Goddess* (Bloomington: Indiana University Press, 1989), 134.

4. Rāmānuja, *Rāmānuja on the Bhagavadgītā*, translated by J. A. B. van Buitenen (Delhi: Motilal Banarsidass, 1968), 109.

5. Ibid., 161.

6. Mādhva, *The Bhagavad-Gita*, translated by S. Subba Rau (Madras: Nungambakkam, 1906), 188.

7. See Anne Mackenzie Pearson, *"Because It Gives Me Peace of Mind": Ritual Fasts in the Religious Lives of Hindu Women* (Albany: State University of New York Press, 1996).

8. Jeanne Openshaw, *Seeking Bāuls of Bengal* (Cambridge: Cambridge University Press, 2002), 131–132.

9. Ibid., 225–233.

10. R. Anananthakrishna Sastri, ed., *Pāśupata-sūtra with Kauṇḍinya's Pañcārthabhāsya Commentary* (Trivandrum: University of Travancore, 1940), 219–221.

11. Daniel H. H. Ingalls, "Cynics and Pāśupatas: The Seeking of Dishonor," *Harvard Theological Review* 60 (1962): 291–292.

12. David N. Lorenzen, *The Kāpālikas and Kālāmukhas: Two Lost Śaivite Sects* (Berkeley: University of California Press, 1972), 145, 157–158.

13. Ibid., 87, 83.

14. See George W. Spencer, "The Sacred Geography of the Tamil Shaivite Hymns," *Numen* 17 (1970): 232–244.

15. Abhinavagupata, *The Tantrāloka of Abhinava Gupta with Jayaratha's Commentary* (hereafter TĀ), 12 volumes, edited by Mukunda Rama Sastri and M. S. Kaul (Allahabad: Indian Press, 1918–1938), 29. 98cd.

16. Ibid., 15. 577.

17. J. A. Schoterman, ed., *The Yonitantra* (New Delhi: Manohar Publications, 1980), 2. 22–24.

18. David Gordon White, *Kiss of the Yoginī: "Tantric Sex" in its South Asian Contexts* (Chicago: University of Chicago Press, 2003), 101.

19. David Gordon White, *The Alchemical Body: Siddha Traditions in Medieval India* (Chicago: University of Chicago Press, 1996), 234–235.

20. Abhinavagupta, *TĀ* 29. 150ca–153.

21. Ibid., 29. 162cd–163.

22. See the connection between devotion, madness, and play discussed more fully by Carl Olson, *The Mysterious Play of Kālī*: An Interpretive Study of Rāmakrishna (Atlanta: Scholars Press, 1990).

23. Jeffrey J. Kripal, *Kālī's Child: The Mystical and the Erotic in the Life and Teachings of Ramakrishna* (Chicago: University of Chicago Press, 1995), 2.

10

Sthūlabhadra's Lodgings: Sexual Restraint in Jainism

Paul Dundas

Popular prejudice often appears to interpret celibacy, whether embedded in a wider nexus of communal disciplinary practice characteristic of organized religious renunciation or undertaken by an individual as an elective mode of life, in terms of (sometimes irregular) self-sacrifice and denial of the natural reproductive instinct. Recent scholarship, however, has preferred to highlight the transformative qualities of sexual restraint effected by means of a willed and affirmative control over the body and its workings.[1] Indeed, the apparent transcultural propensity toward celibacy and other modes of asceticism might reasonably be explained, at least in part, as an innate human disposition that manifests itself most dramatically in contexts where the self and body are regarded as separate, and often becomes as much a component of public discourse as of inner experience.[2]

Hagiography provides the historian of Indian religions with the most extensive sources for assessing the various modalities and contexts of sexual restraint, and Jainism, the subject of this chapter, is particularly rich in this genre. Jainism, a soteriological tradition named after a supposedly endless successions of omniscient figures called Jinas, "conquerors," who are the source of its authority, had its historical origins in the Ganges basin with the teachers Pārśva (ca. seventh century BCE) and Mahāvīra (ca. fifth century BCE), who came to be regarded as the twenty-third and twenty-fourth Jinas of this time cycle. Although frequently represented as a philosophy centered around nonviolence and compassion, Jainism can be more accurately described as a discipline of the body rooted in a strong ascetic rationale aimed at inculcating moral transformation through corporeal control and modification.[3] Celibacy inevitably plays a vital role in effecting such control, and accordingly sexual intercourse is stated by the *Daśavaikālika Sūtra*, the ancient scriptural text that more than any other work has determined the parameters of renunciant practice throughout Jain history, to be the root of all irreligiosity.[4] In Jain hagiographical narrative, the moral ascendancy of the celibate life is frequently confirmed by a renunciant protagonist's rejection of the very object of desire that had previously represented the main focus of his worldly aspirations. There are few better examples of this theme than the story of Sthūlabhadra, whose confrontation of sexual passion and affirmation of the power of celibacy has remained a byword within Jainism's cultural tradition, both elite and popular, up to the present day.[5]

Sthūlabhadra's Victory over Sexual Desire

The earliest developed version of the story of Sthūlabhadra, that of Jinadāsa's *Āvaśyaka Cūrṇi*, which dates from around the sixth century CE, commences in a world of courtly intrigue and eroticism not dissimilar to that found in the Sanskrit epics, the *Mahābharata* and the *Rāmāyaṇa*, and representing the clear moral obverse of Jain ethical values.[6] Sthūlabhadra was the son of Śakaṭāla, the minister of King Mahāpadma, whose idle and carefree mode of life enabled him to spend no less than twelve years in amorous dalliance with the exquisite courtesan Kośā. In the wake of Śakaṭāla's death at the hands of his other son Śrīyaka, which had been engineered by a malevolent brahman courtier as a test of loyalty, Sthūlabhadra rejected the chance to succeed his father as minister and instead renounced the world at the feet of the Jain teacher Saṃbhūtivijaya to become a monk and subsequently a profound scholar of the scriptures. In Sthūlabhadra's absence, Kośā pledged her loyalty to her former lover, and Śrīyaka accordingly engaged the courtesan and her sister to destroy the brahman who had been the cause of the death of the brothers' father.

In due course, Sthūlabhadra and three other monks resolved in front of their common teacher Saṃbhūtivijaya to take vows of intense austerity during the period of the obligatory four-month rain retreat. Sthūlabhadra's colleagues respectively undertook to take up their abode in three particularly dangerous places—near a cave that was the lair of a lion, by a snake's hole, and in the bottom of a well, fasting all the while. Sthūlabhadra, however, went to a still more perilous abode, his former lover Kośā's house, where he was given lodgings in the courtesan's garden. He remained imperturbable when Kośā approached him fully ornamented to tempt him from his vows, and she eventually became a Jain laywoman after hearing the monk discoursing on the faith; she promised to be faithful to any man on whom the king would bestow her. Sthūlabhadra returned to Saṃbhūtivijaya after having lived in the vicinity of his erstwhile lover without breaching his vow of celibacy for four months, and received his teacher's acclaim. The other three monks were jealous, thinking that Sthūlabhadra had received favor because of his rank as a minister's son. The monk who stayed near the lion's cave attempted in the face of Saṃbhūtivijaya's warnings to emulate Sthūlabhadra's self-control, but was vanquished by Kośā's charms. When the monk rebuked her after she had contemptuously rejected a present offered by him, Kośā asked him why he did not grieve for himself and his intended breach of celibacy, at which he became enlightened and went back to Saṃbhūtivijaya, who confirmed the greatness of Sthūlabhadra's deed.

We need not follow further the narrative of Sthūlabhadra, who becomes at a later point in his career a vital agent of the preservation of the Jain scriptural canon, after the ruinous effects of a twelve-year famine on the renunciant community.[7] However, it is noteworthy that later versions of the story amplify some of Jinadāsa's thematic material to highlight the hero's celibate fortitude still more dramatically. So Hemacandra (twelfth century) describes how Sthūlabhadra spent the four-month retreat lodging in a picture gallery in Kośā's house that contained representations of intensely erotic scenes, thus directly confronting the world of courtly sensuality in which he had ceased to participate.[8] A full-scale poetic treatment of the Sthūlabhadra narrative, the *Sthūlabhadraguṇamālākāvya*, "Poetic Description of Sthūlabhadra's Garland of Qualities," of Sūracandra (early seventeenth century), emphasizes the difficulty and length of the monk's renunciant sojourn in the house of Kośā, who in the latter portions of the work is portrayed in accordance with the conventions of Sanskrit erotic poetry as a *virahiṇī*, a lady separated from her lover, with her diverse and intense emotions portrayed against the resonant backdrop of the changing seasons.[9]

Part of the force of the Sthūlabhadra story derives from its juxtaposition of what can be viewed from the early Indian perspective as two opposing conceptual realms that mutually define each other: that of courtly or urban sexual relations, in which desire functions as a major component of the transient pleasure which characterizes human emotional experience, and that of renunciation, where celibacy represents the heroic overcoming of desire and affirmation of the inadequacy of worldly entanglements.[10] Sthūlabhadra, who, as a prominent seventeenth-century poet puts it, "killed the god of love with sword of his meditation,"[11] is not the only Jain monk who is portrayed as having had a close relationship with a courtesan or as having been tempted by the attractions of a previous relationship.[12] The story of his career does, however, foreground particularly clearly the fact that abandonment of sexual activity is an act of psychological bravery underpinning the conquest of passions that should characterize the life of every renunciant. This point is made clearly by the *Daśavaikālika Sūtra* when it describes the attempt by a monk to return to his former life of sex and comfort as equivalent to eating one's vomit.[13]

Sthūlabhadra came to be regarded within Jain tradition as an exemplar impossible to be imitated by those living in this debased period of time.[14] This confirms the judgment of another important scriptural text, the *Uttarādhyayana Sūtra*, that the intense requirements of a vow of celibacy are particularly difficult to enact for somebody who has fully experienced the pleasures of sex.[15] The story of Sthūlabhadra's lodgings, in which a monk faces simultaneously, as it were, two of the most intense areas of human experience, sexual relations and ascetic control of the body, provides a useful introductory frame of reference for a broad consideration (based mainly on classical sources) of the Jain understanding of celibacy as a behavioral modality that significantly informs the conduct of both the renunciant and householder way of life.

Sexual Restraint in Early Jainism

The ideology of the earliest stage of South Asian religious history, usually called the vedic period after the Veda, the corpus of brahmanical scripture whose codification dates from ca. 1200–800 BCE, strongly privileged the householder state and sexual reproduction within it, envisaging a male offspring as a means of ensuring continuity and safety after death through his assumption of the father's identity. It was also the son who performed the crucial ritual role of making the *śrāddha* offerings of rice balls and water, which as a form of symbolic corporeal remolding served to bind the dead ancestors together.[16] During the vedic period, celibacy seems to have been acknowledged as a possible temporarily assumed *vrata*, or vow, which could imbue a householder carrying out a socially sanctioned role with a necessary degree of purification that would ensure the successful completion of the undertaking.[17] Typical of types of individuals for whom such a state of purity was enjoined were members of a warrior band or sodality setting out on a seasonal raiding expedition; patrons of a large-scale sacrificial ritual; and students obliged to spend a considerable period of time in a teacher's household prior to entering into married life. The standard Sanskrit term for celibacy, *brahmacarya*, seems in fact to have derived from the obligatory practice characteristic of the *brahmacārin*, or brahman student.[18]

This temporarily assumed physical alterity began to attain more institutional solidity when renunciant teachers such as Mahāvīra and the communities of ascetics who followed them began to reconfigure vedic ideology. They claimed that individuals were now morally complete entities whose continuity did not derive from assimilating their ancestors' transmitted essence, and instead advocated a homeless and wandering mendicant life in the wilderness, outside the village, the symbolic and actual locus of the householder who craved continuity through offspring. The authority of these renunciants to claim transcendence over the mundane values of the householder derived from their positioning themselves outside the reproductive imperative on which vedic society was grounded, and so celibacy was now envisaged as an essential component of the lifelong practice of asceticism that effected the inner transmutation eventually leading to liberation, the realm beyond the conditioning effects of time.[19] In this interpretation of human existence, sexual desire was regarded as a product of ignorance, and the continuity that it brought about, called saṃsāra, was viewed in negative terms as an inferior temporal mode of life that endlessly replicated itself in varying unsatisfactory forms of existence.

It is unclear whether it was Mahāvīra who promoted the expression *mahāvrata*, "Great Vow," to designate the five main areas of physical and mental activity that had to be abandoned by renunciants, and that to this day constitute the basis of the way of life followed by all Jain monks and nuns of whatever order. These are abandonment of violence, lying, taking what has not been given, sexual activity, and acquiring possessions.[20] Jain tradition contrasts the ascetic regime prescribed by Mahāvīra, which included celibacy as one of the five Great Vows, with that of the earlier teacher Pārśva who, supposedly living in somewhat less corrupt times than his successor, had subsumed this requirement within abandonment of possessions on the grounds that his followers had not required sexual inactivity to be singled out specifically.[21] Irrespective of the veracity of this tradition, the evidence suggests that the five Great Vows, at least in textual guise, coalesced only gradually within Jainism as a formal renunciant code.[22] The earliest scriptural stratum makes clear that violence and contact with women were linked together as the two sinful actions which had to be avoided above all.

The ancient first chapter of the *Ācārāṅga Sūtra*, which describes the rigorous mode of life followed by Mahāvīra, may be regarded as representative in linking these two together and advocating withdrawal from motivated action: "Practicing the sinless abstinence from killing, he performed no actions, neither himself nor with the assistance of others; he to whom women were known as the causes of all sinful actions, he saw the true state of the world."[23] The capacity of women to destabilize ascetic quiescence of the passions that are the root of violence, and so destroy the inner calm of a monk is made clear by the same text:

> The greatest temptation in the world is women. . . . When strongly vexed by the influence of the senses, the monk should eat bad food, mortify himself, stand upright, wander from village to village, take no food at all, withdraw his mind from women. First troubles, then pleasures; first pleasures, then troubles: in this way women are the cause of strife. Considering this and well understanding it, one should teach oneself not to cultivate sensuality. Thus I say. He should not speak of women, nor look at them, nor converse with them, nor claim them as his own, nor do their work. Careful in his speech and guarding his mind, he should always avoid sin. He should maintain this monastic state.[24]

In Christian tradition the generally enclosed nature of monastic life served as a form of protection from the dangers of worldly relationships. The Jain monk, however, lived a continually peripatetic life, only suspending it for the annual four-month rain retreat, which exposed him not just to temptation but in particular to what the scriptures depict as predatory women who desired sex with a celibate renunciant so that they might get a gifted son.[25] So the *Uttarādhyayana Sūtra* claims that it is as dangerous for a celibate monk to stay in the house of a woman as it is for mice to live in the vicinity of a cat.[26] The *Sūtrakṛtāṅga Sūtra*, another ancient text of the scriptural canon, makes clear in a section entitled "Knowledge of Women" the dangers of females for the monk and their incorrigible sexuality, particularly those of the family he has left behind:

> Sometimes women offer the monk as alluring devices couches or seats; these he should recognize as dangerous snares. He should not fix his eye on those women, nor should he consent to women's inconsiderate acts, nor should he walk together with them: thus his self; thus he guards himself. As men by baiting with a dead animal ensnare a lion, fearless and solitary as he is, in a trap, even thus women ensnare even a restrained and solitary monk. Then afterward he will repent, as if he had eaten a milk dish mixed with poison. Even with his daughters and daughters-in-law, with nurses and female servants, whether adult or immature, the houseless monk should not become intimate. Even when people see an unconcerned

> ascetic some become angry with him, or they suspect the fidelity of their wives on account of the food given by them to the monk.[27]

Obviously written in awareness of these perils, the opening portion of the sixteenth chapter of the *Uttarādhyayana Sūtra* prescribes ten ways for maintaining the "contemplative mental disposition which is celibacy" (*bambhacerasamāhi*) with which a monk can guard himself and his senses and so proceed "without carelessness" (*appamatta*) in the world. I list them here.

1. The monk should not sleep or rest in places frequented by women, cattle, or *paṇḍagas*.[28] The reason for this is that doubt may arise about his celibacy or he may experience a pang of desire or remorse for the world he has left behind. Alternatively he may fall prey to passion or illness and desert the Jain path.

For the same reasons

2. The monk should not converse with women.
3. The monk should not sit together with women on the same seat.
4. The monk should not look at directly or contemplate the delights of women.
5. The monk should not, behind a screen, curtain, or wall, listen to the screeching or screaming or singing or laughing or crying of women.
6. The monk should not recall the pleasure and amusements which in the past he enjoyed together with women.
7. The monk should not eat over-spiced food.
8. The monk should not eat or drink excessively.
9. The monk should not wear ornaments or decorate his body lest he become an object of desire to women.
10. The monk should not be influenced by sounds, colors, tastes, smells, and feelings.[29]

These methods of maintaining celibacy are approximately the same as the stipulations concerning the renunciation of sexual pleasure embodied in fourth of the five Great Vows found for the first time in the second chapter of the *Ācārāṅga Sūtra* 2.15.4.4, which is not in fact part of the oldest scriptural stratum.[30] In that text the idiom of abandonment, as with the other four Great Vows, is couched in the first person. The monk undertakes to avoid all sexual activity, including that with gods (who despite their apparent lofty state are rooted in the world of rebirth), men and animals, and further resolves not to cause anybody else to engage in such activity nor to approve of anybody engaging in it.[31] He resolves to confess and repent of such sins whether committed physically, mentally, or vocally throughout his life. Five supporting "realizations" (*bhāvaṇā*), which are couched in a general third person idiom and overlap with the stipulations of the *Uttarādhyayana Sūtra*, reinforce the overall context of the Great Vow of celibacy. According to these, a monk does not speak about topics relating to women, does not look at women, does not remember former pleasures with women, does not eat and drink excessively or partake of alcohol or highly seasoned food, and does not use a bed or couch accessible to women, animals, or *paṇḍagas*.

It might be added that the obligation incumbent on the Jain monk not to wash or pay heed to vermin in his clothing and to tear out his hair in order to avoid the killing of life forms was no doubt also intended to effect a reduction in his sexuality.

Food and Sexual Desire

In his version of the story of Sthūlabhadra, Hemacandra describes how the hero consumed large meals in the house of the courtesan Kośā rather than the exiguous nourishment generally prescribed for Jain renunciants, no doubt to highlight the monk's bravery in taking his confrontation with his erstwhile lover to the very limit of what could be endured.[32] As can be deduced from the rejection of seasoned food enjoined by the "realizations" of the vow of celibacy just described, Jainism makes a clear correlation between food and erotic desire, with the basic instinct for physical nourishment perceived as conditioning the craving for sexual activity; the act of sexual intercourse, accordingly, is often compared to eating poisoned food.[33]

The *Uttarādhyayana Sūtra* makes clear the interrelationship between food and sexual desire:

> As the crane arises from the egg and the egg arises from the crane, the enlightened ones say that in the same way desire is based on delusion and delusion is based on desire. Passion and hatred stem from karma and karma has its origins in delusion, so they say. Karma is the origin of old age and death, and old age and death are suffering, so they say. The one who does not have desire has destroyed delusion. The one who does not have greed has destroyed desire. The one who has destroyed desire does not have greed. The one who has nothing has destroyed greed. I will explain in order those means which must be undertaken by the man who wishes to remove root and branch desire, hatred and delusion. Food with a pleasant taste should

> not willingly be taken, for as a rule that increases men's energy. And desires overwhelm the energetic man as birds do a tree with sweet fruit. The fire of the senses of a man who eats as he wishes is like a fire in a forest full of tinder which does not abate when whipped up by the wind. This does not bring about good for any celibate man. Passion, the enemy, will not overwhelm the mind of those who spend their time in solitary habitations, who take unsavoury food and who have controlled their senses. It is overcome, like a disease by medicines.[34]

Food often seems to play a greater part in Jain ascetic prohibitions than sex, no doubt in acknowledgment that the satisfaction engendered by the ingestion of nutrients is perhaps the human experience closest to sexual gratification.[35] Accordingly Jainism, perhaps more than any other tradition, assigns a particularly prominent position to fasting within its practical religious culture as a means of diminishing sexual desire. To this day Jain renunciants, and frequently lay people, follow formalized regimens of withdrawal from eating or, alternatively, consumption of meager quantities of flavorless and unappetizing food that can be structured in such a way as to last for lengthy periods of time.[36] Eating food after sunset is held by one influential medieval writer to be on a par with masturbation and sexual intercourse, and monks who engage in these practices must be expelled from the order.[37]

The attempt to control and subdue the natural workings of the body is typical of dualist metaphysical perspectives, such as that advocated by Jainism apparently from its very beginnings.[38] Jain teachers envisaged the life principle or, loosely, soul (*jīva*), which in its pristine form is pure energy and knowledge, as having become debased through the actions of the body that encases it and it is consequently embedded in a world of gross physicality. The body is surrounded by innumerable life forms whose destruction (inevitable because of the continual karmically conditioned operation of the passions and ensuing physical, mental, and vocal action) leads to further degradation of the soul's status through infinities of rebirth. Liberation is conceived in Jainism as being the achievement by the soul of a radical isolation from physical entrammelments and full activation of its innate but hitherto occluded qualities. This is achieved by means of the progressively intense performance of asceticism, which effects a distancing from the natural world though the suppression of the operation of sensual activity.

Intake of food and sexual activity are the two most obvious ways in which the integrity of the soul is threatened by the surrounding physical world, and control of them is vital to those who strive to gain liberation. Asceticism thus serves as the means of reconfiguring the physicality of the body in order to render it a suitable receptacle for the soul.[39] However, complete suppression of intake of nourishment can only be effected in the heroic death of *sallekhanā*, in which the renunciant (and sometimes the layperson) progressively diminishes his consumption of food and water and radically recreates himself, abandoning life in measured and fully conscious manner. Such a death by alimentary reduction, while idealized by Jain tradition since ancient times, is obviously less easy to effect than cessation from sexual activity.

Regulation of Renunciant Celibacy

Jainism increasingly came to view the first Great Vow, which enjoins cessation from destruction of life forms, as conditioning the succeeding four and regarded any breach of them as leading to the infliction of violence on living creatures either directly or indirectly. Thus sexual intercourse was deemed reprehensible not simply because it was a product of the operation of the passions which, to quote a modern Jain scholar, "immediately initiates the process of an augmentation of all defilements and a diminution of all merits," but also because a multiplicity of life forms that inhabit semen were regarded as being destroyed in every act of ejaculation.[40] Prohibition of sexual activity, which by this analysis represents a form of violence, was thus doubly significant in Jain renunciant ideology.

The *cheda sūtras*, the Jain texts that lay down the expiations for breaches of renunciant behavior, reveal a world in which there are possibilities for lapsing from celibacy that are reckoned to be omnipresent. The authors of these texts carefully proscribe any activities by monks that might be undertaken with a view to procuring sexual intercourse, and make clear that public and private interaction with women requires formal expiation.[41] Contact with relatives is deemed to be particularly dangerous because of the possibilities for sex that might arise.[42] Although the *cheda sūtras* are not overly preoccupied with same-sex physical relations, they do firmly state that homosexuals are to be expelled from the order and that males who are in some way sexually or physically compromised, such as *paṇḍagas*, should not be given renunciant initiation.[43]

Because of the existence throughout Jain history of a substantial number, probably a majority, of female renunciants in the ascetic community, the act of renunciation could never automatically entail absence of contact between the sexes, and the practicalities of relations between monks and nuns required careful regulation in order to maintain the practice of celibacy. The *Sthānāṅga Sūtra*, a canonical text dating from around the early common era that reflects a renunciant background somewhat different from the sternly individualistic world described in the most ancient Jain scriptures, discusses those occasions when monks and nuns can come together without breaking their vow of celibacy. So while ostensibly it would be highly inappropriate for male and female renunciants to cohabit in the same place during the inevitable intervals in their mendicant wanderings, the *Sthānāṅga Sūtra* allows for them to rest and study together for practical reasons such as the impossibility of getting lodging or the need for nuns to be protected from possible assault. Even a monk who has taken the extreme vow of abandoning clothing, the *Sthānāṅga Sūtra* adjudges, may live with nuns if he is suffering from some form of psychological illness and no other help is possible.[44] In general terms, the *Sthānāṅga Sūtra* allows a monk to come into direct physical contact with a nun for what amount to chivalrous reasons: to protect her from attack by wild animals, to support her if she is stumbling on difficult terrain or sinking into mire or water, when she embarking or disembarking from a boat, or if she is weak or out of her wits for some reason, or if she is in danger of breaching her vow of celibacy.[45]

The specific stipulation of the *Sthānāṅga Sūtra* that monks and nuns should not wander together from village to village in the early monsoon time was no doubt prompted by the standard Jain belief that the possibility of inadvertently harming a wide variety of life forms was greater during the rainy period than at any other season of the year. Yet even a possible breach of the vow of nonviolence in this context could be countenanced when there were circumstances such as general danger, famine, expulsion from a village, flood, or the threat of injury from barbarians that necessitated a speedy change of location by renunciants.[46] However, the potential compromise of the celibacy of monks and nuns through sharing the wandering life became in the late sixteenth and early seventeenth centuries the subject of a dispute between the two most prominent Śvetāmbara Jain lineages, the Tapā Gaccha and the Kharatara Gaccha. For teachers of the former group, the scriptural tradition provided ample support for the undesirability of nuns traveling without the supportive and protective company of their male counterparts. However, one of the most significant textual sources adduced by the Tapā Gaccha, namely *Ācārāṅga Sūtra* 2.3, in fact refers to the wandering of a monk or a nun, rather than the two together.[47] Kharatara Gaccha teachers accordingly adopted an altogether sterner view, interpreting the overall stance of Jain teaching as forbidding the close proximity of celibate male and female renunciants in both restricted and public environments on the grounds of the popular opprobrium that might be roused.

Women and Sexual Restraint

It might seem obvious that celibacy could hardly be enjoined as a practical choice on all nonrenunciant Jains, impelled as they must be by the necessity to reproduce themselves and so perpetuate the community to which they belonged. Notwithstanding this, the uncompromisingly negative view of sexual intercourse described above was extended in Jainism from the realm of purely renunciant values to that of lay behavior. Throughout the medieval period, as the Jain laity expanded in numbers and significance, monastic teachers continually advocated that the idealized householder, the lay representative of Jain values par excellence, be obliged to exercise extreme restraint in sexual activity, restricting himself to limited access to his wife in order to avoid the excitement and physical exhaustion that would interfere with his religious duties. However, even such a paragon of virtue is deemed no more capable of escaping the fever of lust that will keep him in thrall to rebirth than, as Hemacandra puts it, a fire is likely to be extinguished by oblations of ghee.[48] All sexual activity, whether with one's own wife or another woman, is accordingly stigmatized in negative terms in the literature produced by Jain monks.

Quite clearly this perspective on sexuality is thoroughly androcentric. Although concern is continually shown in the *cheda sūtras* for the chastity of nuns,[49] the safeguarding and confirmation of this virtue is invariably the task of monks, and it can be concluded that celibacy has largely been presented within the Jain learned tradition in male terms. Jainism does not explicitly correlate storing semen within the body and the generation of the creative inner heat (*tapas*) of manliness in quite the same manner as Hinduism.[50] However, Gayatri Reddy has recently pointed out that celibacy in South Asia has generally been conceptualized in terms of a "retention of semen" model, in which the spilling of male seed is equated with diminution of virility and male life force. She argues for a more expansive understanding of celibacy in the Indian context and suggests that rather than restricting the conceptualization of sexual withdrawal to a male preoccupation with generative fluids and the permeability of the body, female experience of chastity as involving "moral purity, a lifetime of self-control or self-restraint and emotional detachment" should be equally foregrounded.[51] It is precisely these qualities that regularly distinguish female exemplars of chastity within Jain tradition.

Although monks such as Sthūlabhadra have undoubtedly achieved great fame because of their ability to overcome sexual temptation in what is regarded as a typically virile fashion, in the Jain imagination sexual restraint is more normally associated with women who, despite their supposed innate susceptibility to erotic passion, are regarded as being capable to a far greater extent than males of controlling its influence through the regular performance of fasting. Sexual restraint is in these terms closely linked to social reputation, and the following of a public regime of fasting reflects on the moral reputation and public standing of a laywoman's family. Furthermore, the centrality of chastity in the Jain laywoman's life and the religious power that it is believed to embody readily overlap with the renunciant vocation, where sexual restraint is a paramount discipline. In these terms it is surely not accidental that there are many more Jain nuns than monks.[52]

All Jains are familiar with the stories of the *satīs* or *mahāsatīs*, great female followers of Jainism of ancient times.[53] The term *satī*, literally "virtuous," is well known in Hinduism as referring to a woman who chooses to share her deceased husband's funeral pyre. This connotation of self-sacrifice in total dedication to the marital partner does not, however, regularly inform the term *satī* in Jainism, where it is used more generally of a chaste woman who does not succumb to the passions.[54] The stories of the *satīs* often not only serve to inform moral practice but can also provide a commentary on the difficulties of transactions between males and females in differing emotional contexts. Here I refer to the story of Subhadrā, the earliest version of which occurs around the sixth century CE, which although not entirely congruent with the overall themes of contemporary vernacular *satī* narrative, where marital love is not always a major consideration, nonetheless represents a memorable example of this type of narrative.[55]

Subhadrā was a pious Jain girl who became the object of the affections of a Buddhist boy. So enamored was he of Subhadrā that in order to win over her family he pretended to take lay Jain vows, and eventually he attained *samyaktva*, true religious insight. However, the ensuing marriage proved difficult for Subhadrā, and her refusal to pay homage to Buddhist monks infuriated her husband's female relatives, who were staunch adherents of Buddhism. On one occasion, a Jain monk who was suffering from an infection of the eye came to Subhadrā on his alms round. Subhadrā, aware that the monk's ailment would impair his ability to perform the basic Jain renunciant discipline of *īryā*, care in walking to avoid harming life-forms, delicately cleaned the diseased eye with the tip of her tongue, despite knowing that women should not come into close physical proximity to monks. Unfortunately she inadvertently transferred onto the monk's forehead her painted *tilaka* mark, which was taken by her Buddhist relatives as evidence of her adultery. Publicly accused, Subhadrā became dismayed at the opprobrium, which might possibly be cast on the Jain religion, and took to the performance of austerities. A deity was drawn to Subhadrā by her manifest piety and undertook to help her establish her chastity, magically sealing the gates of the city and proclaiming that they would only open to a truly chaste woman who could sprinkle them with water from a sieve that does not drip. After many women had failed, Subhadrā miraculously carried out the task, to the astonishment of all, through sincerely declaring her chastity and love for her husband.

In this story chastity and the glory of Jainism are equated through the performance of a miracle, while even what would normally be taken as an infringement of the normally guarded relationship between monk and laywoman is transformed into a confirmation of the central Jain principle of nonviolence. An action bordering on the lascivious takes on a chastely religious garb, and the integrity of sexually restrained Jain womanhood is confirmed.

Conclusion

Throughout Jain history celibacy has been admired as a cardinal virtue, although it has naturally been enacted with different levels of intensity in the renunciant and lay contexts, with householders and their wives in current times generally choosing to abandon sexual activity only late in life.[56] Although ideally a lifelong vocation, celibacy was judged by the eminent teacher Vijayasenasūri (sixteenth to seventeenth centuries) to be highly efficacious if followed for only one day with the right intention.[57] And it is intention that Vijayasenasūri identifies as the most important factor determining the nature of sexual restraint, as can be seen from his assessment of who is the more worthy, the man who adopts the vow of celibacy and then breaks it because of the influence of karma or the man who refuses to adopt such a vow for fear of breaking it.

For Vijayasenasūri, the karma that is gained by the purity of intention involved at the moment of adopting a vow of celibacy will unquestionably yield positive results such as enlightenment, rebirth, heaven, and long life. If the vow is eventually broken though the influence of karma, then the reproach and opprobrium directed toward the defaulter will nonetheless still have a purifying effect on him and lead to eventual diminution of negative karma. But the individual who for whatever reason does not adopt the vow at all gains more negative karma because he derives none of the inevitable benefit from being celibate even for a short while.[58] All in all, Jainism holds that there is greater incentive to adopt a celibate life of sexual restraint than not to.

NOTES

1. See, for example, Peter Brown, *The Body and Society: Men, Women, and Sexual Renunciation in Early Christianity* (New York: Columbia University Press, 1988). For the type of popular prejudice I refer to, consider a bus advertisement seen in York

during June 2003, which attempted to entice visitors to the ruins of the great medieval Cistercian foundation of Fountains Abbey with the words "Visit scenes of human sacrifice. Such as celibacy."

2. Cf. Johannes Bronkhorst, "Asceticism, Religion, and Biological Reproduction," *Method and Theory in the Study of Religion* 13 (2001): 374–418.

3. For Jain history, see Paul Dundas, *The Jains* (London: Routledge, 2002); and for the interaction between Jain practice and ideology in contemporary India, see John E. Cort, *Jains in the World: Religious Values and Ideology in India* (Oxford: Oxford University Press, 2001), 118–141. Unless otherwise specified, I am throughout this chapter referring to Jains of the Śvetāmbara sect.

4. *Daśavaikālika Sūtra*, edited by Ernst Leumann and translated by Walter Schubring in Walter Schubring, *Kleine Schriften* (Weisbaden: Franz Steiner, 1977), 6.10.

5. See Olle Qvarnström, *The Yogaśāstra of Hemacandra: A Twelfth-Century Handbook on Śvetāmbara Jainism*, Harvard Oriental Series (Cambridge: Harvard University, Department of Sanskrit and Indian Studies, 2002), 71–72, for some further sources for the Sthūlabhadra narrative. Mohanlāl Cunīlāl Dhāmī's Gujarati novel *Rūpkośā* testifies to the attraction of the story in modern times. My thanks to Whitney Kelting for making a copy of this available to me. *Ārya Sthūlabhadra* and *Mahāyogī Sthūlabhadra* are, respectively, numbers 43 and 44 of the Divākar Citrakathā illustrated series, a Jain equivalent of the Amar Citrakathā series famous for its retelling of Hindu legends and history.

6. Jinadāsa, *Āvaśyakacūrṇi*, vol. 2 (Ratlām: Ṛṣbhdevjī Keśarmaljī Śvetāmbara Saṃsthā, 1928), 183–186.

7. There is no doubt a structural parallel in the story between the length of the famine and Sthūlabhadra's twelve-year sojourn with Kośā.

8. Hemacandra, *The Lives of the Jain Elders*, translated by R. C. C. Fynes (Oxford: Oxford University Press, 1998), 155–168.

9. Sūracandra, *Sthūlabhadraguṇamālākāvya*, edited by Vinayasāgara (Ahmadabad: Śāradāben Cimambhāī Ejyukeśanal Senṭar, 2005), chapters 10–14.

10. Cf. Daud Ali, "Technologies of the Self: Courtly Artifice and Monastic Discipline in Early India," *Journal of the Economic and Social History of the Orient* 41 (1998): 159–184.

11. Devavimala, *Hīrasaubhāgyamahākāvya*, edited by Shivadatta and Kashinath Sharma (Kalandri: Śrī Kālandrī Jain Śve. Mū. Saṃgh, 1985), 4.35. Despite regularly reworking Hindu mythology from the perspective of Jainism, Jain writers seem to have taken no serious interest in the standard Hindu personification of eroticism, the god of love Kāmadeva, for whom see Catherine Benton, *God of Desire: Tales of Kāmadeva in Sanskrit Story Literature* (Albany: State University of New York Press, 2006). In fact, the name Kāmadeva is used in Jainism of a pious layman who remained steadfast in his moral principles despite the torments inflicted on him by an inimical deity. See Jinadāsa, *Āvaśyakacūrṇi*, 1:452–454.

12. For example, Nandiṣeṇa, for whom see Hemacandra, *Triṣaṣṭiśalākāpuruṣacarita, or the Lives of the Sixty-Three Illustrious Persons*, vol. 6, translated by Helen M. Johnson (Baroda: Gaekwad's Oriental Series, 1962), 164–166.

13. *Daśavaikalika Sūtra* 2.2–9. This passage is linked to the story of the nun Rājīmatī, who rebuffs a monk intent on sexual intercourse with her; *Uttarādhyayana Sūtra* 22; see Ludwig Alsdorf, *Kleine Schriften* (Wiesbaden: Franz Steiner, 1974), 178–185. Rājīmatī had in fact become a nun after her husband-to-be Nemi, eventually to become the twenty-second Jina of this time cycle, had rejected marriage after hearing the anguished cries of the animals that were to be killed in the wedding feast. Another celebrated Jain example of rejection of marriage is that of Mahāvīra's disciple Jambū who, on the day after his wedding to eight beautiful wives, became a monk committed to the vow of celibacy. See Hemacandra, *Lives of the Jain Elders*, cantos two and three.

14. Guṇavinaya, *Dharmasāgarīyotsūtrakhaṇḍana* (Surat: Śrī Jinadattasurijñāṇḍhāndāgar, 1933), 30b–33b.

15. *Uttarādhyayana Sūtra* 19.28. Note that Digambara Jain tradition claims that Mahāvīra never married prior to his renunciation of the world. The Śvetāmbara version of Mahāvīra's life accepts that he married and fathered children but, unlike the biography of the Buddha, no stress is made on the pleasures of marital life he experienced. Neither Jain sectarian version of Mahāvīra's life depicts him after renunciation as being tempted by the possibility of a resumption of sexual pleasures, as the Buddha was by Māra, the god of death. As if to underscore their transcendence of sexuality, the Jinas, who are the most developed of human beings in moral terms, are typically represented iconically in genderless form. See Marcus Banks, "The Body in Jain Art," in *Approaches to Jaina Studies: Philosophy, Logic, Rituals and Symbols*, edited by Narendra Wagle and Olle Qvamström (Toronto: University of Toronto Centre for South Asian Studies, 1999), 316–317.

16. For the Vedic attitude toward procreation, see Michael Witzel, "Prajātantu," in *Harānandalaharī: Volume in Honour of Professor Minoru Hara on His Seventieth Birthday*, edited by R. Tsuchida and W. Wezler (Reinbek: Dr. Inge Wezler, 2000), 456–480.

17. The term *vrata*, in standard Sanskrit "vow," "calling," occurs for the first time in the ṚgVeda, where a range of meanings such as "rule," the "laws" over which the gods preside, and "rule of ritual observance" has been identified. See Timothy Lubin, "Vrata Divine and Human in the Early Veda," *Journal of the American Oriental Society* 121 (2001): 655–679.

18. Jan Gonda, *Change and Continuity in Indian Religions* (New Delhi: Munshiram Manoharlal, 1985), 292. In its broadest sense, *brahmacarya* can be regarded as encompassing disciplinary qualities beyond celibacy. For the temporary assumption of celibacy in the vedic period, see J. C. Heesterman, "Non-Violence and Sacrifice," *Indologica Taurinensia* 12 (1984): 124.

19. See Patrick Olivelle, *Saṃnyāsa Upaniṣads: Hindu Scriptures on Asceticism and Renunciation* (New York: Oxford University Press, 1992), 42.

20. See Klaus Bruhn, "The Mahāvratas in Early Jainism," *Berliner Indologische Studien* 15–17 (2003): 3–98.

21. The main contrast between the teachings of the two Jinas is described in the twenty-third chapter of the *Uttarādhyayana Sūtra*, which records a (no doubt fanciful) discussion between Kesin, a follower of Pārśva, and Gautama, a disciple of Mahāvīra,

over the respective validity of their forms of renunciant practice, the former enjoining four areas of disciplinary restraint, the latter five. This discrepancy is explained by Gautama by reference to the differing capabilities of Jain monks over the ages. He describes the most ancient as being morally upright and slow-witted, while the more recent were morally flawed and slow-witted. The monks who came in between, however, were both morally upright and intelligent. Cf. Padmanabh Jaini, "Cātuyama-saṃvara in the Pali Canon," in *Essays in Jaina Philosophy and Religion*, edited by Piotr Balcerowicz (Delhi: Motilal Banarsidass, 2003), 119–126.

22. Bruhn, "Mahāvratas in Early Jainism."

23. Hermann Jacobi, *Jaina Sutras*, part 1 (Oxford: Clarendon Press, 1884), 81, slightly emended.

24. Ibid., 48–49, slightly emended.

25. Cf. *Ācārāṅga Sūtra* 2.2.1.12, translated by Jacobi, ibid., 124. For the later medieval perspective on this, see S. B. Deo, *The History of Jaina Monachism from Inscriptions and Literature* (Poona: Deccan College Research Institute, 1954–1955), 435–436.

26. *Uttarādhyayana Sūtra* 32.13.

27. *Sūtrakṛtāṅga Sūtra* 1.4–5, 8, 10a and 14–15; translated by Alsdorf, *Kleine Schriften*, 259, emended.

28. The conventional translation of *paṇḍaga* is "eunuch" or "hermaphrodite," although the term most likely signifies "impotent," "sterile." In traditional Indian classificatory systems, inclusion within supposedly irregular sexual or gender categories was determined by abnormality of reproductive ability rather than particular forms of sexual activity. See Leonard Zwilling and Michael J. Sweet, " 'Like a City Ablaze': The Third Sex and the Creation of Sexuality in Jain Religious Literature," *Journal of the History of Sexuality* 6 (1996): 361 and 363–364.

29. I follow Hermann Jacobi, *Jaina Sutras*, part 2 (Oxford: Clarendon Press, 1895), 74–75; the prose is amplified by a series of seventeen recapitulating verses. Cf. Deo, *History of Jaina Monachism*, 207–209.

30. *Ācārāṅga Sūtra* 2.15.4.4. See Jacobi *Jaina Sutras*, 1: 207–208, and cf. Bruhn, "Mahāvratas in Early Jainism," 34–37. The second chapter of the *Ācārāṅga Sūtra* may tentatively be dated to around the second or first centuries BCE.

31. Here the category of *paṇḍaga* is not mentioned.

32. Hemacandra, *Lives of the Jain Elders*.

33. Cf. Jacobi, *Jaina Sutras*, 1: 83 n. 23 and see also, for example, Haribhadra, *Aṣṭakaprakaraṇa with the Commentary of Jineśvarasūri*, edited by Vijayajinendra Sūri (Shuntiputi: Śrī Harṣapuṣpāmṛta Jin Granthamāla, 1991), 20.8.

34. *Uttarādhyayana Sūtra* 32.6–12; translated by Jacobi, *Jaina Sutras*, part 2: 185–186.

35. See Padmanabh Jaini, *Collected Papers on Jaina Studies* (Delhi: Motilal Banarsidass, 2000), 284–286, and cf. Patrick Olivelle, "From Feast to Fast: Food and Indian Asceticism," in *Rules and Remedies in Classical Indian Law*, edited by Julia Leslie (Leiden: E. J. Brill, 1991), 17–36, for a similar perception in brahmanical tradition. As with many other renunciant orders, breach of celibacy, an unrestrained

attitude to food, and excessive preoccupation with personal appearance were reckoned to be the most public causes of a Jain monk being treated with scepticism by potential lay supporters. The Jain textual tradition, however, tends to view these as prejudicing the inner, spiritual development of a monk. Cf. *Daśavaikālika Sūtra,* 8.56: "ornaments, contact with a woman, spiced food are like deadly poison for a man striving after self."

36. Cf. Cort, *Jains in the World,* 128–133.

37. Saṇghadāsa, *Bṛhatkalpabhāṣya,* in *Bhadrabāhu: Bṛhat-Kalpa-Niryukti* and Sanghadāsa: *Bṛhat-Kalpa-Bhāṣya* (three volumes), edited by W. B. Bollée (Stuttgart: Franz Steiner, 1998), vv. 4877–4968. For the Jain prohibition of eating food after sunset, see Dundas, *Jains,* 159.

38. Cf. James Laidlaw, *Riches and Renunciation: Religion, Economy, and Society among the Jains* (Oxford: Clarendon Press, 1995), 230–239.

39. Cf. Banks, "Body in Jain Art," 318.

40. *Sukhlalji's Commentary on Tattvarthasutra of Vacaka Umasvati* (Ahmedabad: L. D. Institute of Indology, 1974), 296. See also R. W. Williams, *Jaina Yoga* (London: Oxford University Press, 1963), 91.

41. *Niśītha Sūtra,* edited by Yuvācārya Miśrīmaljī and Muni Kanhaiyālāljī (Byavara: Śrī Āgamprakāśan Samiti, 1991), 6.1–78, 7, and 8.1–9. Cf. Deo, *History of Jaina Monachism,* 5:380–381 and 435–436.

42. Cf. Saṇghadāsa, *Bṛhatkalpabhāṣya,* vv. 5234–5262 for the expiatory punishment for a sick monk or nun being embraced by relatives of the opposite sex and so being induced to engage in sex. See also note 27 above.

43. Saṇghadāsa, *Bṛhatkalpabhāṣya,* v. 5025, and vv. 5138–63 for *paṇḍagas* and impotent men (v. 5164) not to be allowed in the renunciant order. See also note 28 above.

44. *Sthānāṅga Sūtra* with the commentary of Abhayadevavasūri, 3 vols., edited by Muni Jambūvijaya (Amadāvād/Bhāvnagar: Siddhi-Bhuvan-Manohar Jain Ṭrasṭ/Jain Ātmānand Sabhā, 2002), 417.

45. Ibid., 439.

46. Ibid., 413.

47. Jacobi, *Jaina Sutras,* part 1, 136–148.

48. See Williams, *Jaina Yoga,* 84–92, esp. 91.

49. Cf. Deo, *History of Jaina Monachism,* 380–382. One might note the care prescribed by the *cheda sūtras* for a raped nun who, even though giving birth to a child, is not to be expelled from the community. However, it is made clear that she should not be exposed to the laity while in her compromised state. See Deo, *History of Jaina Monachism,* 490–491.

50. This can be concluded from consulting Jain texts. However, compare Laidlaw, *Riches and Renunciation,* 74 and 254, and for the general context see Carl Olson, *The Indian Renouncer and Postmodern Poison: A Cross-Cultural Encounter* (New York: Peter Lang, 1997), 62–66.

51. Gayatri Reddy, *With Respect to Sex: Negotiating Hijra Identity in South India* (Chicago: University of Chicago Press, 2005), 39.

52. Cf. Laidlaw, *Riches and Renunciation*, 257, and for extensive general contextualization, Sherry Fohr, "Gender and Chastity: Female Jain Renouncers," Ph.D. dissertation, University of Virginia, 2001. See also Anne Vallely, *Guardians of the Transcendent: An Ethnography of a Jain Ascetic Community* (Toronto: University of Toronto Press, 2003), 139, for the "demonic possession" afflicting a nun, interpreted as a means by which a woman who is isolated from sexually charged emotions can channel and experience worldly desire.

53. For their names, see Nalini Balbir, "Women and Jainism in India," in *Women in Indian Religions*, edited by Arvind Sharma (New York: Oxford University Press, 2002), 82.

54. Whitney Kelting, *Singing to the Jinas: Jain Laywomen, Maṇḍaḷ Singing and the Negotiation of Jain Devotion* (New York: Oxford University Press, 2001), 211 n. 3.

55. I follow the version of the *Kathākoṣaprakaraṇa* of Jineśvarasūri (eleventh century), although the story is found several centuries earlier in Jinadāsa's *Āvaśyaka Cūrṇi*, 2: 269–270. Cf. V. M. Kulkarni, *A Treasury of Jain Tales* (Ahmedabad: Sharadaben Chimanbhai Educational Research Institute, 1994), 260–261.

56. Jainism has never countenanced any form of interstitial noncelibate clergy, nor has it at any point produced an esoteric or antinomian form of sexually centred practice of the sort that has come to be called Tantra in the West, although it is ironic that Bhagvan Rajneesh, later named Osho, the Indian teacher most widely known in the twentieth century for advocating uninhibited sexual activity as a means to self-discovery, came from a Digambara Jain background.

57. *Senapraśna*, compiled by Śubhavijaya (Mumbai: Devcand Lalbhāī Jain Pustakoddhār Granthamālā, 1919), 104a.

58. Ibid., 56b–57a.

11

Celibacy in Indian and Tibetan Buddhism

John Powers

It would be better . . . if your penis had entered the mouth of a terrifying and poisonous snake than a woman's vagina. . . . It would be better . . . if your penis had entered a charcoal pit, burning, blazing, aflame, than a woman's vagina.

Vinaya III.20–23, attributed to the Buddha

In a pleasant place where there are no distractions, in secret, you should take a woman who has desire. . . . Then make your throbbing vajra (penis) enter the opening in the center of the lotus (vagina). Give 1,000 thrusts, 100,000, 10,000,000, 100,000,000 in the three-petalled lotus. . . . Insert your vajra and offer your mind with pleasure.

Caṇḍamahāroṣaṇa Tantra VI.22–24

Early Buddhism in India

The story of Buddhism begins with the Buddha, who was born in the Terai Lowlands of present-day Nepal and probably lived during the fifth century BCE. Traditional biographies report that his father, Śuddhodana, was the ruler of a small kingdom whose capital city was Kapilavastu. His mother, Māyā, conceived him after a dream in which a white elephant entered her womb, and she subsequently asked her husband's permission to take a vow of celibacy. He agreed, and after that regarded her like his mother or sister.[1]

After the child was born, several astrologers were asked to predict his future. All agreed that he would be a great king, but one stated that if he were to be confronted by the negative aspects of existence prior to ascending the throne he would renounce his royal heritage and become a buddha ("awakened one," a person who has awoken from the sleep of ignorance in which most beings spend their lives). The king named his son Siddhārtha (He Whose Aims Are Accomplished), indicating his wish that the child follow in his footsteps. He ordered all his servants to ensure that the prince would never see any signs of suffering and would be constantly surrounded by sensual pleasures. "I was comfortable, extremely comfortable, incomparably comfortable," he is quoted as saying. "My father's mansion had lotus pools of blue, red, and white all for my benefit. . . . Day and night a white canopy was held over me to protect me from the cold, heat, dust, chaff, or dew. I had three palaces, one for winter, one for summer, and one for the rainy season. During the rainy season, I was in the palace suited for the rains surrounded by female entertainers, and was never left alone."[2]

As he grew, Siddhārtha excelled at all sports and martial arts. He had a perfect body and a melodious voice, and he was also highly intelligent. At the age of sixteen he married a beautiful princess named Yaśodhārā, and she subsequently gave birth to a son. By this time, however, Siddhārtha was becoming disenchanted by the sumptuous life of the palace, and he named the child Rāhula (Fetter), indicating that he was one of the factors restraining him from renouncing the world and pursuing the religious life. The king provided him with scores of beautiful women, and traditional biographies report that he indulged in every sort of sexual activity. One day after an extended orgy, however, he alone remained conscious, and the beautiful courtesans were passed out on the floor, their bodies slumped in unflattering positions, their clothes disheveled, makeup smeared on their faces. Some snored, and others drooled. Siddhārtha was disgusted by the sight and concluded that their former attractiveness was merely superficial. He experienced an overwhelming feeling of revulsion and resolved that he would leave the palace that very night and renounce the world.

For the next six years he wandered and practiced austerities, but eventually concluded that extreme asceticism is just as useless as hedonistic indulgence for those who seek liberation from cyclic existence (*saṃsāra*). According to Buddhism, all beings are born, die, and are reborn again in accordance with their volitional actions (*karma*), which are driven by a fundamental ignorance (*avidyā*) concerning the true nature of reality. They mistakenly imagine that the pursuit of sensual pleasures, wealth, power, and fame can bring true satisfaction, but because all worldly things are transient they eventually lose whatever they have gained; relationships turn sour, former friends turn into bitter enemies, and everyone inevitably ages, becomes sick, loses people and possessions that are treasured, is forced to endure situations that are unpleasant, and finally dies. As long as one's actions are motivated by misguided attitudes, one will inevitably create cognitive attachments to transitory worldly things, which will result in continued rebirth.

Buddhism does not deny that there are enjoyments to be found in the world, of course, but from the beginning Buddhist teachers have pointed out that all mundane delights eventually end and that the pain of separation from what one desires is often more intense than the original pleasures. As long as one's actions are motivated by ignorance, one will create the conditions for successive lifetimes in which the same process will repeat itself.

Siddhārtha eventually found a way to overcome ignorance and put an end to the pointless cycle of birth, death, and rebirth in which deluded beings are ensnared. One night he sat under a tree—referred to in traditional biographies as the "Tree of Awakening," near modern-day Bodhgaya—and he attained a series of successively more profound meditative states, culminating in buddhahood. A buddha sees reality as it is, no longer creates karma that will lead to further rebirths within cyclic existence, and has a mind that is perfectly at peace.

Beginnings of Buddhist Monasticism

Shortly after his experience of awakening, the Buddha taught five of his former companions in asceticism the path he had found, and they were subsequently ordained as the first Buddhist monks. In common with other ascetic movements of the time, Buddhist monastics were required to adhere to a strict regimen of conduct and were forbidden to engage in any sexual acts, to kill living beings, to take anything not given to them, or to make false claims regarding attainment of supernatural powers. Any who violated these fundamental norms were to be immediately expelled from the monastic order (*saṃgha*), with no possibility of reinstatement. These offenses are referred to as "defeats" (*pārājika*) in the code of conduct for Buddhist monastics (*vinaya*) because those who commit them are defeated by their passions and sever their ties with the order. In order to ensure that no one could claim ignorance of the rules, the Buddha ordered that all monks or nuns residing in a particular area must meet every fortnight and recite them. To make recitation easier, the regulations were condensed into a text entitled *Individual Liberation* (*Prātimokṣa*). The first of these regulations states that a monk "who has engaged in sexual intercourse with anyone, even a female animal, has committed an expulsionary (*pārājika*) offense and is no longer a part of the monastic community."

As Buddhism developed, different versions of the rules emerged, and today there are three main Vinaya traditions: 1. the Theravāda Vinaya, which is normative in most of Southeast Asia, including Thailand, Burma, Laos, Cambodia, and Sri Lanka; 2. the Dharmaguptaka Vinaya, which is the standard for monastics in East Asia, including China, Korea, Japan, Vietnam, and Taiwan; and 3. the Mūlsarvāstivāda Vinaya, which is followed by monks and nuns in Tibet, Mongolia, and the Himalayan region. The only one of these codes that survives today in an Indic language is the Theravāda Vinaya, which was written in a language called Pāli (and so the Theravāda scriptural collection is commonly referred to as the "Pāli canon").

Details vary between these three codes, but all agree on the central importance of celibacy (*brahmacarya*). This is also stressed throughout the sections of the Pāli canon that contain discourses (*sutta*; Sanskrit *sūtra*) attributed to the Buddha. Although these were only compiled after his death by his monastic followers, there can be little doubt that the Buddha and the early monastic community placed a high value on self-restraint, particularly in terms of sexuality. The first rule that monks and nuns recite during the fortnightly convocation (*uposatha*) is the vow to avoid any sexual intercourse, and a large number of supplementary statutes go into extensive detail regarding what sort of actions constitute sexual misconduct. In most cases, the regulations were promulgated when an inventive monk or nun found a potential loophole in the existing codes, forcing the Buddha to consider the situation and pronounce new restrictions on the community's behavior.

An example is the monk Sudinna, who decided to leave his wife and become a monk. One day during his alms round he passed his family's house, and his parents rebuked him for joining the order before leaving them with an heir. He was their only son, and now that he was celibate there would be no one to inherit the family fortune or care for them in their old age. They asked him to return to his wife's bed and get her pregnant, but he initially refused, on the grounds that sexual intercourse is forbidden to Buddhist monks. They pointed out that they were not asking him to do anything he had not done before: he had previously had sexual relations with his wife, and he could return to the order as soon as she became pregnant. He agreed with their logic, and successfully impregnated her, but afterward became troubled, and his health began to suffer. He asked the Buddha if his conduct was acceptable, and he was rebuked in the strongest terms: "It is not allowed, foolish man, it is not becoming, it is not proper, it is unworthy for a monk, it is not lawful, it ought not to be done. . . . For that reason, foolish man, you should go to death, or to suffering like unto death . . . for this reason, foolish man, at the destruction of the body after death, you will enter into distress, to bad rebirths, the pit of hell."[3]

Buddhism denies that there is any enduring essence or soul. Living beings are conceived as collections of parts (the matter of their bodies, sensations, thoughts, emotions, karmic latencies, and so on) that change from moment to moment, flowing like a river that is in constant motion. Cells die and are replaced, thoughts emerge one after another, emotional responses to the environment change, and nothing endures forever. The psychophysical continuum of a living being is brought into being by causes and conditions, changes from moment to moment as a result of causes and conditions, and eventually degenerates and dies. Taking monastic vows represents a profound shift in this continuum, and certain actions that one performed previously are prohibited. Sexual activity is permitted for laypeople, but a monk or nun who has sexual intercourse violates a fundamental vow, and the Vinaya states that anyone who breaks this vow is no longer a monastic, even if the offense is not discovered. One may still wear robes and claim membership in the community, but one has committed a grave and unpardonable offense and is subject to immediate expulsion if discovered. One who has committed such a misdeed can never retake the vows.

There are exceptions, however. If a person is insane, drugged, or sleeping, there is no offense. The Vinaya contains a story of a monk who fell asleep with an erection, and a group of women passing by noticed and mounted him one by one. He never woke up, and they left praising him as a "bull of a man," but when other monks noticed a stain on his robe, he was reported to the Buddha. Because he was not conscious, did not consent, and did not enjoy it, he was not guilty of an infraction, but the Buddha cautioned his monastic followers to sleep behind closed doors after that.[4]

The Buddha was committed to the ideal of monastic celibacy, which is declared to be essential for those who aspire to liberation.[5] It is possible for laypeople to successfully practice meditation and become free of desire, anger, and delusion (the three primary factors that enmesh living beings in cyclic existence), and they can even become *arhats* (female: *arhatı*, those who have overcome all negative mental states, who have freed themselves from worldly attachments, and who will never be reborn in cyclic existence). An arhat will attain nirvana at the completion of his or her life, and nirvana is declared to be a state of perfect peace, of ultimate bliss, and the supreme goal of the religious path. If a layperson becomes an arhat, however, he or she must immediately take ordination as a monk or nun, because the state of arhathood is incompatible with lay life. A layperson who fails to take ordination will soon die, and then pass into nirvana.

Celibacy is not a problem for arhats; they have overcome even the slightest inclination toward pleasures of the senses, but many of the Buddha's followers developed highly creative (and sometimes bizarre or amusing) ways of testing the limits of the rules. One limber monk, for example, was able to perform auto-fellatio, and another well-endowed monk could perform auto-sodomy.[6] The Vinaya reports that two monks ejaculated after penetrating an open sore on a corpse, and another had a female monkey with whom he had sexual relations. He was reported to the Buddha after other monks saw the monkey bending over, expecting that they would have intercourse with her. As a result of these and many other permutations of sexuality, the Buddha promulgated a number of rules—along with various stipulations and exceptions—designed to cover as many types of sexual acts as possible. The second section of the *Prātimoksa* states that monks are prohibited from: (1) intentional seminal emissions; (2) having any bodily contact with a woman, holding hands, or touching a woman's hair or any part of her body; (3) inviting a woman to sexual intercourse or speaking lewdly to her; (4) speaking to a woman about "ministering to his sexuality," that is, indicating to her that this is a virtuous activity because he is a monk; or (5) acting as a go-between in order to bring a man and a woman together, regardless of whether their liaison is a one-time affair or leads to marriage and a stable relationship.[7]

As these rules indicate, Buddhist monks are forbidden to have anything to do with sexuality, either for themselves or for the benefit of others. The ideal is asexual indifference to worldly attractions, and many of the lesser rules relate to acts leading up to coitus, all of which are forbidden. Anyone who commits these lesser offenses is required to confess the transgression during the fortnightly recitation of the *Prātimoksa*. Those who have remained pure should stay silent when asked if they have broken any of the norms they have just recounted. If any member of the assembly has violated a rule, he or she should publicly confess, and in some cases this is sufficient. More serious matters require a meeting of the monastic community (*saṃgha-karma*) to decide on the seriousness of the offense and to mete out punishment (often a period of suspension for actions relating to sexuality).[8]

Commentaries on the Vinayas go into even greater detail regarding exactly what constitutes an offense and the proper punishments. According to one Vinaya text, sexual intercourse involves penetration of any orifice "as far as the width of a sesame seed," and so even if one begins intercourse and subsequently calls it off, one is still guilty.[9] Forbidden orifices are also listed, and they include the vagina, the anus, the mouth, as well as orifices of animals or openings in inanimate objects. For nuns, any penetration using a severed penis, vegetables, dildos, or self-stimulation, or even washing themselves in a way that produces sexual pleasure, is forbidden. Monks are enjoined to avoid letting women bathe or massage them, from intentionally indulging in any act that they expect will lead to seminal emission, and from any form of masturbation. In one story, a monk is bitten by an insect on his penis and subsequently finds that he is aroused when the sore rubs against his robes. The Buddha forbids this too, along with blowing on one's penis, inserting it into keyholes or a bunch of flowers, sand, mud, or water.

In one Vinaya story, a young monk named Seyyasaka was having difficulty with the rigors of the monastic life and had become thin and jaundiced from practicing austerities. A senior monk, concerned about his condition, advised him to masturbate regularly. He took the advice, and soon became robust and healthy. The other monks asked him what medicine he had taken for his remarkable recovery, but when he told them what he had been doing, they were appalled and asked him if he used the same hand for masturbation and for collecting alms. When he answered that he had, he was reported to the Buddha, who told him: "Imbecile, you publicly hold out your hand to receive alms, and with the same hand you commit abominations." He then promulgated a rule: "Afraid that this imbecile may later have imitators, I prescribe the following text: . . . If a monk, touching his genitals, causes the semen to flow, this monk must confess his offense in front of the community and be submitted to canonical penance. . . . But if one experiences a pollution during sleep it does not fall under this prohibition."[10]

The Problem with Women—and How to Deal with It

As a general rule, it appears that the order of nuns had fewer problems maintaining vows of celibacy than their male brethren. There are stories of nuns who transgress their vows, but far more about men, and there are more cautions for monks regarding the attractions of the opposite sex. The Buddha exhorted his disciples, "The thing that enslaves a man more than anything else is a woman. Her body, her voice, her smell, her attractiveness, and her touch all beguile a man's heart. Stay away from them at all costs."[11] In *So It Has Been Said,* women are compared with monsters and demons, and later with poisonous snakes.[12] In one sermon the Buddha states that "a monk is better off embracing a fire than a woman."[13]

Buddhist monks and nuns strive to become asexual. They are required to shave their heads; they leave their homes and wander from place to place with no fixed abode, and the Vinaya enjoins them to clothe themselves in robes made of cast-off rags and dyed saffron. They are expected to devote their time to religious pursuits, and the monastic life is designed to develop a calm mind, untroubled by worldly concerns or attachments, a dignified comportment, and an attitude of detachment from the vicissitudes that afflict ordinary beings.

Some monks appear to have been austere and unattractive to the opposite sex, but others, such as the Buddha's cousin and personal attendant Ānanda, were often beset by advances by women. Ānanda was reportedly a handsome man with a charming personality, and when he asked the Buddha how he should relate to women, he was told, "Do not look at them Ānanda." "But what," he wondered, "if I do see them?" The Buddha responded, "Do not speak to them." "But what," Ānanda continued, "if we must speak with them?" The Buddha cautioned, "Maintain mindfulness and self-control."[14]

There is a vast amount of discussion of the faults of sexual intercourse and various forms of sensual indulgence, along with advice on how to overcome desire and live a life of monastic purity. The focus of these instructions is not the sexual organs, however, but a far more important organ: the brain. The mind is the source of desire, and it is also the key to overcoming it. There are several stories of monks who severed their penises because they could not control lustful tendencies, but the Buddha issued rules forbidding any sort of self-mutilation. The goal of meditative training is to eliminate even the slightest vestiges of desire, and castration cannot accomplish this. When the arhat Bakkula was asked by a friend how many times he had indulged in sexual intercourse during his eighty years as a monk, he replied that the question was improperly formed, and that the correct one was how many times perceptions of sensual pleasures had entered his mind during those eighty years. To this question, he replied, "My friend, during these eighty years, no perception of sensual pleasures has arisen in my mind."[15]

The Pāli discourses and the Vinaya texts provide a number of mental trainings designed to overcome lust, including learning to visualize all women as one's mother, sister, or daughter.[16] Through this they cease to be objects of sexual desire. There are also extensive descriptions of meditative practices that involve observing corpses in various stages of decomposition. One begins with a mental image of a person of the opposite sex whom one finds particularly attractive, and then one visualizes her as a corpse, going through various stages: rigor mortis, becoming blue and bloated, decomposing, being torn apart by wild animals and devoured by insects, and as a skeleton whose bones are first scattered and then reduced to dust. In another meditation, monks are taught to consider the foulness of the constituents of their bodies and those of potential sex partners, which include blood, snot, urine, feces, bones, muscles, internal organs, hair, and so on. These induce revulsion when separated from the body and laid on the ground, and one should realize that the body is composed of many foul substances and is not worthy of desire. Men should further consider that when they have sex with a woman they are lying on her full bladder and that her body contains various smelly and unpleasant materials.[17]

The Vinaya recounts the story of a young monk who zealously tried to maintain his vows but was obsessed by the beautiful courtesan Sirimā. One day she unexpectedly died, and the Buddha requested that her corpse not be cremated but instead left in a cemetery. After the body had begun to decay, he brought the young monk and several others to view it, and he pointed out that a few weeks ago many men willingly paid a thousand gold coins for one night of sexual ecstasy with her. He asked who would now pay a hundred gold coins, but there were no takers. He gradually reduced the price, and finally offered the body for free to anyone who wanted it. No one had any interest in the rotting corpse, and the young monk became an arhat at that moment and never again had any sexual desire.[18]

As an indication of how important renunciation of sexual passion is in the Vinaya, the only view that is unconditionally prohibited for monks is the assertion that there is nothing wrong with it. A monk named Ariṭṭha reportedly made this claim, and he even accused the Buddha of overstating the danger of sensual pleasures. He said that attempting to prohibit sex is like trying to fence in the ocean; all beings have desires, they are a natural aspect of the world, and there is no possibility of truly eliminating them. In response, the Buddha declared this to be a false view, and compared those who might hold it to a man who tries to capture a poisonous snake by grabbing its tail and is bitten.

> He dies or suffers mortal agony. In the same way, monks, some stupid men study the teaching (*dharma*), but in studying it they do not wisely reflect on the aim of the teaching. Because they do not consider its aim, the teaching does not increase their mental acuity. They only study the dharma in order to criticize it or to refute others in debate. They are not capable of reaching the goal to which the study of the dharma should lead. This doctrine, incorrectly received, will lead them to sin and suffering for a long time, because they did not approach the teaching in the correct manner.[19]

In many Asian countries, Buddhist monks are believed to possess magical power, which is related to their taking and maintaining monastic vows. In Theravāda lands, monks are referred to as "fields of merit" (*puñña-khetta*; Sanskrit: *puṇya-kṣetra*), meaning that gifts donated to them yield greater merit than those given to less worthy recipients. Because of their moral character (closely tied to celibacy), they are resources for the entire community and serve as moral exemplars. Their power is easily lost, however, and this may occur not only through sexual intercourse but through a range of other activities connected with sensuality. For this reason, Theravāda monks will generally avoid sitting on the same car seat as a woman, even if there is a man between them, and any physical contact with women is considered an infraction. They are forbidden from being alone in a room with a woman with the door closed,[20] and during their ordinations are instructed to remain as physically distant as possible in the presence of women and to keep their eyes on the ground. Some monks will even avoid walking under a line on which women's clothes are hanging.

The Vinaya regulations remain normative for monks and nuns today throughout the Buddhist world. Shortly before he died, the Buddha reportedly told Ānanda that in the future monastics could forego some of the minor rules, but Ānanda neglected to ask what these were. As a result, the Theravāda tradition—which regards itself as the most rigorous in maintaining monastic discipline and as the only truly orthodox order of Buddhism—enjoins monks to adhere to all of them. In the Tibetan cultural area and in East Asia, some restrictions are considered to be minor and are often ignored, but there is no dispute regarding celibacy.[21] Monks and nuns in Tibet, Mongolia, China, Korea, and Vietnam are expected to refrain from any type of sexual intercourse (whether heterosexual or homosexual), and breach of this rule is an expulsionary offense. Despite the theoretical strictness with which celibacy is regarded, there have been numerous sex scandals in Theravāda countries, as well as in other parts of the Buddhist world.[22] There have also been several high-profile cases of misconduct in North American Buddhist centers, some of which involve Asian teachers, some offenses committed by Western Buddhists in positions of authority.[23] This has not significantly affected the general rule that celibacy is expected of monks and nuns, just as the fact that there are thousands of murders in the United States every year has not led anyone to seriously propose that murder ought to be decriminalized.

Sex and the Single Bodhisattva: A New Buddha, A New Buddhism

Several centuries after the death of the Buddha, new discourses attributed to him began to appear in India. Those who advocated their authenticity referred to their tradition as the "Great Vehicle" (Mahāyāna) and denigrated their opponents as belonging to a "Lesser Vehicle" (Hīnayāna). The new texts were entitled *sūtras*, implying that they were spoken by the historical Buddha, but their adherents claimed that they had only been revealed to advanced disciples and later hidden until the time was right for their dissemination. Many of these portray the Buddha as a godlike figure who is able to abrogate the laws of physics and whose lifespan and powers are immeasurable. In the *Lotus Sūtra of the True Doctrine* (*Saddharma-puṇḍarīka-sūtra*), the Buddha appears on Vulture

Peak and informs an astounded audience that he did not really die, but only appeared to do so in order to give his followers a sense of urgency regarding their training. He then asserts that his birth, life in the palace, renunciation, practice of austerities, attainment of awakening, and his subsequent teaching career were all a show for the benefit of sentient beings. In fact he became a buddha countless eons ago and has been tirelessly engaged in compassionate activities. His physical form was merely an emanation created by him, and he resides in a "pure land" where he is still accessible to advanced practitioners.

Many of the doctrines and practices contained in Mahāyāna *sūtras* are also found in earlier discourses, but there are some striking differences. One of the most important of these is the relegation of the arhat—valorized in early Buddhist literature as an advanced practitioner of meditation who has brought an end to all mental afflictions and attained the supreme goal of nirvana—to an inferior position. The Mahāyāna texts describe the arhat as selfish and limited, only concerned with personal salvation, and as lacking "great compassion" (*mahākaruṇā*). They admit that arhats have some compassion and that they willingly help others to follow the path and attain nirvana, but they are castigated for being primarily concerned with their own salvation.

The Mahāyāna texts extol the figure of the *bodhisattva* (literally "awakening-being"), who is not content with settling for the quick and (relatively) easy nirvana enjoyed by arhats and instead is devoted to the welfare of all sentient beings. The bodhisattva eschews personal nirvana and resolves to become a buddha, even though this process requires a minimum of three countless eons (*asaṃkhyeya-kalpa*) to complete. It is possible to become an arhat and attain nirvana in as little as three human lifetimes, and so the bodhisattva's commitment is vastly more ambitious, and along the way he or she develops such qualities as wisdom, morality, generosity, patience, and compassion to their highest degree.

Their opponents viewed this ambition as wildly misguided and contended that only a minuscule number of beings have the capacity to become buddhas. There were buddhas before Siddhārtha (who is referred to as Śākyamuni or "Sage of the Śākyas" to distinguish him from other buddhas), and there will be buddhas in the future, but most beings ought to recognize their limitations and opt for the more achievable goal of becoming arhats and putting an end to cyclic existence as quickly as possible. The Mahāyānists, however, reject this notion, and contend that all Buddhists should devote themselves to nothing short of buddhahood in order to help others to attain liberation.

One of the main aptitudes that bodhisattvas develop during their training is "skill in means" (*upāya-kauśalya*), which enables them to cleverly adapt Buddhist teachings and practices to the proclivities and level of realization of trainees. Bodhisattvas can even engage in actions that are forbidden in the Vinaya if by doing so they benefit living beings and contribute to their spiritual advancement. In the *Concentration of Heroic Progress Sūtra*, for example, the bodhisattva Māragocarānulipta (Defiling the Domain of Māra) has sex with females in Māra's entourage in order to convert them, but he accomplishes this by emanating physical holograms of himself who satisfy their passion, convert them to the dharma and extinguish all lustful thoughts, and then disappear.[24] In the *Skill in Means Sūtra*, the bodhisattva Jyotis practices celibacy for 42,000 years, and then journeys to a city, where he is spotted by a woman who falls passionately in love with him. She declares her love/lust, but he informs her that he is celibate and cannot return her affections. She threatens to kill herself unless he does, and out of compassion he consents, even though he might go to hell as a result. Their relationship lasts for twelve years, following which he returns to his meditative practice. He dies soon afterward, however, but because his sexual interlude was motivated by compassion rather than lust, he is reborn in the heaven of Brahmā. The Buddha informs his audience that he was Jyotis, and Yaśodharā was the woman who lured him to her bed. He concludes the story by stating that he could engage in sexual acts with impunity because of his advanced understanding of skill in means: "That which leads other beings to hell leads a bodhisattva who is proficient in skill in means to rebirth in the realm of Brahmā."[25]

The focus of early Buddhist practice is celibate monks and nuns, and it is assumed in the Vinaya and the collections of discourses that anyone who is serious about attaining liberation will renounce worldly life and enter the *saṃgha*, but Mahāyāna greatly expanded the role of the laity, and there are even *sūtras* attributed to lay men or women that portray them as advanced practitioners. In the *Sūtra Spoken by Stainless Action* (*Vimalakırti-nirdeśa-sūtra*), for example, the bodhisattva Vimalakırti is described as a wealthy householder with a harem and a son, but he is also celibate. Because of his lay status, he can go places forbidden to monastics and work for the benefit of sentient beings in ways that monastics cannot. He frequents bars and brothels, but only in order to awaken the patrons to the pitfalls of their debauchery and lead them to the dharma. In justifying his actions, he says, "without entering the great sea it is impossible to obtain precious pearls; similarly, without entering the sea of passion it is impossible to develop the thought of omniscience."[26]

Vimalakırti's ability to walk into the morass of sensuality and remain undisturbed by it is said to be an indication of the depth of his realization. Others might succumb to temptation, but Vimalakırti remains pure and chaste. Even when a bodhisattva manifests as a courtesan, she has no desire, but only takes that form in order to provide a teaching opportunity for men who would never willingly enter a Buddhist center but who frequent prostitutes. The goal of this sort of skillful means is essentially the same as what we saw earlier: helping beings to overcome desire in order that they might successfully pursue the path of dharma and eventually attain nirvana. In his famous poem *Entry into the Bodhisattva Deeds* (*Bodhicaryāvatāra*), Śāntideva extols bodhisattvas who cleverly manifest in various forms in order to benefit sentient beings, and describes the skillful means they use to attract students who are motivated by desire and then set them on the path of dharma, but he is adamant that they must not succumb to passion themselves.

No sword, no poison, no fire, no cliff, no enemies can compare with the passions when one remembers the torments in hell and other lower realms. Thus one should recoil from sensual desires and cultivate delight in solitude and tranquil wildernesses free from contention and strife.[27]

He also warns aspiring bodhisattvas to view women in ways that are reminiscent of passages we saw earlier in the Vinaya and the discourses of the Pāli canon: "Even though it does not move, you are afraid of a skeleton when you see it like this. Why do you not fear it when it moves as if it were animated by a vampire? [Women] produce both spit and shit from a single source of food. You do not want the shit from it. Why are you so fond of drinking the spit?"[28] Even when bodhisattvas manifest as prostitutes, they remain essentially sexless and have no desires. Sexuality is closely associated with awakening (*bodhi*) in Buddhism, whether it is suppressed or skillfully used, but there are descriptions in many Mahāyāna texts of the clever stratagems bodhisattvas employ to avoid succumbing to temptation, along with exhortations to retain mindfulness and to be aware of the dangers of uninhibited indulgence in passions. Bodhisattvas and buddhas can immerse themselves in the sea of sensuality without being affected by it, but ordinary beings are slaves to their desires, and this is the reason why it is so important to be able to confront them where they live and play. Moreover, most Mahāyāna texts that speak of bodhisattvas having sex with lust-obsessed women or men portray them as laypeople and not monastics, and so the ideal of monastic celibacy is maintained. Even when bodhisattvas use passion skillfully it is still clear that the end goal is eradication of desire and that sexual congress is merely an opportunity for facilitating a cognitive shift in deluded beings.

Vajrayāna: Sex Is Good

Around the end of the seventh century, a new wave of texts began to appear in India. Like the discourses of the Pāli canon and the Mahāyāna *sūtras*, they purported to have been spoken by the historical Buddha, even though he had been dead for over 1,000 years. Most of them were entitled *tantra* (and sometimes *sūtra*), and they followed the general outlines of the Mahāyāna path. They used the standard opening formula of Pāli and Mahāyāna discourses attributed to the Buddha ("Thus have I heard at one time..."), but where the former generally situated him in a location in India associated with his preaching, the *Hevajra Tantra* and a number of others begin with the Buddha engaged in sexual intercourse with female consorts.

The opening phrase of the *Hevajra Tantra* states: "Thus have I heard at one time: The Bhagavan [Buddha] dwelt in the vagina (*bhaga*) of the Vajrayoginī who is the body, speech, and mind of all buddhas."[29] In chapter two, the Buddha instructs his audience, "You should kill living beings, you should speak lying words, you should take things that are not given, you should frequent others' wives."[30] These actions are explained symbolically, but are obviously intended to shock orthodox Buddhists.[31] He later urges them to "have sex with women in various modes of existence in the three worlds," and assures them that these "fearful and terrible actions" are "conducive to the awakening of a buddha." The assembled bodhisattvas are so stunned at seeing the Buddha in flagrante delicto and propounding teachings that contravene his earlier dispensations that they collectively faint. He revives them with his magical power and informs them that the new methods they are learning are simply more advanced versions of what he previously taught.

Like the earlier Mahāyāna discourses, the tantras valorize the bodhisattva and proclaim buddhahood as the supreme ideal for religious practitioners, but they describe radically new techniques that they claim can shorten the period required to attain it to as little as one human lifetime. These techniques include meditative visualizations in which trainees generate a vivid image of a buddha and then imagine that their bodies merge with the visualized deity and that they are transformed into buddhas, with the body, speech, and mind of buddhas, performing compassionate actions for the benefit of sentient beings.

The tantras also describe sexual yogas in which men and women engage in ritualized coitus. These are linked with a mystical physiology of the "illusory body" (*māyā-deha*), consisting of subtle energies called winds (*prāṇa*) and drops (*bindu*) and the channels (*nāḍī*) through which they circulate. There are 82,000 channels, the most important of which are: (1) the central channel, roughly contiguous with the spine; (2) the right channel, which is parallel to it on the right side and associated with compassion and skill in means; and (3) the left channel, which runs parallel on the left side and is associated with wisdom. At several places called *cakras* the right and left channels wrap around the central channel and constrict the flow of energies. By loosening the constrictions and causing winds and drops to move through the central channel, meditators are able to manifest subtle levels of mind, and these practices enable them to make more rapid progress than is possible through the standard Mahāyāna path.

Adherents of the tantras referred to their path as a new vehicle, the "Adamantine Vehicle" (Vajrayāna). The *vajra* is a core symbol in the tantras: it is said to be the hardest substance, and is equated with the union of wisdom and compassion perfected to the highest degree in the mind of a buddha. Iconographically the *vajra* is a five-pointed scepter that is frequently held by tantric buddhas in statues or paintings. It is also associated with the penis, which is commonly referred to as *vajra* in tantric texts.

Vajrayāna follows the earlier Mahāyāna *sūtras* in declaring that all phenomena are empty (*śūnya*) of inherent existence, that is, they are collections of parts brought together by causes and conditions, which change from moment to moment. They have no enduring substance or essence. The same is true, as we have seen, of humans and other beings. According to the *Hevajra-tantra*, there is no real difference between cyclic existence and nirvana (*saṃsāra-nirvāṇa-abheda*): "when the essence is declared, pure and consisting in knowledge, there is not the slightest difference between cyclic existence and nirvana."[32]

Ordinary beings falsely imagine that they have enduring souls and that things in their environment have essential natures, and they grasp after them, whereas buddhas have eliminated all false conceptuality and have no cognitive attachments to the fleeting phenomena of the world. The difference between the two is one of perspective; the world does not change when one becomes a buddha, only one's perception of it. The *Tantra of Fierce Great Passion* echoes Shakespeare's statement that "nothing is either good or bad, but thinking makes it so": "The mind precedes all things good or bad, and distinctions of one's situation, location, etc., are merely forms created by the mind."[33]

Some Vajrayāna texts propose a radical reversion of the norms found in the monastic codes. Sexual desire is the primary factor that enmeshes sentient beings in cyclic existence, but some tantras contain techniques for transmuting this energy and using it in the path to buddhahood. According to the *Tantra of Fierce Great Passion*, "The same terrible acts that lead beings to hell will certainly lead them to liberation if they are conjoined with method."[34] Its practices are prescribed "for the sake of acquisition of supernatural powers (*siddhi*) by the lustful." Far from being an impediment, lust is said to be a necessary prerequisite for anyone wishing to attain buddhahood. The *Hevajra-tantra* asserts:

> That by which the world is bound,
> By the same things it is released from bondage.
> But the world is deluded and does not understand this truth,
> And one who does not possess this truth cannot attain perfection.[35]

Some tantric texts even rewrite the biography of Śākyamuni Buddha in order to make it conform to the notion that sexual yogas are essential for the attainment of buddhahood—even though no mention is made of them in the earlier accounts of his life. *The Compendium of the Truth of All Buddhas* (*Sarva-thatāgata-tattva-saṃgraha*) asserts that he was sitting under the Tree of Awakening meditating during the night he attained buddhahood, but a number of buddhas interrupted him and informed him that it is impossible to complete the path without engaging in sexual yogas. He realized that they were correct, and then left his physical body behind and traveled to a transcendant tantric realm in a magically created body. He was given the highest consecrations, which empowered him to engage in sexual yogas with a physical consort (*karma-mudrā*, literally "action seal"). After his brief rendezvous, he returned to his place beneath the Tree of Awakening and resumed his meditations.

In addition to sexual acts, some tantras also urge trainees to ingest forbidden substances such as meat and intoxicants in order to overcome their aversion to them. Restrictions of diet, behavior, and passion are appropriate for beings of lesser capacities, but for advanced practitioners any preference for some things or aversion toward others becomes an impediment, a lingering vestige of conventional thought that must be overcome in order for one to become a buddha. Buddhas view all things with absolute equanimity; none are inherently good or bad, desirable or repellant, and those who have attained awakening have completely surpassed ordinary notions of conduct or behavior. The *Hevajra-tantra* declares that the advanced tantric practitioner:

> has passed beyond oblations, renunciation, and austerities,
> and is liberated from *mantras* [incantations] and meditation.
> There is nothing that one may not do, and nothing that one
> may not eat.
> There is nothing that one may not think or say,
> nothing that is either pleasant or unpleasant.[36]

Tantric adepts (*siddha*) are described in a number of Vajrayāna texts. Some belong to despised castes and make their living by the lowliest occupations. Some Indian siddhas wandered naked or seminaked, clothed in animal skins and wearing bone ornaments, their hair matted and sometimes smeared with ashes from cremation grounds, and they often had antisocial actions ascribed to them. They gathered in cemeteries for tantric "feasts" (*ganacakra*), in which they fornicated with multiple partners and ingested forbidden substances such as elephant meat, wine, and drugs. Their biographies contain descriptions of the negative judgments of these iconoclastic figures by mainstream Indians, and they appear to revel in their unconventionality.[37]

The *Tantra of Fierce Great Passion* urges aspiring siddhas to have sexual intercourse numerous times, and it contains a catalogue of positions, along with ritualized activities before and after coitus. After the two partners have become exhausted, the male yogin is advised to ply the female yoginı with meats and intoxicants so that they can regain strength and arouse desire again, following which they should engage in more sexual yoga (2.7). The tantra also includes extensive lists of forbidden substances that they should ingest, including meat and seminal fluids.

Sexual Tensions in Tibet: Siddhas and Monks

Tibetans began importing Buddhism in the seventh century. Traditional histories report that the second of Tibet's Buddhist kings (*chos rgyal*), Trisong Detsen (ca. 740–798) extended an invitation to the Indian scholar-monk Śāntarakśita to travel to Tibet and spread the dharma, but his visit was marred by natural disasters, which were attributed to attempts by Tibet's indigenous demons to obstruct his mission. The king reluctantly asked Śāntaraksita to leave the country, but before he did he advised the king to invite the tantric master Padmasambhava to quell demonic resistance.

When Padmasambhava arrived at the border, a huge snowstorm created by the demons made further progress impossible, and so he retreated into a cave and meditated. The power of his meditation stopped the storm, and he then challenged the demons to personal combat. One by one, they were defeated by the power of Padmasambhava's *siddhi* and the mantras he chanted. The demons offered up their "life force," but Padmasambhava spared them in exchange for a vow that they would henceforth become protectors of Buddhism. Śāntaraksita was asked to return, and he, Padmasambhava, and Trisong Detsen subsequently consecrated Tibet's first monastery, which was named Samye (ca. 767).

The figures of Śāntaraksita and Padmasambhava represent a dichotomy that still characterizes Tibetan Buddhism. Celibate monasticism is a key feature of each of Tibet's four Buddhist orders, but all of them also inherited lineages that are traced back to nonmonastic Indian siddhas, who often denigrated monastics as plodding and conventional, and asserted that the siddhas' own paths—which included the practice of sexual yogas—were a more rapid path to buddhahood than those of their celibate coreligionists.[38]

The Nyingma (Old Translation) order claims that its roots lie in the first period of Buddhism's dissemination to Tibet (seventh to ninth centuries), and it follows the early translations of tantric texts. Many of its core practices are traced back to Indian siddhas, and some Nyingma monks engage in sexual yogas despite taking monastic vows.

The Kagyupa (Teaching Lineage) order views the Indian siddhas Tilopa (988–1069) and his student Nāropa (1016–1100) as its progenitors, and Nāropa's Tibetan follower Marpa (1012–1097) and his student Milarepa (1040–1123) are among the most important figures in the tradition. Milarepa's student Gampopa (1079–1153) instituted a monastic order whose members take vows of celibacy, but the two strands of lay siddhas and monastics continue to be central aspects of the Kagyupa lineage.

The Sakyapa (Grey Earth) order traces its tantric practices to the Indian siddha Virūpa, and it also maintains a monastic order that emphasizes study and celibate monasticism along with the tantric tradition of "path and result" (*lam 'bras*).

The Gelukpa (System of Virtue, founded by Tsong Khapa (1357–1419), is the newest and largest of Tibet's Buddhist traditions. Tsong Khapa was a reformer whose writings and biography indicate he was deeply concerned with the rising popularity of sexual yogas and practices that he considered to be problematic. Tsong Khapa and the Gelukpa tradition are adamant about the necessity of practice of sexual yogas for the attainment of buddhahood, but at the same time he sought to restrict them to elite practitioners. He believed that for most people celibate monasticism is the surest way to advance on the path, and he denounced monks who violated their vows by engaging in sexual practices, believing that Vajrayāna vows supersede those of the Vinaya. In his commentary on Asaṅga's "Chapter on Ethics" (*Śıla-parivarta*) in the *Bodhisattva Levels* (Bodhisattva-bhūmi), Tsong khapa writes that some Buddhists say of adherence to monastic vows:

> "We are Bodhisattvas; we are [practitioners of] secret *mantra*. Thus we should 'transcend' [the monastic vows], and the higher [vows] will purify [the transgression of lower vows]." They say this and enter into laxity. When one has adopted the two higher vows [bodhisattva vows and tantric vows], the major transgression of contradicting bodhisattva precepts creates an even larger [transgression] that contradicts the tantric vows in the context of this [Buddhist] teaching.... In light of this formulation, how can those who claim to be Mahāyānists but who do not maintain either of the two vows [of laypeople and monks] have the slightest basis for asserting this? Thus they pollute the Teacher's dispensation with the filth of their sick thoughts, and so we who desire what is best should avoid them like poison.[39]

Such concerns were not unique to Tsong Khapa, and were echoed by other Tibetans from the first importations of siddha tantric lineages to Tibet. In the tenth century, King Yeshe Öd of Guge in western Tibet issued an ordinance that denounced tantrists who engaged in sexual yogas while remaining monks:

> You tantrists, who live in our villages,
> Have no connection to the three paths of Buddhism
> [Hınayāna, Mahāyāna, and Vajrayāna];
> And yet you claim to follow the Mahāyāna.
> Not maintaining the moral strictures of Mahāyāna,
> You claim, "We are Mahāyānists."
> This is like a beggar claiming to be a king.
> Or a donkey dressed in the skin of a lion.[40]

He goes on to accuse such people of being bereft of both shame and true compassion, and characterizes them as "more beset by lust than a donkey or an ox in heat." He warns that those who violate monastic vows in this way will be reborn in hell or as intestinal worms.

Despite Tsong Khapa's strong feelings on the subject of monastic celibacy, he agrees with those who claim that sexual yogas are an essential part of the path to buddhahood, but he holds that only practitioners with unusually keen compassion who are in a hurry to complete the training in order to be of benefit to others should even consider them. Moreover, only those who have directly realized emptiness (*śūnyatā*) should engage in sexual yogas, because successful completion of these techniques requires the ability to generate vivid images of buddhas from the wisdom consciousness directly realizing emptiness. Direct realization of emptiness is considered to be a high level of attainment in Tibetan Buddhism, and only a handful of practitioners would claim to have achieved it. Thus sexual yogas ought to be restricted to a small spiritual elite, and the rest should realize that their progress is best guaranteed by taking and maintaining monastic vows, along with study and practice of meditation that does not involve sexual intercourse.

According to Gelukpa tradition, Tsong Khapa was a physical emanation of Mañjuśrī, the buddha of wisdom, and thus could have engaged in sexual practices without violating his vows, but he feared that if he did it would send a contradictory message to his followers, and so during his life he maintained strict adherence to the Vinaya and expected it of his students. After he died, however, he performed sexual yogas in the intermediate state (*bar do*) between lives in a subtle body, and thus avoided any infraction of monastic conduct. This has been taken as the ideal by successive generations of Gelukpas, but some lineages of the other orders claim that Vajrayāna practice transcends monasticism, and so it is permissible to engage in sexual yogas if they are integral to one's progress and one has been advised to do so by one's teacher (*bla ma*).

All orders of Tibetan Buddhism, including the Gelukpas, also have lay tantrikas (*sngags pa*), who may marry and have families, but are full-time religious practitioners. Many of Tibet's most popular saints were laypeople, and it is also possible to retract one's monastic vows if one reaches a point in one's practice at which sexual yogas are appropriate. This is generally easy to do, and there is no animus toward former monks and nuns who leave the order to further their training. Some may subsequently retake the vows after successful completion of advanced tantric meditation.

Vajrayāna sexual techniques are vastly different from popular notions of "tantric sex" in the West. Most practitioners who engage in them do so only after an extended period of preparation that includes long sessions of solitary meditation and development of advanced levels of realization. Moreover, according to biographies of those who practice them, sexual yogas are only used at particular junctures of meditative training, and are not orgiastic or licentious. For example, the "liberation story" (*rnam thar*) of Yeshe Tsogyel (ca. 757–817)—one of Tibet's greatest female yogins—recounts that she practiced solitary meditation for lengthy periods, following which her lama Padmasambhava advised her to take a consort and practice sexual yogas in order to help her progress on the path. Following each of these periods, she returned to solitary meditation, and the descriptions of the practices portray them as highly ritualized and not particularly erotic.[41]

The goal is to utilize the power of desire in order to access subtle levels of mind, but because of the danger of unrestrained lust practitioners must have engaged in previous mental training and have the ability to manipulate the winds and drops, and they should have at least the inception of direct realization of emptiness. Sex is not done for its own sake, but rather as a means for achieving advanced states of consciousness, and according to Vajrayāna theory one result of these techniques is transcendence of sexual desire. A popular analogy holds that just as two sticks rubbing together produce a fire that consumes them both, so sexual yogas use the power of desire in order to eradicate it. So in the final analysis, these techniques claim to produce the same result as the Vinaya trainings of celibate monasticism, but through radically divergent means.

NOTES

1. The mother of a buddha need not be a virgin—and there is no indication that this was a virgin birth—but after a woman conceives a buddha all lustful thoughts disappear, and even after giving birth she will never again engage in sexual activity. The Buddha's mother is said to have died seven days after he was born, but even if she

had lived she would have remained celibate. He was raised by his stepmother, Prajāpatı, who later became a nun.

2. *Aṃguttara-nikāya*, edited by Richard Morris (London: Pali Text Society, 1961), I. 145ff.

3. *Vinaya Pitakam*, edited by Shermann Chenberg (London: Pali Text Society, 1964), III.20–23. This passage also contains the quote in the first epigraph at the beginning of this chapter.

4. *Vinaya* I.60ff.

5. Rules prohibiting any type of sexual intercourse may be found throughout the *Vinaya*. An example is *Vinaya* VI (*Parivāra*), in the "Great Differentiation" (*Mahā-vibhaṃga*) section (VI.33): "Through indulging in sexual intercourse one falls into three offenses: If one indulges in sexual intercourse with a body that is not dead there is an expulsionary offense. If one indulges in sexual intercourse with a body that has partially decayed this is a grave offense. If without touching the penis one causes it to enter an open mouth this is an offense of wrong-doing." According to this calculus, sexual intercourse with a living woman rates among the five worst possible offenses for a monk, and is more serious than intercourse with a corpse. There are also a number of similar passages in other parts of the Pāli canon, including: the "Sā-maññaphala-sutta" (*Dıgha-nikāya* I.63); "Apāyika-vagga" (*Aṃguttara-nikāya*), edited by T. W. R. Rhys Davids and J. E. Carpenter (London: Pali Text Society, 1947), I.265–273; the "Indriya-vagga" (*Aṃguttara-nikāya* II.141–148); the "Tevijjā-sutta" (*Dıgha-nikāya* I.246–247); and *Sutta-nipāta*, translated by S. Saddhatissa (London: Curzon Press, 1985), 400, 609, 814, 835.

6. See *Dharmaguptaka Vinaya Vinaya 1. 56* (*Sifen lu*), 55.

7. Heterosexuality is the presumed orientation in the Vinaya. There are numerous examples of monks engaging in homosexual acts, but no sense that they are "homosexuals." Rather, it appears that the authors of these texts assumed that men will only engage in homosexual acts when women are not available or as a form of experimentation. There is no indication that there are some men who prefer sexual relations with men; as Foucault noted regarding Europe prior to the nineteenth century, when the concept of "the homosexual" developed, homosexuality is seen as something one does, rather than something that one is. Buddhaghosa asserts that those who engage in sex with other men are unable to attain some advanced meditative states (*Visuddhimagga* I.77), but he does not appear to consider this a differing orientation. Prohibitions against homosexual acts can be found in *Vinaya* IV.287–288, 341–344 (*Pācittiya* rules 31, 32, 90, 91, 92, 93).

8. Any intentional emission of semen requires a formal *saṃgha-karma* (*Vinaya* VI.34). If a monk intentionally rubs his body against that of a woman, this also requires a *saṃgha-karma* (VI.34). Even if he strokes an article of her clothing with his hand, or rubs his clothing against hers, this constitutes a serious offense requiring formal expiation (VI.34). Similarly, speaking to a woman about satisfying his sensual desires requires a *saṃgha-karma* (VI.34).

9. See, for example, *Sphuṭāthata Srıghanacara-saṃgraha-ṭıkā* III.1–3, which stipulates that even the slightest penetration of any orifice for purposes of sexual

enjoyment constitutes an expulsionary offense: J. Duncan Derrett, *A Textbook for Novices* (Turin: Instituto di Indologia, 1983), 52–53. The Vinaya (e.g., *Vinaya* III.28–29) indicates that any sexual congress with women, men, animals, eunuchs, humans, or nonhumans constitutes an expulsionary offense. See also *Vinayamukha* I.4.1, which states that any monk who engages in sexual intercourse immediately loses communion (*saṃvāsa)* with the monastic community, that is, ceases to be a monk. This text goes on to say (I.4.1) that any penetration, even to the width of a sesame seed—even if he does not finish the action, and even if his or her partner's sexual organ is covered, and whether the intercourse occurs with living or dead humans, living or dead animals, with trees or inanimate objects, and even if he initially resists but subsequently enjoys it—is an expulsionary offense.

10. *Vinaya* I.192. Masturbation is also prohibited in *Vinaya* III.109 (*saṃghādisesa* rule 1). Masturbation by nuns is forbidden in *Vinaya* IV.259–261 (*Pācittiya* rules 3 and 4).

11. *Aṅguttara-nikāya* I.1–2.

12. *Itivuttaka*, 114. The *Itivuttaka* is the fourth book of the *Khuddaka-nikāya* section of the *Sutta-pitaka* of the Pāli canon.

13. *Aṅguttara-nikāya* IV.128. Earlier in the same collection, the Buddha states: "In truth, women are a snare devised by Māra [the Buddhist Satan, who tempts people into ignorance]. It is better for you to argue with a man carrying a sword than to speak alone with a woman. It is better for a monk to quarrel with a friend than to speak alone with a woman. It is better for a monk to sit next to a dangerous snake than to speak alone with a woman" (*Aṅguttara-nikāya* III.68).

14. *Dīgha-nikāya* II.141.

15. *Majjhima-nikāya* edited by V. Trenckner (London: Pali Text Society, 1964), III.126–128.

16. See *Saṃyutta-nikāya* IV.110, where the arhat Pindola tells King Udena that the Buddha advised monks to perceive women in these three ways.

17. This technique worked for some, but according to one story the Buddha taught monks this "meditation on the foul," following which he went into meditative retreat. When he returned, he observed that there were fewer monks, to which Ānanda replied that some monks had become so disgusted with the foulness of their own bodies that as many as thirty committed suicide in one day. The Buddha then wisely decided to emphasize other techniques for eradicating desire.

18. Interestingly, both the *Visuddhimagga* of Buddhaghosa (p. 184) and the *Aṅguttara-nikāya* (III.68, IV.42) state that men should not meditate on female corpses because they might find them attractive, although in the case of Sirimā this seems fairly unlikely.

19. *Majjhima-nikāya* I.133–134.

20. See *Vinaya* IV.20, *pācitiya* rule 7.

21. The main exception to this is Japan, where priests commonly take the monastic vows but have no intention of actually keeping them. Many get married and have children, and it is generally thought that the world has entered a time in which the dharma will inevitably degenerate (*mappō*) and that humans have become too

depraved to practice as the Buddha's followers did. As a result, monks cannot be expected to maintain the vows they take.

22. See, for example, Sanitsuda Ekachai, *Keeping the Faith: Thai Buddhism at the Crossroads* (Bangkok: Bangkok Post, 2002). The author is a features editor at *The Bangkok Post*; the book chronicles examples of misdeeds by the Thai *saṃgha*, many of which pertain to sexual misconduct.

23. For a discussion of some of the scandals and how Western Buddhists have attempted to deal with the problem, see James W. Coleman, *The New Buddhism: The Western Transformation of an Ancient Tradition* (New York: Oxford University Press, 2001).

24. See Étienne Lamotte's translation: *Śūraṃgamasamādhisūtra: The Concentration of Heroic Progress* (Richmond: Curzon, 1998), 177–178.

25. *Upāya-kauśalya-sūtra*, chap. one. See Mark Tatz's translation of this text: *The Skill in Means Sūtra* (Delhi: Motilal Banarsidass, 1994), 34–35. Although some Mahāyāna texts portray skillful use of desire to lure lustful beings into Buddhist practice as a special feature of the "Great Vehicle," there are precedents in the Pāli canon. An example is the story of how the Buddha had his half-brother Nanda kidnapped shortly before his wedding to a beautiful woman and against his will. The Buddha then brought the still-protesting Nanda to a celestial realm, where he saw nymphs who were far more beautiful than any human woman. Nanda agreed that they were in fact more attractive than his fiancée, and then the Buddha informed him that rebirth in such realms was the result of meditative practice. Hoping to have sex with them, Nanda assiduously applied himself to meditation, but along the way his desire was eliminated. He eventually became an arhat and lost all interest in the nymphs.

26. *Vimalakırti-nirdeśa-sūtra*, chap. 7.3. See Étienne Lamotte's translation of this passage: *The Teaching of Vimalakırti (Vimalakırtinirdeśa)*; English translation by Sara Boin-Webb (London: Pali Text Society, 1976), 179.

27. *Bodhicaryāvatāra*, edited by V. Bhattacharya (Calcutta: The Asiatic Society, 1960), chap. 8:84–85.

28. *Bodhicaryāvatāra*, chap. 8:48–49.

29. *Hevajra-tantra* I.1. My translation (and the translations of other passages from this tantra) follows the Sanskrit text of David Snellgrove: *The Hevajra Tantra: A Critical Study* (London: Oxford University Press, 1959), but differs from his translation. Snellgrove translates this passage more delicately: "Thus have I heard—at one time the Lord dwelt in bliss with the Vajrayoginı who is the Body, Speech, and Mind of all the Buddhas." But his own text vol. II: 2 clearly indicates that he "dwelt in [her] vagina" (*bhagesu vijahāra*).

30. *Hevajra-tantra* II.3, 29.

31. In the following verses, the Buddha explains that "killing living beings" involves cultivating "singleness of thought" (*eka-citta*); "speaking lying words" refers to the vow to save all sentient beings; "what is not given" is a woman's bliss (presumably in sexual yoga); and "frequenting others' wives" is meditation focused on Nairātmyā, Hevajra's consort. This point is also emphasized in the *Commentary on the Condensed*

Meaning of the Hevajra-tantra (*Hevajra-pindārtha-tıkā*; Tib. *Kye'i rdo rje bsdus pa'i don gyi rgya cher 'grel pa*), which cautions that "the rites of ritual slaying and so forth that have been described [in the tantra] are intended to frighten living beings in order to subdue them, and thus establish them [on the correct path]. If one were really to kill them, one would be violating a vow of the great seal (*phyag chen po'i dam tshig*) and would fall into Avıcı hell" (15.86b, 5–6).

32. *Hevajra-tantra* I.10, 12.

33. *Caṇḍamahāroṣaṇa-tantra*, sDe dge edition, 6.33. "Great Fierce Passion" is the name of the main buddha discussed in the text.

34. *Caṇḍamahāroṣaṇa-tantra* 7.33.

35. *Hevajra-tantra* I.9, 19.

36. *Hevajra-tantra* I.7, 24.

37. The most popular of these is Abhayadatta's (ca. twelfth century) hagiography, *Lives of the Eighty-Four Adepts* (*Caturśıti-siddha-pravrtti*).

38. This ongoing tension is the central theme of an excellent study of Tibetan Buddhism by Geoffrey Samuel, *Civilized Shamans: Buddhism in Tibetan Societies* (Washington, D.C.: Smithsonian Institution Press, 1993).

39. Tsong kha pa, *Byang chub sems dpa'i tshul khrims kyi rnam bshad byang chub gzhung lam* in *Peking Tripitaka* (Tokyo: Suzuki Research Foundation, 1981), vol. 154, p. 69a.5–8.

40. See Samten G. Karmay, "The Ordinance of lHa Bla-ma Ye-shes-'od," *Tibetan Studies in Honour of Hugh Richardson*, edited by Michael Aris and Aung San Ssu Kyi (Warminster: Aris & Philips, 1980), 150–152. The Tibetan text is on p. 156. The translator Rinchen Sangpo 958–1055) echoed these sentiments in his *Refutation of Errors Regarding Secret Mantra* (*sNgags log sun 'byin*).

41. Her meditative training, including practice of sexual yogas, is described in her biography, *The Secret Life and Songs of the Tibetan Woman Yeshe Tsogyel* (*Bod kyi jo mo ye shes mtsho rgyal gyi mdzad tshul rnam par thar pa gab pa mngon byung rgyud mangs dri za'i glu 'phreng*), which has been translated by Keith Dowman as *Sky Dancer: The Secret Life and Songs of the Lady Yeshe Tsogyel* (London: Arkana, 1984). Padmasambhava's advice to take a consort and practice sexual yogas can be found on p. 44.

12

Celibacy in East Asian Buddhism

John Kieschnick

Hundreds of years after the birth of Buddhism in India, in the final decades of the first century of the Common Era, we begin to see rare but unmistakable signs of the arrival of Buddhism in China: a Buddha-like figure among indigenous Chinese deities in a tomb mural; an account of a regional ruler worshiping a strange new god; chance references to exotic foreigners living in communities and espousing a new religion. In the centuries that followed, Chinese Buddhists propagated newly produced legends, explaining that the first image of a Buddha came to China in an emperor's dream. On waking, the emperor sent out envoys to bring back a real image along with the scriptures of this great and mysterious holy man. In fact, the entrance of Buddhism to China was much more prosaic, a gradual process of centuries of transmission and acculturation, interaction with indigenous Chinese culture and innovation that continued long after Buddhism disappeared from India. Once Buddhism had taken hold in China and become a powerful cultural force there (by, say, the late fifth century), it began to spread to the emerging regional powers of Korea and Japan, and later to Vietnam. Unlike areas of Southeast Asia, such as Thailand and Cambodia, which were influenced more directly by India and Ceylon, cultures in East Asia were heavily influenced by Chinese culture and, with it, by the Buddhist experience in China.

During the first few centuries of its life in China, Buddhism introduced a host of new ideas, practices, and artifacts first formed in India or, in some cases, in Central Asia. The idea of rebirth and karma (the moral order that governs rebirth), though not originally exclusively Buddhist concepts in India, first came to China with Buddhism, eventually becoming so widespread in China that even those who did not identify themselves as Buddhist accepted karma and rebirth as fundamental parts of the natural order. Buddhism introduced as well a new repertoire of deities, rituals, and vocabulary that were eventually incorporated into Chinese culture. But perhaps no idea was so strange or faced so many obstacles to success as the notion of celibacy, embodied in the Buddhist reverence for an order of trained religious professionals with shaved heads and distinctive robes who swore to renounce all sexual activity.

In what follows, I will attempt to describe just what the obstacles to celibacy were and how Chinese Buddhists, nonetheless, successfully created and nurtured a large celibate clergy of monks and nuns that continues to flourish to this day wherever Chinese Buddhists have sufficient numbers to sustain them. Under Chinese influence, the notion of a celibate Buddhist clergy took root in Vietnam, Korea, and Japan in medieval times. In the second part of this chapter, I will turn to Japan and the curious question of how, after centuries of adhering to the celibate ideal, Japanese Buddhists abandoned it for a married clergy in the nineteenth century.

Celibacy in Chinese Buddhism

Well before Buddhism reached China, Chinese writers expressed reservations about sex and warned of the dangers of unbridled desire. In general, the focus in pre-Buddhist China was on improper sex, in particular sex with other men's wives, but early Chinese writers directed their criticism as well at excessive indulgence in sex at the expense of moral and social duties.[1] At least one ritual manual advised temporary sexual abstinence during the period of mourning, but continence for long periods of time seems to have been unheard of.[2] Although abstinence for a number of months or even a few years could be seen as an admirable sacrifice and mark of respect for a deceased family member, a number of deeply ingrained Chinese ideas worked against the practice of more long-term sexual abstinence. For one thing, regular sexual activity, extending into old age, was supported on medical grounds. A number of early sources composed before the entrance of Buddhism to China testify to the belief that abstention from sex was unhealthy; for, as one second-century BC author put it, sex served to "settle the blood" and "steady the heart."[3] An early bibliography lists a series of sex manuals (no longer extant), the titles of which reveal that sex was from early on considered a useful exercise, imperative for maintaining health.

Perhaps an even more fundamental obstacle to the practice of lifelong celibacy was the importance of lineage and ancestor worship in China. The earliest extant Chinese writings are inscriptions on turtle shells and animal bones (the "oracle bones"), which record communications between rulers and the spirits of their deceased ancestors. Later sources demonstrate that the practice of making offerings to one's ancestors was common at all social levels in ancient China. In other words, beyond the more general and virtually universal desire to continue the family line and insure a source of financial support in one's old age, in early Chinese religion, the ancestors depended on their descendants to feed them through sacrifice. In short, given beliefs about sex and reproduction already in place in China before the entrance of Buddhism, to take a vow of abstinence before one had an heir would usually have been considered extremely eccentric, physically unhealthy and, considering views of life after death, dangerously short-sighted.

As the previous chapter on celibacy in Indian Buddhism has shown, celibacy was a key feature of the Buddhist monastic order in India from early on. Early Buddhist texts make clear the juxtaposition between the pursuit of sexual satisfaction and spiritual advancement, and on repeated occasions the monastic regulations state explicitly that monks and nuns were to renounce sex and marriage on joining the order. Equally influential was the model of the Buddha, who himself renounced sex when he left his wife and family to begin the spiritual quest that led to his enlightenment. And although it is true that the Buddha's wife had already conceived a son when the Buddha left his home, eventually this son became a monk before he had had children, effectively ending the Buddha's family line.

In China, Buddhism was always linked to suspicion of sensuality, both by Buddhists and by their opponents, and Buddhist monks and nuns were, from the beginnings of Buddhism in China, always expected to be celibate. Given that China had no tradition of celibate religious professionals, it is not surprising that the sexual renunciation of the first monks and nuns in China attracted attention. One of the earliest references to a monk in China comes not in a Buddhist work but in a secular poem that describes the Chinese capital city in the second century CE. In order to highlight the incomparable beauty and seductive powers of the city's dancing girls, the poet remarks in passing that even a *sramana* (that is, a Buddhist monk) "could not help but fall under their spell."[4]

In the centuries that followed, while ordinary people continued to marvel at the fierce vows of the Buddhist monk, monks themselves proudly proclaimed their adherence to their own rules. Refusal to marry and abstinence from sex were taken for granted; biographies of eminent monks focus instead on the lengths monks went to ensure their separation from women in every respect, even when sexual intercourse is not at issue. Take, for instance the opening lines of a biography of a relatively obscure seventh-century monk named Fachong:

> He continually chanted the *Lotus Sutra* and recited the large version [of the *Perfection of Wisdom Sutra*] innumerable times. He also founded a monastery, devoting himself to its administration. In his later years he lived at the Huacheng Monastery at Banding on Mount Lu where he practiced meditation. He did not lightly involve himself in non-monastic affairs, frequently advising the monks to allow no woman to enter the monastery, for "at the highest level this harms efforts to spread Buddhism, and at a lower level gives rise to vulgar rumors."[5]

As in this quotation, the emphasis in references to celibacy in Chinese Buddhist texts is on the external effects created by monks who break their vows, rather than on the act itself. That is, the problem is not so much that a monk has committed a sin that affects his own spiritual cultivation as that through sexual misconduct he has damaged the reputation of Buddhism. The monastic regulations composed in India, but translated into Chinese in medieval times, on the contrary place great emphasis on intention, stating that if a monk accidentally engages in a sexual act but does not gain pleasure from it he is not guilty of an infraction of the code. In the case of wet dreams, for instance, as long as the monk does not enjoy or supplement the sexual experience on waking, he need not confess the act.[6] But this sort of subtlety of interpretation is absent from Chinese accounts of monks, who avoid sex at all costs, regardless of the circumstances or the monk's state of mind. In the story of a medieval monk named Guangyi, for example, the monk castrates himself in order to repel the advances of a particularly persistent seductress.[7] It is said that the Central Asian monk Kumarajiva, who came to China at the end of the fourth century, eventually becoming one of the most influential monks in Chinese Buddhist history, was on several occasions forced to have sex by powerful rulers unsympathetic to his vows of chastity and determined that the great monk should produce heirs. Buddhist sources insist that in none of these cases did Kumarajiva give into temptation; it was simply that he was forced to have sex against his will. Nonetheless, the same sources state that afterward he lived in quarters separated from the other monks.[8] In other words, while Chinese monks could theoretically have drawn on remarks in canonical Buddhist texts that argued that the importance of sexual transgression was in the intention of the monk rather than the act itself, they rarely if ever did so.

Similarly, a variety of Buddhist scriptures promote the doctrine of nonduality. Every concept relies on others to give it meaning: without ugliness there can be no beauty; without good, no bad. In some cases this doctrine was invoked to explain apparent violation of the monastic code. For instance, stories of eminent monks who ate meat and drank wine—both strictly forbidden in Chinese Buddhism—could be explained away by claiming that such monks had achieved such a high level of spiritual cultivation that for them conventional distinctions between meat and vegetable, wine and water, good and bad were irrelevant.[9] The same doctrine could conceivably have been invoked to justify violation of the vows of celibacy, but it was not. Further, although tantric texts were translated into Chinese during the medieval period, and tantric Buddhism did exert an influence on Chinese Buddhist art and ritual, sexual yoga—whether purely symbolic or actually practiced—of the sort described in the last chapter is virtually absent from Chinese Buddhism. In short, the taboo against monastic sex was so strong that there was no room for exceptions of any kind.

In addition to the order of monks, an order of nuns also took shape early in the history of Chinese Buddhism and has continued to flourish to this day. Although writings by and about nuns are relatively rare until very recently, what documents do exist make it clear that nuns were, like monks, expected to remain celibate. And accounts of eminent nuns, like their masculine counterparts, include stories of nuns who resist the sexual advances of powerful officials and other unsavory men in order to preserve their chastity.[10]

The rules defining the conduct and accoutrements of the monk and nun are as clear as they are copious, allowing for little flexibility. Lay people, however, have always had many more options when determining what it means to be "Buddhist." For instance, although Chinese monks and nuns are expected to be lifelong vegetarians, and some lay people too adopt lifelong vows of vegetarianism, some lay people choose to eat vegetarian food only on certain days of the month or not at all. In general, the Buddhist clergy in China has been tolerant of lay practices, encouraging the laity to adopt the more rigorous habits of monks and nuns but not insisting that they do so. This flexibility is readily apparent in the case of celibacy. Buddhist scriptures invite lay people to adopt various sets of precepts, the most common of which are five: do not kill, do not steal, do not engage in sexual misconduct, do not lie, and do not drink alcoholic beverages. In this list of taboos, the precise meaning of "sexual misconduct" for the laity was open to interpretation. One influential scripture described the precept as follows:

> If at an improper time or place one has sexual contact with women other [than one's wife], one commits the offense of sexual misconduct.... If at a time of difficulty, war, tyranny, or fear, one has one's wife renounce the home life and later maintains a sexual relationship with her, one commits the offense of sexual misconduct. If the contact involves the three organs [oral sex with the male or female mouth, and anal sex], the offense of sexual misconduct is committed. If on the roadside at a place beside a stupa, temple, or a place where people gather, one engages in impure conduct either by oneself or with another, one commits the offense of sexual misconduct. Whether one is protected by one's parents, one's brothers, or a king, whether one has set a date, whether one promises, or whether one is paid or invited, if one engages in impure conduct beside statues or dead bodies, one commits the offense of sexual misconduct. If one [has sexual intercourse with one's wife but] thinks her another, or thinks another's wife is one's own, one commits the offense of sexual misconduct.[11]

Another, equally influential, text also lists as illicit sex with one's wife when she is pregnant or nursing and sex with a young girl.[12] In the case of the precept enjoining Buddhist lay people to refrain from "killing," many simply interpreted the rule as meaning they were not to slaughter the animals they ate, while others went a step farther, taking the rule to mean they were to keep a vegetarian diet regardless of who did one's butchering. The same is true for the precept regarding sexual misconduct. That is, many throughout Chinese history vowed not just to abstain from "sexual misconduct" but to avoid sex altogether. The theme of the man or woman who swears off sex to devote him or herself to Buddhist cultivation is common from the early history of Buddhism in China up to modern times.[13] Most of the references to those who vowed to "renounce the bed chamber" (*jue fangshi*) in early Chinese writings were elite men who normally did so only after they had at least one son to continue the family line. The same was often, but not always, true in accounts of women who took vows of perpetual chastity. At times, such vows were directly related to the lay precepts laid out in Buddhist scriptures; but sexual continence was also justified as a part of a general regimen of spiritual cultivation, or as a mark of sorrow and respect on the death of a loved one.

Growing up alongside somber Buddhist admonitions warning monks and nuns of the dangers of sexual desire, and pious biographies of monks, nuns, and even lay people who strictly observed vows of celibacy, are pointed references to monks and nuns who broke their vows, together with salacious stories, vulgar jokes, and doggerel that criticize and ridicule monks and nuns for their supposed sexual exploits. Recall the quotation cited earlier of an eminent Chinese monk who refused to allow women on monastery grounds because "at the highest level this harms efforts to spread Buddhism, and at a lower level gives rise to vulgar rumors." Ample evidence demonstrates that the monk's fears of "vulgar rumors" were well founded. Suspicions of the ability of monks and nuns to control their sexual cravings at times took a relatively mild form, as in the following comments from the raucous seventeenth-century erotic novel the *Carnal Prayer Mat*:

> Any young man joining the [Buddhist] order has certain problems he must face. However strongly he tries to rein in his lusts, however firmly he tries to extinguish his desires, prayer and scripture reading will get him through the day well enough, but in the wee hours of the morning that erect member of his will start bothering him of its own accord, making a nuisance of itself under the bedclothes, uncontrollable, irrepressible. His only solution is to find some form of appeasement, either by using his fingers for emergency relief or by discovering some young novice with whom to mediate a solution. (Both methods are regular standbys for the clergy.)[14]

The passage is notable not so much for its accusations, which as we will see were common, but for its sympathy, in particular its tolerance of homosexual relations between supposedly celibate monks and their novices.[15] The sixteenth-century erotic novel the *Plum in the Golden Vase* is harsher in its assessment of sex in the monasteries, referring to monks as "sex-starved hungry ghosts" and noting that, since they are not required to work for their food like lay people, "they are able to devote all their attention to lust."[16] Suspicion that monks were in fact far from celibate was widespread in medieval times as well. Outraged officials periodically memorialized the throne, complaining of the perverse conduct of monks. "In the morning," wrote one sixth-century official, "imperial consorts enter the monks' quarters, while at night young men sleep in the nuns' rooms." And a famous fifth-century persecution of Buddhism was justified in part by the claim that monks carried on secret sexual affairs with women "of good families" in hidden chambers beneath a monastery. Periodic court sex scandals involving monks further reinforced the image of monks as depraved hypocrites who, far from renouncing the physical pleasures, use their status as a cover to indulge the basest cravings without restraint. A prominent seventh-century monk, for example, was executed when he was found to have been carrying on a relationship with one of the emperor's daughters.[17] The most celebrated sexual scandal involving a monk was the alleged relationship between the seventh-century Empress Wu and her monk-lover Huaiyi.[18]

It is probably impossible to assess the accuracy of such accounts from the premodern period. Already in the tenth century, Buddhist historians dismissed as slander accounts that the prominent seventh-century monk Kuiji was a womanizer.[19] Even official court documents and legal cases may in many cases be the products of hearsay and calumny. The fifth-century persecution of Buddhism just mentioned, for instance, was carried out in large measure for ideological, political, and economic reasons. When immediate justification was needed for such campaigns it was a simple matter to fabricate shocking accounts of the lascivious behavior of renegade monks, providing convenient moral grounds for attacking powerful monks and wealthy monasteries. Stories of the relationship between Empress Wu and her monk-lover were propagated by male historians who reviled Wu as an ambitious woman who usurped a throne that rightfully belonged in the hands of men.

The same holds true more clearly for stories of monks and nuns in fiction. That is, the sexually avaricious nun and lustful monk very early on became stock characters—accurate reflections of lay fantasies but only obscurely related to actual practice. The same dynamics are very much at work even today: however ardently leading Chinese monks and nuns defend the general level of sexual abstinence in the Buddhist clergy, pornographic films and erotic literature continue to delight in recounting the secret sexual lives of monks and nuns, and rumors of a wide variety of levels of veracity continually swirl about the sexual habits of prominent Buddhist figures. Nevertheless, although it remains difficult to determine with precision the extent to which the celibate ideal is being carried out among Chinese monks and nuns, we can safely say that the ideal itself is as powerful as ever. Buddhist monks and nuns in China have always been expected to remain celibate, and any violation of the vow swiftly results in public scandal, ridicule, and condemnation.

Married Monks in Japanese Buddhism

Chinese Buddhism for centuries exerted a major influence on regions surrounding China. In the second century, Buddhism entered Vietnam, which provided a flourishing center for monks and merchants traveling between China and India. Buddhism began to have a significant influence on Korean culture from the fourth century, and on Japan from the sixth. In all three of these regions—Vietnam, Korea, and Japan—Buddhist texts were in premodern times read in Chinese, and Chinese missionary monks played an active role in promoting Buddhism abroad. Hence it is not surprising that, allowing for some degree of regional variation, the early history of Buddhist celibacy in these regions followed the pattern we have already seen for China. That is, although stories of lascivious monks and nuns appear in secular sources, and there is even an occasional reference to lofty monks who appear to break the monastic rule of celibacy for greater ends, in general monks were expected to be celibate.[20] On the rare occasions when biographies of monks mention women at all, it is to emphasize that, even when they attempt to seduce a monk, his heart remains unmoved; or women appear in quotations from monastic sermons in which monks warn laymen of the dangers of adultery.[21]

In nineteenth-century Japan, however, the history of Buddhist celibacy took an unexpected turn, leading to the decision to abandon the requirement of celibacy for the Buddhist male clergy.[22] At present, approximately 90 percent of all male Buddhist clergy in Japan are married, a fact that leads some scholars of Buddhism to prefer the term "cleric" to "monk" in the Japanese context. This practice is far from raising suspicion and discontent among practicing Buddhists; in fact, most lay Japanese Buddhists now prefer clerics who are married. The common practice of passing down the abbacy of a temple from cleric to son further increases pressure on Buddhist clerics in Japan not only to marry but also to produce male descendants.

In early medieval times, Japanese attitudes toward Buddhist celibacy were not very different from those we have already seen for China. As in China, Japanese monks had to defend themselves from the charge that by not marrying and producing heirs they were unfilial. As in China, one reaction to the celibate clergy was the emergence of lewd, fornicating monks and nuns as stock characters in popular literature. And the sexual misconduct of the Buddhist clergy was a standard focus of attention whenever the state decided to act against the interests of the Buddhist church. Finally, as in China, there were cases of men who underwent ordination chiefly to avoid taxes and corvée, and whose dedication to maintaining the precepts was superficial, leading no doubt to frequent violation of monastic precepts against sex.

Medieval accounts of monastic indiscretions are notoriously slippery and difficult to assess (which are mere rumor, which invented to destroy a rival monk or explain away an unwanted pregnancy?). Nonetheless, beyond scandalous stories of monks frequenting brothels or carrying on clandestine relations with promiscuous nuns or fallen laywomen, the practice of monks marrying and even passing their temples on to their sons seems to have been much more common in Japan than elsewhere.[23] Male homosexuality in the monasteries was apparently more widespread and certainly more open in Japan than elsewhere.[24] More striking still, in the thirteenth century the charismatic monk Shinran openly married and raised a family, while even then not entirely renouncing his clerical status. By declaring himself "neither monk nor layman," Shinran laid the foundation for a new type of Buddhist cleric in the Jodo Shinshu tradition, a prominent branch of Japanese Buddhism that hailed Shinran as its founder.[25]

The justification for Shinran's decision was rooted in the doctrine of the "decline of the Dharma," influential throughout the history of Buddhism in East Asia, which held that Buddhist teachings rose and fell together with the general moral tenor of the world in grand cycles of thousands of years. Shinran, like many monks before him, believed that he was living in a stage in this endless cycle in which the moral capacities of human beings were weaker than they had been in previous eras. In such an age, it was hopeless to attempt to cultivate oneself through diligent study of complex doctrine or demanding ascetic practice; the only hope was instead through reliance on faith, as expressed in the practice of recitation of the name of the Buddha. In the same way, although monks in the Buddha's day had been able to keep themselves chaste through sheer determination, none could now hope to emulate them. In other words, Shinran's decision to marry was not so much a critique of celibacy per se as it was an admission of the difficulties of carrying out a noble practice in a degenerate age.

In later times, clerics belonging to the Jodo Shinshu denomination, such as the seventeenth-century cleric Chiku, continued to defend their practice of marrying. They argued that their own denomination, led by a married clergy, had flourished, while others had declined, and they drew attention as well to famous "fallen monks" of the past, including some we have already seen such as Kumarajiva and Kuiji, who nonetheless were still regarded as important, eminent figures in the history of Buddhism. Through such figures, he claimed, monks could find noble precedent for the decision to openly marry. In a standard Buddhist rhetorical move, Chiku further argued that the Buddha established the rule of celibacy as an "expedient device," suitable for that age, but with the understanding that it could be abolished at such time as it was no longer appropriate. Removed from the Indian origins of Buddhism by more than two centuries, remote from the Buddha's original context both geographically and culturally, modern Japanese Buddhists clearly needed new guidelines for practice. Finally, employing the same sort of rhetoric that had been used against monks for centuries throughout Buddhist history, Chiku complained that sexual misconduct was rampant among monks of other denominations that insisted on celibacy; only through marriage could Buddhist clerics channel their natural desires and avoid the rank hypocrisy of monks who only pretended to be celibate while secretly engaging the services of prostitutes or sleeping with married women, and hence exposing the clergy in general to ridicule, resentment, and shame.

Supported by such arguments as well as the growing weight of tradition, members of the Jodo Shinshu denomination followed Shinran's example and married. Nonetheless, Japanese clerics of other denominations continued to promote the celibate ideal more or less as it had been since the early years of Buddhism in ancient India. In addition to pressure from within the Buddhist tradition, celibacy for Buddhist monks in Japan was enforced by the state. The state closely monitored monastic behavior and enforced strict penalties on monks deemed guilty of sexual misconduct. The penalties could be extraordinarily harsh. In the eighteenth century, monks judged guilty of fornication were at times forced to kneel in public before a plaque detailing their crimes. Others were paraded down public streets, stripped naked, imprisoned, and crucified. "Sexual misconduct" focused on sex with prostitutes and married women, but included as well any sexual contact with women. Again, however common clerical marriage may have been as a tacitly accepted tradition at the local temple, monastic authorities and the state still expected monks to remain celibate.

Pressure for the abolition of celibacy among Buddhist clerics developed slowly and came from various quarters. In part as a response to the state-sponsored crackdowns on sexual misconduct among Buddhist clerics, the monk Otori Sesso (1814–1904) repeated the now familiar argument that the traditional rules of celibacy were unenforceable; far from protecting the clergy from distraction and preserving an image of purity, celibacy rules had become a hindrance to proselytizing and were destroying the image of the Buddhist monk. Otori went on to argue, in a petition to the secular authorities to abolish the ban on clerical marriage, that it was fundamentally wrong to suppress "human emotions" and that marriage was a necessary step in the modernization of Japanese Buddhism.

Arguments like these were well received by nineteenth-century reformers within the Japanese government—generally hostile to Buddhism—who argued for the necessity of eliminating the special status of Buddhist clerics under the law as one part of a larger program of modernization and reform that included the elimination of special privileges for nobles and samurai. Calls for the reform of state regulations for Buddhist monks culminated in an edict in 1872, which announced that "From now on Buddhist clerics shall be free to eat meat, marry, grow their hair, and so on. Furthermore, they are permitted to wear ordinary clothing when not engaged in religious activities."[26] In this way, the state encouraged monks to abandon all that makes the Buddhist monk distinctive, from his shaven pate and peculiar garments to his eating habits and vow of sexual abstinence. Outraged by the edict, many Buddhist leaders responded with vigorous defenses of the tradition of celibacy, arguing that open marriage damaged the reputation of the clergy and would inevitably lead to fewer donations and difficulties in proselytizing. Sexual desire, they insisted, increases attachment, is a hindrance to spiritual cultivation, and is expressly condemned in Buddhist scriptures. Defenders of the edict, including members of the clergy, countered that celibacy was an old-fashioned, fanatical abnegation of the world, unfit for the modern predicament that Buddhists now faced, threatened as it was by competition from Christianity and declining interest in Buddhism among the laity.

Overall, the leaders of almost all denominations of Buddhism opposed clerical marriage, announcing that although the state had no objections to the practice, they certainly did. That is, while it was now acceptable under state law for a monk to marry, most of the Japanese Buddhist leadership encouraged their followers to conform to a higher standard in keeping with the call for sexual abstinence instituted by the Buddha. The trend among the rank and file of the clergy, however, was toward marriage. For example, by 1936, the overwhelming majority of clerics in the Soto school had married, despite opposition from their leadership.[27] The celibate ideal lost ground with surprising rapidity. Increasingly, celibacy was seen as misogynist, unnatural, and an obstacle to modernity. In the conception of modern life, the family was the fundamental unit, and champions of modern science insisted that sex was a biological necessity, rendering celibacy a threat to one's physical and psychological health. Reformers, enthusiastically embracing the new drive toward modernization, argued that through marriage the clergy could improve the Buddhist genetic stock, and that the imposition of celibacy was a violation of "human rights." On a more mundane level, clerics realized the benefits of sharing the duties of running a small temple with a capable wife; others sympathized with the plight of wives of clerics and their children, unrecognized by the Buddhist leadership. During World War II, many clerics were drafted, leaving the role of running their temples to their wives and families, the value of whom even the Buddhist leadership now had to acknowledge. Conservatives who had argued that the laity would lose respect for the clergy once they took wives apparently underestimated the flexibility of the laity, who came to see married clergy as perfectly normal and even preferable to celibate monks.

Although the practice of marriage for Buddhist clerics is now firmly entrenched in Japanese Buddhism, it continues to create problems and uneasiness, particularly as Buddhist monks from different parts of the world come into contact with one another more frequently at international conferences and, more generally, because of the globalization of travel and commerce. Monks from other countries often view Japanese clerics with suspicion and scoff at their arguments for abandoning celibacy. Although marriage has been legal for clergy now for over a century, most Buddhist denominations have yet to explicitly condone it. And clerics continue to find the need to justify marriage as a sign of human frailty rather than as an innately superior way of life.

Curiously, the story of Buddhist nuns in Japan developed quite differently. Although nuns, like monks, were permitted by the state to marry in an edict promulgated in 1873, very few nuns have taken advantage of the opportunity. The reasons for this difference are very much open to question. Part of the answer lies in the fact that, unlike male clerics, nuns in general do not have the pressure to pass on their temples to children. But more diffuse and as yet unexplored reasons for the decision of Buddhist nuns to remain celibate lie no doubt in the history of nuns in Japan and in the history of gender relations in Japan more generally.

Conclusion: The Future of Celibacy in East Asian Buddhism

The Japanese decision to reconsider the necessity of a celibate Buddhist clergy had a major impact on Korea, which was for the first half of the twentieth century a Japanese colony.[28] During the colonial period, many Korean monks openly married. As in Japan, the decision to abandon celibacy came with a combination of pressure from the Japanese imperial government and from Buddhist intellectuals who, in the early decades of the century, quickly became familiar with the practice of clerical marriage in Japan and began to openly discuss its merits.

Perhaps the most influential Korean Buddhist to call for clerical marriage was the monk Han Yongun (1879–1944), who traveled to Japan as a young man, an experience that impressed on him the need to modernize Korea and, more specifically, Korean Buddhism. Yongun submitted several petitions to the ruling Japanese cabinet and to the official monastery supervisory board, asking that restrictions on clerical marriage be lifted. His arguments included many of the same points we have already seen in the case of Japan. The clergy, he argued, was rapidly losing monks; by abandoning the celibacy requirement, the Buddhist establishment could more easily recruit new Buddhist clergy. Further, since restrictions against sex were largely ignored anyway, legalizing clerical marriage would put an end to the hypocrisy of pretending that monks were celibate and would channel their sexual energy into monogamous marriage instead of unseemly, illicit relationships. Open marriage and childbirth among the clergy would establish model Buddhist families that could compete with the rising popularity of Christianity in Korea. And by having children, monks could finally put to rest charges that they were unfilial, while at the same time contributing to the nation's need for an expanded population. As for the traditional prohibitions against sex and marriage, clearly stated in Buddhist scriptures, these were expedient devices designed for a time that had long since passed, and inappropriate for modern Korea.

The combination of Japanese imperial pressure and arguments by Koreans such as Yongun led in 1926 to the official repeal of the prohibition against clerical marriage in Korea. Again, as in Japan, while some monks readily accepted the arguments for clerical marriage, others vehemently opposed the practice. Unlike the case of Japan, however, in Korea clerical marriage was for many closely associated with a foreign imperial power, a form of spiritual pollution to be extirpated as much for nationalistic as for religious reasons. After the end of World War II, celibate monks sought to restore the practice of celibacy for all monks, leading in 1955 to a presidential order calling for the resignation of all "Japanese" monks from monastic positions. In the decades that followed, the tension between the two groups—married and celibate clergy—remained intense, involving as it did not only issues of Buddhist orthodoxy and nationalism but property rights as well (since married monks hoped to pass their temples on to their children). The debate over whether or not Korean monks should be celibate, and the tension between the two camps, continues to this day.

In sum, responses to celibacy in East Asian Buddhism are divided along national lines. At the moment, Japanese clerics show no signs of reverting to the previous requirement of celibacy for all Buddhist clergy. Nor do Chinese monks and nuns show any indication that they are moving toward the Japanese model. In fact, as monks and nuns have in recent years become increasingly prominent in Taiwan and in mainland China, the image of the monk and nun there continues to be inextricably bound up with celibacy. But if the history of Buddhism in the twentieth century teaches us anything, it is that Buddhism can take radically different directions in the space of a few decades. On the one hand, Japan demonstrates the possibility for Buddhist monks to renounce celibacy; on the other, Korea shows that a counter movement back to celibacy is also possible. Nor is it easy to gauge the effects of the rapid dissemination of pornography and sex-based advertising in modern Asia, which is as likely to produce revulsion for sex as attraction to it.

But throughout the history of Buddhism in East Asia, the discourse over celibacy has involved more than the potential dangers of sexual pleasure for spiritual cultivation. It has engaged as well the question of distinction and the authority that comes with it, whether it be distinguishing monk from layman or Buddhist from non-Buddhist. Equally fundamental to debate over the celibate option was the conception of the family. Is continuing the family line through marriage and childbirth a part of a child's duties to his parents? Is the traditional sharing of domestic and public duties between husband and wife a more efficient means of negotiating the incessant challenges of daily life than living in a community of unmarried men or women? Just as the concept of modernity played a key role in debates over celibacy in the twentieth century, the rapidly changing concept of the family and gender roles are sure to shape the debate in the future as men and women, clerics and lay continue to assess the place of monasticism in East Asian society.

NOTES

1. For examples of sexual misconduct in pre-Buddhist Chinese literature and discussion of the place of sex in early Chinese historical, literary, and philosophical rhetoric, see Paul Rakita Goldin, *The Culture of Sex in Ancient China* (Honolulu: University of Hawaii Press, 2002). For a general overview of sex in premodern China, see R. H. Van Gulik, *Sexual Life in Ancient China: A Preliminary Survey of Chinese Sex and Society from ca. 1500 B.C. till 1644 A.D.* (originally published in 1961) with a new introduction and bibliography by Paul R. Goldin (Leiden: E. J. Brill, 2003).

2. *LiKi*, book 19, part 2, section 20, translated by James Legge ([1895]; Richmond: Curzon, 2001), 192. The practice of maintaining sexual abstinence during the mourning period continued into modern times. The great eighteenth-century novel *Story of the Stone*, for instance, includes several episodes in which characters avoid sex while in mourning.

3. Van Gulik, *Sexual Life in Ancient China*, 69.

4. I discuss the passage in more detail in Kieschnick, *The Eminent Monk: Buddhist Ideals in Medieval Chinese Hagiography* (Honolulu: University of Hawaii Press, 1997), 17–18, which includes a brief section on attitudes toward sex as reflected in medieval biographies of monks.

5. For references, see Kieschnick, *Eminent Monk*, 20.

6. See Bernard Faure, *The Red Thread: Buddhist Approaches to Sexuality* (Princeton: Princeton University Press, 1998), 76. This book contains a wealth of information on Buddhist sexuality, particularly for China and Japan.

7. For references, see Kieschnick, *Eminent Monk*, 22. For the Buddha's pronouncements on self-castration and Japanese examples, see Faure, *Red Thread*, 34–36.

8. Kieschnick, *Eminent Monk*, 18–19.

9. Ibid., 51–63; Faure, *Red Thread*, 151–153.

10. For a translation of a sixth-century collection of biographies of Chinese nuns, see *Lives of the Nuns. Biographies of Chinese Buddhist Nuns from the Fourth to Sixth Centuries*, translated by Kathryn Ann Tsai (Honolulu: University of Hawaii Press, 1994).

11. *The Sutra on Upasaka Precepts*, translated by Bhiksuni Shih Heng-ching (Berkeley: Numata Center for Buddhist Translation and Research, 1994), 173.

12. Vasubandhu, *Abhidharmakosa bhasyam*, French translation and annotation by Louis de La Vallée Poussin, translated into English by Leo M. Pruden (Berkeley: Asian Humanities Press, 1991), 652.

13. For examples see Kieschnick, *Eminent Monk*, 22; Patricia Buckley Ebrey, *The Inner Quarters: Marriage and the Lives of Chinese Women in the Sung Period* (Berkeley: University of California Press, 1993), 164–165; Susan Mann, *Precious Records: Women in China's Long Eighteenth Century* (Stanford: Stanford University Press, 1997), 71, 110–111.

14. Li Yu, *The Carnal Prayer Mat* (*Rou pu tuan*), translated by Patrick Hanan (New York: Ballantine Books, 1990), 304.

15. On Buddhist attitudes toward homosexuality more generally (and in particular homosexual relations between monks and novices in Japan), see Faure, *Red Thread*, 207–278.

16. *The Plum in the Golden Vase or Chin P'ing Mei*, translated by David Tod Roy (Princeton: Princeton University Press, 1993), 1: 166.

17. For references, see Kieschnick, *Eminent Monk*, 19–20.

18. Stanley Weinstein, *Buddhism under the T'ang* (Cambridge: Cambridge University Press, 1987), 43–44; 162 n. 16.

19. Kieschnick, *Eminent Monk*, 167 n. 239.

20. For a rare example of a monk who transgresses the rule of sexual abstinence apparently to prove his high level of spiritual cultivation, see the discussion of legends of the seventh-century monk Wŏnhyo in Faure, *Red Thread*, 5.

21. The man whose heart "could not be moved" is the seventh-century Korean monk Ŭisang (see Kieschnick, *Eminent Monk*, 22). For a brief fourteenth-century sermon in Vietnam on the dangers of adultery, see Cuong Tu Nguyen, *Zen in Medieval Vietnam* (Honolulu: University of Hawaii Press, 1997), 147.

22. The following discussion of celibacy in Japanese Buddhism is based on Richard M. Jaffe's *Neither Monk nor Layman; Clerical Marriage in Modern Japanese Buddhism* (Princeton: Princeton University Press, 2001), a clear and detailed account of the policies and debates concerning clerical marriage in modern Japan.

23. Ibid., 11.

24. In general in Buddhism, male homosexuality was seen as only a minor infraction of the vows of celibacy, if that. Faure, *Red Thread*, 81–82, 207–278.

25. For more on Shinran and the Jodo Shunshu, see James C. Dobbins, *Jodo Shinshu: Shin Buddhism in Medieval Japan* (Honolulu: University of Hawaii Press, 1989).

26. Jaffe, *Neither Monk nor Layman*, 72.

27. Ibid., 225.

28. My discussion of celibacy in Korean Buddhism is based on Robert E. Buswell, Jr., *The Zen Monastic Experience: Buddhist Practice in Contemporary Korea* (Princeton: Princeton University Press, 1992), 25–36.

13

Sexual Control and Daoist Cultivation

Livia Kohn

Sexual control is very important in Daoist cultivation. But this does not mean that celibacy, the deliberate abstention from sexual activity and feelings, is a major ideal or that Daoists strive to eliminate or suppress the sexual drive. On the contrary, human sexual energy is considered the root power of all life, the core of inner strength, health, and of all spiritual attainment. It has to be harnessed and properly refined, so that the ultimate goal of Daoist cultivation can be reached: immortality, an extended lifespan, and mystical vision on earth followed by a continued spirit existence in the heavens after this body has fallen away. Sexuality is recognized and experienced fully, sometimes with the help of a partner, sometimes in solo exercises, then transmutated into subtler forms of vital energy that eventually lead to the realization of higher states of awareness and cosmic salvation.

Daoists of all different schools and in all historical periods have made use of sexuality for the cultivation of long life and immortality. They all subscribe to the fundamental vision of the body as consisting of a cosmic, vital energy known as *qi*, which is closely connected to the greater universe and whose harmonious flow can and will influence social, natural, and celestial events. They also follow the Chinese medical understanding that in ordinary people *qi* naturally transforms at regular intervals into a slightly grosser and more tangible force, known as essence or *jing*. This *jing* is what we call sexual energy. It is experienced by the person as sexual arousal and is lost through sexual activity (semen) and the natural cycles of the human body (menstruation). To attain the Daoist goal, this ordinary pattern has to be interrupted and the transformative process reversed, so that *jing* once felt is not emitted but moved back up inside the body and returned into *qi*, more potent now that it has undergone a semi-alchemical transformation. This technique is known as "reverting the sexual energy to nourish the brain" (*huanjing bunao*), and is at the core of all Chinese sexual cultivation.

It is also possible to use the reversion of *jing* not only for religious goals but also for healing and enhanced youthfulness. To this end, Chinese medicine prescribes sexual practices with partners, during which intercourse is undertaken in accordance with the medical prescription—the specific times, rhythms, and methods depending on the diagnosis received. By the same token, some practitioners have used sexual methods to extend life further and create more vitality, engaging in intercourse with multiple partners to bring them to orgasm and thus cause a release of their *jing* without, however, losing their own. This practice of the so-called bedchamber arts is documented since the Former Han dynasty (206–23 BCE) and may still be pursued among Chinese today.

Another use of sexual power in Daoism appears among the first organized schools in the early centuries of the Common Era. Here especially the Celestial Masters (Tianshi) stand out. They used sexuality less toward personal refinement and more for the establishment of cosmic and communal stability. They practiced a set of rites known as the "harmonization of energy" (*heqi*) which involved the controlled, ritualized intercourse among nonmarried couples for the purpose of establishing an overall balance of yin and yang within practitioners, among group members, and in the larger universe. With the establishment of more personally oriented Daoist schools, such as that of Highest Clarity (Shangqing) in the fourth century, these rituals were sublimated into visionary experiences with divine entities as well as into internal transmutations of body energies. The latter, moreover, became the dominant theme in the most recent form of Daoist cultivation, a practice called "inner alchemy" (*neidan*), which has been the mainstay of Daoist meditation since the Song Dynasty (960–1268). In all these forms of sexual cultivation, Daoists have tended to acknowledge the importance and even superiority of the female. Not only were they not threatened by female sexuality but they also found in it an inspiring model for the creation of an immortal embryo, the alter ego that would travel to the heavens and survive the death of this body. As a result, they have for the most part treated women with respect and recognized that they had equal, if not better, chances at attaining the desired goal.

The Medical Vision: *Jing* and *Qi*

From the earliest sources on Chinese medicine, notably the *Huangdi neijing suwen* (The Yellow Emperor's Classic of Internal Medicine: Simple Questions), sexual essence or *jing* has been described as the root of life and the barometer of vitality.[1] For example, the text says:

> When a girl is seven years of age, the kidney *qi* [jing] becomes abundant. She begins to change her teeth and the hair grows longer. At 14, she begins to menstruate and is able to become pregnant. The movement of the great pulse is strong. The menses come regularly, and the girl is able to give birth.
>
> At age 21, the energy is steady, the last tooth has come out, and she is fully grown. When she reaches the age of 28, her tendons and bones are strong, her hair has reached its full length, and her body is flourishing and fertile. At 35, her yang brightness pulse begins to slacken, her face begins to wrinkle, her hair starts falling out.
>
> When she reaches the age of 42, the pulse of the three yang regions deteriorates in the upper part of her body, her entire face is wrinkled, and her hair turns gray. At age 49, she can no longer become pregnant, and the circulation of the great pulse is decreased. Her menstruation is exhausted, and the gates of blood are no longer open. Her body declines, and she is no longer able to bear children.[2]

The same pattern holds also true for males, for whom the cycle proceeds in eight-year intervals, linking vitality, procreative power, and physical beauty to the presence and activity of sexual energy.

Why is this *jing* so important? To begin, it is the *qi* of the kidneys, associated with the water system in the human body, which is responsible for the elimination and purification of substances. It is also linked closely with sexuality and procreation, as well as with the psychological power of will or determination. In general, *jing* is the source of a person's charisma, sexual attraction, and sense of wholeness. In phase energetics, moreover, *jing* is described as the indeterminate aspect of *qi* or as *qi* in transition from one determinate form to another. A classic example is man's semen that carries life from the parents to the offspring. Another is the essence that the body takes from food pending full assimilation. *Jing* is no longer the *qi* of the eggs in the omelet and not yet the *qi* gained from the eggs in the body of the eater. It is neither yin nor yang, but marks energy in transit. Thus Michael Winn suggests: "*Jing* is perhaps best understood in Western terms as primal energy.

It is the raw fuel that drives the pulsating rhythm of the body's moment-to-moment cellular division and reproduction of itself."[3]

Another reason for the importance of *jing* in Daoist cultivation is that it is tangible and can be controlled more easily than the subtler and more elusive *qi*. *Jing* as sexual energy—semen in men and menstrual blood in women—develops from pure *qi* that sinks down from the energetic center of the body. This *qi*-center is located in the abdomen in men, where it is known as the Ocean of Qi, and in the center between the breasts in women, where it is known as the Cavern of Qi. It develops due to sexual stimulation in men and on the basis of the menstrual cycle in women, in each case becoming tangible and visible as sexual sensations and fluids. In ordinary life, *jing* is emitted from the body, causing loss of *qi* which in over time leads to bodily weakness, disease, and death. This loss can be moderate, in which case vital essence will diminish over a lifetime and lead to disease and death only gradually, as outlined in the life-cycle description cited earlier. It can also be excessive, resulting in crippling illness and untimely demise. Or it can be limited and controlled, leading to enhanced vitality and a longer life, and thus form the basis for the subtler levels of Daoist cultivation, those that lead to immortality.

To regulate and slow down the process of *jing* loss, Chinese medicine may use acupuncture and herbs as well as prescribe physical exercises. Daoists and longevity seekers, on the other hand, control sexual energies and retain their *jing* with both physical disciplines and meditation practices. Never ignoring or denying sexual energy, they allow the *qi* to sink down and transform into *jing*, thereby rendering it tangible as sexual arousal, but then prevent it from being emitted and instead revert it to become *qi* once again. Moved consciously around the body in various cycles, the refined *qi* is further rarified into *shen* (spirit), which is a third form that *qi* assumes in the body. *Shen* is understood as the inherent higher vitality of life, the power of consciousness, and the ability to think. It is closely associated with the individual's outlook and personality and is said to reside in the central organ of the heart. It governs the emotions and has the most impact on the mystical transformation. Ultimately, spirit is the goal of Daoist attainment: the transformation of a baser *qi*-being into an entity of pure spirit—but in all cases the holy work begins with *jing*, with the sexual nature and most essential vitality of humanity.

Partner Practice: The Bedchamber Arts

The first practice known in China that involves the cultivation and control of sexual energies is known as *fangzhong shu* or "bedchamber arts." Its earliest documentation is in a set of manuscripts discovered in 1973 at Mawangdui near Changsha (Hunan). Dated to 168 BCE, the finds include about fifteen important early texts that discuss ways to harmonize yin and yang, find alignment with the Dao, nourish life through herbs, stabilize and deepen breathing, absorb *qi*, abstain from grains, undertake therapeutic gymnastics, and engage in sexual techniques. The manuscripts focus largely on healing and describe various modalities of healing, such as moxibustion, spells, rituals, gymnastics, sexual practices, drugs, massages, cupping, bathing, and fumigation.[4]

Information contained in these texts was later codified in works on medicine and longevity techniques. Asexual practices are especially described in classics that have women as masters and instructors as, for example, the "Book of the Simple Woman" (*Sunü jing*), the "Book of the Colorful Woman" (*Cainü jing*), and the "Book of the Mysterious Woman" (*Xuannü jing*). Each of these supernatural ladies served to instruct the Yellow Emperor (Huangdi), who is also the main interlocutor and learner in the medical texts.[5] Another important source on sexual practices is chapter 28 of the *Ishimpō* (Essential Medical Methods; dated 984).[6] This is a major handbook of Oriental medicine compiled in Heian Japan by the court physician Tamba no Yasuyori on the basis of Chinese texts, many of which are otherwise lost. The chapter forms the basis of most English accounts of Chinese sexual techniques.[7]

According to these sources, the bedchamber arts come in two major types. One is directed at health and healing; it encourages practitioners to engage in sexual activities regularly and in a controlled manner so that diseases can be not only prevented but even cured. The other is the more flamboyant exploitation of multiple partners for the sake of gaining as much *jing* as possible, becoming strong and long lived by using another.

As prescribed by the healing mode, sexual exchange with a loving partner should be undertaken regularly. However, at certain times it can be detrimental to your health: after a heavy meal, when intoxicated, after strenuous activity or an acupuncture treatment, when acutely ill, during emotional upheaval, when suffering pressure in the bladder or bowels, and during menstruation. All these are situations that upset the internal *qi*-balance of the person. They need to be resolved before successful sexual activity can be experienced. The medieval Master of Pure Harmony (Chonghezi), cited in the *Yufang bijue* (Secret Instructions of the Jade Chamber), a Tang text contained in the Japanese *Ishimpō*, points out some more details:

> If you have sex at midnight, before you have fully digested your evening meal, you may develop chest pain and fullness of *qi*. Indications are a pulling sensation beneath the ribs and pressure in the

> breast, as if it were being torn. You will lose your appetite for food and drink, feel a blocking knot beneath your heart, sometimes even vomit green and yellow bile. Your stomach will feel tense with the fullness of energy and there will be a slow and irregular pulse. Sometimes in addition there may be nosebleeds, hardness or pain beneath the ribs, and sores on the face. To heal this, have intercourse after midnight and close to the approach of dawn. . . .
>
> If you have intercourse when overdue for urination you may experience incontinence, *qi* pressure in the lower abdomen, and difficulty in urinating. There is pain in the jade stalk [penis] and a frequent urge to grip it with the hand. After a moment one feels like urinating again. To get better, first urinate, then lie down and settle yourself. After a little while, have intercourse at your leisure.
>
> Intercourse when overdue to move the bowels causes piles and difficulty in vacating the bowels. After some days and months there will be dripping pus and blood, and sores will appear around the anus resembling bee hives. Straining at stool, the bowels do not move in timely fashion. In this pain and bloating, you find no rest even by lying down. To cure this by means of sexual techniques, rise at cockcrow and use the bathroom. Then return to your bed, settle yourself comfortably and slowly engage in playful dalliance. When your entire body is deeply relaxed, cause your partner to be slippery with secretions, then withdraw. The illness will be wonderfully cured. The same method also helps in female maladies.[8]

To enhance sexual enjoyment and performance, certain herbs and teas are recommended, including ginseng, cinnamon, cardamom, nutmeg, ginger, and other warming, yang-inducing substances.[9] Before engaging in sexual activity, partners should create a pleasant atmosphere in a clean environment and prepare by taking a bath or shower. They should take plenty of time in foreplay, making sure both are ready and aroused, focusing on the exchange of *qi* in mouth, breasts, and genitals—stimulating the jade spring (saliva), the white snow (nipple *qi*), and the moon flower (vaginal excretion). Frequent sucking and kissing are recommended. Once both partners are ready, the male has a variety of thrusting styles: left and right, under and over, in and out, deep and shallow, and so on. Each thrust, moreover, can be executed at various levels, be it shallow, medium, deep, or very deep. Longer and more frequent thrusting is said to be good for health, and many diseases are cured by practicing eighty-one strokes nine times daily, for a period of nine days.

Some sexual techniques, moreover, can be used to improve eyesight, hearing, and other bodily functions. The Master of Pure Harmony says:

> To improve your eyesight, wait for the impulse to ejaculate, then raise your head, hold the breath, and expel the air with a loud sound, while rolling your eyes to the left and right. Contract your abdomen and revert the *jing* upward so that it enters the hundred vessels of the body.
>
> To prevent deafness, wait for the impulse to ejaculate and then inhale deeply. Clench the teeth and hold the breath. Produce a humming sound in the ears, then contract the abdomen, concentrate on your *qi* and circulate it mentally throughout the body until it becomes strong. Even in old age you will never lose your hearing.
>
> To improve the functioning of your five organs, facilitate digestion, and cure the hundred ills, wait for the approach of ejaculation, then expand your belly and mentally move the *qi* around the body. Next, contract your belly again so that the *jing* disperses and reverts to the hundred vessels. Then penetrate your partner nine times shallow and once deeply between her zither strings and grain ears. Good *qi* will return, ill *qi* will depart.[10]

All these practice instructions are primarily directed at men, who are to create a state of arousal in a sexual encounter, wait for the urge to ejaculate, then—holding their breath, clenching their teeth, and maybe pressing against the perineum—prevent themselves from ejaculating and instead mentally guide the aroused *jing* back into the body, moving it up along the spine and circulating it through the torso, in an effort to "revert sexual essence to nourish the brain."

In a more extreme version of the same practice, the bedchamber arts also taught men to have intercourse with as many women as possible, preferably young and healthy ones, and bring them to orgasm so they would emit their sexual fluids, while the men never had an ejaculation themselves. Practitioners were to experience arousal and prevent their sexual essence from flowing out, making it rise up along the spine toward the head. Although occasionally lauded for the sexual finesse and great satisfaction this technique would bring to women, it is commonly seen today as a form of sexual vampirism that encourages men to value women for their *qi* and discard them after use.[11]

The doctrine behind the technique assumes that women possess an inexhaustible supply of yin-essence and will not suffer from the practice. Still, it is also assumed that they will not voluntarily agree to it, and the literature describes the practices as a form of war that could best be won if the opponent remained ignorant of the game. Thus Chonghezi says:

> A man who intends to nourish his yang essence must not permit women to learn this art. Her knowledge of it will do him no good, and can even make him ill. This is the meaning of the proverb: "Do not lend another a dangerous weapon."
>
> In fact, if you encounter a knowledgeable woman, it is best to gather up your weapons, because you will not win. Similarly the long-lived Pengzu affirms that if a man wants to reap great profits from the sexual act, he must preferably do so with a woman who is ignorant of this art.[12]

Although most women are kept in ignorance of these practices, some use the very same techniques to their own benefit. The most prominent among them is the leading Daoist goddess Xiwang mu (Queen Mother of the West), who is said to have exploited men with such methods and thereby attained immortality. She presents the image of a strong woman who dominates the power exchange, using men—preferably young men—to acquire *jing* and revert it to nourish her own health and longevity. Her practice is described as the model for female cultvation by Chonghezi. He says:

> When having intercourse with a man, first calm your heart and still your mind. If the man is not yet fully aroused, wait for his *qi* to arrive and restrain your emotions in order to attune yourself to him. Do not move or become agitated, lest your yin-*jing* become exhausted first. If this happens, you will be left in a deficient state and be susceptible to illnesses due to wind and cold....
>
> If a woman is able to master this method and has frequent intercourse with men, she can avoid all grain for nine days without getting hungry. Even those who are sick or have sexual relations with ghosts attain this ability to fast. But they become emaciated after a while. So, how much more beneficial must it be to have intercourse with men?[13]

Women engaging in these practices can enhance their inner essences and increase their potential for health, beauty, and vitality.[14] They dedicate themselves to the attainment of pleasure and power, using enchantment to realize their sexuality and giving free reign to what mainstream society would consider shameful and dangerous behavior. The obvious disapproval of such behavior in women has allowed only few stories about their practice to come down through the ages, and although Daoist women were often less restricted than their lay counterparts, most texts still encourage them to be chaste and obedient, serving husband and family and creating cosmic harmony rather than using their inborn powers of yin for personal transformation.[15]

Communal Control: Harmonizing Yin and Yang

The sexual partner practices of ancient China as originally undertaken by longevity seekers of the Han Dynasty can be described as proto-Daoist in that they evolved as part of longevity practices before the beginning of Daoism as an organized religion. Daoism took them over, but has had a mixed and complex relationship to them over the millennia—both rejecting and embracing them in various contexts.

Among the earliest organized groups of the second century CE, the Way of Great Peace (Taiping dao) and the Celestial Masters (Tianshi), the sexual partner practices were sublimated in ritual intercourse. Characterized by their strong millenarian belief systems, ritually based hierarchies, moral life-style, and intense community cohesion, these groups formed the backbone of the organized Daoist religion as grew over the millennia. As in mainstream culture, mothers and matrons were highly honored and played leading roles as wives of leaders and as senior priests or libationers. Beyond that, younger women were key participants in initiatory rites of passage, known as the "harmonization of *qi*" (*heqi*), which essentially consisted of controlled and ritualized sexual intercourse.

Sexuality in this context was understood as the most direct and most obvious way of harmonizing and integrating the forces of yin and yang. In ancient China this exchange was considered necessary not only for the individual's well-being but also for the proper functioning of the universe. The emperor as intermediary between heaven and earth had a regulated sex life in harmony with the evolution of the universe's yin and yang *qi*. "Ladies of the court called *nüshi* [female masters] were experts in the regulation and supervision of the sexual relationship of the king and his wives. They made sure that the king received them on the good days in the calendar according to the cycle established by the *Book of Rites* for each rank."[16] In the countryside villagers similarly celebrated the renewal of spring with festivals during which sacred unions were commonly practiced.

Daoists saw the interaction of yin and yang as leading to a state of unitary *qi* and thus to harmony with the Dao; it could occur as bodily, spiritual, or intellectual intercourse.[17] Each partner in this interaction had his or her role: the yang creating and engendering, the yin transforming and transmuting. In the sexual act as conceived by Daoists, adepts learned to detach themselves from desire and to dissociate orgasm from pleasure. The act itself was less important than its effect of setting the *qi* in harmonious motion along the inner bodily circuits of the participants, where it provided sustenance and nourishment instead of being wasted either by physically flowing out of the body or through passionate outbursts of emotion. In the sexual act, Daoists prioritized the internal over the external, the invisible over the visible, in order to allow full empowerment of the harmony of the two forces, thereby benefiting themselves, their community, and the cosmos at large.[18]

Both in the Way of Great Peace and among the Celestial Masters, sexual rites were of central importance. All members of the community were initiated into a religious life that comprised a strict moral code and various psychophysiological practices. Their key initiatory rite, the harmonization of *qi*, consisted of highly complex ceremonies during which male sexual energies (known as yellow *qi*) and female sexual energies (red *qi*) joined together in a total harmony in accord with cosmic forces.[19] They were practiced in the oratory or quiet chamber, in the presence of a master and an instructor. Adepts began with slow, formal movements accompanied by meditations to create a sacred space, then established the harmony between their *qi* and the cosmic *qi* through visualizations. For example: "May each person visualize the *qi* of his or her cinnabar field [below the navel] as large as a six-inch mirror, leaving the body through open space. Its light progressively increases to illuminate the head and bathe the entire body in radiance, so that the adept can clearly discern the five inner organs, the six viscera, the nine palaces, the twelve lodgings, the four limbs, as well as all the joints, vessels, pores, and defensive and nutritive *qi* within the body and without."[20]

Next, adepts informed their master and various divinities that they were going to undertake the harmonization of *qi*. This involved ritualistic movements in precise directions and according to astronomically defined positions, as well as the concentration and firm maintenance of bodily essence and vital spirits through the retention of sexual fluids. Reverted away from orgasmic expulsion, these fluids were moved up along the spinal column and into the head to nourish the brain and enhance personal and communal harmony. The risen *qi* would also communicate with the gods of the heavens, who in turn erased the names of all participating members from the registers of death and instead inscribed them in the ledgers of long life and immortality.[21]

In this practice, control of sexual urges and desires was essential. As the *Zhenren neili daojia neishi lü* (Esoteric Rites of the Perfected and Rules for Taoists in Attendance in the Inner Chamber), a text cited in a later Buddhist polemic, says: "Do not fail to observe the proper order of attendance in the inner chamber. Do not harbor desire for the ordinary way [of intercourse] nor fail to observe the teachings of [sexual] control. Do not lust for relations with outsiders nor fail to observe the rituals of the proper nourishing of the inner chamber. Do not lust to be first nor fail to observe the rules of cultivation of the inner chamber."[22]

Although not celibacy in the sense of a complete cessation of sexual activity, the rite of harmonizing the energies was thus a form of bodily restraint, a way of making the body with its most essential and potent instincts subject to a higher power and a greater sense of community. The body becomes a vessel for the divine interaction of yin and yang to take place; the individual is transposed into a larger setting; the sense of self is transcended in favor of a larger identity with the community and the cosmos.

The Great Sublimation: Ecstasy with the Divine

Neither the Great Peace movement nor the Celestial Masters were able to practice their harmonization of *qi* for long. The Great Peace movement, believing their leader to be the next rightful emperor of China, in 184 CE rose in rebellion against the Han and was eliminated in a series of military campaigns; the Celestial Masters were caught up in political power struggles and surrendered their domain to the warlord Cao Cao in 215. Following this, they were forced to migrate to different parts of north China and began to form small enclaves among the larger populace, who tended to view their sexual and energetic practices with suspicion and disdain. In due course several sets of new revelations grew from the mixture of Celestial Masters practices and local beliefs, denouncing and transforming sexual initiations and at the same time shifting the vision of women and the female to yet another dimension.

The first major set of such revelations occurred in 364–370 in south China, among a group of southern aristocrats who had been displaced in their political power by the northern court on flight from Central Asian forces. They engaged in visionary interactions with their ancestors and other dead heroes and, with the help of the powerful medium Yang Xi, learned of an entirely new level of heaven called Highest Clarity (Shangqing), located far beyond the more ordinary celestial realms known so far. The gods and immortals in these higher spheres kindly supplied information on their organization and denizens as well as instructions on how to engage in ecstatic excursions and interact with the perfected.[23]

Practitioners of Highest Clarity were married householders, but their religious practice was solitary and meditational. They abstained from ordinary sexual intercourse and began to engage in a sublimated form of *heqi,* harmonizing their energy with that of supernatural and immortal figures. They preserved the theme of sexual intercourse as an initiation and rite of communion by transposing it into the realm of the imagination and the supernatural.[24] Thus Yang Xi, the key recipient of the revelations and chief interlocutor for the perfected, obtained a celestial wife, the concubine Nine-Flowers; the *Zhen'gao* (Declarations of the Perfected, DZ 1016), the main collection of Highest Clarity materials, dated to about 500 CE says: "When a perfected person is in the presence of a spirit-light companion, he must first prize the union with that light and the love between their two lights. Although they are called husband and wife, they do not practice marital acts. Speaking of them as a couple is merely a way of making understood that which can be revealed. But if the perfected person hangs on to ideas of the yellow and red [actual sex], he shall never see the supernatural spirits manifest themselves, nor have them for companions."[25]

Meditation instructions are very specific. For example, according to another early document, the *Mingtang xuanzhen jing jue* (Scripture and Instructions of the Mysterious Perfected from the Hall of Light, DZ 424), adepts visualize the pure energy of the sun or the moon, then imagine a goddess in their midst. The goddess grows stronger and more vivid with prolonged practice, until she is felt present in the flesh. Pressing her mouth to that of the adept, she dispenses celestial vapors to increase his vitality. The text says:

> Make the sun or the moon stand right in front of your mouth, about nine feet away. The rays of their light should be directed straight toward your mouth so they can easily enter.
>
> Now visualize a young lady in the sun or the moon. On her head she is wearing a purple cap, her cloak and skirt are of vermilion brocade. She calls herself Jade Maiden of Cinnabar Morning Light of Greatest and Highest Mystery. Her taboo name is Binding Coil and she is also known as the Secret Perfected.
>
> From her mouth she now emits a red energy, which fills the space between the light rays of the sun or the moon. See how the light rays merge and combine with the morning light of the Jade Maiden. When they have amalgamated completely, let them enter your mouth.
>
> Hold on to the light and swallow it, then visualize the Jade Maiden emit another stream of light. Practice this nine times ten, then stop.[26]

This celestial form of the French kiss may, after prolonged practice and regularly repeated visualizations, even lead to a sexual union. The text notes, "if you practice this for five years, the Jade Maiden of Greatest Mystery will descend to you and lie down to share your mat. She may even divide her shape for you into a host of like jade maidens who will serve your every whim."[27] The state thus attained is one of utter perfection, when the inner energies in the adept's body, his *jing* and *qi*, have been fully pervaded by celestial vapors and he lives only in response to divine impulses. He is free to travel widely through the spirit realm and will not be hindered in his ultimate immortality by the mere falling away of his earthly shell. He can "embody pure life and develop a jade-like glow, command the myriad spirits and ascend to the halls of the emperor-on-high."[28]

Another variation of this theme of interiorized sexuality is the adept's visualization of the joining of interior yin and yang energies or of male and female divinities within the body, such as the father of the Dao in the brain in his union with the mother of the Dao in the kidneys. The *Laozi zhongjing* (Central Scripture of Laozi, DZ 1168) of the fourth century, for example, locates a deity named Yellow Lord Lao of the Central Ultimate in the center of the stars, the Dipper, and as the human body, where he resides in the Yellow Court in the abdomen. His female aspect, or queen, is a jade maiden called Mysterious Radiance of Great Yin (*Taiyin xuanguang yunü*). Wearing robes of yellow cloudy energy, they join to give birth to the immortal embryo.[29]

To activate the pair, adepts visualize a sun and moon in their chests underneath their nipples, from which a yellow essence and a red energy radiate. These vapors rise up to enter the Scarlet Palace in the heart and sink down to the Yellow Court in the abdomen. Filling these internal halls, they mingle and coagulate to form the immortal embryo, which grows gradually and becomes visible as an infant facing south, in the position of the ruler. As he is nurtured on the yellow essence and red energy still oozing from the adept's internal sun and moon, all illnesses are driven out and the myriad disasters are allayed.[30]

In contrast to this sublimated and highly spiritual form of sexual practice, physical intercourse was relegated to a minor rank and was no longer thought to lead to the highest level of realization. As the *Zhen'gao* says:

> One shall never obtain the Dao by taking plant drugs without knowing the bedroom arts and the methods of guiding and inducing *qi*. . . . A person cannot attain immortality either if he only knows the bedroom arts and the methods of guiding *qi*. One must acquire the methods of the divine elixir, which will suffice to become

> immortal. Even better, if one gets hold of the *Dadong zhenjing* (Perfect Scripture of Great Profundity), even the way of the golden elixir will become irrelevant. Reciting this text ten thousand times is sufficient to become immortal.[31]

Further, "The way of the yellow and the red, the art of commingling *qi*, only constitutes one of the minor methods commended for becoming one of the elected as espoused by [the first Celestial Master] Zhang Daoling. The perfected [of Highest Clarity] do not make use of such practices. Although I have observed some people interrupting their decline by practicing these methods, I have never met anyone who has attained eternal life through them."[32]

Moving far beyond the physical harmonization of yin and yang, however ritualized, the practitioners of Highest Clarity began a practice that joined celibacy in this world with a spiritual exchange in the other, an exchange often described in terms of sexual intercourse or the union of internal deities. They sublimated and transformed sexuality into a mode of interaction with the divine, creating ecstasy and harmony on a more intercosmic than mere human level, and thereby laid the foundation for the most recent form of Daoist meditation and sexual control: inner alchemy.

Internal Realization: The Immortal Embryo

Inner alchemy can be traced back to the ninth and tenth centuries. It has flourished in many different schools since then, and is still the dominant form of practice today.[33] Inner alchemy, like ancient longevity techniques and bedchamber arts, begins with the active stimulation and transformation of *jing* into *qi* by reverting it up the spine and toward the head. From there, it then transmutes *qi* into spirit (*shen*), which appears in the form of an immortal embryo who can then travel to the heavens and merge with the Dao in cosmic emptiness. The *Zhonghe ji* (Collection of Balance and Harmony), an early description of the system, says:

> Making one's *jing* complete, one can preserve the body. To do so, first keep the body at ease and make sure there are no desires. Thereby *jing* can be made complete.
>
> Making one's *qi* complete, one can nurture the mind. To do so, first keep the mind pure and make sure there are no thoughts. Thereby *qi* can be made complete.

> Making one's *shen* complete, one can recover emptiness. To do so, first keep the will sincere and make sure body and mind are united. Thereby *shen* can be returned to emptiness....
>
> To attain immortality, there is nothing else but the refinement of these three treasures: *jing, qi, shen.*[34]

To begin the practice, adepts first pursue longevity techniques to make the body healthy and strong, then engage in mental concentration to make the mind tranquil and stable. Then they start by focusing on *jing,* the tangible form of *qi* that develops in the human body by sinking down from the Ocean or Cavern of Qi. They allow *jing* to develop and manifest, but instead of allowing it to leave the body, they work to refine and revert it, restoring their sexual essence back to its original form as *qi* and preventing its future disintegration.

To accomplish this, men should get aroused almost to the point of ejaculation, then mentally concentrate on making the semen flow upward and along the spine into the head. Once a man has reached proficiency in the practice and will no longer ejaculate, texts say that he has "subdued the white tiger." Men then proceed to circulate the reverted energy—parallel to the reverted cinnabar in operative alchemy—along a cycle inside the torso known as the "microcosmic orbit."

This cycle follows the course made up of the Governor and Conception Vessels, central acupuncture meridians that run straight along the spine and in the front of the torso. To establish the inner cycle, men close the various outer orifices of the body to prevent *jing* from escaping and outside energies from entering. Most commonly seven orifices are described in the face (ears, eyes, nostrils, and mouth) plus two at the base of the pelvis. They are seen as important venues for communication and interaction, allowing different aspects of celestial nature to enter the human body but also a potential source of leakage and danger to alchemical transformation. With prolonged practice of the microcosmic orbit, the practitioner's *qi* will be refined and begin to form a divine "pearl of dew" in the lower cinnabar field. This is a first coagulation of stronger and purer *qi* that lays the foundation for the next level.

In women, the first stage of reverting *jing* to *qi* begins with daily breast massages, a change in diet to lighter foods, and a series of meditations in which menstrual blood is visualized rising upward and transforming into clear-colored *qi.* After several months of this, menstruation ceases, an effect called "decapitating the red dragon." It serves to stabilize the *qi,* which will then come to nurture the pearl of dew. Unlike men, women have the "pearl of dew" naturally from birth, but if it is left untended it will dissipate with every menstrual cycle. The beginning of inner alchemical practice is, therefore, the reversal of this natural tendency.

The second stage is the same for men and women. It focuses on the transformation of *qi* into *shen* or spirit. The pearl of dew is developed into the "golden flower" with the help of transmuted *qi*.[35] For this, yin and yang are identified as different energies in the body and described with different metaphors, depending on the level of purity attained. Typically there are the following:

yang = heart = fire = trigram *li* = pure lead = dragon = red bird;
yin = kidneys = water = trigram *kan* = pure mercury =
tiger = white tiger.

The texts describing these advanced practices tend to be rather obscure and highly metaphoric, and images show the curling yang dragon playing with the pearl over the alchemical cauldron. Similarly, the *Huandan gezhu* (Annotated Songs on Reverting Cinnabar) says:

> The red bird is harmonized and nurtured; it brings forth the golden flower. The red bird is the phase fire. Among directions it corresponds to the south. In the sky it is the planet Mars; on earth it is fire; in human beings it is the heart.... It greatly encompasses heaven and earth, minutely reaches into the smallest nook and cranny. Control it and it will obey, let it go free and it will run wild. In the scriptures it is called the bright fire....
>
> To harmonize it, isolate pure water from the Jade Spring Palace in the upper cinnabar field [in the head]. Join this with the fire of the heart and refine it until it enters the lower cinnabar field [in the abdomen]. Secure it behind the Jade Prison Pass. Once locked in, treat it further with yin alchemy. Naturally a new spirit soul and a separate sun and moon are brought forth. After nourishing them for a long time, their color will turn brilliant. They combine to form a new entity, called the Golden Flower. (Verse 4)

At each stage of the transmutation process, the energies are given a different name and different metaphors are employed. Eventually adepts learn to not only mix them in the abdomen but to revolve them through an inner-body cycle that includes not only the spine and breastbone but leads all the way to the feet and is known as the "macrocosmic orbit." Gradually the bodily substances are refined to a point where they become as pure as the celestials and form the golden flower, the first trace of the immortal embryo in the lower cinnabar field. The process is complex and time-consuming, and must be timed in exact correspondence with the cosmic patterns of yin and yang. As the *Huandan gezhu* says: "At midnight call forth the tiger; in the early morning summon the dragon. This has to do with time calculation. Midnight and tiger belong to yin. Yin in turn belongs to the female, and the female has the disposition of water. Thus it is associated with the north and the position of water... The dragon belongs to the phase wood. Wood is associated with the east. It is the position of fire" (Verse 7).

Once the embryo is started, adepts switch their practice to employ a method called "embryo respiration" to nourish it for ten months. This is an inner form of breathing, combined with the meditative circulation of *qi,* which allows the embryo to grow and makes the adept increasingly independent of outer nourishment and air. Unlike the first phase, which was easier for men, the process at this stage is easier for women because they are naturally endowed with the faculty to grow an embryo. After ten months, the embryo is complete.

Adepts then proceed to the third stage. As Despeux and Kohn describe in *Women in Daoism* (2003), the as yet semimaterial body of the embryo is transformed into the pure spirit body of the immortals, a body of pure *yang*, of cosmic *life*, not of life as opposed to death or yang as opposed to yin. To attain its full realization, the embryo has to undergo several phases. First it is nourished to completion and undergoes a spiritual birth by moving up along the spine and exiting through the Hundred Meeting acupuncture point at the top of the head, which is now called the Heavenly Gate. The first exiting of the spirit embryo is known as "deliverance from the womb." It signifies the adept's celestial rebirth and is accompanied by the perception of a deep inner rumbling, like a clap of thunder. When the Heavenly Gate bursts wide, a white smoky essence can be seen hovering above the adept. The spirit passes through the top of the head and begins to communicate with the celestials, transcending the limitations of the body.

Once the embryo has been born, it is further grown through meditative exercises known as "nursing for three years." It gradually gets used to its new powers, moves faster and travels further afield until it can go far and wide without any limitation. As the spirit enters into its cosmic ventures, the adept exhibits supernatural powers, including the ability to be in two places at once, move quickly from one place to another, know the past and the future, divine people's thoughts, procure wondrous substances, overcome hazards of fire and water, and having powers over life and death. Known as "spirit pervasion," this indicates the freedom achieved by the spirit and manifest in the practitioner.

However, even this high level of attainment is not the ultimate goal of inner alchemy, which is only realized after further meditative practice, known as "wall gazing." This technique is adopted from Chan Buddhism, whose first patriarch Bodhidharma is said to have realized full enlightenment by sitting in a cave and gazing at a wall for nine years. In this final phase of the process, the adept whose body is already transformed into pure light has yet to fully overcome its limits and melt into cosmic emptiness.

Practitioners of inner alchemy were celibate in the sense that they for the most part abstained from physical sexual intercourse and lived in monastic communities—although there were also some schools that encouraged *shuangxiu* or "twosome practice," which involved the stimulation and reversal of *jing* with the help of a partner. Most adepts were and are members of the school of Complete Perfection (Quanzhen), which arose in the late twelfth century and under the Mongols became the dominant religious organization of China.[36] Structured along the lines of Chan Buddhist institutions, Complete Perfection monasteries were centers for spiritual cultivation that prescribed strict moral rules and a tight schedule of meditative and other exercises. Rules included prohibitions of killing, stealing, lying, and sexual activity of any sort, and carefully prescribed how to interact with members of the opposite sex. Thus the most elementary set of precepts, found in the *Chuzhen jie* (Precepts of Initial Perfection, JY 278) has a rule among its ten precepts that says: "Do not be lascivious or lose perfection, defile or insult the numinous energy. Always guard perfection and integrity, and remail without shortcomings or violations." And the next higher group of rules, a set of three hundred precepts, has the following:

80. Do not secretly spy on women or give rise to even a minor thought of debauchery.
81. Do not stay among a group of mixed men and women.
82. Do not eat together with a woman or exchange clothing with her.
83. Do not give private instruction to a woman.[37]

These rules closely echo similar precepts found in early Celestial Masters and medieval monastic codes, circumscribing interaction with women to prevent practitioners from falling into the "ways of the world." Celibacy here is a fundamental condition for the concentration on the inner energies and the in-depth meditation practices necessary for successful transformation. It establishes an otherness, a social separation, a sacred space essential for the refinement of the self and the attainment of higher cosmic states. Still, even here sexuality is acknowledged and valued as a fundamental human force, and the sacred work itself is couched in images and metaphors of sexual union, procreation, gestation, and birth.

Conclusion

In the course of two thousand years of history, Daoism has developed various ways of sexual control, some involving physical celibacy, others encouraging the controlled application of intercourse. The earliest sources describe ways of using sexual methods for health and healing, and laud methods to gain as much sexual essence from a partner as possible without ever losing one's own. The earliest Daoist communities use sexual intercourse as the most visible form of the interchange of yin and yang, creating stylized rites of initiation that serve to enhance personal health, community coherence, and cosmic harmony. This is already a sublimation and refinement of the cruder bedchamber arts of the longevity seekers. Following in the wake of the early communities, medieval Daoists continued to refine sexual practices, sublimating them from a physical encounter with a living person into a spiritual union with a divine personage and beginning to use sexual imagery for the interchange and cross-fertilization of different subtle energies within the body. In the practice of inner alchemy, finally, still undertaken today, all sexuality is internalized and both intercourse and conception occur within the adept's own body as part of the creation of an alter ego, a spirit identity that can survive forever.

Celibacy is relevant only in the last phase of this long history, and even there it is questionable, since some practitioners work with partners even into the higher stages. Unlike India and the West, where the body is often seen as an obstacle to salvation and the purity of the soul, and sexuality is the most pronounced and most difficult force to tame within the body, Daoism considers the body the basis for transformation, and highly values sexual energy as the one form of *qi* that can be actively aroused and consciously felt at the beginning of the path. Thus celibacy in Daoism was predicated on the retention, inner circulation, and refinement of *jing* or "essence," and the avoidance of sexual intercourse was not to subdue the body but, on the contrary, to enhance its inner strength and cosmic connection.

This has a strong impact on the vision of women in the religion. Men in Daoism had to actively confront and use their sexuality rather than deny, suppress, and eradicate it. Women, representative of sexual enticement in all cultures, were accordingly seen in a positive light—as sources of sexual fluids, partners in the arousal and enhancement of sexual energies, and teachers of sexual methods and bodily control. More than that, women were admired for their inherent power of yin, a power men wished to refine and cultivate, and for their natural ability of pregnancy, a state men needed to attain in a spiritual way while pursuing immortality. The very substances and states in a woman's body most polluting and most offensive in mainstream Chinese society and other religions—her menstrual blood and the birth of a child—in Daoism come to be key factors in the cultivation of immortality: blood as the female form of *jing* and thus the equivalent of semen; the birth of the embryo as the ultimate liberation of the spirit from the constraints of this world.

This birth is still practiced today, notably among followers of the Healing Dao system, developed by Mantak Chia and enhanced by Michael Winn. In a discussion of sexual practices, Winn mentions that he, at some point in his intensive training, developed the ability of exiting in his spirit. As a result, he found his sleep needs drastically reduced and experienced different spiritual powers, "ranging from bursts of telepathy and foreknowledge of the future to experiences of the entire universe collapsing into a single point."[38]

He also reports on a dramatic experience of cosmic merging in a semi-sexual situation of twosome cultivation with his wife:

> We had sat naked for a few minutes, facing each other in cross-legged meditation position to tune in. We were both suddenly overtaken by a powerful energy field with extremely intense and unusual vibrations. Not a word was spoken, as our mental, emotional, and speech faculties were completely suspended, but we later confirmed having an identical experience.
>
> One aspect of our consciousness began experiencing a very yang orgasm, expanding out of the bedroom faster than the speed of light, whizzing through galaxies, exploding supernovas, and then beyond. Another part of us was orgasmically imploding inward with opposite and equal force, grounding and concentrating the great intensity in our physical bodies.[39]

Here the energy fields of the two practitioners merge in an explosive and powerful manner, moving both outward as their spirits travel into the planetary vastness of the otherworld and inward as the body is opened to cosmic emptiness and primordiality. The experience is overwhelming and transcendent, yet firmly grounded in the energetics of the body, the result of years of practice and the cultivation of subtle forms of *qi*. Inner alchemy and Daoist sexual cultivation are still alive and pursued actively not only in Chinese monasteries but also in the West. They require long periods of dedicated training and involve strong sexual control, but they result in a heightened empowerment and a cosmic merging that is described, time and again, in sexual terms.

NOTES

1. Ilza Veith, trans., *The Yellow Emperor's Classic of Internal Medicine* (Berkeley: University of California Press, 1972). See also Maosing Ni, trans., *The Yellow Emperor's Classic of Medicine* (Boston: Shambhala, 1995).

2. Veith, *Yellow Emperor's Classic,* 98–99.

3. Michael Winn, "The Quest for Spiritual Orgasm: Daoist and Tantric Sexual Cultivation in the West," paper presented at the Conference on Tantra and Daoism, Boston University, Boston, 2002.

4. See Donald Harper, "The Sexual Arts of Ancient China as Described in a Manuscript of the Second Century," *Harvard Journal of Asiatic Studies* 47 (1987): 459–498; and *Early Chinese Medical Manuscripts: The Mawangdui Medical Manuscripts* (London: Welcome Asian Medical Monographs, 1999).

5. Robert H. van Gulik, *Sexual Life in Ancient China* (Leiden: E. J. Brill, 1961), 121–125.

6. Emil C. H. Hsia, Ilza Veith, and Robert H. Geertsma, trans., *The Essentials of Medicine in Ancient China and Japan: Yasuyori Tamba's Ishimpō,* 2 vols. (Leiden: E. J. Brill, 1986).

7. See, for example, Akira Ishihara and Howard S. Levy, *The Tao of Sex* (Yokohama, 1968); Douglas Wile, *Art of the Bedchamber: The Chinese Sexology Classics* (Albany: State University of New York Press, 1992).

8. Wile, *Art of the Bedchamber,* 103.

9. See Wile, *Art of the Bedchamber.*

10. *Yufang bijue;* Wile, *Art of the Bedchamber,* 104.

11. For studies of these sexual practices, see Joseph Needham et al., *Science and Civilisation in China,* vol. 2, *History of Scientific Thought* (Cambridge: Cambridge University Press, 1956); Gulik, *Sexual Life in Ancient China;* Jolan Chang, *The Tao of Love and Sex: The Ancient Chinese Way to Ecstasy* (New York: Dutton, 1977); Mantak Chia and Michael Winn, *Taoist Secrets of Love: Cultivating Male Sexual Energy* (Santa Fe, N.M.: Aurora, 1984); Isabelle Robinet, "*Sexualité et taoïsme,*" in *Sexualité et religions,* edited by Marcel Bernos (Paris: Cerf, 1988), 51–79; Daniel P. Reid, *The Tao of Health, Sex, and Longevity* (New York: Simon & Schuster, 1989); Valentin Chu, *The Yin-Yang Butterfly: Ancient Chinese Sexual Secrets for Western Lovers* (Los Angeles: J. P. Tarcher, 1994).

12. *Yufang bijue,* cited in Hsia, Veith, and Geertsma, trans., *Yasuyori Tamba's Ishimpō* 28.5b–6a.

13. Ibid., 28.7b–8a; Livia Kohn, *Daoism and Chinese Culture* (Cambridge, Mass.: Three Pines Press, 2001), 156; Ishihara and Levy, *Tao of Sex;* Wile, *Art of the Bedchamber,* 102–103.

14. Charlotte Furth, "Rethinking Van Gulik: Sexuality and Reproduction in Traditional Chinese Medicine," in *Engendering China,* edited by Christine Gilmartin et al. (Cambridge: Harvard University Press, 1994), 134.

15. See Suzanne Cahill, *Transcendence and Divine Passion: The Queen Mother of the West in Medieval China* (Stanford: Stanford University Press, 1993), and Catherine Despeux and Livia Kohn, *Women in Daoism* (Cambridge, Mass.: Three Pines Press, 2003).

16. Gulik, *Sexual Life in Ancient China*, 42–43.

17. Barbara E. Reed, "Taoism," in *Women in World Religions*, edited by Arvind Sharma (Albany: State University of New York Press, 1987), 163–166.

18. Catherine Despeux, *Immortelles de la Chine ancienne. Taoïsme et alchimie feminine* (Paris: Pardes, 1990), 36.

19. Kristofer M. Schipper, "Le monachisme taoïste," in *Incontro de religioni in Asia tra il terzo e il decimo secolo* B.C., edited by Lionello Lanciotti (Florence: Leo S. Olschki, 1984), 203.

20. *Shangqing huangshu guodu yi*, DZ, 1294, 2a; Despeux and Kohn, *Women in Daoism*, 12. This text is a fourth-century Highest Clarity document that contains various remnants of earlier practices that date from the second or third centuries; Kristofer M. Schipper, *The Taoist Body*, translated by Karen C. Duval (Berkeley: University of California Press, 1994), 252. Titles in the Daoist canon are abbreviated DZ and numbered according to Kristofer M. Schipper, *Concordance du Tao Tsang: Titres des ouvrages* (Paris: Publication de l'Ecole Française d'Extrême Orient, 1975); Louis Komjathy, *Title Index to Daoist Collections* (Cambridge, Mass.: Three Pines Press, 2002).

21. See Rolf Stein, "Remarques sur les mouvements du taoïsme politico-religieux au IIe siècle ap. J.-C." *T'oung Pao* 50 (1963): 1–78. Also see Yan Shanzhao, "Shoki dōkyō to kōshi konki hōchūjutsu," *Tōhōshūkyō* 97 (2001): 1–19.

22. *Bianzheng lun*, T. 2110; 52.545c. "T" abbreviates *Taishō daizōkyō* and provides the number of the text in the Buddhist canon, followed by volume and page number.

23. On Highest Clarity, see Isabelle Robinet, *La Révélation du Shangqing dans l'historie du taoïsme*, 2 vols. (Paris: Publications de l'Ecole Française d'Extrême-Orient, 1984); Stephan Peter Bumbacher, "Abschied von Heim und Herd: Die Frau im mittelalterlichen Daoismus und Buddhiismus," *Asiatische Studien/Etudes Asiatiques* 52 (1998): 673–694; Stephen Peter Bumbacher, *The Fragments of the Daoxue zhuan* (Frankfurt: Peter Lang, 2000).

24. Bumbacher, *Fragments of Daoxue zhuan*, 521.

25. Zhen' gao 2.1a; Baumbacher, "Abschied von Heim un Herd," 691; Despeux and Kohn, *Women in Daoism*, 15.

26. DZ424, 2ab; Livia Kohn, *The Taoist Experience: An Anthology* (Albany: State University of New York Press, 1993), 269; Edward H. Schafer, "The Jade Women of Greatest Mystery," *History of Religions* 17 (1978): 387–397.

27. DZ 424, 4a.

28. Ibid., 4ab.

29. DZ 1168, 18.7a.

30. Ibid., 18.7ab.

31. Zhen'gao, 5.11b.

32. Despeux and Kohn, *Women in Daoism*, 16.

33. On inner alchemy, see Needham et al., *Science and Civilisation in China*; Isabelle Robinet, "Original Contributions of Neidan to Taoism and Chinese Thought," in *Taoist Meditation and Longevity Techniques*, edited by Livia Kohn (Ann Arbor: University of Michigan, Center for Chinese Studies, 1989), 295–338; and *Introduction*

à l'alchimie intérieure taoïste: De l'unité et de la multiplicité (Paris: Editions du Cerf, 1995); Kuan-yü Lu, *Taoist Yoga—Alchemey and Immortality* (London: Rider, 1970); Thomas Cleary, *Understanding Reality: A Taoist Alchemical Classic by Chang Po-tuan* (Honolulu: University of Hawai'i Press, 1987); Richard Wilhelm, *The Secret of the Golden Flower: A Chinese Book of Life* ([1929] Harmondsworth: Penguin Books, 1984); Farzeen Baldrian-Hussein, *Orocédé secrets du joyau magique: Traité de l'alchimie taoïste de XIe siècle* (Paris: Les Deux Océans, 1984); Muriel Baryosher-Chemouny, *La quéte de l'immortalité en Chine: Alchimie et payasage intérieure des Song* (Paris: Dervy Livres, 1996).

34. Kohn, *Daoism and Chinese Culture*, 146.

35. On practices involving the Golden Flower, see especially Wilhelm, *Secret of the Golden Flower*, 1, and Thomas Cleary, *The Secret of the Golden Flower: The Classic Chinese Book of Life* (San Francisco: Harper, 1992).

36. Tao-chung Yao, "Ch'üan-chen: A New Taoist Sect in North China during the Twelfth and Thirteenth Centuries," Ph.D. dissertation, University of Arizona, Phoenix, 1980.

37. See Heinrich Hackmann, *Die dreihundert Mönchsgebote des chinesischen Taoismus* (Amsterdam: Koninklijke Akademie van Wetenshapen, 1931).

38. Winn, "Quest for Spiritual Orgasm," 8.

39. Ibid., 26.

14

Shinto and Celibacy

C. Scott Littleton

Let me begin by asserting categorically that Shinto, the indigenous animistic religion of Japan, does *not* practice celibacy, especially male celibacy. The fundamental reason for this is that unlike most of the Buddhist sects with which it has coexisted for the past 1,500 years, Shinto is primarily concerned with this world rather than the next one. Indeed, it is sometimes said that in Japan Shinto is the "life religion," while Buddhism is the "death religion." As a Japanese friend once explained it to me, "I live as a Shintoist, but I die a Buddhist." This attitude is reflected in the fact that, while almost all Japanese are buried according to Buddhist rites in cemeteries adjacent to *otera*, or Buddhist temples, the overwhelming majority are married according to Shinto rites.

In short, Shinto celebrates life and procreation; asceticism, including celibacy, is foreign to its essence. In order to understand the extent to which Shinto is embedded in the Japanese psyche and why it rejects celibacy, it is necessary to take a brief look at the myths, beliefs, and practices of this ancient religion, whose roots lie deep in mists of Japanese prehistory.

Shinto Mythology

Like belief systems everywhere, Shino is rooted in a shared mythology which, although rarely if ever taken literally, at least in modern times, nevertheless serves to ground it metaphorically in the minds of its practitioners. The oldest and most sacred Shinto text—and the most ancient of any surviving Japanese text—is the *Kojiki,* or "Record of Ancient Matters," compiled by a poet/scholar named Ōnō Susumu in 712 CE in Nara (near Kyoto), the first Japanese imperial capital. It is essentially a chronicle of the Imperial or Yamato Dynasty (unlike China, Japan has so far had only one dynasty), from the creation of the world to a century or so before the *Kojiki* was complied. Less than a decade after Ōnō presented his work to the empress (there were still reigning empresses at that time, although their days were numbered), in 720 CE, a committee of court scholars complied a second version of the same basic story called the *Nihon Shoki,* or "Chronicle of Japan," which is modeled on Chinese historical texts and takes into account the variants told by the several major clans, or *uji,* that formed the imperial court. This was the prime reason for the second compilation.

Although the more recent sections of both works are almost wholly genealogical, the basic mythic narrative can be summarized as follows. After seven generations of invisible heavenly deities, a primordial pair of corporeal deities, Izanagi and his sister/consort, Izanami, were created and sent down from heaven to solidify the world, which at that time was conceived to be a roiling mass of molasses-like brine. Standing on the "Bridge of Heaven" (almost certainly a metaphor for a rainbow), Izanagi dipped his jeweled spear into the brine, and, as he lifted it out, the drops formed an island called Onogoro. The gods ordered them to descend to this newly created terra firma and begin procreating. But a problem occurred when Izanami, the female, spoke first. Their first offspring was a monster, which they floated away on a small boat. The next time they tried, Izanagi spoke first, as a man should, and they begin procreating in earnest.

After giving birth to innumerable gods, as well as islands, rivers, mountains, and so on, Izanami was burned to death by giving birth to the fire god and went to Yomi, the primordial realm of the dead, which lies deep beneath the earth. But Izanagi, eager to see his beloved spouse again, found the entrance and, despite Izanami's admonition not to look at her corpse, he lit a tooth from one of his hair combs and saw her corpse being consumed by maggots. This angered Izanami, and she and the "Hags of Yomi" chased Izanagi until he managed to wedge a large boulder across the entrance, thus blocking further pursuit. (Yes, this story bears a striking resemblance to the story of Orpheus and Eurydice in Greek mythology, and some scholars have gone so far as to posit a very ancient connection between them.)

After his ordeal, and to cleanse himself of the pollution he acquired in his brief stay in Yomi, Izanagi bathed in a river, and gave birth androgynously to a host of additional deities, called *kami* in Japanese. Eventually, he wiped his left eye, and gave birth to Amaterasu, the sun goddess. Then he wiped his right eye, produced Tsuki-yomi, the moon god. Finally, he wiped his nose, and out popped Susanō, the "Raging Male," or storm god.

At this point, like many a Japanese emperor in premodern times, Izanagi decided to retire and turn over his sovereignty to Amaterasu. Her brother, Tsuki-yomi, immediately swore fealty to his sister. But Susanō, who was assigned by Izanagi to be the lord of the sea, rebeled and claimed that *he* deserved overall sovereignty. He raged up to heaven and confronted Amaterasu. After a disputed divine contest between Amaterasu and her recalcitrant brother, in which each deity attempted to outdo the other in procreating children, the gods endorsed her sovereignty. However, Susanō refused to admit defeat and committed all manner of depredations, including defecating in the heavenly rice paddies, throwing a "piebald horse" through the roof of the divine weaving hut, and killing one of Amaterasu's handmaids who was working at the loom. In disgust, Amaterasu retired to a dark cave, and as a result the sun disappeared from the sky.

To trick her out of the cave, the gods assigned a beautiful young goddess named Ama no Uzumei, or "Heaven's Dawn Woman," to perform a lewd dance in front of the cave mouth. The guffawing of the gods piqued Amaterasu's attention. She poked her nose out of the cave, whereupon they thrust a mirror in her face and asserted that there was another sun goddess greater than she. This brought her all the way out, whereupon a magical rope was immediately strung across the cave mouth, preventing her from returning. After Dawn led the Sun out of darkness, the rice crop once again ripened, order was restored, and Susanō was banished to the Reed Plain, or the mortal world.

This episode is the single most sacred Shinto myth, as it underscores the sun goddess's fundamental importance in the scheme of things. Indeed, almost every Shinto shrine, or *jinja,* has a sacred rope, or *shimenawa,* that symbolizes the one that ensured Amaterasu's continued presence, and thus the persistence of the life-giving sun.

Later on, Amaterasu dispatched her grandson Honinigi to extend her realm to the Reed Plain. He did so after a brief conflict with Susanō's descendant, Ōkuninushi. A deal was struck; Ōkuninushi became the perpetual protector of the land and especially of the future imperial family. Honinigi's great-grandson was the first emperor, Jimmu Tennō, who set out from Kyushu and marched eastward along the north coast of the Inland Sea until he reached the Yamato region of central Honshu, where he established the Imperial Dynasty. From this point on, we are dealing with legend that gradually merges into history proper toward the end of the narratives.

Kami and Oni

The most important concept in Shinto is that of *kami*. Although the word is usually translated as "deity" or "god," it covers a much wider semantic range than its English equivalents. It refers to the entities created by Izanagi and Izanami, including Amaterasu and her divine siblings, plus an infinite number of spirit beings that animate lakes, waterfalls, rocks, moon, mountains, and rivers, and all other natural phenomenon, animate as well as inanimate, human as well as animal. It is for this reason that Shinto, like other religions that venerate such a plethora of spirit beings, is generally held to be a manifestation of what anthropologists call animism. However, as we have seen, some *kami*, such as Amaterasu, Tsuki-yomi, Susanō, and Ama no Uzumei do come close to approximating the Western concept of god (or goddess); that is, divine entities with highly developed personalities and functions that are broadly analogous to the gods and goddesses of ancient Greece and Rome. Among a great many other major Shinto *kami* are Hachiman, the war god, who in part reflects a quasi-legendary emperor named Ōjin (ca. third century CE); the aforementioned Ōkuninushi; Toyoyuke, the god of harvests; Tenjin, who incarnates scholarship and learning; and Inari, the rice god, who is also a patron of merchants and is thus widely venerated.

There is also a vast number of *oni*, or demons, which can possess unwary persons and cause them intense grief. Among the most malevolent of these demons are fox-spirits, or *kitsune-oni*, which must be avoided at all costs. But fox-spirits can also be benevolent and are thought to be the guardians of the aforementioned rice god, Inari; indeed, almost every Inari shine is guarded by a pair of sculpted foxes. There are other examples of ambivalent demons, such as Tengu, whose most recognizable physical trait is a long, Pinocchio-like nose, and who is often as helpful as he is malicious.

Some Core Shinto Beliefs

Although the concept of *kami* lies at the heart of Shinto theology, it is framed in terms of some fundamental beliefs about the essential goodness of nature and the absence of any sharp line between the "real" world and the realm of the divine. As Shinto scholar J. W. T. Mason asserts, "The fundamental idea of Shinto remains that man and Kami or divine spirit are the same." Unlike most other major religions, Eastern as well as Western, Shinto does not posit a truly "other" supernatural reality, either analogous either to the Judeo-Christian concept of the Kingdom of Heaven or to the Hindu-Buddhist idea of nirvana. Rather, Shinto is primarily focused on immediate existence and its management by the *kami*. All life experiences have divine implications, including sex. The divine is transcendent, subsuming all things into its being. This is why Shinto places little emphasis on the afterlife. As I indicated earlier, in the division of supernatural labor that has emerged between Shinto and Buddhism in the course of the last millennium and a half, it is Buddhism to which the vast majority of Japanese turn when it comes to matters concerned with death and dying. There are, in fact, only two or three Shinto cemeteries in all of Tokyo.

Shinto Shrines

The focal point of Shinto ritual is the shrine, or *jinja*. There are tens of thousands of *jinja* in Japan, ranging from tiny altars devoted to local *kami* barely known outside of a single village to massive religious complexes, like the Inner and Outer Shines at Ise, which are collectively known as the Ise-jingu. The Outer Shine at Ise is dedicated to the rice god, Toyoyuki, while the Inner Shine, or *Naiko*, is dedicated to the queen of the Shinto pantheon, Amaterasu. It is by all odds the single most sacred place in the Shino universe. This is reflected in the fact that the entire Ise complex has been rebuilt at twenty-year intervals for more than a thousand years and is therefore at once very old and very new. Thus, the potency and vigor of the deities enshrined there is regularly renewed, and, by extension, so is the well-being of the country. (The emperor is expected to make an annual visit to Ise and report to his divine ancestor on the state of the nation.)

Although the Ise-jingu is the only shrine complex in Japan that is periodically rebuilt in this predictable fashion, the idea of renewal is extremely important in Shinto, and a great deal of Shinto ritual is devoted to it. Again, this encompasses human reproduction and runs contrary to the idea of celibacy. Shinto's concern with human sexuality is reflected in the presence of *jinja* that enshrine the phallus as a *kami* and parade images of it in sacred processions during their annual festivals.

Unlike Western religious institutions, Shinto shrines, even large ones like the Ise-jingu, are for the most part not places for communal worship. Rather, they are typically visited by single individuals who pray to the enshrined *kami* for good health, success in school or business, or a personal favor. When one approaches a shrine, one passes beneath a *torii* gate, a simple post-and-lintel entrance, and then washes both hands and mouth so as to be as pure as possible when approaching the *kami*. Indeed, the well-known Japanese emphasis on personal cleanliness and hygiene, including the daily bath and removing one's shoes before entering a house, is inextricably bound up with Shinto. This applies to nature as well, which is why some rural Shinto shrines have been in the forefront of the environmental movement in modern Japan, pressuring the government to clean up rivers, steams, and lakes. Nature is revered in Shinto and should not be defiled.

Another important locus of Shinto devotion is the *kamidana*, or household "god shelf," which is typically presided over by a senior member of the family. The *kami* enshrined there are ancestral spirits, represented by tablets bearing their names, which are invoked to keep the family healthy and prosperous. Although, as I have said, Shinto places little emphasis on the afterworld, the spirits of recently deceased family members are believed to linger nearby and to watch over their families' well-being, at least for a time, after which they merge with the rest of the ancestral spirits and are supplicated collectively.

The Priesthood

Jinja are staffed by priests known as *kannushi*, literally, "those who nurture the *kami*." *Kannushi* perform periodic rituals, both to honor the enshrined *kami* (sometimes there will be more than one) and to purify both individuals, such as brides and newborn infants, and the village, town, neighborhood, a new house, and so on. These rituals, which are called collectively *oharai*, typically include chanting *norito*, or Shinto prayers, and waving a sacred *sakakai* branch (the *sakaki* is a species of pine tree native to Japan and believed to have supernatural power, especially in the hands of a *kannushi*) in front of the person, place, or object to be purified.

The head priest of a shrine is called a *guji*. In addition to presiding over the shrine's affairs, secular as well as religious (today, some urban *jinja* operate day-care centers for working mothers), the *guji* and his family usually occupy a leadership position in the local social hierarchy, and are generally deferred to when it comes decisions affecting the shrine and its precincts, as well as the community as a whole.

Matsuri

In many respects, the most important single Shinto ritual occurs in the context of the neighborhood's or village's annual (in some cases, semiannual) *matsuri*, or shrine festival, which honors the local *kami*. The *guji* ceremoniously places an image of the deity inside a *mikoshi*, or portable shrine. It is then carried around the community, up one street or lane and down another, on the shoulders of chanting young people. This sacred procession, or *gyōretsu*, serves to sanctify both those who bear the deity and the region through which it is carried. The *miksohi* is carried in an undulating fashion, while the carriers chant nonsense phrases like "Wa-shoi!" It is thus not a solemn event. On the contrary, it is typically fueled by vast amount of beer and sake. Although few Japanese of my acquaintance actually believe it today, the tradition is that the *kami* possesses the participants in the *gyōretsu*, and that they become one with the deity as they carry the *mikoshi*. As you can imagine, the achievement of this "godlike" feeling is greatly facilitated by the consumption of alcoholic beverages.

Matsuri usually occur over a two- or three-day period. There may be several processions during this period, and the participants drop in and out of them frequently. The shrine grounds are covered with vendors' stalls, and the whole effect is remarkably similar to a Latin American fiesta.

Women and Shinto

Until quite recently, the *mikoshi* carriers were almost exclusively male. Before the introduction of Buddhism from China and Korea in the latter part of the sixth century CE, many Japanese women played extremely prominent roles both in Shinto and in the society at large. Indeed, there were even, as I mentioned earlier, reigning empresses, one of whom, the quasi-legendary Himiko (ca. 300 CE), was famed both as a warrior and as a shaman. But thanks to the profound impact of Chinese civilization and its patriarchal, Confucian ideology, the importance of women in Japan declined steadily, and this new state of affairs was, of course, reflected in Shintoism.

However, as feminist ideas began to have an impact on Japan in the late 1960s and 1970s, things began to change. Young women began to take their place in the ranks of the *mikoshi* carrying teams, wearing the same traditional costume—including a *happi* (a short, workman's jacket tied around the waist) and a *hachimaki*, or ritual headband—as their brothers. In 1980, I studied the discussion and debate that preceded this change (it occurred in 1978) in the annual *matsuri* at a small Tokyo neighborhood shrine. One of the arguments made by the local *guji* in favor of allowing young women to carry his shrine's *mikoshi* was that in ancient times there were Shinto priestesses as well as empresses, the most important of whom was the high priestess of Amaterasu at Ise. That the shrine in question is devoted to Amaterasu appears to have facilitated this decision, although the new custom has now spread to the great majority of Shinto shrines, rural as well as urban.

Moreover, in recent years the number of female *kannushi* has steadily increased—in part due to the difficulty of persuading young men to forego lucrative careers in business and enter the priesthood. Female *kannushi* are still very much in the minority, but their ranks are growing.

Miko

One aspect of Shinto in which young women still play an inherently subordinate role is as *miko*—for the most part, teenage virgins who today can best be described as "altar girls." At major shrines, they assist the *kannushi*, or priests, in conducting rituals; sell talismans and fortunes; and occasionally perform sacred dances in which they are symbolically possessed by the *kami*. These dances are a survival of their ancient shamanic heritage, which goes back to the dancing goddess, Ama no Uzumei, although today's *miko* do not perform lewd dances. (In a few remote, mountainous regions of the country, there are still some *miko* who actually practice shamanism. But they are a dying breed in modern Japan, as are their male counterparts, the Yamabushi, or "Mountain Warriors," who are also shamans and healers.)

In any case, a *miko* must be a virgin, and this is about as close as Shinto comes to a rule of celibacy. But there is no expectation that *miko* will remain unmarried virgins, and in a great many cases, current *miko* are the daughters of former *miko*. There is usually a ceremony in which former *miko* "present" their teenage daughters to their neighborhood or village *kami* (or *ujigami*, as such tutelary spirits are called) as novice *miko*. To be chosen to serve as a *miko* at a shrine like the Ise-jingu or the Meiji-jingu in Tokyo, where the first modern emperor, Meiji (reigned 1868–1912), is enshrined, is a great honor to both the girl and her family.

If Ama no Uzumei was the prototypical *miko*, the most celebrated one was Ōkuni, a renegade dancer from the Izumo Taisha shrine in what is now Shimane Prefecture, the most sacred Shinto shrine after Ise. In 1603, she fled with her lover to Kyoto and began performing in a dry riverbed on the outskirts of the city. Her performances, which soon became popular, eventually evolved into Kabuki theater—from which, ironically, women were barred in the 1620s.

The Shinto Attitude toward Marriage

Although there is no specific requirement for them to marry, at least today, the vast majority of *kannushi* and *guji* do have wives and families. And in rural villages, it is often expected that priests will sire sons who will eventually take their places at the local *jinjas*. Moreover, such shrines are typically hereditary in their leadership, with the position of *guji* passing from father to son. This is yet another reason why Shinto has long rejected the celibacy practiced by the majority of Japanese Buddhist priests, along with other aspects of asceticism. To be sure, some Buddhist sects, most notably Jōdō Shinshu, founded by the thirteenth-century Buddhist "Pure Land" reformer Shinran (1173–1263), have long permitted their priests to marry—Shinran himself renounced celibacy and married a Buddhist nun—but the majority of them, including the Zen and Nichiren sects, continue to practice celibacy, at least among their priesthoods, despite the 1872 edict issued by the newly installed Meiji government that allowed all Buddhist priests to marry without incurring penalties from the state, as had been the case during the previous Edo period (1603–1867).

Shinto and the State

Until the Meiji Restoration in 1868, Shinto, which by then had developed a number of sects including Teni-kyo, founded by a woman in the 1830s, and twelve other "churches," as they came to be called, was a haphazard affair. Even the label "Shinto" itself is fairly modern. Outside of the sects, each local shrine was an independent entity, and there was little unity among them. To be sure, the Ise-jingu and the equally ancient Izumo Taisha shrine, where Ōkuninushi is enshrined, were generally regarded as places of pilgrimage, but there was no controlling authority.

However, with the end of the Shōgnate in 1867 and the restoration of the emperor a year later as the actual as well symbolic head of state, an attempt was made to establish shrine Shinto as the state religion. This did not work, largely because there were too many people who practiced both Shinto and Buddhism, let alone a budding Christian community. Nevertheless, a Bureau of Shrines was established, and most *kannushi* became in effect government employees. Orthodoxy in rituals and ceremonies was strictly enforced. The reason behind this was to instill a deep sense of loyalty to the emperor and a fervent nationalism. Shrine Shinto became the "state cult"; to perform Shinto rites was tantamount to saluting the flag or bowing to the emperor.

The culmination of this nationalistic, Shinto-based mindset was Japan's ill-fated attempt to establish the Greater East Asia Co-Prosperity Sphere in the late 1930s, and its crushing defeat at the hands of the Allies in 1945. One of the first things the American Occupation authorities did was to "disestablish" Shinto. As a result, contemporary shrine Shinto returned essentially to what it had been before 1868. To be sure, there is a national Association of Shinto Shines, but it has no authority to prescribe (or proscribe) any rituals or beliefs, and serves primarily as a source of funding for poor shrines—of which there are thousands—and to oversee the training of apprentice *kannushi* at several Shinto universities. However, each local shrine is governed solely by its *sodai-kai*, or elders' association—what I sometimes think of as the deacons—and it can hire and fire *guji* and other *kannushi* at will.

Although nothing could be further from the monotheistic theology expressed in the Old Testament than Shinto's almost infinite number of *kami*, great and small, when it comes to celibacy, as well as other matters, the Shinto priesthood is remarkably similar to the Jewish rabbinate. Like rabbis, who are also expected (but also not required) to marry, *kannushi* are conservers of the sacred tradition and intermediaries between the community and the divine, rather than persons set apart from the community through an "apostolic succession" or by a qualitatively closer relationship with the divine through the achievement of some form of enlightenment. Both rabbis and Shinto priests fully participate in—and celebrate—the life of their respective communities, and that includes marriage and the procreation of children. All in all, the concept of celibacy is as inherently foreign to Shinto and the central core of its theology as it is to Judaism.

15

A Social-Cultural Analysis of Celibacy among the Yoruba: Oyo Alafin's Servants as a Case Study

Oyeronke Olajubu

The Yoruba people, who occupy the southwest of Nigeria, are a highly researched ethnic group in Africa. The people can boast of a rich cultural heritage, manifested in their history, sociology, and philosophy. The Yoruba are bound together by a common progenitor called Oduduwa, a common language, and a rich spirituality. Yoruba religion and culture are two sides of the same coin, and balance is always sought in both religion and culture. Yoruba value procreation highly because of the desire to perpetuate continuity in the family. In other words, both personal and collective immortality are salient ambitions that are pursued vigorously by the Yoruba, through bearing children, especially sons.[1]

The Oyo people in Yorubaland occupy a prominent place politically, economically, and religiously. The ancient Oyo settlement (Oyo-Ile) founded around 1400 CE was the most politically important Yoruba settlement from the mid-seventeenth century to the late eighteenth century. The Oyo empire at this time held sway not only over other Yoruba states but also over the Fon kingdom of Dahomey (now in the Republic of Benin). After the disintegration of old Oyo (Oyo-Ile) around 1796, the capital was moved to the present site of Oyo-Alafin, founded around 1835.[2] Oyo town is primarily a farming town, but other products include textiles, leather goods, and different utensils and decorative items carved from shells and calabashes.

The political stature of the kings, called Alafin, in Yoruba historiography was large. The Yoruba describe their kings as *alase ekeji orisa*, meaning "the one with authority, second only to the orisa"(spirits); the Alafin lived this dictum by wielding tremendous powers. There were, however, traditional provisions for checks and balances within Yoruba social structures; for example, the king ruled in consonance with a council of male and female chiefs. The palace of the Alafin was and is an empire within an empire that comprised freeborn, servants, and slaves. The practice of celibacy was found among specific groups of slaves and servants of the Alafin. It seems apparent that the practice of celibacy in any form within a culture that prioritizes procreation as the Yoruba do cannot be separated from issues of class and consequently power.

Celibacy has been described as "a state of being unmarried, especially as a result of a religious promise."[3] Celibacy could be undertaken for religious or secular purposes, and its scope could cover the entirety of a person's life or part of a lifetime; it could also involve castration, or not.

The agenda of this chapter is twofold: to explicate the practice of celibacy among the servants of the Oyo-Alafin and to offer a sociocultural analysis of the practice with its implications for the contemporary Yoruba setting. The methodology for the work includes interviews and the use of secondary sources such as books, journal articles, and the internet.

Theoretical Framework

On the grounds of both fact and reason, it has been postulated that it is necessary and expedient that some people should rule and others be ruled.[4] Consequently, class stratification is an unavoidable component of social structure in human sociology, though the various modalities for its implementation remain debatable. Usually, class stratification operates with stated and assumed obligations and responsibilities for both the ruled and the ruler. These prescribed obligations and responsibilities may or may not be documented, but they are agreed charters by members of the society and are informed by a people's philosophy, mores, and values.

Slavery is a poignant phenomenon that has elicited diverse reactions from different people over the centuries. Aristotle holds that slavery is natural, in other words, some people are naturally slaves whereas others are masters.[5] He identifies a correlation between a weak mind and a strong body for a natural slave. Such individuals he likens to beasts of burden except that, unlike beasts, human slaves recognize that they need to be ruled. Another dimension of the issue of slavery is the perception that slavery is conventional and legitimate through its link with war.[6] Accordingly, it has been argued that all prisoners of war could be legitimately enslaved irrespective of whether the war is "just" or "unjust." Consequently, "if you lose the battle and are captured, you may be enslaved legitimately."[7] This position thus postulates that "might is right," though opposition to this stance abounds.

Slavery was one of the means of control and regulation in African communities before the advent of the trans-Atlantic slave trade. Theoretically, the trans-Atlantic slave trade is to be differentiated from slavery among African ethnic groups because the two phenomena differ in modalities of operation as well as in purpose. Slavery among African ethnic groups was usually informed and guided by principles that are derived from the people's worldview and belief system, but the trans-Atlantic slave trade was conducted to exploit and displace the Africans for the furtherance of capitalism in the Americas and Europe.

Celibacy: Religious and Secular Purposes

One of the earliest manifestations of celibacy occurred in the institution of monasticism, which is based on the dualistic philosophy that regards matter as evil and low, whereas the spirit is good and high.[8] Some have opined that celibacy is a practice based on guilt founded on false religious teachings that are developed to control people. They argue further that celibacy is physically unnatural and could give rise to health problems.[9] The Roman Catholic Church is known for the practice of celibacy in Christendom, whereas examples of secular celibacy may be located in some political structures such as the Yoruba Oyo-Alafin's palace.

This writer has addressed the practice of celibacy in the Roman Catholic Church in Nigeria in an earlier work, but some points therein are worthy of being reiterated.[10] First, the distinction is made in some quarters between chastity and celibacy. Oftentimes, the vow of celibacy includes the vow of chastity, but not always. According to the canon law, the vow of chastity is broken if the priest marries but not if he engages in sexual relations.[11] He could obtain pardon for sexual relations by confessing to a fellow priest. Second, participation in the practice of celibacy in the Roman Catholic Church is not compelled; it is voluntary. Moreover, the participants are not castrated but function with their normal sexual feelings and facilities. Consequently, a great deal of self-control is imperative for these celibates. Whereas human sexual feelings are recognized by the Roman Catholic Church, the aim is to control them, and not the other way round. Celibacy in the church is a lifetime experience, because the celibate enters the convent or monastery at an early age and normally remains there for life. The stated objectives are rejection of all distractions and total concentration of all energies on the worship of God and service to humanity. There are no biblical injunctions that prescribe celibacy for Christians, however. Third, celibacy as practiced in the Roman Catholic Church is at variance with cultures in Nigeria, where the individual's sense of fulfillment is intertwined with the ability to marry and produce children; hence tension is unavoidable. Again, celibacy is absent in African religions, the nearest being occasional abstinence from sex spanning few days before specific rituals.

The secular practice of celibacy is always connected with issues of power and class. Celibacy could serve as a mark of class distinction among a people or in a group. Also, this type of celibacy is often closely tied with the philosophy and worldview of a people who practice it. Invariably, a people's conceptualization of power structure, power legitimacy, and power accountability could be discerned from their practices of nonreligious celibacy. For instance, nonreligious celibacy is seldom found among rulers or leaders but is present among servants and people of lower class. This sheds some light on the purpose of the practice, which is to control. The ability of an individual of a higher class to control the lives of others who are of a lower class is integral to the practice of nonreligious celibacy. In addition, secular celibacy places a high premium on loyalty in the area of sexuality, hence the loyalty of the celibate to the ruler must be uncompromising.

Both religious and nonreligious celibacy accrue some benefits to the celibate. Financial comfort is often guaranteed by the church and the ruler, respectively. The celibate also receives care because of the utilitarian purposes toward which the services of the celibate are directed. Some level of immunity also accrues to the celibate, which may include political clout, privileges, and delegated authority in different settings.

Sexuality among the Yoruba

Yoruba sexuality is geared toward one goal, which is procreation, to achieve continuity of the human race. Marriage is the prescribed setting for the exercise of human sexuality among the Yoruba, though certain situations may necessitate other measures, such as concubinage. Therefore, marriage is a duty expected of all adult male and female members of Yoruba society. Marriage is one of the characteristics of a mature person, because to be unmarried is perceived as a feature of childhood, irrespective of the individual's age. Marriage conveys a status of responsibility, which may not be true of an unmarried person. This status at marriage is manifested at different levels for the male as well as the female. For the Yoruba woman, marriage is an indication of her maturity because she is able to change residence from her father's house to that of her husband. In addition, it shows her ability to manage both human and natural resources. Also, it bestows on her the privilege to belong to the league of mothers. Marriage for the man is an indication of maturity because he now becomes a provider and guardian of others in the family. Consequently, depending on the level of success of the man as a husband and provider, responsibilities in the larger society may be assigned to him. Again, the status that marriage bestows on both male and female in Yorubaland transcends this life into the hereafter because on it hinges the phenomenon of the ancestors. Marriage is a rhythm of life in which everyone must participate: the ancestors, the living, and the yet unborn.

Having children is essential in Yoruba marriages. Children are the glory of marriages, and the more there are of them the greater the glory.[12] The significance of having children is frequently recorded in Yoruba oral genres including songs, stories, proverbs, dictums, and dirges. Examples of some sayings on the importance of procreation in Yoruba oral genres are: *omo niyi, omo nide, omo l'aso, omo ni i wo 'le de ni l'ojo ale,* meaning "children guarantee prestige," "children are as brass," "children are cloths (because they shield parents from shame)," "children take care of the house (concerns) for parents in old age and after death." Others include: *ina ku 'fi eeru b'oju, ogede ku 'fi omo re ropo, ojo a ba ku, omo eni ni wo 'le de ni,* meaning "when the fire is out, ashes replace it, when the banana tree dies, its child (young one) replaces it, when one dies, it is the children who replaces one." Another example says *omo omo oosin, omo l'afe aye,* meaning "children are worthy to be revered because they constitute the essence of life." Consequently, marriage and procreation are closely tied together among this people.

To die without having children is the greatest calamity that could befall any individual among the Yoruba. A popular Yoruba song aptly sums it up: *ori mi ma je npo 'fo omo lere aye,* meaning "may my destiny not let me be a loser, for children are the gains of living." This explains why Yoruba people, especially females, go to great lengths to ensure that they produce children; to die without children is to become disconnected, to become an outcast, and to lose all links to the human race after death. To produce no children is to be erased and forgotten totally in the memories of one's family members and community.

The proper use of sex therefore is to produce children. Women bear the larger part of the task of procreation through pregnancy and childbirth; hence the Yoruba prescribe more regulations in the form of ritual observance or prohibitions (taboo) for women's sexuality. Sex is recognized as a gift from the creator to both men and women, but its use is monitored to avoid abuse. The Yoruba do not attach any form of guilt to sexual feelings except where they are not properly utilized, such as in incestuous relationships or when they violate specific religious values such as sex on the bare ground or in the afternoon.[13]

Celibacy among the Yoruba

Celibacy (abstaining from sex) as a practice in Yoruba religion is seldom total or final. Cultic functionaries may be required to abstain from sexual relations for the immediate period before officiating at a religious occasion. Because these priestesses and priests often serve also as intermediaries between the Supreme Being and the worshipers, they may be required to shun sex before mediating between these two parties. Again, examples of elderly men and women who are dedicated to some religious deities in Yorubaland may be cited. These elderly people are usually past childbearing age, but have probably been married and had children before this period of dedication. In addition, examples of votary maids in Yoruba religion may be construed as another example of celibacy. Young girls between ten and eleven years old are dedicated to goddesses and required to abstain from sexual relations and marriage until the end of their tenure. Indeed, for some the very day of marriage marks the end of the restrictions from sex as they proceed straight to their marital residence from the last assignment as a votary maid.[14] It is worth noting that such requirements as demanded of votary maids are rarely found among young men in Yoruba religion, and this may be due to the link between women's sexuality and procreation.

Secular celibacy is often found among the lower-class populace in Yoruba society, such as servants and slaves. Victims who are captured due to defeat in war provide the bulk of this population. Such slaves and servants may render services in homes of the rich or in the palace of the ruler. Duties assigned to this class of people range from the domestic to the diplomatic. In specific cases, slaves and servants may be required to practice celibacy, and such celibate status is neither optional nor voluntary. Because these slaves and servants are perceived as properties of their owners, little cognizance is paid to their individual preferences in life; it is the wish of the masters that dictates their lives.

A specific example of the practice of celibacy among the Yoruba is that of some slaves and servants in the Alafin Oyo's palace. Whereas the slaves were known as *iwefa*, the servants were called *ilari*, grown men who served the Alafin. The existence of these classes of servants has been traced to the old Oyo kingdom.[15] The *ilari* were recognized by a special hairdo that divided the hair into three parts (*aaso-meta*). They were messengers to the Alafin and usually went in front of him at any occasion of sacrifice. On ritual occasions, the *ilari*'s apparel was a white wrapper tied on the chest, but on regular days they were usually clad in loose trousers and a gown, known as *atu* and *gbariye*. At any point in time, the *ilari* was armed with a cutlass, just in case there was need to defend the ruler. The Alafin delegated some authority to the *ilari* because they were highly trusted. For example, they collected tributes (*isakole*) from districts, each covering a specified area of jurisdiction. This privileged position granted to the *ilari* was an avenue to exercise power and accumulate wealth, and often they displayed unsanctioned influence in the community.

Ilari practiced celibacy by compulsion. The rationale for this was the imperative to be loyal to the ruler. Treachery was deemed to be sabotage, and the penalty was death. These men (usually married men with sons) were castrated (*te loda*) to ensure that their sexual organs ceased to function, as opposed to relying on self-control to curtail sexual activities. Mention should be made that since these servants lived within the vicinity of the palace grounds, and the ruler often had numerous wives, a major concern was the need to ensure the total absence of any possibility of sexual interaction between the ruler's wives (*olori*) and the slaves or servants. The *ilari* were succeeded by their first son or the son agreed upon by the family to continue the line of service within the palace.

Presently, *ilari* do not practice celibacy, but they do continue to serve in the palace of the Alafin. Once chosen, an *ilari* is required to change residence to the palace of the Alafin, and he may not return to his family compound again except in emergencies, and even then such visits should be brief. The leader of the *ilari* is known as the Kudefu (that is, *iku Alafin de fufu*, meaning "the death of the Alafin is turned to thin air or erased"). He stays at the entrance of the palace, hence he is the first to contact anything or anybody—positive or negative—entering the palace ground. Consequently, he is the first contact for any danger meant for the Alafin.

The Yoruba have a vibrant philosophy of the potency of unseen influences in human endeavor, and so dangerous influences are daily occurrences among the people. Therefore, the Kudefu is usually a strong medicine man (*onisegun ponbele*) because he needs to harness all support to ward off danger on the life of the Alafin. In addition, any gift or tribute brought to the Alafin must of necessity make a first stop with the Kudefu. It is after he has taken his pleasure of such gifts that the remainder goes to the palace. He exercises authority on judicial matters in the Oyo kingdom, and may exercise significant influence on the Alafin on any issue, no matter how serious. The current Kudefu of Oyo-Alafin is Baba 'Laniyi of Ile-Modarikan, Oyo.[16]

Iwefa, slaves, are the second class of celibates in the palace of the Alafin-Oyo. These were people captured at war and conscripted into service, mainly at the domestic level of the palace administration. *Iwefa* were of three classes: Ona-Efa, Otun-Efa, and the Osi-Efa. The Ona-Efa and Otun-Efa were slaves charged with the duties of blessing the ruler by reciting his praise-names, the past heroic deeds of the ruler's ancestors, and the exploits of the ruler—all in a bid to boast the ruler's self-esteem. Further, these two classes of slaves praised the chiefs-in-council who administered the community with the ruler. Also, these slaves acted as interpreters (*ogbifo*) for the rulers when visitors called. This was because of the Yoruba belief that the ruler as the representative of the gods should not communicate with people directly. Presently the Ona-Efa and Otun-Efas' successors still perform the same duties in the palace, though they no longer practice celibacy. They bless and praise the Alafin and chiefs in the palace. Also, they make sure that the ruler is properly dressed by regularly adjusting his flowing gown and attend to his minute-by-minute needs. The mode of dressing for the *iwefa* is the same as that of the *ilari*.

The third class of *iwefa* was the Osi-Efa. They were the ones directly in charge of the ruler's wives (*olori*), hence they were usually castrated and celibate. Because they were castrated, they could move freely among the many wives of the ruler. They were highly trusted and favored by the ruler. They enjoyed tremendous privileges, and the care they received in terms of material blessings and gifts were enormous. All these were geared toward compensating the Osi-Efa for the sacrifice of his sexuality. The last Osi-Efa that was castrated in Oyo-Alafin served the Alafin in the 1960s. According to one informant who knew this particular Osi-Efa in the 1960s, the Osi-Efa was called Baba Busari and was very fat.[17] The current Osi-Efa was installed in 1972; he is Amusa Labintan. Amusa Labintan is neither castrated nor is a celibate, so access to the ruler's wives is restricted.

A Sociocultural Analysis

A comprehensive look at celibacy among the Yoruba shows that it is a practice based on class rather than religion. The Yoruba preference for procreation and marriage buttresses the above assertion. The need to guarantee loyalty is a paramount concern in the practice of celibacy in Yorubaland. This is because as powerful as the Alafin was and is, any act of disloyalty by slaves and servants could endanger his life and that of his family members. This is especially true of the Kudefu and Osi-Efa. Furthermore, any act of sexual impropriety in the palace could lead to bearing bastard children who could infiltrate and consequently contaminate the royal blood. If in the future such an "illegitimate" child were to ascend the throne as Alafin, the ritual repercussions would be enormous for the lineage and the community.[18] Hence, the Osi-Efa's role has implications for the present and future preservation of the sanctity and integrity of the kingship institution in Oyo-Alafin.

The Yoruba philosophy of largeness and pluralism is reflected in the practice of celibacy. The Yoruba say *Karin kapo, yiye ni i ye ni,* meaning "when we walk together in groups, it bestows honor on us all." This implies that individualism in all its ramifications is to be avoided by the people. The retinue of slaves and servants in the Alafin's palace constitute a component of the honor accorded the ruler anywhere within and outside the community. This entourage of slaves and servants symbolizes the largeness of the person and office of the ruler as well as the largeness of the ruler's resources. In plural terms, this retinue of slaves and servants suggests collective ownership of the ruler by the servants. The ruler is the father of everyone in the community and the chief celebrant of any religious festival or ritual, irrespective of his personal religious affiliations.

The practice of celibacy among the Yoruba presents a glimpse into the people's social structure of governance. Aristotle rejected the theory that postulates that "might is right," but the Yoruba uphold the theory, as reflected in their enslavement of captives of war. The parameters to determine whether a war is just or not are complex and dynamic and attended by multifarious factors within and outside each community. Therefore, a war conceived as being just in one community may be termed unjust in another. For the Yoruba any captive of war may be enslaved.

This chapter has attempted to explicate the practice of celibacy among the Yoruba, a people who value procreation and marriage highly. It interrogated the coexistence of celibacy with a high premium accorded procreation. It revealed that secular celibacy among the Yoruba was a case of class stratification and power. In sum, it may be asserted that celibacy among the Yoruba could be described as an exception to the rule. It served a purpose among the people and has now been obliterated because there is no need for the practice any more.

NOTES

1. J. S. Mbiti, *African Religions and Philosophy* (London: Heinemann, 1969), 26.

2. www.reference.allrefer.com.

3. O. Olajubu, "Celibacy in Christianity: Any Relevance to the Contemporary Church in Nigeria," M.A. thesis, Department of Religions, University of Ilorin, 1989, 9.

4. www.dlshq.org/teachings.

5. www.cfp.org.

6. www.pbs.org/religionandethics/week 532/cover.html.

7. www.cfp.org.

8. Olajubu, "Celibacy in Christianity," 11.

9. *Liberated Christians* (2002), www.catholic.com.

10. Olajubu, "Celibacy in Christianity," 9

11. Ibid., 10.

12. Mbiti, *African Religions and Philosophy*, 142

13. Having sexual relations on bare ground is believed to pollute the earth and may result in a poor harvest. Again, having sexual relations in the afternoon is a construed as a sign of laziness because that is the time individuals are expected to be at work earning their living; Yoruba belief is that such sexual relations produce albino children.

14. This is especially true of the Arugba Osun Osogbo, a young maiden dedicated to the goddess until marriage; the other example is the Arugba Otin.

15. Interview with Mallam Lamidi Shittu of Ile-Obashayero, Lagbodoko, Oyo, aged sixty, on September 13, 2006.

16. Interview with Baba Awo Adejare Adisa, the Babasegun Abiwere Oke-Olola, Oyo, aged fifty-eight, on September 13, 2006.

17. Interview with Mallam Lamidi Shittu of Ile-Obashayero, Lagbodoko, Oyo, aged sixty, on September 13, 2006.

18. The Yoruba belief is that children born to unmarried adults are bastards, *omo ale*, and some negative features are ascribed to such children.

16

Celibacy and Native American Indians

Carl Olson

If Native American Indians of the north American continent have anything in common, it is a widespread diversity of beliefs, practices, and regional variations. From the sparsely inhabited Arctic wilderness populated by the Inuit to the subarctic region of the Athapasca-speaking people; extending to the northeast woodlands covered by mixed coniferous and deciduous trees that is home to Algonquian, Iroquoian, and Siouan-speaking peoples; stretching to the southwest woodland with its deciduous forests, savannas, and swamps inhabited by the Iroquoian-speaking Cherokee; covering the tall-grass areas of the prairies and the short-grass plains region of the steppe country occupied by Crow, Cheyenne, and Sioux societies; stretching to the northwest coast with its rough coastline and high mountains that is home to Tlingit, Haida, Tsimshian, and Wakashan peoples; and running to the southwest, desert region populated by Apache, Navajo, and Pueblo peoples, Native American Indians cover a vast geographical area and exemplify lifestyles adapted to their respective natural environments. These various peoples, who have traditionally been dependent on their natural surroundings for survival, do not exhibit any penchant for emphasizing or embracing celibacy. There is instead a proclivity to emphasize sexuality. This does not mean that celibacy is completely absent from such cultures, but it does imply that celibacy is episodic in the lives of these peoples, whereas the necessity of sexuality is central, in part because of its role in the survival and perpetuation of the societies. Because of the plethora of societies in North America and the impossibility of covering them all in a short essay, this chapter will select examples from the eastern woodlands, plains, and southwest to illustrate its argument about the lack of a deeply ingrained observance of celibacy.

Myth and Social Life

Celibacy plays no role in various Native American Indian creation myths because it is not a creative act; it is akin to a sterile refraining from a natural human activity. According to a Seneca creation myth, a great chief and his aged wife lived in the up-above world, in the middle of which grew a cosmic tree with flowers and fruits that provided sustenance for all the people. At the top of the tree was a blossom that illumined the region and emitted a wonderful fragrance, and at the bottom of the celestial tree were white roots that extended to the four directions. In a dream, the chief received a desire for a beautiful maiden. After his dream, his desire came to fruition and the chief married the comely maiden, named Mature Flowers, but he discovered to his consternation that his new wife was pregnant. Feeling deceived and becoming angry, the chief dreamed that he was commanded to uproot the celestial tree in order to punish his unfaithful wife and relieve his distraught spirit. By uprooting the tree, the chief created a huge hole in the up-above world.

As Mature Flowers sat at the edge of the hole peering downward, the angry and vengeful chief kicked her into the gap, but she was able to grasp some seeds shaken from the celestial tree before she fell into the hole. On her way downward, she met a beast with fire streaming from its head, who gave her a small pot, a corn mortar, a pestle, a marrow bone, and an ear of corn, and he instructed her to eat these items because of a dearth of anything at the end of her journey. The fall of Mature Flowers was safely broken by ducks with their wings spread wide; a turtle provided its back as a resting place, and other animals dived into the cosmic waters to retrieve some earth until the muskrat was successful and smeared the earth on the back of the turtle, where it grew. After the earth extended in all directions, Mature Flowers dropped numerous seeds on it that grew, along with a tree that illuminated the world. Finally, Mature Flowers gave birth to a daughter, who was married to the Wind, and the daughter gave birth to two sons: a good one named Good Mind and an evil son called Warty One. When the evil son was born from his mother's armpit, she died and was buried by her good son in the earth, from which sprang stringed-potato, beans, squash, corn, and tobacco, with each plant emerging from a different part of her body. The two antagonistic brothers acted in contrary ways until a battle between them resulted in the destruction of the tree of life, banishment of the evil brother to a cave, and creation of human beings by Good Mind from clay. He entrusted the earth to humans, and taught them to hunt, fish, and eat the fruits of the land, to live together as brothers by treating each other well, and to make offerings of tobacco. Whereupon, Good Mind returned to the sky, leaving his created beings on earth prepared to provide for themselves.

This creation myth embodies many messages about origins of supernatural beings, humans, and animals; good and evil; a transformation of chaos into cosmos; the close relationship between humans and animals; and the reliance of human beings on animals for their continued existence. Furthermore, sexual transgression, anger, resentment, and violence give impetus to creation. Although evil is overcome in the narrative, it continues to lurk on the earth. The narrative takes an ambivalent attitude toward sex because sexual transgression motivates violence, and the sexual congress of Mature Flowers's daughter and the Wind results in the birth of good and evil, which suggest that sex is complex and embodies uncertain results. At the same time, sex is a creative power that provides the impetus for transforming chaos into cosmos or order. In short, there would be no life without sexual relations. This Seneca myth is just one example that stresses the importance of sexual relations for the perpetuation of human life that can be discovered among the creation narratives of Native American Indians.

In comparison to many other cultures in which sex is a taboo subject and not for public discussion, numerous Native American Indian societies are rather open about sexual issues. Among the Cheyenne of the plains region, a man is allowed to treat his wife's sister with the utmost license, such as raising her dress to expose her nakedness. It is only a brother-in-law of outstanding chastity who would forgo such prerogatives with his sister-in-law, who may respond by fondling and teasing the other party.[1] It is also not unusual for a Cheyenne married couple to abstain from sexual relations for long periods of time after the birth of each child, sometimes for as long as ten years, by taking a sacred oath of celibacy in order to give the child time to develop before the arrival of new siblings.[2]

Like the Cheyenne, the Crow Indians agree that a man is expected to gratify his passions under normal circumstances. This type of social expectation reflects a double standard toward sexual behavior, because women are admired for their sexual purity, whereas wanton women lose social prestige, although they are not socially ostracized. The male attitude toward women is expressed in the following way by a member: "Women are like a herd of buffalo, and a husband who cleaves to one wife is like a hunter who has killed the last of the fugitive animals and stays by the carcass because he lacks spirit to pursue others."[3]

This does not suggest that women should mate with just anyone. In fact, the Crow and Cheyenne admired chaste women. For a young Cheyenne girl, sexual seduction was unusual, and any evidence of yielding to sexual advances brought lifetime disgrace, which would compromise her future martial status. In contrast to Cheyenne women, Arapaho women were notorious for their loose sexual morals.[4] Nonetheless, young Arapaho girls were socially pressured to marry young, and others ridiculed girls who were unmarried by their first menses.[5] Overall, chaste men and women were respected, admired, honored, and praised for their virtuous behavior, but the virtue of chastity was not widely emulated, and a long-term commitment to the practice of celibacy was foreign to the social life of the various indigenous peoples, except on particular ritual occasions during a person's life.

Within the context of playing a game similar to lacrosse called *anetsâ*, Cherokee young men abstained from sex for fear of being contaminated by women. The players could also not eat rabbit, a timid creature, or frog, an animal with fragile bones. The players played the game naked with two sticks for each, which they used to throw a deerskin ball until twelve goals were scored, concluding the game. Contests were violent, with few rules to hinder the aggression of the contestants, and the contests were akin to war.[6]

Other examples of short-term celibacy can be discovered among the Inuit and Yup'ik Eskimo during the Bladder Festival, when inflated bladders, which are symbolic of the souls of the sea animals, are returned to the sea to rejuvenate animal life. Couples practice celibacy for one month during the festival. On other occasions, in order to insure success a young hunter will refrain from sexual relations. And after the death of a spouse, the survivor must refrain from sexual relations for twenty days, along with observing other restrictions connected to harvesting, fishing, and hunting activities.[7]

These various examples of North American Indian social practice with reference to sexuality and celibacy can be partly explained by belief in the individual's immanence in the world, within a society that governs speech and actions without ordering or organizing them. What the various examples imply is a social game that members play from habit. This suggests that they enter the game with a practical faith "established in practice between a *habitus* and the field to which it is attuned, the pre-verbal taking-for-granted of the world that flows from practical sense."[8] As embodied beings, Native American do not think out or conceptualize their social actions and choices, which are habitually spontaneous, without consciousness effort, and internalized ways of behaving are accepted modes of common-sense action.

Overt Sexuality of Cultural Figures

Certain culture figures among Native American Indians manifest overt sexual behavior for the edification and amusement of others. The two primary examples are the trickster and clown. Both figures exist on the margins of social life, revel in illogical behavior, and play tricks on others within the context that represents an interplay between social structure and arbitrariness. They often disguise themselves by assuming other forms; they are concerned with survival, and teach that a person must aggressively seek knowledge and power in order to prosper.

Among the Winnebago Indians, the trickster is called the Tricky One; among the Sioux, he appears as the spider Inktomi; within the context of Blackfoot culture, he is called Napi (Old Man); and the Ojibwa call him Nanabozho.[9] Among the Winnebago, comic communication is combined with an origin narrative and male sexuality in the tale of the chipmunk that teases the trickster about his lengthy penis. Vowing to destroy the teaser, the trickster inserts his penis into a hollow tree and instructs it to pursue the chipmunk. After continually inserting more and more of his male organ into the hollow tree to find the annoying chipmunk, the trickster withdraws it to discover to his utter astonishment and horror that only a small piece of his penis remains. Outraged, the trickster kicks the tree to pieces, only to find the chipmunk and the gnawed pieces of his former penis. From these pieces of his male organ, various vegetables and flowers grow, and this episode provides the rationale for the shortness of the male sexual organ. In other tales, the trickster carries his penis in a box for safekeeping.

In addition to the adventures of his penis, many Native American tricksters also manifest an insatiable sexual appetite. By expressing insatiable cravings for food and sex, the trickster figure manifests hidden, universal urges that need to be addressed before humans can find social equilibrium.[10] It is assumed that social balance and harmony cannot be achieved by observing celibacy, because natural, biological impulses are frustrated. According to one narrative, the trickster spied the chief's daughter from across a lake, and desiring to have sexual intercourse with her, he instructed his penis to lodge itself in her. After he dispatched his penis on its cross-lake adventure, it went sliding on the surface of the water. Realizing that the women on the far shore would see it, he tied a stone to it, but his penis sank to the bottom of the lake. Replacing the larger stone with a smaller stone, the trickster successfully launched his submarine-performing penis that hit its designated target. Males and females on the far shore could not dislodge it, but a knowledgeable old woman straddled the penis and struck it a few times with a sharp instrument, causing the organ to be suddenly and forcefully withdrawn, and throwing the old woman a great distance. Even though the trickster withdraws without completing his task, the narrative promises that he will return at an unspecified future time.

Among the Blackfoot Indians, their trickster figure Old Man, or Napi, does not allow his advanced age to interfere with his sexual exploits, which are in fact comically enhanced by his maturity and the enormous length of his male organ. Tricking the daughter of the chief by smearing her dress with smelly excrement and motivating her to ask him to clean her dress, the Old Man insists on a prior sexual relationship before providing his cleaning service. Upon seeing the size of his penis, the chief's daughter requests the Old Man to tie a stick across his organ in order to prevent extreme penetration of her body. Although initially agreeing to her request, the Old Man removes the stick during intercourse, with dire consequences for the Indian maiden. The sexual adventures of the trickster remind us that sexuality is ambivalent, tricky, dangerous, and a powerful force. As the last narrative suggests, sexuality can lead to order and continued existence, or it can lead to disorder when it is uncontrolled. Our need for sex can also motivate us to make imprudent choices, although a person can shape a more harmonious social world and ensure survival by wise choices.

The absurd and self-contradictory features characteristic of a Native American trickster can also be discovered in clown figures. Wearing a mask of scraped rawhide, moccasins, and a G-string on his painted body, an Apache clown goes about mostly naked.[11] The Sioux *heyoka*—a person who receives a vision of a Thunder Being—does everything the opposite of normal people: he rides his horse backward, for instance, and wears heavy clothing in the summer and goes naked in the winter.[12] The clown's contempt for status is evident among the Pueblo and Hopi Indians, where clowns burlesque the Kachina dancers by performing out of time and rhythm, and stumbling around and grimacing in an undignified manner.[13]

Indian clowns often parody human sexuality: male clowns impersonate women and publicly exposing their huge, false vulvas, or they don large, artificial male sexual organs to lampoon men, and fake copulation publicly with a female clown, illustrating the clown's willingness to break social taboos.[14] Other sexually obscene examples are reported among Indian societies such as the Tewa, where an observer reported witnessing a clown snatch off the breechcloth of another clown and drag the unfortunate victim by his penis.[15] A fake reenactment of sexual intercourse is reported of two Pueblo clowns who simulated intercourse with a woman at different locations of her body, while meanwhile a third clown heightened the absurdity and unreality of the scene by masturbating in the center of the plaza.[16] An inventive Arapaho clown used a phallic-like root by which he pretended to magically paralyze the woman of his desires.[17] From the perspective of his disordered nature, the Indian clown lampoons a very personal act and brings it into the open for the amusement of everyone. Paradoxically, the clown creates a social chaos with infinite potentiality and creative possibility, which are features necessary for survival of the society. Likewise, while the absurd behavior of the clown promises potential social disorder, the clown's antics, as well as the importance of sexual behavior for continued existence and welfare of the group, more lucidly define normal social values and behavior.[18]

In comparison to the trickster and clown, the shaman or medicine man is a cultural figure who does not overtly exhibit his sexuality. It is not unusual for a shaman to seek his powers by adopting a celibate lifestyle for a period of time until he acquires them. Among the Shusway, a member of the Salish family located in British Columbia, a young man seeks such powers after reaching puberty and before engaging in any sexual relations.[19] This type of practice is understandable, because a seeker of shamanic powers needs to maintain intense concentration in order to obtain visions that determine his career, and celibacy helps one to achieve one's aim by encouraging focus on the ultimate goal. Oftentimes, shamans will acquire a spiritual spouse with whom they have sexual relations.[20] This type of spiritual, although sexual, relationship is condoned by the society.

Soul and Body

According to Sioux conception, the universe is composed of a finite amount of energy, which can be either good or evil, both controlled by Wakantanka, the Great Spirit. A human being can harness either type of energy by propitiating Wakantanka, who controls both sources of energy, or by appeasing *wakan sica* (evil sacred). Human beings are subordinate to both forms of the sacred, although *waken sica* is inferior to Wakantanka. The energy of the universe can be either visible or invisible, and the latter form is feared by humans. Overall, life and death are *wakan* (sacred) because life, or the visual aspect of what was once invisible, is transformed.

The Sioux believe that humans have three souls: a breath soul (*ni*) that leaves the body at death; an immortal and guardian soul (*sicun*) that represents a powerful potency and ability to protect a person from evil, which can be accumulated by a person; and the shadow soul (*nagi*), an eternal counterpart of every animate and inanimate object in the world. After losing one's breath soul (*ni*), the shadow soul lingers on earth after death, and becomes a dangerous *wanagi* (ghost) because it grieves for loved ones and attempts to entice family members to join it. In order to appease the *wanagi*, a relative will keep it for a year by feeding it. At the conclusion of the year, the *wanagi* is released by means of a rite that involves placing it into a wooden bowl and placing it in front of two holy men within a lodge. Four virgins enter the lodge and assume their places in the northern direction, which is associated with the power of purity. The keeper of the sacred pipe addresses the soul, feeds it sacred food at a hole at the base of the soul post, and covers the food with dirt, which symbolizes the final meal of the soul. After the four celibate women eat sacred buffalo meat and drink cherry juice, they are instructed about their receiving the spiritual seed of the departed soul, which will cause them and their progeny always to be holy.[21]

In contrast to the Sioux, the Ojibwa conceive of two souls: a body- or ego-soul that animates a person and is located in the heart, and can move within or without the body; and a free-soul that is located in the brain and maintains a separate existence from the body, although it can travel during sleep, is sensitive, can perceive distant objects, and warn one of danger during conflict or hunting. Even though each soul exists separately from the body, it yet acts in harmony with the body.[22] The body-soul proceeds to the afterworld upon death, whereas the free-soul is transformed into a ghost, although both souls are united eventually in the afterworld.

The beliefs of the Sioux and Ojibwa suggest a soul-body dualism among Native American Indians. That is, they believe in the soul's activity and its survival of the death of the body; the body is equated with a covering of ignorance for the soul, and the decay and destruction of the body enhances its differentiation from the soul. The soul is considered superior and dominates the body, and the soul also animates the body; the soul is immortal and the body is perishable, and the body cannot exist without the soul.[23] This dichotomy between body and soul might be expected to contribute to an emphasis on celibacy, but it does not among Native American Indian societies. What might explain this?

The answer resides with the conception of sexuality as a powerful force. Writing from the context of a discussion about Indian health, Hultkrantz writes, "Sex is everywhere regarded as a normal expression of life. . . . Sexual power is namely a great and dangerous power since it is creative."[24] There are a few exceptions, when celibacy is needed for a short period of time, as described above. One such occasion is ritual, and the Sun Dance and vision quest are prominent examples of the relationship between celibacy and ritual.

Celibacy, Ritual, and Vision Quest

Traditionally, the Sun Dance of the Sioux was an annual rite held during the full moon of June or July, during a period when the grass of the northern plains turns green and flowers bloom, which associates the rite with a time of rejuvenation and renewal of individuals, dancers, tribe, and universe. If these periodic ceremonies are not enacted, it is believed, life-sustaining powers will cease and the society will cease to exist.[25]

Not only does the rite celebrate rebirth but it also combines ascetic elements with purification and self-inflicted violence. A Sioux male may vow to participate for a variety of reasons, which include the following: to fulfill a previously made vow; to obtain supernatural assistance for another person; to gain the same aid for oneself; or to acquire supernatural powers for himself.[26] Even though a participant's motivation for performing the dance may be noble and within acceptable norms, the prospective dancer must possess and be able to demonstrate to both his tribe and the sun that he possesses four major virtues: bravery, generosity, fortitude, and integrity.[27] If he is not judged to have the necessary virtues, a prospective dancer's request to perform the rite can be denied by the tribal council, which suggest that the Sioux society is the custodian of the ceremony The virtue of chastity and the practice of celibacy are glaringly absent as prerequisites for the rite.

Assuming that a person is worthy of participating in the ceremony, in the estimation of the Sioux society, it is necessary to secure a teacher, whose function is to provide instruction and guidance in the essentials of the ritual. Taking a present, a pipe, and tobacco, a person proceeds to the tipi of the chosen teacher, enters the tent, lays down the present, fills and lights the pipe, and presents it to his potential mentor; this is a reversal of normal smoking etiquette, because a host is normally the person who fills and lights the pipe in a gesture of friendship. By reversing the normal etiquette, the aspirant signifies his high respect for his potential teacher and a willingness to assume a subordinate position in their relationship. By smoking in communion, the teacher accepts the aspirant as his student, and then appoints a friend of the candidate to be his attendant, with the understanding that the friend would substitute for the instructor in case of an emergency.[28] There is a social expectation that the sun dancer and his attendant will remain close friends for the rest of their lives.

After a time is set for the Sun Dance, the tribal council invites other tribes to the rite, which fosters social cooperation and cohesion among the various groups. After sending the invitations, the candidate is prepared for the rite by participating in a sweat lodge ceremony, which purifies him, stimulates his vital breath, and invigorates him.[29] The instructor also purifies the candidate by painting his hands red, which consecrates them and thereby enables him to handle sacred things. If he can successfully complete the Sun Dance, the candidate is granted the privilege of painting his own hands red for the balance of his life, and he is also allowed to attach a braid of sweet grass to his person and wear on his chest a special design painted red by his teacher, representing a visible sign that he danced the second, third, or fourth forms (or most painful ways) of the rite.[30] The aspirant also receives instruction about the rules associated with the ceremony, the required conduct, the religion of the people, and their social customs.

With the candidate prepared, the rite begins. Its initial phase is spread over four days and includes organizational matters and a feast on the second day. On the third day participants are informed about the roles of certain people, a buffalo head is decorated, the power of the Buffalo god is invoked by the leader of the rite within the confines of three concentric circles, and a feast of buffalo tongues is prepared. On the fourth day, the names of two women who are renowned for their industriousness and hospitality are announced; they are selected to chop the sacred tree. This represents an important honor that allows these women to wear a red stripe of paint across their foreheads for the remainder of their lives. After the names of further female attendants are announced, each maiden must stand and declare her virginity, and others may challenge them, although a woman can prove her innocence by biting a snake and vowing her virginity. The feast of the maidens follows this.[31] The fourth day ends with an offering of the sacred pipe to the Four Winds and prayers for favorable weather for the rite and blessings on the people.

The second phase of the rite takes another four days to complete. On the initial day, while aspirants pray and offer the sacred pipe to the Four Winds, others charge the ceremonial camp, shouting war cries and shooting arrows as if engaged in a confrontation with an enemy; this is done to expel evil spirits. The aspirants return in a spiral fashion to the sacred spot, which is represented by the hole for the sacred tree. After the center is marked by a stake and the Buffalo god is propitiated, the digger drives sixteen stakes into the ground four paces apart to form the sun trail to the sacred lodge that symbolizes the universe; it is constructed of twenty-eight forked sticks, a number connected to phases of the moon, days of a month, the twenty-eight ribs of a buffalo, and the same number of feathers in a war bonnet. The other major events of this initial day is the erection of the sacred lodge, placing the ornamented buffalo head beside the altar, and search for the enemy or sacred tree, which must be a cottonwood tree that is painted with red circles on all sides. This particular kind of tree is significant for the Sioux because its leaf serves as a pattern on which their tipis are modeled, and it represents the presence of the Great Spirit in the form of a five-pointed star that one can see by cutting crosswise an upper limb of the tree. After a scout reports finding the tree and reports this news to camp, the day concludes with the Buffalo Feast, which includes a circumambulation of the camp four times in order to propitiate the Buffalo god and the Whirlwind god. Following the feast, young people meet at trysting places outside of the camp, which negates any emphasis on celibacy.

On the second day of the rite, the most important event is the capture of the sacred tree, which symbolizes the enemy. The chopping of the tree begins when a renowned warrior strikes it four times, and he is followed by the chosen women, who finish the task. After the tree is trimmed, unpainted hands must not touch it. Thus it is carried back to camp by sticks placed underneath it. While the sacred pole is being painted, instructors and students sit in a circle around the black-painted figures of a buffalo and man, each depicted with exaggerated genitals in order to impart the potency of Iya, patron god of libertinism, to the aspirant, and the sexual potency of Gnaski, a crazy buffalo and patron deity of licentiousness, to the buffalo. According to Black Elk's non-risqué interpretation of the images, the buffalo represents all the four-legged animals on the earth, and the male figure signifies all people.

If the figures of Iya and Gnaski promote sexuality, this aspect is further enhanced when their effigies are hung from the sacred tree, planted as a pole, on the third day. Moreover, when the sacred tree is placed into the earth, it functions to connect the masculine powers of the sky with the feminine powers of the earth. The people shout the names of the two sexually potent deities suspended from the sacred tree, and sexual banter occurs among men and women. Then warriors perform a war dance to drive these obscene gods from the camp, and end by shooting and striking the figures until they fall from the sacred pole.

The Sun Dance reaches its climax on the fourth and final day, which begins with candidates circling the sacred lodge four times. Each candidate is painted red, symbolic of all that is sacred, from his waist upward by his mentor, and an aspirant's face is framed by a black circle, a sign of Wakantanka (Great Spirit), who like a circle is without end. After some additional bodily painting, dancers process along the trail of the sun marked by the sixteen stakes, at any of which one is permitted to make an offering to the sun.

Before processing four times around the dance lodge and placing the ornamented buffalo head on the altar facing the sacred pole, each candidate pauses at the entrance to the lodge and weeps. In order to harmonize themselves with the potency of the Buffalo God, the aspirants smoke the sacred pipe in communion with each other, and sweet grass is burned. Upon the command to stand, the candidates are given a whistle that is made from the largest bone in an eagle's wing and instructed to blow it, while they dance gazing at the sun. A Buffalo Dance may follow these actions.

The final phase of the Sun Dance occurs within a martial context; there are four phases of the dance: capture, torture, captivity, and escape. Once the dancers are captured, their flesh is pierced in accord with the form of the dance previously chosen by the dancer from among four possible ways: gazing at the sun from dawn to dusk; having wooden skewers inserted into his chest, which are tied to rawhide ropes secured about half way up the sacred pole; having wooden skewers inserted into the chest of the dancer, who is then suspended about a foot off the ground; or having wooden skewers inserted to which thongs are attached to one or more buffalo skulls, which he must drag along the dance area. The sacrifice is not complete until the flesh of the dancer is torn through, representing the death and rebirth of the person. It is permissible for others to assist by pulling on the ropes to end a dancer's agony. Since the torn flesh is symbolic of ignorance, this rite stresses a rejection of the body, which functions as the sacrificial offering. This aspect of the rite would appear to favor celibacy, but other sexual aspects of the ritual mitigate against this possibility.

Although there is apparently no injunction for the dancers to remain celibate during the days of the ritual, there are obviously periods during which celibacy is enforced on a dancer by the ritual pattern of the rite. Overall, the Sun Dance stresses fertility, sexual potency, suffering for the people, renewal, and rejuvenation. This type of scenario can be discovered in other Native American Indian rites. Among the Navaho, male and female virgins grind medicine for the Flint Chant, making chastity a ritualistic ideal, whereas the primary purpose of ritual is to promote reproduction.[32] Among the Cheyenne, leadership roles for the Sun Dance are reserved for chaste males, although no mention is made of celibate males. In either case, such figures are rare.[33]

There are times when Native Americans combine participation in the Sun Dance with going on a vision quest, which also embodies ascetic features that include enforced celibacy. The typical vision quest follows a pattern that includes preparation by participating in purifying baths or sweat lodge ceremony, sacred smoking, nightly vigil, meditation, and visit by one or more spirits. After preparation, a person on a quest is isolated in a deserted location and may engage in various forms of self-mortification, such as the Blackfoot practice of "feeding the sun" with bits of one's body. A Cheyenne suppliant is isolated, tied to a pole by means of wooden pins driven through his flesh, instructed to walk back and forth on the sunward side of the pole, praying continuously, fixing his eyes on the sun, and attempting to tear the pins from his flash. The pieces of torn flesh are held toward the sun, sky, the four directions, and finally buried. Meanwhile, the aspirant waits for a vision. Central Algonquian societies, such as the Winnebago, Menominee, and Fox, use fasting and thirsting to become pitiable before the spirits, whereas the Sioux erect a central pole from which offerings are hung and additional poles at the four directions, where a person laments and prays until a vision arrives that gives the seeker protective guardians and powers.

These visions of spirits, which usually assume animal form, may impart medicine songs for social benefit, and describe the appearance of a medicine bundle and its contents, which functions as a visible sign of the spirit's presence. For seekers, visions help to reduce anxiety associated with uncertain and dangerous situations, giving a seeker confidence; they may ease the transition to new social roles, solidify a person's identity, provide a rationale for the differential distribution of power and prestige within society, and enhance social cohesion. Once a vision is successfully acquired, it is important to put it into action, which legitimizes it. Overall, the strict ascetic regime of the vision quest presupposes a period of celibacy by the very nature of the rigors of the quest, even though sexual abstinence is not especially stressed.

Celibacy plays a negligible role in the religious cultures of Native American Indians in comparison to other religious traditions such as Christianity, Hinduism, Buddhism, and Jainism. The observance of celibacy is imposed by certain religious contexts that often occur during ritual. As the discussion of the Sun Dance makes clear, there are numerous references to sexual power and not an emphasis on celibacy, although sometimes aspects of chastity are stressed. But the virtue of chastity is not the same as the intentional practice of celibacy.

For Native American Indians, to practice celibacy in normal circumstances is to behave in an antisocial manner, although there are ritualistic contexts, accepted social customs, and religious persons that serve as examples of exceptions to the general custom of sexual activity for every mature adult. By practicing celibacy outside of these accepted social and religious contexts, a person also assumes a position on the margins of the social order. The celibate person does not have the same social stake or interest in a given society as do sexually active members. In general, it is possible to assert that to practice celibacy is to be an antisocial being and to risk becoming an outcast.

NOTES

1. George Bird Grinnell, *The Cheyenne Indians*, 2 vols. ([1923] Lincoln: University of Nebraska Press, 1972), 1: 28.

2. Ibid., 1: 149.

3. Robert H. Lowie, *The Crow Indians* ([1935] Lincoln: University of Nebraska Press, 1983), 48.

4. Grinnell, *Cheyenne Indians*, 156.

5. Lowie, *Crow Indians*, 45.

6. Grace Steele Woodward, *The Cherokees* (Norman: University of Oklahoma Press, 1963), 51; William G. McLoughlin, *Cherokee Renascence in the New Republic* (Princeton: Princeton University Press, 1986), 15.

7. Ann Fienup-Riordan, *Boundaries and Passages: Rule and Ritual in Yup'ik Eskimo Oral Tradition* (Norman: University of Oklahoma Press, 1994), 285, 166, 233.

8. Pierre Bourdieu, *The Logic of Practice*, translated by Richard Nice (Stanford: Stanford University Press, 1990), 68.

9. See Paul Radin, *The Trickster: A Study in American Indian Mythology* (New York: Philosophical Library, 1956); Christopher Vecsey, *Traditional Ojibwa Religion and Its Historical Changes* (Philadelphia: American Philosophical Society, 1983), 84–100; Mac Linscott Ricketts, "The North American Indian Trickster," *History of Religions* 5.4 (1966): 327–350.

10. Calvin Luther Martin, *The Way of the Human Being* (New Haven: Yale University Press, 1999), 61–62.

11. Morris Edward Opler, *An Apache Life-Way* (New York: Cooper Square Publishers, 1956), 105.

12. John G. Neihardt, *Black Elk Speaks* (New York: Washington Square Press, 1972), 159–163.

13. Mischa Titiev, *The Hopi Indians of Old Oraibi: Change and Continuity* (Ann Arbor: University of Michigan Press, 1972), 255.

14. *Hopi Journal of Alexander M. Stephen*, edited by Elise Clews Parsons, 2 vols. (New York: Columbia University Press, 1936), 1: 386; Charles Lange, *Cochiti* (Carbondale: Southern Illinois University Press, 1968), 304; N. Ross Crumrine, "Čapakoba, The Mayo Easter Ceremonial Impersonator: Explanations of Ritual Clowning," *Journal for the Scientific Study of Religion* 8.1 (Spring 1969): 6.

15. *Hopi Journal of Alexander M. Stephen*, 491.

16. Lange, *Cochiti*, 6.

17. Alfred Kroeber, "The Arapaho," *Bulletin of the American Museum of Natural History* 18 (1902–1907): 192.

18. Sam D. Gill, *Native American Religions: An Introduction* (Belmont, Calif.: Wadsworth, 1982), 28.

19. Mircea Eliade, *Shamanism: Archaic Techniques of Ecstasy*, translated by Willard R. Trask (New York: Pantheon, 1964), 100.

20. Ibid., 71–73, 79–81.

21. Brown, *The Sacred Pipe: Black Elk's Account of the Seven Rites of the Oglala Sioux* (Norman: University of Oklahoma Press, 1953; reprinted Middlesex: Penguin, 1971), 27–28.

22. Christopher Vecsey, *Traditional Ojibwa Religion and Its Historical Changes* (Philadelphia: American Philosophical Society, 1983), 59–62.

23. Åke Hultkrantz, *Soul and Native Americans* (Woodstock, Conn.: Spring, 1997), 173–175.

24. Åke Hultkrantz, *Shamanic Healing and Ritual Drama: Health and Medicine in Native North American Religious Traditions* (New York: Crossroad, 1992), 164.

25. Joseph Epes Brown, *Teaching Spirits: Understanding Native American Religious Traditions* (New York: Oxford University Press, 2001), 13.

26. J. R. Walker, *The Sun Dance and Other Ceremonies of the Oglala Division of the Teton Dakota* ([1917]; New York: AMS Press, 1979), 60.

27. Ibid., 62.

28. Ibid., 63.

29. Ibid., 66.

30. Ibid., 71.

31. Ibid., 96–99. In addition to Walker's work, I have also used the following for an accurate account of the Sun Dance: Joseph Epes Brown, ed., *The Sacred Pipe* (New York: Penguin, 1979), chapter 5; J. Owen Dorsey, *A Study of Siouan Cults*, Eleventh Annual Report of the Bureau of American Ethnology, Washington, D.C., 1894; Ella C. Deloria, "The Sun Dance of the Ogala Sioux," *Journal of American Folklore* 42 (1929): 354–413; William K. Powers, *Ogala Religion* (Lincoln: University of Nebraska Press, 1977), 95–100.

32. Gladys A. Richard, *Navaho Religion: A Study of Symbolism* (Princeton: Princeton University Press, 1950), 135–136.

33. Grinnell, *Cheyenne Indians*, 48.

17

Abstinence, Balance, and Political Control in Mesoamerica

Jeanne L. Gillespie

In Mesoamerica, sex, like birth and death, was considered a very powerful force that allowed humans to come close to the divine. The power of uncontrolled sexuality could threaten the fabric of life by unleashing uncontainable supernatural or divine forces. Midwives and healers involved in any aspect of birth, sexual disease, or death were thought to carry great power, and must perform ritual cleansing rites to limit the potential damage this power could cause. Sexual misconduct was often related to other indulgences, especially drunkenness. Adulterers also could cause social or actual damage by unleashing supernatural powers, but the control of sexual activity was manifested in specific codes of conduct that varied depending on age, socioeconomic class, and civil status. At the same time, the underlying metaphors of the cosmos, of agrarian success, and of military prowess were derived from a meditation on the codes of human reproduction.

Before we can understand abstinence and celibacy in the Mesoamerican context, we must first understand the role of sexuality in the cosmology, ritual practice, and daily life of Mesoamerica. In seeking information about attitudes toward sexuality in Mesoamerica, several issues arise with regard to primary sources. First, some of our general knowledge about pre-Hispanic Mesoamerica comes directly from the archaeological record, from public art, from polychrome ceramics, and from a handful of bark-paper books that survived the conquest. This information is partial and fragmentary, and we do not have the voices of the creators of this art to interpret it for us.

Most of the information we have from pre-Hispanic Mesoamerica, however, comes from the documents prepared by the Catholic priests whose charge it was to prepare the native populations for their conversion to Catholicism and to assure their continued practice of Christian conduct. By far the greatest portion of the published accounts of Mesoamerican life comes from the Mexica-Tenochca (better known as the Aztecs), who rose to power in the fifteenth century. This group intermarried with local populations and adapted many of their practices to the lifestyles of the local inhabitants, but culture in Mesoamerica was not monolithic. Many different ethnic and linguistic groups inhabited the region. As the Mexica-Tenochca empire expanded, they incorporated the practices and divinities of conquered people. Attitudes toward sex, ethnicity, social status, and ritual were as a result very complex and often contradictory.[1]

From pre-Hispanic sources, we can determine that social control, fertility, and military prowess were important aspects of society, and that all of these were connected to sexuality and to the practice of ritual abstinence. In the eyes of the missionary priests who first arrived in central Mexico, many of these populations were deemed "the perfect Christians" because they had not been contaminated by the "polluting" influences of European society. The missionary ethnographers and many of the European explorers often remarked that the native populations were very "clean" people—offering further evidence of the potential for converts well suited to Christian ideals. The rigorous codes of conduct suited the priests' ascetic aesthetic, even if the philosophy behind the codes differed.

At the same time, cultural attitudes toward sexual activity were perceived by the missionaries as problematic to the salvation of these populations. The priests identified "lust" as the most prolific sin in the Americas. For the European priests, the stain of original sin at the moment of human birth was enough to demand a lifetime of avoidance of sexual activity in order to better reach the Divine. Celibacy, along with the mortification of the flesh, on the part of the clergy helped remove them from the natural (and therefore contaminated, from a European perspective) urges and desires of their bodies. These missionaries were ill-equipped to deal with a society that celebrated pleasure in the sexual act and that used motifs of birth and satiation as organizing principles of the universe. In fact, the encounter between European Catholic priests and Mesoamericans represented polar opposites in terms of the need for the practice of celibacy and abstinence. These priests performed extensive ethnographic investigations to attempt to discover and dispel cultural practices that led Amerindian bodies down the paths of sin and paganism. They also developed detailed confessional texts with questions designed to continually reinforce the seriousness of the transgressions of the flesh. Serge Gruzinski points out that more than 60 percent of the questions in the confessionals developed in the Americas specifically targeted this one mortal sin.[2]

Mesoamerican Constructions of Sexuality

What was perceived as the greatest threat to the new Catholic Amerindians was also an issue in Mesoamerican conduct; however, sexual activity between spouses was seen as a positive and healthy force if practiced in moderation. It was only when sexual transgressions occurred outside of appropriate codes of conduct (such as incest and adultery) that they became issues of social importance or issues that might cause damage to the community. For example, missionary ethnographer Fernando de Sahagún noted that it was believed that when a person who had engaged in adultery passed by a turkey enclosure, the turkey chicks died on the spot.[3] Sexually transmitted diseases and illnesses involving the genital area were also blamed on improper sexual conduct. Ruíz de Alarcón devotes an entire chapter of his *Tratado de supersticiones* (Treatise on Superstitions) to diseases caused by *amor ílícito* (illicit love) and the treatments of those diseases by local healers.[4] In this discussion from the early seventeenth century, Ruíz de Alarcón establishes that it is an "excess of adulteries" that causes the diseases to married or engaged people.[5] Later the missionary priest explains that all of these diseases have the same cure: bathing in the sweat baths with incense, smoke, and steam, as is customary. When the cleansing is over, the healer speaks to the Milky Way, turning the patient over to the care of this celestial entity to help guide the sufferer's pathway. The connection between this cleansing ritual and Christian baptism is not lost on Ruíz de Alarcón. He states that "en este baño, pretendio nuestro enimigo imitar el santo sacramento de bautismo" (in this bath, our enemy [the devil] attempts to imitate the holy sacrament of baptism).[6] Because of the potential for disaster, sexuality and practices related to life and death (which of course are the result of sexual activity) had to be strictly controlled. In these types of events, abstinence and cleansing were vital to returning balance and harmony to the community.

Additionally, there was a specific patroness of sexual activity, Tlazoteotl (Eater of Filth), who was responsible for removing the "filth" or "dirtiness" caused by inappropriate sexual activity. For example, couples who were expecting were, like all other citizens, expected to practice sexual activity in moderation. When a baby was born covered with a coating of vernix, a thick milky substance commonly found on newborns, Mesoamericans believed that this was evidence that the parents engaged too frequently in sex during gestation. While the fluids from sex were necessary to strengthen the fetus, too much activity could cause the infant to be born covered with "filth." The "indiscretion" was made public by the manifestation of the vernix, and it was the responsibility of the midwives who delivered the baby to "clean" this "dirtiness"; to right the transgression.[7] Midwives and healers served Tlazoteotl, and they were responsible for removing the "original" dirtiness that results from being born. For Mesoamericans, the moment of birth was regarded as one of the most sacred of times, when one was most connected to the divine. Newborns brought with them the power of the divine; however, this power could be very dangerous if not properly regulated. Therefore, people who regularly dealt with these moments, such as midwives and healers, were also regarded as people under the influence of the potential power of the divine. As long as strict rituals especially related to ritual cleansing were observed, that sacred power did not become dangerous.

The cleansing of the mother and baby after childbirth was vital to prevent infections and to ensure the continued health of both. Mesoamericans relied heavily on their sweat baths for cleansing themselves both physically and ritually. Even today, in many rural areas indigenous people still practice the sweat baths. Ritual purification as part of the practice of delivering babies would be all part of the duties of midwives in service to Tlazoteotl, and the idea of "dirtiness" at birth or at other times was the concept best exploited by Catholic priests to connect to the European concept of "sin," especially original sin.

Sexual Conduct and Socialization in Mexica Society

One of the most explicit narratives of sexual behavior was recorded by pioneering ethnographer Bernardo de Sahagún. The Mexica called these narratives the *huehuetlatolli* (the discourse of the elders).[8] In these discourses, fathers and mothers explained proper codes of conduct to their children. In one text, the voice of a ruler counsels his precious daughter not to "covet carnal things" or to "wish for experience." Ruling-class women were advised to give themselves "not to the wanderer, [nor] to the restless one who is given to pleasure, [nor] to the evil youth." Young women were also advised not to abandon the one with whom they "will endure."[9] In the *huehuetlatolli*, elders also specifically address the importance of pleasure and of sexuality in marriage. In one passage, an elder explains to young men that they must have "enough honey" to please their wives, so they are encouraged to practice premarital sex in moderation so that they will not "dry up" and cease to be able to please their wives. One interesting point here is that body fluids were thought to be finite, so eventually one would run out of blood, semen, and so on. This is an interesting explanation for impotence.

On the other hand, an entire group of women called the *auiani* (joy women) were, like the Japanese geisha, schooled in pleasing Mexica-Tenochca warriors with song, with food, and with their bodies. Members of the military were afforded special privileges with regard to sexual pleasure, while members of the elite ruling class were expected to practice abstinence and control over their sexual desires. For ruling-class leaders who were schooled in the *calmecac*, a school devoted to the worship of Quetzalcoatl, abstinence was expected. For the military class, who studied in the *telpochcalli* and who served Tezcatlipoca, specific periods of abstinence were prescribed, but they were also allowed to indulge in sexual activities as part of the rewards for their service. It appears that nonelite women were also schooled in the arts of pleasure, including singing, dancing, and food preparation, as well as in the arts of physical pleasure. Again, this represents different expectations for different social classes.

For the Mexica-Tenochca, an excess of food also led to serious imbalances. As in the admonition to moderation in sexual conduct, the connections between food and drink and elimination also were understood as practices of taking in and giving back to the fertile earth. Only small amounts of food were to be consumed at a time, and feces and urine were collected in public storage areas to fertilize crops and to use in dye production. Sexual activities, especially those out of balance, were often also related to elimination practices or metaphorically referred to with scatological terms. At the same time, it was through this process of "filth" that the world was renewed, and in order to be "clean" one must first have had to be "dirty."

Cleanliness and the process of renewal were so important to the Aztecs in the late fifteenth century that Tlazoteotl was responsible for all of the cleansing rituals that would occur in the event of physical or psychic "dirtiness"; however, the idea of "dirtiness" did not have the same connotation as in Europe, since "dirtiness" or "contamination" was not necessarily a bad thing, merely a result of imbalance or of excess.[10] Tlazoteotl, therefore, and cleanliness by extension, was responsible for putting things right. Different expectations of abstinence occurred with regard to particular festivals and celebrations and the sacrifices required in those. One constant, however, was that abstinence was a practice, like fasting and bloodletting, designed to return balance to a specific person or to the community. In *Primeros memorials,* Sahagún described the judgment of a youth who has made himself "old-womanish" (indulged too much in insatiable sex), and who has thereby caused a lack of rain and an ensuing famine, which was blamed on a lack of sacrificial captives to feed the gods. "Because of him there was accusing, because of him there was assembling, because of him there was spreading of fear," further explaining the crime: "It was said that he impeded something in battle; he hindered the eagle jaguar warriors. And it was said that he ill used, he defiled the upright drum, the watching of the city." Because of this transgression, "none of the noblemen, the eagle jaguar warriors took captives."[11]

Sexual Imagery and Mesoamerican Cosmology

It is especially interesting that struggles between forces dedicated to Quetzalcoatl and those in service to Tezcatlipoca represented terrestrial reflections of cosmological conflict. Although these two figures were perceived in concrete terms, they also represented celestial bodies and cosmological balance. Quetzalcoatl and Tezcatlipoca are the personifications of the planet known in the European tradition as Venus Morningstar and the sun, respectively. Each of these celestial bodies travels out from the earth's body, across the sky and returns to the earth in its cycle.

The mountainous terrain of central Mexico, the earth as Mesoamericans knew it, metaphorically resembles the ridges of a crocodile's back. The female earth divinity Tlalteotl, also known as Cihuacoatl (Woman Serpent), who is portrayed as a saurian creature, participates in a violent struggle between these two important tutelary figures in Mesoamerica who are battling over the control of the sun. Quetzalcoatl and Tezcatlipoca grab the limbs of Tlalteotl. In this battle, Tlalteotl succeeds in biting off the foot of Tezcatlipoca. This foot is replaced by the smoking mirror that is the symbol of his name. The battle becomes so fierce that the body of the earth monster rips into two pieces, and she becomes the earth and the night sky. The earth monster wails for sustenance, and she does not offer forth the corn and other crops humans will use to nourish themselves until she is satiated with human hearts and blood.[12] The celestial bodies emerged from her body and returned to it. This female divinity is the destination and the embodiment of birth and death. Everything comes from her and returns to her.

The importance of images of renewal and rebirth can be seen in the terms used for precious materials such as gold and silver. Gold deposits were referred to as the "excrement of the sun" and silver the "excrement of the moon." This mimics the return of body waste to the earth and its precious nature in fertilizing sustenance crops. Blood and water were called jade for their precious, life-giving essence. Precious rain flows from the heavens to the earth and gives life to the crops. The process requires continual sacrifice and offering of precious fluids to assure adequate food for Mesoamerican society.

The metaphor of a woman's body as a cave or a gorge that must be satiated, reflects, by extension, an earth who continually demands the proper sacrifices to produce enough sustenance. Bernard Ortiz de Montellano cites the discourse from an adultery trial of elderly women who had engaged in sexual activities with younger men. In their defense, the women explain to Nezahualcoyotl that they are "never satiated, nor do [they] stop liking it." They further comment that women's bodies are "like a cave, a gorge that swells and receives whatever is thrown in and still wants and demands more."[13] Interestingly, these women also comment on the need for moderation on the part of young men. They complain, "You men cease to desire sexual pleasure when you are old because you indulged in your youth and because human potency and semen run out." They further suggest that the ruler "live cautiously and discreetly; so you will go step by step and not hurry with these ugly and harmful businesses."[14] The idea of male celestial bodies emerging from and returning to a female body, an insatiable body that demanded warrior hearts to feed her, will later establish a precedent for the "flowery wars" in which Mexica-Tenochca warriors went into battle to secure captives whose hearts they could sacrifice. The image of the fertile female is central in Mesoamerican cosmology, especially among the agrarian groups. These groups in Mesoamerica celebrated fecundity and bountiful harvests. They venerated divinities dedicated to rain, water, and to the crops that they raised, especially corn. The earliest artifacts that present at least the consequences of sex, as in many other cultures, are ceramic figurines of pregnant women. These abound in the archaeological record throughout Mesoamerica. The metaphor of a "pregnant earth" was also common in Mesoamerican stories. Many mountains and volcanoes (especially dormant ones) were personified as females. Caves marked the entrance into the underworld and often also became linked with the idea of the earth as a female crocodile or other saurian animal swimming in a great sea, from whose body the sun emerges each day.

In accounts narrated by central Mexican groups, the settled communities are often referred to as Toltecs and the nomads as Chichimecs. The Mexica-Tenochca represent the last group of Chichimecs to arrive in the Valley of Mexico before the Europeans. Over a period of two hundred years, the Mexica-Tenochca established themselves as the central power in the region. The mother of the Mexica-Tenochca tutelary figure Huitzilopochtli, Coatlicue, was portrayed as a mountain while she was pregnant, although, like many important mothers, Coatlicue did not become pregnant in the usual way. While she was sweeping, a ball of feathers fell between her breasts into her lap and made her pregnant. Her sons, the Mimixcoa (Four Hundred), and her daughter, Coyolxauqui, were horrified at their mother's apparent adultery and decided to kill her for her transgressions. As they swarmed up the mountain to dispatch her, Huitzilopochtli burst from her womb as a fully grown warrior, causing her demise.

Hutzilopochtli then defeated his sister and brothers, slicing his sister into pieces and throwing her down the mountain. In the excavations of the Mexica city, Tenochtitlan, a giant stone disk with a representation of Huitzilopochtil's sister Coyolxauqui was discovered at the base of his pyramid. This mythic battle was recreated in the city's architecture, and it can be assumed that this battle was reenacted on the pyramid on a regular basis. That Huitzilopochtli's mother, Coatlicue, died in the act of giving birth and in the midst of a cosmic battle elevated her to a doubly important status, since women who died in childbirth and warriors who died in battle or sacrifice went to the same paradise, Tamoanchan. Louise Burkhart remarks that only sexually pure (that is, inexperienced) warriors were chosen by the sun to die in battle, and that women who died in childbirth had not successfully completed their mission to deliver warriors to the empire.[15] At the same time, these women and warriors were all residents of the terrestrial paradise known as Tamoanchan, and were responsible for the movement of the sun across the sky. The warriors brought the celestial ball out of the body of the earth and accompanied it to the zenith, where the women who had perished in childbirth took the sun back to the earth. Although advice on chastity and abstinence seemed appropriate for ruling-class women, the fertility of the women of all classes provided warriors for the empire. Nevertheless, the power of the divine that was associated with the bodies of women who died in childbirth was so great that warriors would attempt to seize parts of the defunct women's body while the husband and the midwives were in the process of burying it.[16] These women were buried at the crossroads of travel routes, places where the temptation to slip into excess or to err in judgment was also especially strong. The ghosts of these women were said to harass travelers and to seduce them, causing extremely dangerous imbalances.

Birth, Death, Adultery, and Abstinence

The entire cycle of Aztec warfare opens with the celebration of the birth of the corn divinity, Cinteotl. He is the product of adultery; his mother, known as

Toci/Teteo inan/Tlazoteotl and Xochiquetzal, was abducted from her home in paradise and seduced, causing her expulsion for "gathering flowers." When she delivers Cinteotl, his body provides all the plants and grains typical of the Mesoamerican diet. He is especially associated with the ripe ear of corn. In her aspect as Tlazoteotl, she is often portrayed as giving birth to Cinteotl. In this case, the sexual transgression resulted in the delivery of sustenance on earth.

In "Three Nahuatl Hymns on the Mother Archetype," Willard Gingerich offers a fascinating study of the songs dedicated to Teteo inan/Xochiquetzal and other female divinities in Mexica society. Gingerich points out that the veneration of these female warrior-mothers represents a mobilizing force behind its imperial expansion and the fierce and violent military domination of the entire region.[17] Female sexuality in Mesoamerica appears to have been principally dedicated to the process of making new warriors for the state or of cementing political alliances. Although large cities existed in Mesoamerica from 250 BCE on, settlement patterns also indicate that at the same time nomadic societies were moving into the region from the north. These societies were often powerful military forces who either conquered the local communities or dedicated themselves to their service to help protect the resources of the settlements. Agrarian societies also needed to protect themselves, so connections between images of fertile females and powerful warriors abound in the pre-Hispanic record.[18] In southern Mexico, in the present-day state of Oaxaca, diverse communities established alliances to protect themselves from the threat of newcomers. One way in which these alliances were established was through marriages between the ruling families.

In various codices, images of couples who have engaged or are engaging in sexual activity reflect Mesoamerican attitudes toward sex and illustrate the level of political control that regulated society. In one scene of the *Codex Zouche-Nuttall*, one of eight pre-Colombian texts that survived the conquest, a couple is portrayed in their wedding bed after they have undergone the ritual cleansing.[19] This portion of the text narrates the military alliance between two towns in southern Mexico that was cemented by the marriage of the son of one ruler to the daughter of the other in 957 CE.[20] It is especially significant that the consummation of the marriage under a blanket in their bed was the highlight of this event. Apparently the act of copulation (and perhaps of producing a child) offers the most powerful symbol of the alliance.

Whereas marital alliances could cement power, the taking of another's mate caused ruin for Quetzalcoatl and success for Tezcatlipoca. This reiterates the different codes of conduct for different social classes, however, and communicates the idea that many unfortunate events, like the fall of Quetzalcoatl, could be and were blamed on activities "out of balance." It was a lack of respect for balance that caused the most damage in Mesoamerican accounts. The illicit conduct seemed to be the most damaging force. Although no penalty existed for premarital sex (except for the possible loss of potency in marriage) certain forms of "adultery" were, like drunkenness, punishable by death. And males and females who engaged in this improper activity were both punished. It appears that adultery may be more specific than sex with a married woman; it may be more like "sex with someone else's woman" or "sex with an inappropriate partner." Colonial accounts discuss the ease of dissolution of marriage, and frequent breaks in married life were common practices that the priests had difficulty changing as they attempted to instill the idea of matrimony as a monogamous relationship.

Perhaps the most ambivalent account of the wages of adultery comes from the narrative of the goddess Xochiquetzal's fall from grace.[21] Xochiquetzal has been identified in Mesoamerican natives as the first adulteress, but she is also the mother of the divine Cinteotl, whose body becomes the food that sustains humans. Xochiquetzal was expelled from Tamoanchan for "cutting trees and gathering flowers," a reference to a perceived sexual indiscretion. According to Tlaxcalan mestizo chronicler Diego Muñoz Camargo, this divine female was very well guarded and served by jesters, dwarves, hunchbacks, and buffoons to entertain her. Her job was to spin and weave beautiful creations. (The spindle and whorl are frequently used as a metaphor for sexual activity.) Xochiquetzal resided in the land of the flowering tree, and if anyone was touched by the flowers of the tree that person would be happy and faithfully loved.

In this paradise, Xochiquetzal was the consort of Tlaloc, the water divinity. She was accused of "gathering flowers" with Tezcatlipoca, who apparently kidnapped and seduced her. Xochiquetzal's original consort, the most prominent male divinity associated with water—called Tlaloc in the Mesoamerican highlands, Cha'ac in the Maya area, and Cosijo in the Mixteca—was responsible for rain and the oceans. In some accounts, Xochiquetzal, also called Chalchihuitlicue, controlled water that was contained, as in lakes and ponds. The metaphor of the male raining down from the sky into a female vessel or container offered a very powerful image of fertility for agrarian groups. This metaphor also celebrates the offering of "rain" as a fertilizing activity that produces sustenance. Mesoamericans reenacted this action on the part of the divinity by offering blood—humans' own "precious fluid"—to thank Tlaloc/Cha'ac/Cosijo for good crops and the proper amount of rainfall. In fact, when rainfall was too much or too little, that is, out of balance, the result was crop failure and starvation, so in order to keep the precious fluid flowing in the proper amount, the sacrifices were extremely important.

While blood sacrifice often came in the form of human sacrifices, Mesoamericans also performed auto-sacrificial rituals to appease the rain divinity. Priests in service to Tlaloc in the city of Teotihuacan are portrayed piercing their hands to draw blood for a sacrifice. In Maya glyphs, the image of a hand with droplets that epigraphers call the "scattering" glyph indicates that a priest or a ruler performed the proper sacrifice. In addition to the hands, tongues and penises were important spots of the body for bloodletting.[22] In the Maya region, incredibly ornate penis perforaters have been found in the archaeological record of many sites. In central Mexico, a ritual that involved penis perforation with maguey spines and then a spinning dance to splatter the sacrificial blood onto a paper skirt was documented in murals found at Cacaxtla that date from around 750 CE.[23] Specific festivals, such as Panquetzaliztli dedicated to Huitzilopochtli, called for periods of abstinence. In this festival, "there was eating, but no one washed himself with soap or took a steam bath; no one slept with a woman" for eighty days.[24] In the festival of Atamalcualiztli (The Eating of Water Tamales), which was celebrated every eight years, citizens practiced seven days of abstinence. If anyone was discovered engaging in sexual activity, those people were punished.[25]

Marta Foncerrada de Molina has discussed the connections between Tlaloc and military prowess at both Teotihuacan and Cacaxtla. Connections also can be made between Tlaloc and Tezcatlipoca in Tlaxcala and in the Mexica-Tenochca region. By taking Tlaloc's wife, and by having a child with her, Tezcatlipoca has established himself as the more powerful divinity. His "adultery" causes them to be expelled from Tamoanchan, but both the Mexica-Tenochca and their enemies served Tezcatlipoca as the ultimate warrior and dedicated their battles to Ipalnemoani (He by Whom We Live), just as the Christian forces dedicated themselves to Santiago (Saint James), the patron saint of Spain.

It is not surprising that Tlazoteotl was an avatar of Xochiqueztal or that the idea of divine excrement would also be linked to her. The power of Tlazoteotl to purify others results directly from her fall from paradise and from the idea identified by Cecilia Kline as "divine excrement": things that have become dirty, old, used up, will return to service through purification rituals and cleansing to become precious again (like gold).[26] What is most interesting, however, is that in mestizo and European sources, Tlazoteotl, especially in her role as Teteo inan, is closely linked to the Virgin Mary. The missionary priests chose Quetzalcoatl as the divinity most representative of Christ because of his ascetic nature, and Tezcatlipoca was often considered the devil as Catholic priests attempted to downplay discourse on warfare and human sacrifice. In addition, the constant battle between Quetzalcoatl and Tezcatlipoca helped explain, at least in a superficial way, the conflict between Christ and Satan.

While the story above of the struggle between Quetzalcoatl and Tezcatlipoca represents a cosmic struggle between two powerful male divinities over control of the earth female, another story of political struggle between Quetzalcoatl and Tezcatlipoca adds the elements of overindulgence and sexual misconduct. Again, a female is involved in the result. The trickster Tezcatlipoca encourages the ruler of Tollan, Quetzalcoatl Topiltzin, to become drunk on pulque. As a result, the noble Quetzalcoatl also apparently had sexual relations with his sister. Consumed with shame at abandoning the ritual practices of avoiding alcohol and engaging in sexual conduct, Quetzlacoatl fled the city and abandoned his kingdom to the military class in service to Tezcatlipoca. Overindulgence in alcohol that led to sexual indulgence and compromised the practice of balance and abstinence caused the loss of a great empire. The link between drunkenness and sexual misconduct is strong. The penalty in Mesoamerica for public drunkenness and for serious or excessive adultery was death. It is especially interesting that the elderly were permitted to indulge in drunkenness, possibly because they were no longer able to reproduce, and therefore could not summon the dangers of the supernatural.

As we have seen, for the Mesoamericans excesses were often the cause of being out of balance—when one was out of balance, one would slip, fall down, and become "dirty." Measure, balance, and equilibrium were the most important ideals for which to strive. Although ritual cleansing of both physical and psychic "dirt" was of utmost importance, the idea that bodily functions and fluids were important offerings and part of the cycle of birth and death regulated not only sexual activity but all other body functions as well. Care must be taken to offer the proper respect for all body functions, including eating, drinking, elimination, menstruation, breast feeding, ejaculation, and urination, as well as sexual activity, and the events of birth and death.

Mesoamerican accounts of the situation before the arrival of the Europeans offer some insight into pre-Hispanic practices, and the documents prepared in the colonial era reflect an awareness of both European and Amerindian sources and a mestizo voice that was permitted by the priests in charge of the missionary processes. As we continue to explore the pre-Hispanic record for clues about sexuality and the practices of abstinence, we find that meditations on fertility, on the consequences of premarital sex and adultery, on reproduction for the purpose of providing great warriors to the Mesoamerican state, and on maintaining balance in all things were the most important themes of texts that recount history as well as those that portray religious practices.

NOTES

1. For a detailed discussion of Aztec body image, see Alfredo Lopez Austin, *The Human Body and Ideology: Concepts of the Ancient Nahuas*, translated by Thelma Ortiz de Montellano and Bernard R. Ortiz de Montellano (Salt Lake City: University of Utah Press, 1988).

2. Serge Gruzinski, "Confesión, alianza y sexualidad entre los indios de Nueva España: Introcucción al estudio de los confesionarios en language indígenas," in *El placer de pecar y el afán de normar* (Mexico City: Joaquín Mortiz-INAH, 1987), 36.

3. Bernardo de Sahagún, *Florentine Codex: General History of the Things of New Spain*, edited by Arthur J. O. Anderson and Charles Dibble, 13 vols. (Santa Fe: School of American Research and University of Utah Press, 1950–1982), 5: 191–192.

4. Hernando Ruíz de Alarcón, *Tratado de las Supersticiones y costumbres gentilicas que oy viene entre los indios naturals desta Nueva España* ([1629] Mexico City: Museo Nacional, 1892), in *El alma encantada: Anales del Museo Nacional de México*, edited by Fernando Benítez (Mexico City: Instituto Indigenista/Fondo de Cultura Económica, 1987), 182–184.

5. Ibid., 183.

6. Ibid., 184.

7. See Louise Burkhart, *The Slippery Earth: Nahua and Christian Moral Dialogue in Sixteenth-Century Mexico* (Tucson: University of Arizona Press, 1989), 112–113 on *Florentine Codex* 6, 167; and Inga Clendinnen, *Aztecs* (Cambridge: Cambridge University Press, 1991), 181.

8. See Miguel León-Portilla, ed., *Huehuehtlahtolli: Testimonios de la Antigua palabra* (Mexico City: Secretaria de Educación Pública/Fondo de Cultura Económica, 1991).

9. Sahagún, *Florentine Codex*, 6: 97–98, quoted in David Carrasco, "Uttered from the Heart: Guilty Rhetoric among the Aztecs," *History of Religions* 39.1 (August 1999): 22.

10. See Cecilia Klein's discussion of filth and renewal in "Teocuitlatl, 'Divine Excrement': The Significance of 'Holy Shit' in Ancient Mexico," *Art Journal* 52.3 (Autumn 1993): 20–27.

11. Bernardo de Sahagún, *Primeros memorials*, translated by Thelma Sullivan (Norman: University of Oklahoma Press, 1997), 244.

12. See the "Leyenda de los soles," in *Anales de Cuauhtitlán. Códice Chimalpopoca*, edited by Primo F. Velásquez (Mexico City: Imprenta Universitaria, 1945).

13. See Sahagún, *Florentine Codex* 2, p. 145, quoted in Bernardo Ortiz de Montellano, *Aztec Medicine Health, and Nutrition* (New Brunswick: Rutgers University Press, 1990), 62.

14. Ibid.

15. Burkhart, *Slippery Earth*, 50–51.

16. Clendinnen, *Aztecs*, 176–178.

17. Williard Gingerich, "Three Nahuatl Hymns on the Mother Archetype: An Interpretive Commentary," *Mexican Studies: Estudios mexicanos* 4.2 (Summer 1988): 191–244.

18. For more information on female warrior figures, see Michel Graulich, *Myths of Ancient Mexico*, translated by Thelma Ortiz de Montellano and Bernard R. Ortiz de Montellano (Norman: University of Oklahoma Press, 1997), and Jeanne Gillespie, *Saints and Warriors: Tlaxcalan Perspectives on the Fall of Tenochtitlan* (New Orleans: University Press of the South, 2004).

19. *Codex [Zouche-]Nuttall: A Picture Manuscript from Ancient Mexico*, edited by Zelia Nuttall (New York: Dover, 1975), Lamina 19. For more information on the history of this region, see Bruce E. Byland and John M. D. Pohl, *In the Realm of 8 Deer* (Norman: University of Oklahoma Press, 1994).

20. *Codex [Zouche-]Nuttall*, 19.

21. For a detailed account of Xochiquetzal's fall from grace, see Alfredo Lopez Austin, *Tamoanchan, Tlalocan: Places of Mist*, translated by Bernard Ortiz de Montellano and Thelma Ortiz de Montellano (Niwot: University Press of Colorado, 1997).

22. For a discussion of warriors' sacrificial practices, see Richard Townsend, *State and Cosmos in the Art of Tenochtitlan* (Washington, D.C.: Dumbarton Oaks, 1979).

23. Marta Foncerrada de Molina, "Mural Painting at Cacaxtla and Teotihuacan Cosmopolitism," *Third Palenque Round Table* (Austin: University of Texas Press, 1980), 198.

24. Sahagún, *Primeros memoriales*, 64.

25. Ibid., 68.

26. Klein, "Teocuitlatl, 'Divine Excrement,' " 20–21.

Index